Acts of Literature

JACQUES DERRIDA

EDITED BY DEREK ATTRIDGE

ROUTLEDGE
NEW YORK • LONDON

Published in 1992 by

Routledge
An imprint of Routledge, Chapman and Hall, Inc.
29 West 35 Street
New York, NY 10001

Published in Great Britain in 1992 by

Routledge
11 New Fetter Lane
London EC4P 4EE

Library of Congress cataloging in publication data

Derrida, Jacques.
    Acts of literature / Jacques Derrida : edited by Derek Attridge.
      p. cm.
    Includes bibliographical references and index.
    ISBN 0-415-90056-5   ISBN 0-415-90057-3 (pb)
      1. Derrida, Jacques—Contributions in criticism.
    2. Deconstruction.   3. Literature—Philosophy.   4. Literature—
History and criticism.   I. Attridge, Derek.   II. Title.
    PN98.D43D44 ~~1991~~ 1992
    801.95—dc20   91-30342
                                                  CIP

British Library Cataloguing in Publication Data

Derrida, Jacques, 1930–
    Acts of literature.
    I. Title
    194

    ISBN 0-415-90056-5
    ISBN 0-415-90057-3 pbk

Contents

Act *sb.* A thing done; a deed, a performance (of an intelligent being). . . . A decree passed by a legislative body, a court of justice, etc. . . . Any instrument in writing to verify facts. . . . A "performance" of part of a play. . . . Part of a formula used when signing a legal instrument [*act and deed*]. . . . Pretence (of being what one is not).

Act *v.* To carry out or represent in mimic action (an ideal, incident, or story); to perform (a play). Hence *fig.* in a bad sense: To simulate, counterfeit. . . . To perform on the stage of existence; to perform actions, to do things, in the widest sense. . . . To do the duties of an office temporarily, without being the regular officer.

—*Oxford English Dictionary*

Prefaces

&. From his earliest publications, literature has made demands on Jacques Derrida. His writings abound in responses to a wide range of literary texts in French, German, and English, including drama, poetry, and fiction, as well as texts which find no obvious place in the generic classifications of the literary institution (or indeed in the classification literature/nonliterature). This volume brings together a number of these responses, selected in accordance with several criteria: I have tried to achieve a spread across literary traditions and genres (this has meant leaving out many other French authors about whom Derrida has written, including Flaubert, Valéry, Artaud, Genet, Jabes, Bataille, and Sollers), to choose texts that are relatively accessible to the nonphilosopher, and to maintain a continuing focus on the central question of literature as an institution and literary writing as a practice. I have included both complete texts—sometimes long ones—and excerpts. The selection also constitutes my singular response, at this particular time, to the many demands—imperious, pleasurable, unfathomable— which Derrida's texts have made on me.

&. The specific works to which these texts of Derrida's respond are all acts—doings and records—of literature: that is, works conventionally and institutionally categorized as "literary" (with one borderline case in Rousseau's *Confessions*), but also works which in some way "perform" literature, put it into play, establish and question its laws, operate at some internal distance from the institution and the category which they at the same time confirm. Derrida's responses, too, might be thought of as "acts of literature" in many of these senses. They range from texts written relatively early in his career, at least as an internationally renowned philosopher, to more recent publications; some appear here for the first time in English or in hitherto untranslated revised versions (see the headnotes to "Mallarmé," "Before the Law," the excerpt from *Shibboleth*, and "Aphorism Countertime"). The interview was conducted at Derrida's suggestion, and has not been published previously. Taken together, these texts offer to those who are not well acquainted with Derrida's writing an introduction to his work and to the phenomenon known as "deconstruction"; to those who are, they invite a fresh consideration of the significance of literature—literary texts and the institution of literature—in Derrida's work, and of Derrida's work in literature.

≈ Editors of anthologies conventionally preface their volumes with remarks on the necessary arbitrariness of selection, the inevitable violence of excerpting, the regrettable impossibility of true representativeness. All these disclaimers are as valid for this anthology as for any other, if not more so; Jacques Derrida's work seems especially ill suited, in its arguments as well as in its form, to the neat compartments, the simplified headnotes, the limits on length and detail that typify the genre. The presentation in translation of these untranslatable works requires a further caveat that scarcely needs spelling out. On the other hand, Derrida's work also helps us to appreciate the implicit, and challengeable, assumptions that underlie these conventional apologies: that there is an "original," "whole," seamless oeuvre, free from the operations of translation, that *could* in principle be read or represented in a nonselective, unexcerpted, nonviolent way. In large measure thanks to Derrida, we have become aware that all reading, all memories of reading, all publication and all criticism are processes of fragmenting, anthologizing, and translating, a prey to (but also the beneficiaries of) the random, the contingent, the mediated. Perhaps Derrida's work is *more* open to anthologizing and translation than most ... as long as no single anthology—such as this one—is assumed to have a transcendent or central position among all the possible representations of his writing.

≈ Many of the reprinted translations were originally derived from early versions of Derrida's texts that have subsequently been published in revised form; where necessary, editorial modifications have been

made to reflect the author's final revisions. It has also been necessary
to make some minor alterations in the interests of consistency and
clarity. Translator's notes and editor's notes are indicated by TN and
EN respectively; other notes are Derrida's.

ᴥ Publication details of works by Derrida mentioned in the course of
the volume, whether in editorial matter or in the selections themselves,
will be found in the Selected Bibliography at the end. This list also
incorporates suggestions for further reading on the subject of Derrida
and literature.

ᴥ A collection such as this does not come together by itself, but the
necessary labor has been made a pleasure both by the fascination of
the material itself and by the extraordinary generosity and good will
that prevails among those who have worked closely on and with it.
My first and overriding acknowledgment is to Jacques Derrida, who
was willing to entrust to someone else significant decisions about his
texts and yet to provide assistance whenever it was requested, making
him the ideal collaborator/subject. Peggy Kamuf, whose *Derrida
Reader* was in preparation at the same time as this collection, made
the coexistence of the two projects a matter for fruitful interchange—
to the lasting improvement of this one, at least. The introduction
has benefited greatly from the comments and conversation of Geoff
Bennington, Rachel Bowlby, David Carroll, Tom Keenan, Richard
Rand, Nicholas Royle, and Samuel Weber. The work of the translators
made the volume imaginable in the first place, and many of them
were actively involved in its development; in addition to those already
mentioned, valuable contributions were made by Avital Ronell, Christine Roulston, Gayatri Spivak, and Joshua Wilner. Others who helped
were Marc Chénetier, Uri Eisenzweig, and Penny Wilson. My graduate
class at Rutgers University in the spring of 1989 increased my understanding of many of these texts, without making them seem any less
challenging. The interview was made possible by a grant from the
Research Council of Rutgers University. Bill Germano at Routledge

was a benign critical presence from start to finish. My thanks go to all these, and much more than thanks to Suzanne Hall and Laura Catherine Attridge.

D.A.
Glasgow–New Brunswick–Paris, 1987–90

Acknowledgments

𝒶 The publishers gratefully acknowledge the following sources for selections reprinted or translated in this volume: The Johns Hopkins University Press for ". . . That Dangerous Supplement . . ." (from *Of Grammatology*, trans. Gayatri Chakravorty Spivak) and for "The Law of Genre" (*Glyph* 7); Editions Gallimard for "Mallarmé" (from *Tableau de la littérature française, tome 3: De Madame de Staël à Rimbaud*); The University of Chicago Press and the Athlone Press for "The Double Session" (from *Dissemination*, trans. Barbara Johnson); Indiana University Press for "Before the Law" (from *Franz Kafka and the Contemporary Critical Performance*, ed. Alan Udoff); Syracuse University Press for "Ulysses Gramophone: Hear Say Yes in Joyce" (from *James Joyce: The Augmented Ninth*, ed. Bernard Benstock); the University of Minnesota Press for "Psyche: Invention of the Other" (from *Reading de Man Reading*, ed. Lindsay Waters and Wlad Godzich); Columbia University Press for "Signsponge" (from *Signéponge/Signsponge*, trans. Richard Rand); Yale University Press for "Shibboleth: For Paul Celan" (from *Midrash and Literature*, ed. Geoffrey Hartman and Sanford Budick); and Editions Galilée for "Aphorism Countertime" (from *Psyche: Inventions de l'autre*).

INTRODUCTION

DERRIDA AND THE QUESTIONING OF LITERATURE

Derek Attridge

> When and how does an inscription become literature and what takes place when it does? To what and to whom is this due? What takes place between philosophy and literature, science and literature, politics and literature, theology and literature, psychoanalysis and literature?
> —"The Time of a Thesis"

> Deconstruction . . . is a coming-to-terms with literature.
> —"Deconstruction in America"

ᴥ What is literature? This question, which must be a central one for anybody committed to literary studies, has also—since Plato and Aristotle—repeatedly been asked within the Western tradition of philosophy. It is, after all, a philosophical, not a literary question; it asks for a statement of the essence of literature, for that which distinguishes literature from all that is not literature. And among the things from which literature has traditionally been distinguished, in order more clearly to establish the properties of both, is philosophy.

We need not be surprised, therefore, that Jacques Derrida, as a philosopher (and especially as a philosopher who feels strongly the continuing pressure of the entire philosophical tradition), should find this question haunting him.[1] He does not, however, attempt a strictly philosophical answer, much less a sociological, political, or psychological one, for it is first of all the question of the question that fascinates him. It is articulated, like all questions, in language, and one of Derrida's constant concerns is to remind us, and the philosophical tradition, that this fact is not negligible. What Derrida dwells on in the question is the relationship of "What is . . .?" to "literature": might it not be the case, he asks, that something in the final word retroactively challenges the first two, with their assumptions about essence, identity, and truth?[2] And *this* is a question upon which abstract philosophical speculation can gain no purchase; it requires that one read a number of texts called "literary," and that one do so with particular attention to the ways in which they potentially confirm or unsettle philosophical presuppositions without themselves offering philosophical arguments. Literary texts, one might say, are acts of writing that call forth acts of reading: though in saying this, it is important to remain aware of the polysemy of the term *act*: as both "serious" performance and "staged" performance, as a "proper" doing and an improper or temporary one, as an action, a law governing actions, and a record documenting actions.[3]

1. In addition to the testimony of Derrida's repeated engagement with literary texts and with the question of literature, there are such autobiographical witnesses as the statement in his thesis defense of 1980: "[M]y most constant interest, coming even before my philosophical interest I should say, if this is possible, has been directed towards literature, towards that writing which is called literary" ("The Time of a Thesis," 37), and the comment in a 1983 interview with *Le nouvel observateur*: "My 'first' inclination wasn't really towards philosophy, but rather towards literature, no, towards something that literature accommodates more easily than philosophy" ("An Interview with Derrida," 73). The qualifications in these comments are important, however; see also the opening response in the Interview below.

2. For some of the ramifications of this question see—for example—"The First Session" below.

3. In the extract from *Signsponge* reprinted here, Derrida says of the signature: ". . .the work of writing designates, describes, and inscribes itself as *act* (action and archive)" (see below, p. 363), and in a later part of the book he remarks that "the signature, as act, splits *immediately* into event and legend, and cannot be at one and the same time what it immediately is, event and legend" (108). The term *act*, that is, transgresses the boundaries that separate happening and object, speech and writing, *parole* and *langue*, original and copy, time and space. Of course, in any given context— such as the phrase "speech act theory" and the ideology it represents—these border-crossings are inhibited, though they always continue as covert operations. Noting the connection between *act* and terms such as *active* and *actual* (with their connotations of self-present intentionality), Derrida remarks, "[T]he value of the *act* (used so generally

In their questioning of philosophical questioning, Derrida's acts of reading literature impinge directly upon philosophy, and are closely connected with his readings of philosophical, linguistic, theological, constitutional, judicial, aesthetic, and other kinds of nonliterary text.[4] But they demand equal attention within the discipline of literary studies: not just because any strong and conscientious reading of a literary text is of interest to those who work with and take pleasure in such writing, but because it is Derrida's contention that in spite of literature's potential challenge to philosophy, literary studies are dominated by philosophical assumptions quite as much as philosophy is—perhaps even more so, given philosophy's long tradition of critical reflection on its own assumptions. Literary theory, or poetics, has always consciously worked under the sign of philosophy. But literary criticism, too, has operated for the most part within the bounds established by classical Greek thought, taking for granted the rules of syllogistic reason, the ultimate priority of meaning over its mode of articulation, and such fundamental and absolute oppositions as the intelligible and the sensible, form and matter, subject and object, nature and culture, presence and absence.[5] Literature has often been read in terms of a dominant meaning or of a dominant form; although a given critical tradition may emphasize one of these at the expense of the other, or insist on their interdependence, this does not diminish the determining

and analyzed so little in the theory of speech acts), like that of event, should be submitted to systematic questioning" (*Limited Inc*, 58). Much of *Limited Inc* is concerned with the impoverishment of terms such as *act* in speech act theory and the philosophical tradition it participates in; see also the references to speech act theory in "Psyche" and "Ulysses Gramophone" below.

4. To call Derrida's engagements with texts, literary or philosophical, "readings" is inadequate to the extent that this term suggests a traditional interpretative project; like any alternative term one might use, it needs to be understood in the light of Derrida's practice (which is different for every text he "reads"). Paul de Man's understanding of reading as an act which responds to those aspects of a text which cannot be defined grammatically (that is, according to a general code or program) is useful here, forcing one to face the paradox that reading in the strictest sense is called for by that which is *unreadable* in a text ("The Resistance to Theory," 15–17). See also Weber, "Reading and Writing *chez* Derrida" and the collection *Reading de Man Reading*, ed. Waters and Godzich.

5. Derrida gives as examples of philosophically derived categories that have dominated literature "the values of meaning or of content, of form or signifier, of metaphor/metonymy, of truth, of representation" (*Positions*, 69), and refers to such "reductions and misconstruings" of literature as "thematism, sociologism, historicism, psychologism" (*Positions*, 70).

force of the philosophical categories themselves.[6] Or it has been read as understandable in terms of an origin (biographical, historical, socio-economic, psychoanalytic) or a goal (aesthetic, moral, spiritual, political), or as fundamentally mimetic and therefore answerable to a classical notion of truth. The result has been a representation of literature as itself governed by these oppositions and assumptions, a representation which one cannot simply call "inaccurate" since it responds to a marked tendency in a large part of Western literary writing.

Of course, the literary tradition is far from homogeneous, and some works of literature, criticism, and literary theory have resisted such philosophical categories more than others—not by abolishing mimesis, reference, form, content, genre, origin, intention, and so on, but by staging, suspending, and testing these concepts, showing them to be other than the self-consistent, controlling categories they are usually taken to be. Derrida's own interest has been largely in literary texts whose resistance to these terms is particularly strong, beginning with Mallarmé's unmistakable challenge to the conventions of reading and criticism over a century ago. As his discussion of Shakespeare's *Romeo and Juliet* in this volume indicates, however, this selectivity does not imply an identification of "modernity" or "modernism" with the capacity to unsettle philosophic-critical categories; a concentration on certain works of this century has a strategic value, and also springs from a particular response with very specific historical determinants that Derrida would be the last to undervalue.[7]

꙳ In drawing attention to the philosophical allegiances of most literary criticism and literary theory, and of literature as read through their

---

6. In *Positions*, Derrida comments on the equal inadequacy of "a criticism concerned only with content" and "a purely formalist criticism which would be interested only in the code, the pure play of signifiers, the technical manipulation of a text-object" and adds: "These two insufficiencies are rigorously complementary" (46–47).

7. Derrida has explained his focus on certain writers from Mallarmé to the present as follows: "It is incontestable that certain texts classed as 'literary' have seemed to me to operate breaches or infractions at the most advanced points. Artaud, Bataille, Mallarmé, Sollers. . . . These texts implement, in their very movement, the demonstration and practical deconstruction of the *representation* that was made of literature, it being well understood that long before these 'modern' texts a certain 'literary' practice was able to operate against this model, against this representation. But it is on the basis of these last texts, on the basis of the general configuration to be remarked in them, that one can best

glasses, however, Derrida is not "attacking" this tradition, any more than he is attacking the philosophers he reads with such care and commitment ("I am very fond of everything that I deconstruct in my own manner; the texts I want to read from the deconstructive point of view are texts I like, with that impulse of identification which is indispensable for reading" [*The Ear of the Other*, 87; translation modified].) Derrida's writing on literary texts arises from a strong response to them which is also a strong sense of his *responsibility* toward them, the registering of a demand which they and their signatories make, of a call that seems to come from somewhere outside the orbit within which we comfortably go about our intellectual business— but an outside which cannot simply be classified as exterior. Although the philosophical discourse of ethics is as much subject to Derrida's de-totalizing interrogation as the other branches of philosophy, there has always been an ethico-political dimension to Derrida's writing, manifesting itself particularly in a respect for *otherness*, be it textual, historical, cultural, or personal (to use categories which are by no means separate or self-sufficient). This responsibility toward the other is also a responsibility toward the *future*, since it involves the struggle to create openings within which the other can appear beyond any of our programs and predictions, can come to transform what we know or think we know. (See "Psyche," in this volume, for a discussion of this issue.) Responsibility for Derrida is not something we simply "take": we find ourselves summoned, confronted by an undecidability which is also always an opportunity and a demand, a chance and a risk.[8] Highlighted in Derrida's readings of literary texts are those as-

reread, without retrospective teleology, the law of the previous fissures" (*Positions*, 69; translation modified).

8. Derrida discusses "responsibility," and in particular "academic responsibility," in "The Conflict of Faculties." In preparing for his reading of Kant's *The Conflict of Faculties*, he asks: "Would it not be more interesting, even if it proves difficult or perhaps impossible, to conceive of a responsibility—that is, a summons to be responded to— which would no longer in the final analysis pass by way of the ego, the 'I think,' the subject, intention, or the ideal of decidability? Would it not be more 'responsible' to attempt to think the ground upon which, in the history of the West, the juridical and egological values of responsibility have arisen and imposed themselves? There, perhaps, lies a source of responsibility at once 'older' and—to the extent that it is now newly perceived through the crisis afflicting the classic ideal of responsibility—also 'younger,' or still to come?" See also Derrida's discussion of response and responsibility in "The Politics of Friendship."

pects which make most demands on us, which are most difficult to write about in the conventional discourse of criticism because they shake the foundations of that discourse. And Derrida's argument is that it is those aspects which mark literature *as* literature; while the features that criticism has traditionally foregrounded are features that exist in common across a variety of discourses—which is not a reason for desisting from such criticism, though it may be a reason for not accepting some of the claims it makes. (We shall consider later the further—more difficult and more important—argument that the "literary" aspects of these texts not only trouble the "philosophical" grounds of the critical discourse but are what make this discourse possible.)

   ▸ What I have sketched here may sound like the assertion of a literary essence, a set of detectable characteristics from which one could derive an exact compartmentalization of the literary and the nonliterary; in short, a theoretically clear (if in practice difficult) answer to the question "What is literature?" Let us therefore attend to one of Derrida's engagements with this question, which arises from his reading of Mallarmé's short prose piece "Mimique" (see "The First Session" below):

> If this handbook of literature *meant to say* something, which we now have some reason to doubt, it would proclaim first of all that there is no—or hardly any, ever so little—literature; that in any event there is no essence of literature, no truth of literature, no literary-being or being-literary of literature. And that the fascination exerted by the "is," or the "what is" in the question "what is literature" is worth what the hymen is worth—that is, not exactly nothing—when for example it causes one to die laughing.

The references to the hymen and death by laughter arise from the specificity of Mallarmé's text, and one has to note that the comments on literature are presented not apodictically but contextually and dramatically: as always with Derrida's writing, to wrench a piece out of context is to transform it. But there remains in this passage a challenge to the notion that "literature"—in the sense of those unsettling aspects we have been discussing—operates as a substantial presence or force.

It is barely "there" at all, precarious, fleeting, to be experienced only by means of a certain kind of attention and effort, confirmed by a certain kind of act.

Not only do these "literary" potentialities have no substantial presence in literature, but they do not serve to distinguish it absolutely from other categories of writing. Derrida insists—for instance, in the Interview below—that *no* text is wholly governed by the concepts and oppositions of philosophy, *every* text can be read (though not necessarily without some tough and extended intellectual labor) as "literary."[9] Equally, no text could be *wholly* "literary": all acts of language and interpretation depend on philosophical categories and presuppositions. There can be no absolutely sharp distinction between Derrida's readings of what are conventionally called literary texts and his readings of other types of text; and there is therefore a sense in which the raison d'être of the present volume, as a selection of writings on literary texts, is unmistakably at odds with Derrida's own thinking.

ᐖ What then justifies a selection of Derrida's writing on literary texts? Apart from the inherent interest of these pieces, some of them famous, some little known, their appearance between the same covers may serve to correct some of the biases in the reception of Derrida's work in the English-speaking world.[10] Paradoxically, the works by Derrida most cited and most imitated in readings of literary texts by literary critics are those on philosophical texts. (We may take "philosophy" here to include those disciplines whose procedures and assumptions are fundamentally philosophical, including anthropology, linguistics, aesthetics, structuralism, and political theory.) We have already touched on an explanation for this phenomenon: the tradition of literary criticism is dominated by philosophical thinking, and it is—broadly speak-

9. In view of a frequent misunderstanding, it may be worth stressing that for Derrida the "literariness" of texts conventionally classed as non-literature is not a matter of their employment of metaphor or rhetoric; he argues at length in "White Mythology" that metaphor is a thoroughly (if not simply) philosophical figure, and he frequently includes rhetoric—the study and classification of purely formal features of discourse—within the domain of philosophy. Discovering figurative language in philosophical texts has very little to with the practice of deconstruction.

10. I have discussed this topic further in an essay that overlaps with this Introduction—see "Singularities, Responsibilities."

ing—in many of Derrida's readings of philosophical texts that his procedure most closely approaches such thinking, even while exposing and questioning its foundations. Among the terms Derrida has used of this procedure is *deconstruction*, and although the term has come to stand for a much broader range of practices, many having little to do with Derrida's work, these readings could still be regarded as exemplary of "classical" or "philosophical" deconstruction—one thinks of the reading of Husserl's *Logical Investigations* in *Speech and Phenomena*, of Rousseau's *Essay on the Origin of Languages* in *Of Grammatology*, of Plato's *Phaedrus* in *Dissemination*. Such readings use the same strategies of logical argument and distinction-drawing that can be found in the text being discussed in order to demonstrate the dependence of such strategies on something which they cannot grasp, something which renders their claims of self-sufficiency and exhaustiveness questionable. (That "something" is not a "thing," it must immediately be added; it is not strictly namable at all, since all names are, in the end, governed by philosophy.) These readings, difficult and challenging as they were when they first appeared (and indeed as they still are if approached with the rigorous attention they call for), can seem now to yield fairly readily to an approach in traditional conceptual and logical terms. Such an approach leaves the reader in the odd situation of having had the conceptual underpinnings of his or her thought both shaken and reaffirmed.

This means that it is possible, although inevitably misleading, to summarize "philosophical deconstruction" as a method of reading; this has frequently been attempted in commentaries on Derrida's work, and the summary I am about to offer is as inadequate as any other attempt. By means of a close engagement with its language and its argument, Derrida demonstrates both the text's privileging, in accordance with the habits of what he terms "logocentric" or "metaphysical" or just "philosophical" thought, of one of the two terms in a classical opposition, and also an inverse relation (obscured but detectable), whereby the subsidiary term is characterized by a structure or a movement upon which the other term, and the whole argument of the text being read, depends. (In this volume, the excerpt from *Of*

Grammatology—". . .That Dangerous Supplement. . ."—comes closest to a deconstructive reading in this sense.) Thus the philosophical tradition's repeated preference for speech over writing as a model of language's unmediated relation to meaning, truth, and subjectivity is shown in several varied readings to rely upon a submerged acknowledgment that it is the properties of writing which make speech possible; these properties are necessarily excluded by philosophy since they do not answer to philosophical thought (or, indeed, to "common sense"). They do not obey the logic of identity, they cannot be classed as either spatial or temporal, active or passive, they originate without being an origin. Rather than introducing a new term that would seem to transcend the texts he is discussing, Derrida retains the word *writing* to refer to these properties, sometimes distinguishing the new sense from the literal one by using the terms *arche-writing* or *general writing*.[11] But this is only one of the names—we might call them "nicknames"— Derrida uses to point to a movement or a realm anterior to thought and its concepts and categories; since we can apprehend this realm only by means of an act of reading that displaces the entrenched configurations of our mental habits, it can never be isolated, conceptualized, or named. To call "it" a "movement" or a "realm" that is "anterior" to thought is already to bring it back within conceptual categories, to deny its otherness. Derrida's strategy is therefore to allow the text he is reading to proffer a temporary reference mark, not susceptible of generalization—"writing" (from Plato, Saussure, Husserl, and several others), "the supplement" (from Rousseau), the "hymen" (from Mallarmé), the "trace" (from Nietzsche, Freud, Levinas), and so on. He also coins terms that do not function as simple names, such as "*différance*" and "re-mark," and shows that certain familiar concepts that we take for granted are not concepts at all, since they operate in this undecidable manner, such as "metaphor," "law"—

---

11. Although sometimes misrepresented in this way, Derrida's claims about writing do not refer to its "materiality" or physical and visible substance; on the contrary, such a notion of language, dependent as it is on the opposition between the sensible and the intelligible, is a longstanding metaphysical one. Nor—to counter another misunderstanding—does "writing" mean "literature," even though there is a specific relation between the two terms which demands careful examination.

and, we might conjecture, "literature."[12] Once the anterior movement nicknamed by "arche-writing," "trace," etc., has been demonstrated (it can never be "revealed" as such), a transformation of the whole field is necessarily effected, since the philosophical concepts are now understood not only as owing their existence to this movement but as limited by it—this threat of limitation (dividedness, contamination by that which is exterior) being what produced the suppression of the second term of the opposition in the first place.

𝕚𝕒 It is no doubt the relative summarizability and applicability of deconstruction as found in these readings of philosophy—in spite of their questioning of the notions of summary and application—that has led to the bias in readings of and responses to Derrida's work in the anglophone world.[13] (Titles sometimes imply as much: *Deconstruction—Theory and Practice*, or *Applied Grammatology*.)[14] Jonathan Culler, one of the most effective conduits of Derrida's influence in English-speaking countries, succinctly describes the operation of this preference: "Derrida's own discussions of literary works draw attention to important problems, but they are not *deconstructions* as we have been using the term, and a deconstructive literary criticism will be primarily influenced by his readings of philosophical works" (*On Deconstruction*, 213). Most of those who have written extensive commentaries on Derrida, whether their institutional affiliation is to philos-

---

12. For the relation between law and literature, see, in particular, "Before the Law" in this volume; and note Derrida's comment in the Interview below: "What literature 'does' with language holds a revealing power which is certainly not unique, which it can share up to a point with law, for example with juridical language." Rodolphe Gasché, in *The Tain of the Mirror*, examines the potential of the term "literature" (which he distinguishes sharply from literature as ordinarily understood) as a member of the chain that includes *différance*, arche-writing, supplementarity, the trace-structure, etc. No metaphysical concept, in fact, is free of undecidability and self-difference.

13. Derrida has named the reduction of deconstruction to an applicable and teachable method "deconstructionism" (a word often used by those who take this approach to it, whether to employ it or to dismiss it); "Some Statements and Truisms," 75–76, 83–90. He stresses in this lecture, however, that the border between deconstruction and deconstructionism (or deconstructionisms) is "always being crossed, erased and re-traced" (76).

14. Christopher Norris, *Deconstruction: Theory and Practice*; Gregory L. Ulmer, *Applied Grammatology: Post(e)-Pedagogy from Jacques Derrida to Joseph Beuys*. Ulmer's "application" of Derrida, it should be added, is not the simple philosophical or technical procedure which the term might at first suggest.

ophy or literature, take a strong stand in defense of this "philosophical" deconstruction against what they see as a trivializing "literary" interest. Thus Rodolphe Gasché accuses "deconstructionist critics" of having "chosen simply to ignore the profoundly philosophical thrust of Derrida's thought" (*The Tain of the Mirror*, 3). Christopher Norris distances himself from "those zealots of a limitless textual 'freeplay' who reject the very notions of rigorous thinking or conceptual critique" (*Derrida*, 27). Irene Harvey states (in a prefatory "Open Letter to Literary Critics") that her aim in *Derrida and the Economy of "Différance"* is "to suggest a Derrida and a deconstruction that rely on his textual practice and his own claims concerning the 'theory' behind it in a more rigorously *philosophic* way than hitherto" (x).[15] In making these assertions, all three of these commentators—whose insistence on the philosophical thrust of Derrida's writing has valuably countered one possible imbalance in its reception—are justifying the selectivity of their reading of Derrida: the texts on literature do not figure centrally in any of their books, and we hear little of the delight of Derrida's writing, its pathos, its elegance, its humor.

As might be gleaned from the rather embattled tone of some of these comments, there is another strand in "American deconstruction," one which takes its inspiration from those of Derrida's writings that seek most inventively to exceed the modes and methods of philosophical argument—such writings as *Glas*, "Envois" in *The Post Card*, and *The Truth in Painting*. Thus Gregory Ulmer says of his methodology in *Applied Grammatology*, "I approach Derrida through his style rather than through his philosophical arguments" (318), and in *Saving the Text* Geoffrey Hartman notes that he has "looked at *Glas* as a work of art and bracketed specific philosophical concepts developed by Derrida" (90). Here, in spite of the brilliance with which Derrida's use of "literary" techniques is developed, the tendency is to overlook the

---

15. A similar preference for a "philosophical" as against a "literary" Derrida can be found in Henry Staten, *Wittgenstein and Derrida*—which, it should be added, is, like all these books on Derrida, substantial and illuminating. A study by a philosopher which is more alert to the problematization of the category of the "philosophical" than those mentioned above is John Llewelyn, *Derrida on the Threshold of Sense*. For a meticulous and funny meditation on some philosophically-oriented studies of Derrida, see Geoffrey Bennington, "Deconstruction and the Philosophers (The Very Idea)."

degree to which all Derrida's writing is tenaciously concerned with philosophical problems, and the inseparability of this concern from his "style" and "art."[16] Although Derrida's less orthodox texts have not been as influential as the defenders of his philosophical seriousness often claim, it is true that this version of deconstruction has given rise to some rather pointless verbal antics among those with only a limited first-hand acquaintance with Derrida's work, and has come to stand for deconstruction—especially "American deconstruction"—in the eyes of many of its detractors. However, the popularity of this more "literary" image of deconstruction has not led to a focus on Derrida's readings of literary texts; as Ulmer's remark suggests, the selectivity of its approach to Derrida is based on the style of certain of his works, and not on their subject-matter. Those who favor this approach are just as likely to be basing their understanding of deconstruction on Derrida's readings of philosophy (or on summaries of those readings) as those who attack it.[17]

The academic journals in the field of literary studies of the 1970s and '80s abound with essays that pursue one or other of these visions of a Derridean criticism, sternly philosophical or playfully literary, or that mix the two in an uneasy jostling of the logical and the ludic.[18]

16. One influential American philosopher—Richard Rorty—also devalues Derrida's concern with philosophical problems, regarding this as a phase characteristic of his early writing, and preferring the later Derrida who "offers not a way of reading but a kind of writing—comic writing that does not presuppose 'the discourse of philosophy' as anything more than a butt" ("Two Meanings of 'Logocentrism,' " 212). While right to emphasize Derrida's superb comic prose (which, however, is only one of his many modes), Rorty presents an extremely impoverished view of Derrida's "later" works, failing to appreciate how they draw out and extend the implications of the more obviously philosophical engagement of his earliest writing.

17. Thus a number of the very specific arguments made by Derrida in relation to particular philosophical texts have been generalized *ad absurdum*, and used to legitimate free-wheeling discourses claiming to be deconstructive: all binary oppositions and all indications of presence are illusory or evil, all meaning is indeterminate, there is a place in every text where it undoes itself, language is essentially unreliable or self-reflexive, communication always fails, intention or context or theme are irrelevant, there is no such thing as the referent, etc., etc. A major topic for intellectual historians of our time will be the (mis)appropriation of Derrida's work in this manner, often by intelligent and well-informed commentators.

18. This is not to deny the value of the truly original work carried out during this period, especially in the United States, by literary theorists who read Derrida carefully and responsibly (and therefore from their specific time and place); the most influential mediating figure was, of course, Paul de Man. In a longer study, it would be necessary to take up the complex issue of the relation between Derrida and de Man, vis-à-vis the

Now that this academic trend is, it seems, being supplanted by others, there may be a particular value and timeliness in tackling the difficult question ignored in much of the "American deconstruction" of this period: what is the relation between Derrida's readings of literary texts and his readings of philosophical texts? What, for Derrida, "is" literature?

ঌ The polarization between these two versions of Derrida's work, though understandable, is quite out of keeping with the work itself. The opposition that underlies it—"philosophy" versus "literature"— is an opposition that Derrida has patiently chipped away at in his readings of both kinds of text. Not only is the opposition itself a philosophical one, it is an opposition by means of which philosophy produces, and thus constitutes itself against, its other. (For Derrida, the alterity that we need to attend to is not that by which the same relates to *its* other, which provides only confirmation of the opposition, but a completely heterogeneous alterity that overruns all oppositionality.) The rejection of the "literary" Derrida can be seen as the repetition by philosophy, once again, of its founding move, even when the "philosophical" Derrida who emerges is shown to have profoundly questioned the philosophical tradition. At the same time, any thought of expelling philosophy from the practices of writing in the name of literary "free play" or "textuality" is doomed: philosophy will always come in by the back door—indeed, it will never have left the house. The very notion of literature as ungoverned rhetoricity, as a practice safely "outside" philosophy, is a philosophical notion *par excellence*.

What is necessary, then, is to make the attempt to grasp *together* the literature/philosophy couple, to gain a sense of their co-implication— which is also the double bind in which both are caught—as well as their distinctiveness. One way of doing this is to separate out, as a strategic move, Derrida's writings on literary texts, and to ask what it

question of literature and philosophy. For important contributions to the discussion, see Gasché, " 'Setzung' and 'Übersetzung,' " Gearhart, "Philosophy *before* Literature," Godzich, "The Domestication of Derrida," and—in a discussion which relates de Man to Philippe Lacoue-Labarthe (whose work is also important in this connection)—Carroll, *Paraesthetics*, 11–21. Derrida himself touches on the subject in *Mémoires*, and in the extract from "Psyche: Invention of the Other" reprinted below.

is about these texts that interests him, and what in his own response to them can throw light on the question "What is literature?"—which, as we've seen, is inseparable from the question "What is philosophy?", and is implicated in any consideration of culture, politics, ethics, or history. Derrida's writing on literature is not necessarily more "literary" in style than his writing on philosophy or art criticism or ethics; and the essays in this collection take advantage of a variety of tools, "philosophical" as well as "literary," in pursuing and staging a number of interconnected issues arising out of the peculiar status of literature, and bearing close links with the issues addressed in Derrida's readings of philosophy.

☙ I have already stressed that "philosophical" deconstruction can work only through particular acts of reading (Derrida's reading of a text, my reading of Derrida, my reading of that text in the light of Derrida's reading, my reading of other texts...), that there is no abstractable or applicable argument, concept, or method which could be laid out independently of such readings.[19] (This, of course, is precisely the deconstructive quarrel with philosophy, which is based on the principle of abstraction away from particular acts of language, and responses to language, toward transcendent meaning, truth, or instrumentality). Much of the difficulty of Derrida's work stems from this insistence, since our inclination in any strenuous mental activity is to extract the meaning, the theme, the repeatable program. While Derrida demands that we do not economize on this effort—and there is much in his writing that is systematic and programmable—he also finds ways of thwarting it by placing in its way reminders of the idiomatic, the irreducibly singular, as a necessary aspect of any act of writing.

There is one linguistic practice in which we habitually celebrate the unique, instead of finding it a hindrance, in which we usually have little objection to the impossibility of abstracting a detachable meaning or

---

19. One mark of this is Derrida's repeated acknowledgment of his own unique historical and cultural situation, in contrast to the philosophical goal of writing from a place that transcends such specificities; another is the frequency with which his texts are dated (an issue addressed in the extract from *Shibboleth* in this volume), and bear the traces of the occasion of their composition and delivery.

moral, in which we welcome being obliged to read the text again (in a repetition which is always different) in order to apprehend its power or its value: the practice we call literature. This, at least, is the claim frequently made about the distinctiveness of literature, but we've already had occasion to consider the ease with which the tradition of literary commentary passes to the assertion of generalities, the abstraction of meanings, the uncovering of origins, and many other typically philosophical activities. Against this transcendentalizing and universalizing tendency, Derrida tries to do justice to the literary text as radically *situated*—written and read and re-read at particular times and places—and as possessing a singularity (each time) which can never be reduced by criticism or theoretical contemplation; the presence of this quality in his own writings is therefore a response to what he finds in literary texts—and in philosophical texts when they show themselves to be readable as literary. (It is this singular response to singularity that Derrida's philosophical commentators tend, inevitably, to undervalue.)

However, Derrida places his emphasis not on singularity as such, but on the puzzling yet productive relation between singularity and generality, a relation which for him is not merely a paradoxical coexistence but a structural interdependence. For if the literary text were absolutely singular each time we encountered it, it would have no access to the human world at all; its readability, its possession of "meaning," however subject to change across the particular instances of reading and interpretation, implies a repetition, a law, an ideality of some type. Thus to be interpretable any literary text must belong to a genre or a number of genres, a set of generalized conventions which guide reading; but the relation of "belonging" in this instance, like the status of an individual or an act "before the law," is not one that can be easily handled by philosophical thought (as Derrida shows in "The Law of Genre," reprinted here). Whenever the text signals its own status as writing, as literature, as a member of a specific genre, it does so by means of a mark which is necessarily marked in advance *as* a mark—by what Derrida calls the "re-mark."[20] This is not a self-reflec-

20. The complex operation of the re-mark is usefully summarized—while the difficulty of discussing it in philosophical terms is demonstrated—in Gasché's *The Tain of the Mirror* (217–23).

tion nor a classical *mise-en-abyme* (as in the inclusion within a heraldic shield of a small representation of itself), but a moment at which the categories of form and content, inside and outside, break down; another intimation of the anterior movement—the trace, *différance*, supplementarity—which both produces and restricts the categories of philosophy. Once again, we should note that this does not involve the extraction of an essence of literature; the re-mark is a permanent possibility in all texts, all signs, but literature has the capacity to stage its operation with unusual forcefulness and to produce unusual pleasure in doing so. Or put it the other way round: a text in which the re-mark, and the relation between singularity and generality, are staged with haunting power is, to that extent, "literary."

For Derrida the literary text is not, therefore, a verbal icon or a hermetically sealed space; it is not the site of a rich plenitude of meaning but rather a kind of emptying-out of meaning that remains potently meaningful; it does not possess a core of uniqueness that survives mutability, but rather a repeatable singularity that depends on an openness to new contexts and therefore on its difference each time it is repeated. That which marks out the specific literary text is also a property of the "general text"—and it must be remembered that the general text is not by any means limited to language or graphic signs.[21] Derrida's writings on literary texts are therefore not commentaries in any conventional sense, not criticism, not interpretation (the hermeneutic search for the meaning of a text, however qualified by sensitivity to contextual changes, is still a fundamentally philosophic quest). They do not attempt to place, or master, or exhaust, or translate, or penetrate

---

21. The preference which Derrida evinces for the word *mark* over words such as *sign, signifier,* or *language* is related to his claim that the operations he is pointing to take place over an extremely wide field; beyond what are usually thought of as sign-systems or effects of meaning, beyond, indeed, the realm of the purely human. It is the failure to appreciate the extensive reach of the "text" that has led to the frequent misunderstanding of such aphorisms as "There is nothing outside the text" (see ". . .That Dangerous Supplement . . . ," note 21, below). Among the many clear accounts Derrida has given of this point is the following: "What I call 'text' implies all the structures called 'real,' 'economic,' 'historical,' socio-institutional, in short: all possible referents. Another way of recalling once again that 'there is nothing outside the text.' That does not mean that all referents are suspended, denied, or enclosed in a book, as people have claimed. . . . But it does mean that every referent, all reality has the structure of a differential trace, and that one cannot refer to this 'real' except in an interpretive experience" ("Afterword," 148; see also 136 and 137).

the literary work. Like all valuable readings of literature, they seek to make the text strange (or perhaps strangely familiar), offering not a reduced and simplified version of the text but one which operates at its own level of difficulty. They do not simply represent the operations of a subject with respect to an object; these readings (and any effects of subjectivity and agency they may produce) are also read by the texts they read. (Just as a letter does not simply reach, but participates in the creation of, its addressee, so the literary text in part constitutes its reader.[22]) Each one is different in style, tone, manner, emphasis, argument, as it responds to a text that is different from all others. But it is not merely a matter of writing a poem in response to a poem; Derrida's texts on literature—though they are not more centrally philosophical than they are literary—remain fascinated by philosophical questions, and look for ways of letting the literary text's undoing of philosophy be heard.[23] In doing so, they foreground what is literary about literature; that which makes the word *literature* a term like *writing* or *law*, capable of destabilizing the discourses and institutions within which it has its being.

&. This question of the singular and the universal raises a number of issues of importance in any consideration of literature. One of these is the issue of translation and translatability, about which Derrida has often written. For instance:

> A text lives only if it lives on, and it lives *on* only if it is *at once* translatable *and* untranslatable. . . . Totally translatable, it disappears as a text, as writing, as a body of language. Totally untranslatable, even within what is believed to be one language, it dies immediately. ("Living On/Borderlines," 102–03)

Once again, this is not a feature peculiar to literature; it is equally constitutive of the operation of justice, which relies on an impossible

---

22. See, for instance, Derrida's "Telepathy," 4–6. This epistolary piece, and the related series of letters entitled "Envois" (in *The Post Card*), can be usefully read in connection with the question of the addressee of the literary text.

23. Stephen Heath, in "Modern Literary Theory," makes an intriguing connection between Derrida's responses to literary texts and F. R. Leavis's in that for both of them literature is a "force" that resists or exceeds theory (35–36).

union of a singular occurrence and a general law,[24] and in fact of all discursive events. One name Derrida gives it is "iterability": the necessary repeatability of any item experienced as meaningful, which at the same time can never be repeated exactly since it has no essence that could remain unaffected by the potentially infinite contexts (which are always contexts within contexts...) into which it could be grafted. Moreover, its "first" occurrence is made possible by this openness to change and loss, so there is a sense in which it is never purely and simply "itself." Iterability—which overruns the conventional border-line between substance and accidents, necessity and chance—both makes meaningful items and events possible, and prevents them from being meaningful in the sense that philosophy or linguistics would ideally want—single, self-identical representations of prior, whole, meanings. (For a full discussion, see Derrida's "Signature Event Context.")

Two closely-related instances of this alogical logic of particular importance in considering literature are the *signature* and the *proper name* (among the texts reprinted here, see in particular "Ulysses Gramophone," the extract from *Signsponge*, and—for the proper name— "Aphorism Countertime"). The function of the signature in our legal culture is dependent upon two contradictory properties, its unique affirmation of the here-and-now of the signatory, and its repeatability, recognizability, and reproducibility (which also implies its forgeability). Once again, Derrida extends the notion of the "signature" beyond its literal sense to take in the operation of this impossible double in much wider contexts; every literary text, for instance, has the self-contradictory characteristics of the signature. And like any signature, it does not exist until it calls forth some response that affirms its status as signature, a response that is not a subjective answering to another subject but one that has itself the structure of a signature. It is never merely "I" who signs, and "I" alone never completes the event of the signature: there is always an other who countersigns (an other both unforeseen and yet made possible by the "first" signature).

24. See "Force of Law" for a discussion of justice which, although presented in the context of legal theory, has important implications for all acts of judgment, including those of literary criticism.

The proper name is another instance of the mutually constitutive co-occurrence of the singular and the general: on the one hand the distinctiveness of proper names is that they function *outside* the language system, they are supposed only to refer and not to mean, they are wholly untranslatable, etc.; on the other hand, their "properness" depends on their occurrence within a system of differences, they have to be repeatable (and therefore falsifiable), and they can never be prevented from slipping into the functions of common nouns. Another important feature of both signatures and proper names, which has a bearing on literature, is that neither could begin to function if they were not able to survive beyond the death of the person whom they identify; death is therefore structurally implicit in every occurrence of a signature or a proper name. (See "Aphorism Countertime" for some of the consequences of this; Derrida also discusses survival in "Living On/Borderlines," a text devoted partly to a consideration of *The Triumph of Life* by Shelley and *L'arrêt de mort* by Blanchot.) In another discussion included here, taken from "Psyche," Derrida finds a similar doubleness in the notion of *invention*: a coming into being (whether technical or literary) which is wholly new and yet at the same time recognizable and exploitable. And in *Shibboleth*, reprinted here in part, the necessary uniqueness and repeatability of the *date*—concretely manifested in Celan's poetry—are shown to be a property of any poem.

The literary text, like the signature, the proper name, and the date, is an act (both a doing and an imitation of doing, both a performance and a record, both an event and a law) which displaces and resituates the philosophical opposition between unique and general, concrete and ideal, idiomatic and rule-governed. And each reading of it is a response to both sides of this (non-)opposition, to that which is irreducible, which resists assimilation to what we know and how we think, and at the same time to that which speaks to us of the systems which overarch the text and its readers. Moreover, this dual response involves the apprehension of the interdependence of these two qualities as an oscillation or vibration that underlies, but also undermines, all logic. We have to qualify the term *response*, then, insofar as it carries with it connotations of the Romantic subject reacting to a text out of a developed sensitivity of feelings and intellect, organically united with one another and with the text; the "answer" exemplified by Derrida's reading exists, from the beginning, as language (of some kind), it is itself subject to the contradictory structure we have described, and, like the counter-signature to a signature, it both confirms the text and opens up a new need for confirmation.[25] Its response is tied to responsibility, it is an answer that recognizes that it must always be answerable—both to the laws of the text and to the text as irreducibly other. Because of its uniqueness and its responsiveness to a particular situation, because of its call for another response, such a reading does not claim exhaustiveness or definitiveness, nor does it offer any kind of key to the work. Nor should one think, in accordance with some misconstruals of deconstruction, of the "text" to which such a response is made as simply a verbal entity, words-on-the-page; what deconstruction is concerned to show is that a verbal artifact can never close upon itself, and the other that summons us from literature is not confined within language in the narrow sense. Derrida comments: "I never cease to be surprised by critics who see my work as a declaration that there is nothing beyond language, that we are imprisoned in language; it is, in fact, saying the exact opposite. The critique of logocentrism is above all else the search for the 'other' and the 'other of language' " ("Deconstruction and the Other," 123).

One striking feature of Derrida's responses to literary texts is their predominantly affirmative mode: they affirm what they take the texts to be doing in their most challenging operations, they bring this quality or movement out into the open (as far as it is possible to do so), they celebrate it, they put it to work, they invite a further response to it. By

---

25. Derrida discusses what he calls "the question of the response" in "The Politics of Friendship" (638–41). One might note in particular the close connection between his comments on the relationship to the other in the context of friendship and the relationship to the literary text as we have been discussing it: "One answers before the other because first one answers to the other. . . . In the idiom, the expression 'before' generally indicates the passage to an institutional instance of alterity. It is no longer singular, but is universal in its principle. One answers to the other who can always be singular, and who must remain so in a certain way, but one answers before the law, a tribunal, a jury, some agency (instance) authorized to represent the other legitimately, in the form of a moral, legal, or political community. . . . But is this an alternative? Are there really two different, even antagonistic or incompatible relations? Do not these two relations imply each other at the moment they seem to exclude each other? Does not my relation to the singularity of the other as other pass through the law?" (639–41; translation modified).

contrast, the mode of his writing on philosophical texts may seem neutral or even antagonistic (though Derrida has been at pains to distance himself from the possible negative connotations of the term *deconstruction*).[26] As we have seen, it is the latter mode that has been most influential in literary theory: the appeal of the term *deconstruction* to a wide audience—as against the numerous other terms Derrida has introduced—lies no doubt in its air of mechanical precision and methodological repeatability, seeming to bring into the murky realm of literary studies a much needed technical rigor. Generality, in other words, has been emphasized at the expense of singularity.[27] But it would be wrong to erect another opposition between two kinds or moments of deconstruction, the analytical and the affirmative. The effect of "philosophical" deconstruction is a shaking loose, an opening, which makes possible—while it is made possible by—the coming and the call of the other, the "yes" that precedes all speech and subjectivity (see "Psyche" and "Ulysses Gramophone"), the affirmation of the unpredicted and unpredictable. The two modes are always at work together, implicit in one another, like the two kinds of laugh that Derrida, in "Ulysses Gramophone," responds to in Joyce's writing. If there is an implicit negative in deconstruction, it is directed against those who would reduce and simplify both literature and philosophy, instead of recognizing that the texts to which we give these labels remain always ahead of us, calling to us, making demands on us, laughing at us and with us.

26. See, for example, "Letter to a Japanese Friend": "[T]he undoing, decomposing, desedimenting of structures, in a certain sense more historical than the structuralist movement it called into question, was not a negative operation. Rather than destroying, it was also necessary to understand how an 'ensemble' was constituted and to reconstruct it to this end. However, the negative appearance was and remains much more difficult to efface than is suggested by the grammar of the word (de-), even though it can designate a genealogical restoration [*remonter*] rather than a demolition. This is why the word, at least on its own, has never appeared satisfactory to me (but what word is?), and must always be girded by an entire discourse" (3).

27. This seems to be the case with Gasché's project in *The Tain of the Mirror*. He proposes a "deconstructive literary criticism" which would "proceed from the signifying structures that reinscribe, and thus account for, the differences constitutive of the literary work and the critical discourse," adding: "Except marginally, Derrida has not systematically undertaken to establish the particular infrastructures of the critical discourse" (269). This may be because such a systematic and differentiating analysis would come once more under the aegis of philosophy, and reestablish the opposition philosophy/

ᏨᎳ In a response to the question "What is poetry?" written for an Italian literary magazine,[28] Derrida introduces the phrase "to learn by heart." The poetic, he suggests, is "that which you desire to learn, but from and of the other, thanks to the other and under dictation, by heart." And "heart," here, "no longer names only pure interiority, independent spontaneity, the active self-affection free to reproduce the beloved trace. The memory of the 'by heart' is confided like a prayer—that's safer—to a certain exteriority of the automaton, to the laws of mnemotechnics, to that liturgy that mimes mechanics on the surface." In other words, the poem has the power both to speak to your most intimate feelings and thoughts, and at the same time to reveal how even these private depths are always made possible by otherness and exteriority, always passing through the institution, the law, that which is not you, which calls to you, and without which "you" could not come into being. One corollary of the exteriority at the heart of the literary text is its openness (like the signature or the proper name) to accidents: it cannot set limits to the way it will be read, and the accidents which "befall" it cannot simply be separated from some essence which they unfortunately betray. (Any more than the mis-chances—the contretemps—in *Romeo and Juliet*, or the multiple coin-cidences in *Ulysses*, can be separated from the instituted networks of marks which, while set up to forestall them, make them possible.) This does not mean that there are not, in any given context, appropriate or inappropriate readings, but that the relation between "appropriate" and "inappropriate"—like that between "genuine" and "forged" sig-natures—is not one of absolute heterogeneity, and needs to be thought through with great care. Like a hedgehog rolled into a defensive ball on the freeway, suggests Derrida in "Che cos'è la poesia?", the poem's singular self-possession is also that which most exposes it to accident (and calls forth the desire to make it our own, to learn it by heart).

literature (and philosophy/literary criticism). See also the Interview below. (It should be added that Gasché has written illuminatingly *about* the question of singularity; see, for example, "Edges of Understanding," 218–19).

28. See "Che cos'è la poesia?" Derrida ends this piece by once more problematizing the posing of the question itself: " 'What is. . .?' laments the disappearance of the poem. . . . By announcing that which is just as it is, a question salutes the birth of prose."

☙ If the literary text has no essence and no inherently determined limits, what governs its appearance and operation on the cultural and political scene? What gives it to us as "literature"? The answer to this question is of central importance in any consideration of Derrida's interest in literature, yet it is not one which has been given the attention it demands. What Derrida emphasizes is that literature is an *institution*: it is not given in nature or the brain but brought into being by processes that are social, legal, and political, and that can be mapped historically and geographically. (The same is true, of course, of philosophy—the history of exclusions which Derrida traces from Plato onwards is not to be explained in terms of "natural" or "logical" causes, since this is exactly the kind of explanation being deconstructed.) It is worth stressing this point, lest the attention which Derrida gives to literature seem to indicate a perpetual, ahistorical, privileging. That a body of texts called "literary" can, at a certain historical conjuncture, serve strategic purposes is not the result of any transcendent properties these texts possess, any permanent access to truth. Rather, it is an opportunity that can be seized, just as any individual text (literary or not, verbal or not) may proffer the chance of a productive and important intervention. The institution of literature, especially as we have known it in the Western democracies since the seventeenth or eighteenth century, has certain features that make it an unusual member of the set of verbal practices around us, and Derrida stresses this peculiarity: although the historical origins and geographical limits of this institution can be (roughly) calculated, it cannot simply be *contained* by our usual socio-economic-historical thought about such human constructions, because of the way it takes that thought's founding oppositions to the limits, including the oppositions between the given and the produced, and between nature and its series of others such as culture, art, education, technique, and institution. (Derrida speculates further on the particular function of the literary institution in Western democracies—as a space in which, in principle, anything and everything may be said—in the Interview below.) Never forgetting that literature is an institution also means never forgetting the relations of power within which it exists, nor the laws which keep it in being; in "Before the Law," responding to Kafka's text of this name, Derrida focuses not only on the question "What is literature?" but on the inescapable companion question "Who decides?" And if literature is characterized by a certain structural undecidability, then the act of deciding is not a calculation but an ethical, political act, an act for which we remain responsible since it is not determined in advance by a law we can simply appeal to.[29]

While "literature" names for Derrida a relatively recent cultural institution, differing from the predecessor institutions which we often subsume under the name "literature" as well,[30] in its reappropriated guise—when it names that which resists philosophical conceptuality—it can be found at work over a much longer history, beginning with ancient Greece. In this guise (which is still a historical, not a universal, one), it always functions as the *supplement* of a use of language regarded as "normal"; and, as emerges from Derrida's discussion of Rousseau in ". . .That Dangerous Supplement . . .," this relation of supplementarity always involves a contradictory logic that relates it to the workings of *différance,* both leaving the final determination of what counts as "literary" to economic and political forces and rendering impossible the final control of the literary by those forces.[31] We might observe, too, the paradoxical fact that in such differentiations, litera-

29. "A decision can only come into being in a space that exceeds the calculable program that would destroy all responsibility by transforming it into a programmable effect of determinate causes. There can be no moral or political responsibility without this trial and this passage by way of the undecidable" ("Afterword," 116; see also "Force of Law," 961–71). It should be added that an understanding of "ethics" or "politics" faithful to Derrida's argument here necessarily differs from the traditional meanings— and programs—associated with these terms. For an economical account of Derrida's sense of his relation to the domain of ethics, see *Altérités,* 70–72, 76–77.

30. See Derrida's comments on the distinction between "literature" and "poetry" in the Interview below. In his discussion of glossematics in *Of Grammatology* (59), Derrida equates "the *literary* element" with "what in literature passes through an irreducibly graphic text" and with "something in literature which does not allow itself to be reduced to the voice, to epos or poetry." He notes that the Russian Formalists, "in their attention to the being-literary of literature, perhaps favored the phonological instance and the literary models that it dominates. Notably poetry." Derrida's most striking deployment of this distinction is in "No Apocalypse, Not Now" (26–27), in which he associates the uniqueness of nuclear war with the possibility of the destruction of the entire literary archive, in that "literature produces its referent as a fictive or fabulous referent, which in itself is dependent on the possibility of archivizing, indeed constituted in itself by the archivizing act." By contrast, "poetry or the epic" might "reconstitute their living process and their archive" after a nuclear cataclysm.

31. I have discussed this set of issues more fully in *Peculiar Language,* in relation to a number of specific texts and historical conjunctures.

ture tends to be deprived of its power in the same gesture that exalts it; it is valued for its transcendence of the practical, the social, the economic, the political, and even its moral influence is represented in the most generalized of terms. Like writing in relation to speech, if it is not belittled it is praised in such terms as deny it the radical force it potentially possesses.

❧ As a peculiar institution which sheds light on institutionality, as a site of resistance to the philosophical tradition of conceptual thought, as a series of singular (but repeatable) acts that demand singular (but responsible) responses, as a staging of a number of strategic issues—the signature, the proper name, the date, invention, law, iterability, and many others which will emerge over the following pages—literature is clearly of major importance in Derrida's work. He says in *Positions*, "If we had the time, we could . . . ask ourselves too, why the irreducibility of writing and, let us say, the subversion of logocentrism are announced better than elsewhere, today, in a certain sector and certain determined form of 'literary' practice" (11). To insist upon this importance of literature is not, however, to accord it a position of superiority over other modes of writing (we might note in the comment quoted above that, as so often, Derrida puts "literary" in inverted commas, and stresses that he is talking about a strategic value, at a particular historical moment, rather than a transcendent quality);[32] it is to stress the specific role literature plays in Derrida's work—or rather *roles*, since it is a different one each time, and it is the impossibility of predicting what kind of summons the next literary text will make that is part of literature's importance and power.

If we can use the term *deconstruction* of the essays collected here—

32. In "Institutional Authority vs. Critical Power," David Carroll argues strongly against the use of Derrida's work, or some version of it, as part of an effort to sustain the authority of literature and the institutions that promote it over other disciplines and institutions; and in *Paraesthetics*, chap. 4, he stresses the strategic quality of the privilege given to literature in Derrida's writing. Timothy Clark has clarified the nature of literature's importance for Derrida by contrasting it with the more metaphysically derived privilege accorded to poetry by Heidegger ("Being in Mime"); in spite of this contrast (which one might heighten by adducing Derrida's emphasis on literature as an institution), Heidegger's attention to literature remains a crucial precursory context for Derrida's work.

Derrida has acknowledged that the word has acquired a generality and a celebrity which he did not foresee—it is necessary to revise radically the popular images associated with it. Derrida's practice is neither the bloodless dissection of a scalpel-wielding technician nor the frolicsome play of an exuberant comedian; it is not trapped within the borders of the text (those borders being precisely what it questions),[33] nor does it range with reckless abandon across all borders (their force being one of the things it is most interested in). Deconstruction is not an evil product of the latest stage of multinational capitalism, nor is it a predictable reappearance in new clothes of an ancient philosophical— or literary—game. However, these widespread responses do not come from nowhere; and perhaps the most significant fact about them is the deep contradictions they evince (often within the same hostile response). Deconstruction is indeed contradictory. (It is also impossible, Derrida likes to say—and it doesn't exist.) It *is* both careful and irreverent, it *does* both acknowledge and traverse borders, it *is* both very old—older than philosophy, Derrida claims—and very new, not yet born, perhaps. Deconstruction is radical and, in a strict sense, conservative,[34] and challenges political rhetorics of both left and right. Neither the language of communality and historical laws nor the language of individuality and pragmatic freedom matches deconstruction's insistence on the structural interconnectedness of the absolutely singular and the absolutely general, necessitating a new understanding of both "absolutes"; and there is a strong ethico-political summons implicit in the constant attention in these essays to the uniqueness of the other, the function of alterity in any movement or consciousness of the self, and the call to and dependence upon the other in any

33. Derrida writes of the relation between Nietzsche's "life" and "works": "[W]herever the paradoxical problem of the border is posed, then the line that could separate an author's life from his work, for example, or which, within this life, could separate an essentialness or transcendentality from an empirical fact, or, yet again, within his work, an empirical fact from something that is not empirical—this very line itself becomes unclear. Its mark becomes divided; its unity, its identity becomes dislocated" (*The Ear of the Other*, 44–45). Derrida's own crossing of the boundary between autobiographical and philosophical writing is particularly evident in "Envois" and in "Circonfession," in Bennington and Derrida, *Jacques Derrida*; see also his autobiographical comments in the Interview below, and his use of personal anecdotes in "Ulysses Gramophone."

34. In "Deconstruction in America" Derrida expresses his support for the university's mission to "assure the memory of culture, of thought, of philosophy" (7).

signature and any signed text. Nor is deconstruction manifested only in individual acts; Derrida often uses the term to designate a process constantly at work, whether recognized or not, in cultural, intellectual, and political change.[35]

૨ "What is literature?" It will be evident by now that the question with which we began was being both asked and quoted, used and mentioned (to draw on a distinction from speech act theory which Derrida is fond of using, mentioning, and undermining). It is not, for Derrida, a question that can *simply* be used, since it is always a citation, a quotation from philosophy that puts itself—and philosophy—in question. In every text in this collection, and in every text being responded to, the question is both posed and staged, followed through and subverted. These responses to literature, and to the question of literature, cannot serve as models for a new critical practice, since they shake the foundations of any such mimetic extrapolation. As verbal acts which "belong" both to literature and philosophy the only responsible answer to the demands they make is another act on the reader's part, an invention, a risk, at once singular and general, which will countersign them and so make them happen, again, for the first time.

Works Cited For works by Derrida, see the *Selected Bibliography* at the end of the volume.

Attridge, Derek. *Peculiar Language: Literature as Difference from the Renaissance to James Joyce*. Ithaca: Cornell University Press, 1988.

———. "Singularities, Responsibilities: Derrida, Deconstruction, and

---

35. In "Some Questions and Responses," for instance, Derrida replies to the question of whether "all changes in human thought in the past have been, in some sense or other, covertly, or patently even, deconstructive": "[I]f there is change this means that there is somewhere a structural logic which makes it possible. This has to do with deconstruction. ... Of course deconstruction today designates not only this principle of disintegration or dislocation in any question within a system, but a way of thematising this possibility" (262–63).

the Literary Text." *Deconstruction Reviewed* (provisional title). Ed. Cathy Caruth and Deborah Esch. Rutgers University Press, forthcoming.

Bennington, Geoffrey. "Deconstruction and the Philosophers (The Very Idea)." *Oxford Literary Review* 10 (1988): 73–130.

Bennington, Geoffrey, and Jacques Derrida. *Jacques Derrida.* Paris: Seuil, 1991.

Carroll, David. "Institutional Authority vs. Critical Power, or the Uneasy Relations of Psychoanalysis and Literature." *Taking Chances: Derrida, Psychoanalysis, and Literature.* Ed. Joseph H. Smith and William Kerrigan. Baltimore: Johns Hopkins University Press, 1984. 107–34.

————. *Paraesthetics: Foucault, Lyotard, Derrida.* New York: Methuen, 1987.

Clark, Timothy. "Being in Mime: Heidegger and Derrida on the Ontology of Literary Language." *MLN* 101 (1986): 1003–21.

Culler, Jonathan. *On Deconstruction: Theory and Criticism after Structuralism.* Ithaca: Cornell University Press, 1982.

de Man, Paul. "The Resistance to Theory." *The Resistance to Theory.* Minneapolis: University of Minnesota Press, 1986. 3–20.

Gasché, Rodolphe. "Edges of Understanding." *Responses: On Paul de Man's Wartime Journalism.* Ed. Werner Hamacher, Neil Hertz, and Thomas Keenan. Lincoln: University of Nebraska Press, 1989. 208–20.

————. " 'Setzung' and 'Übersetzung': Notes on Paul de Man." *Diacritics* 11.4 (Winter 1981): 36–57.

————. *The Tain of the Mirror: Derrida and the Philosophy of Reflection.* Cambridge, Mass.: Harvard University Press, 1986.

Gearhart, Suzanne. "Philosophy *before* Literature: Deconstruction, Historicity, and the Work of Paul de Man." *Diacritics* 13.4 (Winter 1983): 63–81.

Godzich, Wlad. "The Domestication of Derrida." *The Yale Critics: Deconstruction in America.* Ed. Jonathan Arac, Wlad Godzich, and Wallace Martin. Minneapolis: University of Minnesota Press, 1983. 20–40.

Hartman, Geoffrey H. *Saving the Text: Literature/Derrida/Philosophy.* Baltimore: Johns Hopkins University Press, 1981.

Harvey, Irene E. *Derrida and the Economy of "Différance."* Blooming-ton: Indiana University Press, 1986.

Heath, Stephen. "Modern Literary Theory." *Critical Quarterly* 31.2 (Summer 1989): 35–49.

Llewelyn, John. *Derrida on the Threshold of Sense.* London: Macmil-lan, 1986.

Norris, Christopher. *Deconstruction: Theory and Practice.* London: Methuen, 1982.

———. *Derrida.* Cambridge, Mass.: Harvard University Press, 1987.

Rorty, Richard. "Two Meanings of 'Logocentrism': A Reply to Nor-ris." *Redrawing the Lines: Analytic Philosophy, Deconstruction, and Literary Theory.* Ed. Reed Way Dasenbrock. Minneapolis: Uni-versity of Minnesota Press, 1989. 204–16.

Staten, Henry. *Wittgenstein and Derrida.* Lincoln: University of Ne-braska Press, 1984.

Ulmer, Gregory L. *Applied Grammatology: Post(e)-Pedagogy from Jacques Derrida to Joseph Beuys.* Baltimore: Johns Hopkins Univer-sity Press, 1985.

Waters, Lindsay, and Wlad Godzich, eds. *Reading de Man Reading.* Minneapolis: University of Minnesota Press, 1989.

Weber, Samuel. "Reading and Writing *chez* Derrida." *Institution and Interpretation.* Minneapolis: University of Minnesota Press, 1987. 85–101.

"THIS STRANGE INSTITUTION
CALLED LITERATURE"

AN INTERVIEW WITH JACQUES DERRIDA

✒ The original interview, of which this is an edited transcript, took place in Laguna Beach over two days in April 1989. The translation is by Geoffrey Bennington and Rachel Bowlby.

D.A. You said to your thesis jury in 1980 that "my most constant interest, coming even before my philosophical interest I should say, if this is possible, has been directed towards literature, towards that writing which is called literary." And you have published a number of texts which present readings of literary texts, about which we shall soon be talking. Yet a large part of your work has been concerned with writing that would be more likely to be called philosophical. Could you expand upon that statement concerning your primary interest in literature, and say something about its relation to your extensive work on philosophical texts?

J.D. What can a "primary interest" be? I would never dare to say that my primary interest went toward literature rather than toward philosophy. Anamnesis would be risky here, because I'd like to escape my own stereotypes. To do that, we'd have to determine what got called "literature" and "philosophy" during my adolescence, at a time when, in France at least, the two were meeting through works which were then dominant. Existentialism, Sartre, Camus were present everywhere and the memory of surrealism was still alive. And if these writings practiced a fairly new kind of contact between philosophy and literature, they were prepared for this by a national tradition and by certain models given a solid legitimacy by the teaching in schools. What's more, the examples I have just given seem very different from each other.

No doubt I hesitated between philosophy and literature, giving up neither, perhaps seeking obscurely a place from which the history of this frontier could be thought or even displaced—in writing itself and not only by historical or theoretical reflection. And since what interests me today is not strictly called either literature or philosophy, I'm amused by the idea that my adolescent desire—let's call it that—should have directed me toward something in writing which was neither the one nor the other. What was it?

"Autobiography" is perhaps the least inadequate name, because it remains for me the most enigmatic, the most open, even today. At this moment, here, I'm trying, in a way that would commonly be called "autobiographical," to remember what happened when the desire to write came to me, in a way that was as obscure as it was compulsive, both powerless and authoritarian. Well, what happened then was just like an autobiographical desire. At the "narcissistic" moment of "adolescent" identification (a difficult identification which was often attached, in my youthful notebooks, to the Gidian theme of Proteus), this was above all the desire to inscribe merely a memory or two. I say "only," though I already felt it as an impossible and endless task. Deep down, there was something like a lyrical movement toward confidences or confessions. Still today there remains in me an obsessive desire to save in uninterrupted inscription, in the form of a memory, what happens—or *fails to happen*. What I should be tempted to denounce as a lure—i.e., totalization or gathering up—isn't this what keeps me going? The idea of an internal polylogue, everything that later, in what

I hope was a slightly more refined way, was able to lead me to Rousseau (about whom I had been passionate ever since childhood) or to Joyce, was first of all the adolescent dream of keeping a trace of all the voices which were traversing me—or were *almost doing so*—and which was to be so precious, unique, both specular and speculative. I've just said "fails to happen" and "almost doing so" so as to mark the fact that what *happens*—in other words, the unique event whose trace one would like to keep alive—is also the very desire that what does not happen should happen, and is thus a "story" in which the event already crosses within itself the archive of the "real" and the archive of "fiction." Already we'd have trouble not spotting but separating out historical narrative, literary fiction, and philosophical reflexion.

So there was a movement of nostalgic, mournful lyricism to reserve, perhaps encode, in short to render both *accessible and inaccessible*. And deep down this is still my most naive desire. I don't dream of either a literary work, or a philosophical work, but that everything that occurs, happens to me or fails to, should be as it were *sealed* (placed in reserve, hidden so as to be kept, and this in its very signature, really like a signature, in the very form of the seal, with all the paradoxes that traverse the structure of a seal). The discursive forms we have available to us, the resources in terms of objectivizing archivation, are so much poorer than what happens (or fails to happen, whence the excesses of hyper-totalization). This desire for *everything* + *n*— naturally I can analyze it, "deconstruct" it, criticize it, but it is an experience I love, that I know and recognize. In the moment of narcissistic adolescence and "autobiographical" dream I'm referring to now ("Who am I? Who is me? What's happening?," etc.), the first texts I got interested in had that in them: Rousseau, Gide, or Nietzsche— texts which were neither simply literary, nor philosophical, but confessions, the *Rêveries du promeneur solitaire*, the *Confessions*, Gide's *Journal*, *La porte étroite*, *Les nourritures terrestres*, *L'immoraliste*, and at the same time Nietzsche, the philosopher who speaks in the first person while all the time multiplying proper names, masks and signatures. As soon as things become a little sedimented, the fact of not giving anything up, not even the things one deprives oneself of, through an interminable "internal" polylogue (supposing that a poly-logue can still be "internal") is also not giving up the "culture" which carries these voices. At which point the encyclopedic temptation be-comes inseparable from the autobiographical. And philosophical dis-course is often only an economic or strategic formalization of this avidity.

All the same, this motif of *totality* circulates here in a singular way between literature and philosophy. In the naive adolescent notebooks or diaries I'm referring to from memory, the obsession with the *protei-form* motivates the interest for literature to the extent that literature seemed to me, in a confused way, to be the institution which allows one to *say everything*,[1] in *every way*. The space of literature is not only that of an instituted *fiction* but also a *fictive institution* which in principle allows one to say everything. To say everything is no doubt to gather, by translating, all figures into one another, to totalize by formalizing, but to say everything is also to break out of [*franchir*] prohibitions. To *affranchise oneself* [*s'affranchir*]—in every field where law can lay down the law. The law of literature tends, in principle, to defy or lift the law. It therefore allows one to think the essence of the law in the experience of this "everything to say." It is an institution which tends to overflow the institution.

For a serious answer to your question, an analysis of my time at school would also be necessary, and of the family in which I was born, of its relation or non-relation with books, etc. In any case, at the moment when I was beginning to discover this strange institution called literature, the question "What is literature?" imposed itself upon me in its most naive form. Only a little later, this was to be the title of one of the first texts by Sartre I think I read after *La nausée* (which had made a strong impression on me, no doubt provoking some mimetic movements in me; briefly, here was a literary fiction grounded on a philosophical "emotion," the feeling of existence as excess, "being-superfluous," the very beyond of meaning giving rise to writing). Bewil-derment, then, faced with this institution or type of object which allows

---

1. TN *Tout dire*, both to "say everything," with a sense of exhausting a totality, and to "say anything," i.e., to speak without constraints on what one may say.

36

one to say everything. What is it? What "remains" when desire has just inscribed something which "remains" there, like an object at the disposal of others, one that can be repeated? What does "remaining" mean? This question subsequently took on forms which were perhaps a little more elaborated, but ever since the beginning of adolescence, when I was keeping these notebooks, I was absolutely bewildered at the possibility of consigning things to paper. The philosophical becoming of these questions goes by way of the content of the texts of the culture I was entering—when one reads Rousseau or Nietzsche, one has a certain access to philosophy—just as much as through naive or marveling bewilderment at remains as a written thing.

Subsequently, philosophical training, the profession, the position of teacher were also a detour to come back to this question: "What is writing in general?" and, in the space of writing in general, to this other question which is more and other than a simple particular case: "What is literature?"; literature as historical institution with its conventions, rules, etc., but also this institution of fiction which gives *in principle* the power to say everything, to break free of the rules, to displace them, and thereby to institute, to invent and even to suspect the traditional difference between nature and institution, nature and conventional law, nature and history. Here we should ask juridical and political questions. The institution of literature in the West, in its relatively modern form, is linked to an authorization to say everything, and doubtless too to the coming about of the modern idea of democracy. Not that it depends on a democracy in place, but it seems inseparable to me from what calls forth a democracy, in the most open (and doubtless itself to come) sense of democracy.

D.A. Could you elaborate on your view of literature as "this strange institution which allows one to say everything"?

J.D. Let's make this clear. What we call literature (not belles-lettres or poetry) implies that license is given to the writer to say everything he wants to or everything he can, while remaining shielded, safe from all censorship, be it religious or political. When Khomeini called for the murder of Rushdie, it happened that I put my signature to a text—

without approving all its formulations to the letter—which said that literature has a "critical function." I am not sure that "critical function" is the right word. First of all, it would limit literature by fixing a mission for it, a single mission. This would be to finalize literature, to assign it a meaning, a program and a regulating ideal, whereas it could also have other essential functions, or even have no function, no usefulness outside itself. And by the same token it can help to think or delimit what "meaning," "regulating ideal," "program," "function," and "critical" might mean. But above all, the reference to a critical function of literature belongs to a language which makes no sense outside what in the West links politics, censorship, and the lifting of censorship to the origin and institution of literature. In the end, the critico-political function of literature, in the West, remains very ambiguous. The freedom to say everything is a very powerful political weapon, but one which might immediately let itself be neutralized as a fiction. This revolutionary power can become very conservative. The writer can just as well be held to be irresponsible. He can, I'd even say that he must sometimes demand a certain irresponsibility, at least as regards ideological powers, of a Zhdanovian type for example, which try to call him back to extremely determinate responsibilities before socio-political or ideological bodies. This duty of irresponsibility, of refusing to reply for one's thought or writing to constituted powers, is perhaps the highest form of responsibility. To whom, to what? That's the whole question of the future or the event promised by or to such an experience, what I was just calling the democracy to come. Not the democracy of tomorrow, not a future democracy which will be present tomorrow but one whose concept is linked to the to-come [à-venir, cf. avenir, future], to the experience of a promise engaged, that is always an endless promise.

As an adolescent, I no doubt had the feeling that I was living in conditions where it was both difficult and therefore necessary, urgent, to say things that were not allowed, in any case to be interested in those situations in which writers say things which are not allowed. For me, Algeria in the forties (Vichy, official anti-semitism, the Allied landing at the end of 1942, the terrible colonial repression of Algerian resistance in 1945 at the time of the first serious outbursts heralding the Algerian war) was not only or primarily my family situation, but it is true that my interest in literature, diaries, journals in general, also signified a typical, stereotypical revolt against the family. My passion for Nietzsche, Rousseau, and also Gide, whom I read a lot at that time, meant among other things: "Families, I hate you." I thought of literature as the end of the family, and of the society it represented, even if that family was also, on the other hand, persecuted. Racism was everywhere in Algeria at that time, it was running wild in all directions. Being Jewish and a victim of anti-semitism didn't spare one the anti-Arab racism I felt everywhere around me, in manifest or latent form. Literature, or a certain promise of "being able to say everything," was in any case the outline of what was calling me or signaling to me in the situation I was living in at that time, familial and social. But it was no doubt much more complicated and overdetermined than thinking and saying it in a few words makes it now. At the same time, I believe that very rapidly literature was also the experience of a dissatisfaction or a lack, an impatience. If the philosophical question seemed at least as necessary to me, this is perhaps because I had a presentiment that there could sometimes be an innocence or irresponsibility, or even an impotence, in literature. Not only can one say everything in literature without there being any consequences, I thought, no doubt naively, but at bottom the writer as such does not ask the question of the essence of literature. Perhaps against the backdrop of an impotence or inhibition faced with a literary writing I desired but always placed higher up than and further away from myself, I quickly got interested in either a form of literature which bore a question *about* literature, or else a philosophical type of activity which interrogated the relationship between speech and writing. Philosophy also seemed more political, let's say, more capable of posing politically the question of literature with the political seriousness and consequentiality it requires.

I was interested by the possibility of fiction, by fictionality, but I must confess that deep down I have probably never drawn great enjoyment from fiction, from reading novels, for example, beyond the pleasure taken in analyzing the play of writing, or else certain naive movements of identification. I like a certain practice of fiction, the intrusion of an effective simulacrum or of disorder into philosophical writing,

39

for example, but telling or inventing stories is something that deep down (or rather on the surface!) does not interest me particularly. I'm well aware that this involves an immense forbidden desire, an irrepressible need—but one forbidden, inhibited, repressed—to tell stories, to hear stories told, to invent (language and in language), but one which would refuse to show itself so long as it has not cleared a space or organized a dwelling-place suited to the animal which is still curled up in its hole half asleep.

D.A.   You have just made a distinction between "literature" and "belles-lettres" or "poetry"; and it is a distinction that comes up elsewhere in your work (in "Before the Law," for instance). Could you be more precise about the difference that is being assumed here?

J.D.   The two possibilities are not entirely distinct. I'm referring here to the historical possibility for poetry, epic, lyric or other, not only to remain oral, but not to give rise to what has been called literature. The name "literature" is a very recent invention. Previously, writing was not indispensable for poetry or belles-lettres, nor authorial property, nor individual signatures. This is an enormous problem, difficult to get into here. The set of laws or conventions which fixed what we call literature in modernity was not indispensable for poetic works to circulate. Greek or Latin poetry, non-European discursive works, do not, it seems to me, strictly speaking belong to literature. One can say that without reducing at all the respect or the admiration they are due. If the institutional or socio-political space of literary production as such is a recent thing, it does not simply surround works, it affects them in their very structure. I'm not prepared to improvise anything very serious about this—but I do remember having used some seminars at Yale (around 1979–80) to look at the appearance of this word "literature" and the changes which accompanied it. The principle (I stress that it's a *principle*) of "being able to say everything," the socio-juridico-politico guarantee granted "in principle" to literature, is something which did not mean much, or not that, in Graeco-Latin culture and *a fortiori* in a non-Western culture. Which does not mean that the

40

West has ever respected this principle: but at least here or there it has set it up as a principle.

Having said that, even if a phenomenon called "literature" appeared historically in Europe, at such and such a date, this does not mean that one can identify the literary object in a rigorous way. It doesn't mean that there is an essence of literature. It even means the opposite.

D.A. Turning to the literary texts you have written on, it is notable that they form a more homogeneous group than the philosophical texts (still using these categories in a highly conventional way): mostly twentieth-century, and mostly modernist, or at least nontraditional (many would say "difficult") in their use of language and literary conventions: Blanchot, Ponge, Celan, Joyce, Artaud, Jabès, Kafka. What has led you to make this choice? Was it a necessary choice in terms of the trajectory of your work?

J.D. In what way would the literary texts I write *about, with, toward, for* (what should one say? this is a serious question), *in the name of, in honor of, against,* perhaps too, *on the way toward*—in what way do they form, as you put it, a more homogeneous group? On the one hand, I almost always write in response to solicitations or provocations. These have more often concerned contemporaries, whether it be Mallarmé, Joyce or Celan, Bataille, Artaud, or Blanchot. But this explanation remains unsatisfactory (there were Rousseau and Flaubert too), the more so as my response to such expectations is not always docile. These "twentieth-century modernist, or at least nontraditional texts" all have in common that they are inscribed in a *critical* experience of literature. They bear within themselves, or we could also say in their literary act they put to work, a question, the same one, but each time singular and put to work otherwise: "What is literature?" or "Where does literature come from?" "What should we do with literature?" These texts operate a sort of turning back, they *are* themselves a sort of turning back on the literary institution. Not that they are only reflexive, specular or speculative, not that they suspend reference to something else, as is so often suggested by stupid and uninformed rumor. And the force of their event depends on the fact that a thinking about their own possibility (both general and singular) is put to work in them in a *singular* work. Given what I was saying just now, I'm brought more easily toward texts which are very sensitive to this crisis of the literary institution (which is more than, and other than, a crisis), to what is called "the end of literature," from Mallarmé to Blanchot, beyond the "absolute poem" that "there is not" ("*das es nicht gibt*"— Celan). But given the paradoxical structure of this thing called literature, its beginning *is* its end. It began with a certain relation to its own institutionality, i.e., its fragility, its absence of specificity, its absence of object. The question of its origin was immediately the question of its end. Its history *is constructed* like the ruin of a monument which basically never existed. It is the history of a ruin, the narrative of a memory which produces the event to be told and which will never have been present. Nothing could be more "historical," but this history can only be thought by changing things, in particular this thesis or hypothesis of the present—which means several other things as well, doesn't it? There is nothing more "revolutionary" than this history, but the "revolution" will also have to be changed. Which is perhaps what is happening...

Those texts were all texts which in their various ways were no longer simply, or no longer only, literary. But as to the disquieting questions about literature, they do not only pose them, they do not only give them a theoretical, philosophical, or sociological form, as is the case with Sartre, for example. Their questioning is also linked to the act of a literary performativity and a critical performativity (or even a performativity in crisis). And in them are brought together the two youthful worries or desires I was talking about a moment ago: to write so as to put into play or to keep the singularity of the date (what does not return, what is not repeated, promised experience of memory as promise, experience of ruin or ashes); and at the same time, through the same gesture, to question, analyze, transform this strange contradiction, this institutionless institution.

What is fascinating is perhaps the event of a singularity powerful enough to formalize the questions and theoretical laws concerning it. No doubt we shall have to come back to this word *power*. The "power" that language is capable of, the power that *there is,* as language or as writing, is that a singular mark should also be repeatable, iterable, as mark. It then begins to differ from itself sufficiently to become exemplary and thus involve a certain generality. This economy of exemplary iterability is of itself formalizing. It also formalizes or condenses history. A text by Joyce is simultaneously the condensation of a scarcely delimitable history. But this condensation of history, of language, of the encyclopedia, remains here indissociable from an *absolutely* singular event, an *absolutely* singular signature, and therefore also of a date, of a language, of an autobiographical inscription. In a minimal autobiographical trait can be gathered the greatest potentiality of historical, theoretical, linguistic, philosophical culture—that's really what interests me. I am not the only one to be interested by this economic power. I try to understand its laws but also to mark in what regard the formalization of these laws can never be closed or completed. Precisely because the trait, date, or signature—in short, the irreplaceable and untranslatable singularity of the unique—is iterable as such, it both does and does not form part of the marked set. To insist on this paradox is not an antiscientific gesture—quite the contrary. To resist this paradox in the name of so-called reason or of a logic of common sense is the very figure of a supposed enlightenment as the form of modern obscurantism.

All of which ought to lead us, among other things, to think about "context" in general in a different way. The "economy" of literature *sometimes* seems to me more powerful than that of other types of discourse: such as, for example, historical or philosophical discourse. *Sometimes*: it depends on singularities and contexts. Literature would be potentially more potent.

D.A. In *Of Grammatology* you observe that "with the exception of a point of advance or a point of resistance which has only very lately been recognized as such, literary writing has, almost always and almost everywhere, in accordance with very different fashions and across very different periods, lent itself to that *transcendent* reading, that search for the signified which we here put in question" (160, translation modified). That phrase "lent itself" [*s'est prêtée d'elle-même à*] suggests that although this mass of literature may invite such a transcendent reading, it does not *oblige* it. Do you see possibilities for re-reading everything that goes under the name of literature in ways which would counter or subvert this dominant tradition? Or would this only be possible for *some* literary texts, as is suggested by your reference in *Positions* to "a certain 'literary' practice" which was able, prior to modernism, to operate against the dominant model of literature?

J.D. You say "lent itself." Does not every text, every discourse, of whatever type—literary, philosophical and scientific, journalistic, conversational—lend itself, every time, to this reading? Depending on the types of discourse I've just named—but there would be others—the form of this lending itself is different. It would have to be analyzed in a way specific to each case. Conversely, in none of these cases is one simply obliged to go in for this reading. Literature has no pure originality in this regard. A philosophical, or journalistic, or scientific discourse, can be read in "nontranscendent" fashion. "Transcend" here means going beyond interest for the signifier, the form, the language (note that I do not say "text") in the direction of the meaning or referent (this is Sartre's rather simple but convenient definition of prose). One can do a nontranscendent reading of any text whatever. Moreover, there is no text which is literary *in itself.* Literarity is not a natural essence, an intrinsic property of the text. It is the correlative of an intentional relation to the text, an intentional relation which integrates in itself, as a component or an intentional layer, the more or less implicit consciousness of rules which are conventional or institutional—social, in any case. Of course, this does not mean that literarity is merely projective or subjective—in the sense of the empirical subjectivity or caprice of each reader. The literary character of the text is inscribed on the side of the intentional object, in its noematic structure, one could say, and not only on the subjective side of the noetic act. There are "in" the text features which call for the literary reading and recall the convention, institution, or history of literature. This *noematic* structure is included (as "nonreal," in Husserl's terms) in subjectivity, but a subjectivity which is non-empirical and linked to an intersubjective and transcendental community. I believe this phenomenological-type language to be necessary, even if at a certain point it must yield to what, in the situation of writing or reading, and in particular literary writing or reading, puts phenomenology in crisis as well as the very concept of institution or convention (but this would take us too far). Without suspending the transcendent reading, but by changing one's attitude with regard to the text, one can always reinscribe in a literary space any statement—a newspaper article, a scientific theorem, a snatch of conversation. There is therefore a literary *functioning* and a literary *intentionality*, an experience rather than an essence of literature (natural or ahistorical). The essence of literature, if we hold to this word essence, is produced as a set of objective rules in an original history of the "acts" of inscription and reading.

But it is not enough to suspend the transcendent reading to be dealing with literature, to read a text as a literary text. One can interest oneself in the functioning of language, in all sorts of structures of inscription, suspend not reference (that's impossible) but the thetic relation to meaning or referent, without for all that constituting the object as a literary object. Whence the difficulty of grasping what makes for the specificity of literary intentionality. In any case, a text cannot by itself avoid lending itself to a "transcendent" reading. A literature which forbade that transcendence would annul itself. This moment of "transcendence" is irrepressible, but it can be complicated or folded; and it is in this play of foldings that is inscribed the difference between literatures, between the literary and the non-literary, between the different textual types or moments of non-literary texts. Rather than periodize hastily, rather than say, for example, that a modern literature resists more this transcendent reading, one must cross typology with history. There are types of text, moments in a text, which resist this transcendent reading more than others, and this is true not only for literature in the modern sense. In preliterary poetry or epic (in the *Odyssey* as much as in *Ulysses*), this reference and this irreducible intentionality can also suspend "thetic" and naive belief in meaning or referent.

Even if they always do so unequally and differently, poetry and literature have as a common feature that they suspend the "thetic" naivety of the transcendent reading. This also accounts for the philosophical force of these experiences, a force of provocation to think phenomenality, meaning, object, even being as such, a force which is at least potential, a philosophical *dynamis*—which can, however, be developed only in response, in the experience of reading, because it is not hidden in the text like a substance. Poetry and literature provide or facilitate "phenomenological" access to what makes of a thesis a *thesis as such*. Before having a philosophical content, before being or bearing such and such a "thesis," literary experience, writing or reading, is a "philosophical" experience which is neutralized or neutralizing insofar as it allows one to think the thesis; it is a nonthetic experience of the thesis, of belief, of position, of naivety, of what Husserl called the "natural attitude." The phenomenological conversion of the gaze, the "transcendental reduction" he recommended is perhaps the very condition (I do not say the natural condition) of literature. But it is true that, taking this proposition to its limit, I'd be tempted to say (as I have said elsewhere) that the phenomenological language in which I'm presenting these things ends up being dislodged from its certainties (self-presence of absolute transcendental consciousness or of the indubitable *cogito*, etc.), and dislodged precisely by the extreme experience of literature, or even quite simply of fiction and language.

You also ask, "Do you see possibilities for re-reading everything that goes under the name of literature in ways that would counter or subvert this dominant tradition? Or would this only be possible for *some* literary texts . . .?"

Another "economistic" reply: one can always inscribe in literature something which was not originally destined to be literary, given the conventional and intentional space which institutes and thus constitutes the text. Convention and intentionality can change; they always induce a certain historical instability. But if one can re-read everything as literature, some textual events lend themselves to this better than others, their potentialities are richer and denser. Whence the economic point of view. This wealth itself does not give rise to an absolute evaluation—absolutely stabilized, objective, and natural. Whence the difficulty of theorizing this economy. Even given that some texts appear to have a greater potential for formalization, literary works *and* works which say a lot about literature and therefore about themselves, works whose performativity, in some sense, appears the greatest possible in the smallest possible space, this can give rise only to evaluations inscribed in a context, to positioned readings which are themselves formalizing and performative. Potentiality is not hidden in the text like an intrinsic property.

D.A. For certain literary theorists and critics who associate themselves with deconstruction, a text is "literary" or "poetic" when it resists a transcendental reading of the sort we have been discussing...

J.D. I believe no text resists it absolutely. Absolute resistance to such a reading would purely and simply destroy the trace of the text. I'd say rather that a text is poetico-literary when, through a sort of original negotiation, without annulling either meaning or reference, it does something with this resistance, something that we'd have a lot of trouble defining for the reasons I was mentioning earlier. For such a definition would require not only that we take into account multiple, subtle and stratified conventional and intentional modifications, but also at a certain point the questioning of the values of intention and convention which, with the textuality of the text in general and literature in particular, are put to the test of their limits. If every literary text plays and negotiates the suspension of referential naivety, of *thetic* referentiality (not reference or the intentional relation in general), each text does so differently, singularly. If there is no essence of literature— i.e., self-identity of the literary thing—if what is announced or promised as literature never gives itself as such, that means, among other things, that a literature that talked only about literature or a work that was purely self-referential would immediately be annulled. You'll say that that's maybe what's happening. In which case it is this experience of the nothing-ing of nothing that interests our desire under the name of literature. Experience of Being, nothing less, nothing more, on the edge of metaphysics, literature perhaps stands on the edge of everything, almost beyond everything, including itself. It's the most interesting thing in the world, maybe more interesting than the world, and this is why, if it has no definition, what is heralded and refused under the name of literature cannot be identified with any other discourse. It will never be scientific, philosophical, conversational.

But if it did not open onto all these discourses, if it did not open onto any of those discourses, it would not be literature either. There is no literature without a *suspended* relation to meaning and reference. *Suspended* means *suspense,* but also *dependence,* condition, conditionality. In its suspended condition, literature can only exceed itself. No doubt all language refers to something other than itself or to language as something other. One must not play around with this difficulty. What is the specific difference of literary language in this respect? Does its originality consist in stopping, arresting attention on this excess of language over language? In exhibiting, re-marking, giving to be re-marked this excess of language as literature, i.e., an institution which cannot identify itself because it is always in relationship, the relationship with the nonliterary? No: for it shows nothing without dissimulating *what* it shows and *that* it shows it. You'll say that that too is true of all language and that we're reproducing here a statement whose generality can be read, for example, in texts of Heidegger's which do not concern literature but the very being of language in its relation with truth. It is true that Heidegger puts thought and poetry *in parallel* (one beside the other). By the same token, we still *have trouble* defining the question of literature, dissociating it from the question of truth, from the essence of language, from essence itself. Literature "is" the place or experience of this "trouble" we also have with the essence of language, with truth and with essence, the language of essence in general. If the question of literature obsesses us, and especially this century, or even this half-century since the war, and obsesses us in its Sartrian form ("What is literature?") or the more "formalist" but just as essentialist form of "literarity," this is perhaps not because we expect an answer of the type "S is P," "the essence of literature is this or that," but rather because in this century the experience of literature crosses all the "deconstructive" seisms shaking the authority and the pertinence of the question "What is . . . ?" and all the associated regimes of essence or truth. In any case, to come back to your first question, it is in this "place" so difficult to situate that my interest in literature crosses my interest in philosophy or metaphysics—and can finally come to rest neither with the one nor the other.

D.A. Could you be more explicit about the ways in which you see the Western tradition of literature and of reading literature as dominated by metaphysical assumptions? You refer in *Positions* to "the necessity of formal and syntactic work" to counter such misconstruings of literature as "thematism, sociologism, historicism, psychologism," but you also warn against a formal reduction of the work. Is it necessary to make a distinction between literature and literary criticism here? Have any kinds of criticism or commentary escaped such reductions in your view?

J.D.: "Metaphysical assumptions" can inhabit literature or reading (you say "reading literature") in a number of ways which should be very carefully distinguished. They aren't faults, errors, sins or accidents that could be avoided. Across so many very necessary programs— language, grammar, culture in general—the recurrence of such "assumptions" is so structural that it couldn't be a question of eliminating them. In the content of literary texts, there are always philosophical theses. The semantics and the thematics of a literary text carry, "assume"—in the English or in the French sense of the word—some metaphysics. This content itself can be stratified, it occurs via themes, voices, forms, different genres. But, to pick up again the deliberately equivocal expression I just used, literature's *being-suspended* neutralizes the "assumption" which it carries; it has this capacity, even if the consciousness of the writer, interpreter or reader (and everyone plays all these roles in some way) can never render this capacity completely effective and present. First of all, because this capacity is double, equivocal, contradictory, *hanging on* and *hanging between, dependent* and *independent,* an "assumption" both assumed and suspended. The terribly equivocal word *fiction* (which is sometimes misused as though it were coextensive with literature) says something about this situation. Not all literature is of the genre or the type of "fiction," but there is fictionality in all literature. We should find a word other than "fiction." And it is through this fictionality that we try to thematize the "essence" or the "truth" of "language."

Although I did not always, or in every respect, agree with him on this point, Paul de Man was not wrong in suggesting that ultimately all literary rhetoric in general is of itself deconstructive, practicing what you might call a sort of irony, an irony of detachment with regard to metaphysical belief or thesis, even when it apparently puts it forward. No doubt this should be made more complex, "irony" is perhaps not the best category to designate this "suspension," this *epochē*, but there is here, certainly, something irreducible in poetic or literary experience. Without being ahistorical, far from it, this trait, or rather *retrait*, would far exceed the periodizations of "literary history," or of the history of poetry or belles-lettres, from Homer to Joyce, before Homer and after Joyce.

Inside this immense space, many distinctions remain necessary. Some texts called "literary" "question" (let us not say "critique" or "deconstruct") philosophy in a sharper, or more thematic, or better informed way than others. Sometimes this questioning occurs more effectively via the actual practice of writing, the staging, the composition, the treatment of language, rhetoric, than via speculative arguments. Sometimes theoretical arguments as such, even if they are in the form of critique, are less "destabilizing," or let's just say less alarming, for "metaphysical assumptions" than one or other "way of writing." A work laden with obvious and canonical "metaphysical" theses can, in the operation of its writing, have more powerful "deconstructive" effects than a text proclaiming itself radically revolutionary without in any way affecting the norms or modes of traditional writing. For instance, some works which are highly "phallocentric" in their semantics, their intended meaning, even their theses, can produce paradoxical effects, paradoxically antiphallocentric through the audacity of a writing which in fact disturbs the order or the logic of phallocentrism or touches on limits where things are reversed: in that case the fragility, the precariousness, even the ruin of order is more apparent. I am thinking here as much of the example of Joyce as of that of Ponge. The same thing goes from a political point of view. The experience, the passion of language and writing (I'm speaking here just as much of body, desire, ordeal), can cut across discourses which are thematically "reactionary" or "conservative" and confer upon them a power of provocation, transgression or destabilization greater than that of so-called "revolutionary" texts (whether of the right or of the left) which advance peacefully in neo-academic or neoclassical forms. Here too I'm thinking of a large number of works of this century whose political message and themes would be legitimately situated "on the right" and whose work of writing and thought can no longer be so easily classified, either in itself or in its effects.

Our task is perhaps to wonder why it is that so many of this century's strong works and systems of thought have been the site of philosophical, ideological, political "messages" that are at times conservative (Joyce), at times brutally and diabolically murderous, racist, anti-semitic (Pound, Céline), at times equivocal and unstable (Artaud, Bataille). The histories of Blanchot or Heidegger, that of Paul de Man too, are even more complicated, more heterogeneous in themselves and so different from each other that this mere association might risk encouraging into confusion some of those who are multiplying ineptitudes on this matter. The list, alas, would be a long one. In the matter of equivocation, heterogeneity or instability, analysis by definition escapes all closure and all exhaustive formalization.

What goes for "literary production" also goes for "the reading of literature." The performativity we have just been talking about calls for the same responsibility on the part of the readers. A reader is not a consumer, a spectator, a visitor, not even a "receiver." So we find once more the same paradoxes and the same stratifications. A critique presenting itself with "deconstructionist" proclamations, theses or theorems can practice, if I may put it this way, the most conventional of readings. And reciprocally. And between the two extremes, right inside each reading, signed by one and the same person, a certain inequality and even a certain heterogeneity remains irreducible.

Your question also refers to "the necessity of formal and syntactic work," as opposed to "thematism," "sociologism," "historicism," "psychologism," but also to the warning against formalist reduction. If I have thought it necessary to make apparently contradictory gestures in this matter, it is because this series of oppositions (form/content, syntax/semantics or thematics) seems to me, as I have often noted, especially in "The Double Session," incapable of getting the measure of what happens in the event and in the signature of a text. It is always this series of oppositions which governs the debates with the socio-psycho-historicist reductions of literature, by alternating the two types of hegemony.

This leads me to the last part of your question: "Is it necessary to make a distinction between literature and literary criticism here?" I'm not sure. What has just been said can have to do with both of them. I don't feel at ease either with a rigorous distinction between "literature" and "literary criticism" or with a confusion of the two. What would the rigorous limit between them be? "Good" literary criticism, the only worthwhile kind, implies an act, a literary signature or counter-signature, an inventive experience of language, *in* language, an inscription of the act of reading in the field of the text that is read. This text never lets itself be completely "objectified." Yet I would not say that we can mix everything up and give up the distinctions between all these types of "literary" or "critical" production (for there is also a "critical" instance at work "*in*" what is called the literary work). So it is necessary to determine or delimit another space where we justify relevant distinctions between certain forms of literature and certain forms of... I don't know what name to give it, that's the problem, we must invent one for those "critical" inventions which belong to literature while deforming its limits. At any rate I wouldn't distinguish between "literature" and "literary criticism," but I wouldn't assimilate all forms of writing or reading. These new distinctions ought to give up on the purity and linearity of frontiers. They should have a form that is both rigorous and capable of taking account of the essential possibility of contamination between all these oppositions, those we encountered above and, here, the one between literature and criticism or reading or literary interpretation.

D.A. To pursue this question a little further, would you say that the tradition of literary criticism has shown itself to be as governed by metaphysical presuppositions as philosophy, and more so than the literary texts it treats of?

J.D.: To give too sweeping a reply, I would say yes. Simply, a work of literary criticism is not, any more than a philosophical discourse, simply "governed by metaphysical assumptions." Nothing is ever homogeneous. Even among the philosophers associated with the most canonical tradition, the possibilities of rupture are always waiting to be effected. It can always be shown (I have tried to do so, for example, in relation to the *chōra* of the *Timaeus*)[2] that the most radically deconstructive motifs are at work "in" what is called the Platonic, Cartesian, Kantian text. A text is never totally governed by "metaphysical assumptions." So the same will be true for literary criticism. In "each case" (and the identification of the "case," of singularity, of the signature or corpus is already a problem) there is a domination, a dominant, of the metaphysical model, and then there are counter-forces which threaten or undermine this authority. These forces of "ruin" are not negative, they participate in the productive or instituting force of the very thing they seem to be tormenting. There are hierarchies, there are relations of force: as much in literary criticism, moreover, as in philosophy. They aren't the same ones. The fact that literary criticism is dealing with texts declared "literary," and of which we were saying just now that they suspend the metaphysical thesis, must have effects on criticism. It is difficult to speak *in general* of "literary criticism." As such, in other words as an institution, installed at the same time as the modern European universities, from the beginning of the nineteenth century, thereabouts, I think it must have tended, precisely because it wanted to be theoretical, to be more philosophical than literature itself. From this point of view, it is perhaps more metaphysical than the literary texts it speaks about. But it would be necessary to look at this for each case. In general literary criticism is very philosophical in its form, even if the professionals in the matter haven't been trained as philosophers, or if they declare their suspicion of philosophy. Literary criticism is perhaps structurally philosophical. What I am saying here is not necessarily a compliment—for those very reasons that we are talking about.

D.A.: Do you also see the demonstration of literature's historical solidarity with the metaphysical tradition as an important task to be

2. EN Jacques Derrida, "*Chôra*."

undertaken by literary critics? Would you in any way wish to question—in a critical sense—the enjoyment which most readers have obtained, and still obtain, from literature of this kind, and from the criticism that promotes it? Is literature, understood and taught in this way, as logocentric and metaphysical, complicit with a particular ethics and politics, historically and at present?

J.D. Let me first quote your question: "Do you also see the demonstration of literature's historical solidarity with the metaphysical tradition as an important task to be undertaken by literary critics?" By "demonstration" you are perhaps hinting at deconstruction: demonstration of a link which must be, if not denounced, at least questioned, deconstituted, and displaced. In any case, I think we should demonstrate this solidarity, or at any rate become aware of the link between literature, a history of literature, and the metaphysical tradition—even if this link is complicated for the reasons given just now.

Contrary to what some people believe or have an interest in making believe, I consider myself very much a historian, very historicist—from this point of view. We must constantly recall this historical solidarity and the way in which it is put together. Deconstruction calls for a highly "historian's" attitude (*Of Grammatology*, for example, is a history book through and through), even if we should also be suspicious of the metaphysical concept of history. It is everywhere.

So this "historical solidarity" of literature and the history or tradition of metaphysics must be constantly recalled, even if the differences, the distances must be pointed out, as we were just doing. Having said that, this task, "an important task" as you correctly say, is not only for literary critics, it's also a task for the writer; not necessarily a duty, in the moral or political sense, but in my opinion a task inherent in the experience of reading or writing. "There must be" this historicity, which doesn't mean that all reading or all writing is historicized, "historian's," still less "historicist." We shall no doubt come back to this problem later on.

There is a sort of paradoxical historicity in the experience of writing. The writer can be ignorant or naive in relation to the historical tradition which bears him or her, or which s/he transforms, invents, displaces.

But I wonder whether, even in the absence of historical awareness or knowledge s/he doesn't "treat" history in the course of an experience which is more significant, more alive, more *necessary* in a word, than that of some professional "historians" naively concerned to "objectify" the content of a science.

Even if that isn't a moral or political duty (but it can also become one), this experience of writing is "subject" to an imperative: to give space for singular events, to invent something new in the form of acts of writing which no longer consist in a theoretical knowledge, in new constative statements, to give oneself to a poetico-literary performativity at least analogous to that of promises, orders, or acts of constitution or legislation which do not only change language, or which, in changing language, change more than language. It is always more interesting than to repeat. In order for this singular performativity to be effective, for something new to be produced, historical competence is not indispensable in a certain form (that of a certain academic kind of knowledge, for example, on the subject of literary history), but it increases the chances. In his or her experience of writing as such, if not in a research activity, a writer cannot not be concerned, interested, anxious about the past, that of literature, history, or philosophy, of culture in general. S/he cannot not take account of it in some way and not consider her- or himself a responsible heir, inscribed in a genealogy, whatever the ruptures or denials on this subject may be. And the sharper the rupture is, the more vital the genealogical responsibility. Account cannot not be taken, whether one wish it or not, of the past. Once again, this historicity or this historical responsibility is not necessarily linked to awareness, knowledge, or even the themes of history. What I have just suggested is as valid for Joyce, that immense allegory of historical memory, as for Faulkner, who doesn't write in such a way that he gathers together at every sentence, and in several languages at once, the whole of Western culture.

Perhaps this should be linked to your question on "enjoyment"? I don't know if this word can be translated by *plaisir* or *jouissance* (that word which is so difficult to translate into English). The experience of "deconstruction," of "deconstructive" questioning, reading, or writing, in no way threatens or casts suspicion on "enjoyment." I believe rather the opposite. Every time there is *"jouissance"* (but the "there is" of this event is in itself extremely enigmatic), there is "deconstruction." Effective deconstruction. Deconstruction perhaps has the effect, if not the mission, of liberating forbidden *jouissance*. That's what has to be taken on board. It is perhaps this *jouissance* which most irritates the all-out adversaries of "deconstruction." Who, moreover, blame those they call the "deconstructionists" for depriving them of their habitual delectation in the reading of the great works or the rich treasures of tradition, and simultaneously for being too playful, for taking too much pleasure, for saying what they like for their own pleasure, etc. An interesting and symptomatic contradiction. These masters of "kettle logic" understand in some obscure way that the "deconstructionists," to use that ridiculous vocabulary, are not those who most deprive themselves of pleasure. Which is sometimes hard to put up with.

Of course the question of pleasure, of the pleasure principle and its beyond, is not simple, above all in literature, and we cannot deal with it here. But if I may be a bit abrupt and aphoristic, collapsing the separate psychoanalytic stages and referring back to what I try to demonstrate about it in *The Post Card*, let's say that there is no efficient deconstruction without the greatest possible pleasure. It's possible—in a provisional way and for convenience, to save time—to present these paradoxes in terms of repression and the lifting of repression. In these terms, literature would lift repression: to a certain extent at least, in its own way, never totally, and according to rule-governed scenarios, but always in the process of modifying their rules in what we call the history of literature. This lifting or simulacrum of a lifting of repression, a simulacrum which is never neutral and without efficacity, perhaps hangs on this being-suspended, this *epochē* of the thesis or "metaphysical assumption" which we were talking about just now. That can procure a subtle and intense pleasure. It can be produced without literature, "in life," in life without literature, but literature is also "in life" in its way, in "real life," as people calmly say who think they can distinguish between the "real life" and the other one. Pleasure is linked to the game which is played at this limit, to what is suspended at this limit. It is also linked to all the paradoxes of the simulacrum and even of mimesis. For if "deconstruction," to use this word again for shorthand, can dismantle a certain interpretation of mimesis—what I have called a mimetologism, a mimesis reduced to imitation—the "logic" of *mimesthai* is undeconstructible or rather deconstructible *as* deconstruction "itself." Which is at once identification and disidentification, experience of the double, thought about iterability, etc. Like literature, like pleasure, like so many other things. The pleasure taken in mimesis is not necessarily naive. The things in play in mimesis are very cunning. And even if there is some naiveté, and irreducible naiveté, to deconstruct does not consist in denouncing or dissolving naiveté, in the hope of escaping from it completely: it would rather be a *certain* way of resigning oneself to it and taking account of it.

So: no deconstruction without pleasure and no pleasure without deconstruction. "It is necessary," if one wants to or can, to resign oneself to it or take it from there. But I give up on proceeding further while improvising. We lack the time or the space.

D.A. The kind of historical re-reading I referred to in my previous question is perhaps most advanced in some feminist criticism, which takes as its goal the demonstration of the phallocentric assumptions of literary texts over a long period, as well as of commentaries on those texts. Does this work overlap with your own? To what extent does "literature" name the possibility of texts' being read in ways that put phallocentrism—along with logocentrism—in question?

J.D.: Another very difficult question. It's true, isn't it, that "feminist" literary criticism, as such, as an identifiable institutional phenomenon, is contemporary with the appearance of what is called deconstruction in the modern sense? The latter deconstructs first of all and essentially what announces itself in the figure of what I have proposed to call phallogocentrism, to underline a certain indissociability between phallocentrism and logocentrism. It was after the war—and even well after a period whose dates and limit could be marked by Simone de Beauvoir—that "feminist criticism" was developed as such. Not before the sixties, and even, if I'm not mistaken, as far as the most visible and organized demonstrations are concerned, not before the end of the sixties. To appear at the same time as the theme of deconstruction, as deconstruction of phallogocentrism, does not necessarily or always mean to depend on it, but at least to belong to the same configuration and participate in the same movement, the same motivation. Starting from that, the strategies can of course be different, be opposed here and there, and inequalities can appear.

But let's go back, if you don't mind, for a little detour, to what we were saying on the subject of literature in general: a place at once institutional and wild, an institutional place in which it is in principle permissible to put in question, at any rate to suspend, the whole institution. A counter-institutional institution can be both subversive and conservative. It can be conservative in that it is institutional, but it can also be conservative in that it is anti-institutional, in that it is "anarchist," and to the extent that a certain kind of anarchism can be conservative. Following this logic, if we come back to the question of what is called "feminist" literature or criticism, we risk finding the same paradoxes: sometimes the texts which are most phallocentric or phallogocentric in their themes (in a certain way no text completely escapes this rubric) can also be, in some cases, the most deconstructive. And their authors can be, in statutory terms, men or women. There are sometimes more deconstructive resources—when you want or at least are able to make something of them in reading—and there is no text before and outside reading—in some texts by Joyce or Ponge, who are often phallocentric or phallogocentric in appearance, than in some texts which, thematically, are theatrically "feminist" or "anti-phallogocentric," be they signed by the names of men or women.

Because of the literary dimension, what "phallogocentric" texts display is immediately suspended. When someone stages a hyperbolically phallocentric discourse or mode of behavior, s/he does not subscribe to it by signing the work, s/he describes and, describing it as such, s/he exposes it, displays it. Whatever the assumed attitude of the author on the matter, the *effect* can be paradoxical and sometimes "deconstructive." But we shouldn't talk generally, there are no rules here such that each singular work would be merely a case or example of them, a sample. The logic of the work, especially in literature, is a "logic" of the signature, a paradoxology of the singular mark, and thus of the exceptional and the counter-example.

Texts like those by Nietzsche, Joyce, Ponge, Bataille, Artaud, violently phallocentric in so many ways, produce deconstructive effects, and precisely against phallocentrism, whose logic is always ready to reverse itself or subvert itself. Inversely, if I can put it that way, who will calmly believe that George Sand, George Eliot, or immensely great modern writers like Virginia Woolf, Gertrude Stein, or Hélène Cixous, write texts that are simply non- or anti-phallogocentric? Here I demand that one look, and closely, each time. There must be refinements, both around the concept or the law of "phallocentrism" and in the possible plurality of readings of works that remain singular. At the moment we are in a slightly "crude" and heavy-handed phase of the question. In polemical argument, there is too much confidence in the assumed sexual identities of the signatories, in the very concept of sexual identity, things are dealt with too generally, as if a text were this or that, in a homogeneous way, for this or that, without taking account of what it is in the status or the very structure of a literary work—I would rather say in the paradoxes of its *economy*—which ought to discourage these simplistic notions.

Whether it is phallocentric or not (and that is not so easy to decide), the more "powerful" a text is (but power is not a masculine attribute here and it is often the most disarming feebleness), the more it is written, the more it shakes up its own limits or lets them be thought, as well as the limits of phallocentrism, of all authority and all "centrism," all hegemony in general. Taking account of these paradoxes, some of the most violent, most "reactionary," most odious or diabolical texts keep, in my view, an interest which I will never give up, in particular a political interest from which no intimidation, no dogmatism, no simplification should turn us away.

D.A.: Would you say, then, that a literary text which puts in question logocentrism does the same with regard to phallocentrism, and does so in the same act and in the same measure?

J.D.: If I could answer in a word, I would say yes. If I had the time to formulate sentences, I would develop this suggestion: although phallocentrism and logocentrism are indissociable, the stresses can lie more here or there according to the case; the force and the trajectory of the mediations can be different. There are texts which are more immediately logocentric than phallocentric, and vice versa. Some texts signed by women can be thematically anti-phallocentric and powerfully logocentric. Here the distinctions should be refined. But in the last instance, a radical dissociation between the two motifs cannot be made in all rigor. Phallogocentrism is one single thing, even if it is an articulated thing which calls for different strategies. This is what is at issue in some debates, real or virtual, with militant feminists who do not understand that without a demanding reading of what articulates logocentrism and phallocentrism, in other words without a consequential deconstruction, feminist discourse risks reproducing very crudely the very thing which it purports to be criticizing.

D.A.: Let me move on to some specific authors and texts. In an interview you once mentioned Samuel Beckett along with other writers whose texts "make the limits of our language tremble." As far as I'm aware, you've never written on Beckett: is this a future project, or are there reasons why you have observed this silence?

J.D.: Very rapidly. This is an author to whom I feel very close, or to whom I would like to feel myself very close; but also too close. Precisely because of this proximity, it is too hard for me, too easy and too hard. I have perhaps avoided him a bit because of this identification. Too hard also because he writes—in my language, in a language which is his up to a point, mine up to a point (for both of us it is a "differently" foreign language)—texts which are both too close to me and too distant for me even to be able to "respond" to them. How could I write in French in the wake of or "with" someone who does operations on this language which seem to me so strong and so necessary, but which must remain idiomatic? How could I write, sign, countersign performatively texts which "respond" to Beckett? How could I avoid the platitude of a supposed academic metalanguage? It is very hard. You will perhaps say to me that for other foreign authors like Kafka, Celan, or Joyce, I attempted it. Yes, at least attempted. Let's not speak of the result. I had a kind of excuse or alibi: I write in French, from time to time I quote the German or the English, and the two writings, the "performative signatures," are not only incommensurable in general, that goes without saying, but above all without a "common language," at least in the ordinary sense of the term. Given that Beckett writes in a particular French, it would be necessary, in order to "respond" to his oeuvre, to attempt writing performances that are impossible for me (apart from a few stammering [and thus oral] tries in some seminars devoted to Beckett in the last few years). I was able to risk linguistic compromises with Artaud, who also has his way of loving and violating, of loving violating a certain French language of its language. But in Artaud (who is paradoxically more distant, more foreign for me than Beckett) there are texts which have permitted me writing transactions. Whatever one thinks of their success or failure, I have given myself up to them and published them. That wasn't possible for me with Beckett, whom I will thus have "avoided" as though I had always already read him and understood him too well.

D.A.: Is there a sense in which Beckett's writing is already so "deconstructive," or "self-deconstructive," that there is not much left to do?

J.D.: No doubt that's true. A certain nihilism is both interior to metaphysics (the final fulfillment of metaphysics, Heidegger would say) and then, already, beyond. With Beckett in particular, the two possibilities are in the greatest possible proximity and competition. He is nihilist and he is not nihilist. Above all, this question should not be treated as a philosophical problem outside or above the texts. When I found myself, with students, reading some Beckett texts, I would take three lines, I would spend two hours on them, then I would give up because it would not have been possible, or honest, or even interesting, to extract a few "significant" lines from a Beckett text. The composition, the rhetoric, the construction and the rhythm of his works, even the ones that seem the most "decomposed," that's what "remains" finally the most "interesting," that's the work, that's the signature, this remainder which remains when the thematics is exhausted (and also exhausted, by others, for a long time now, in other modes).

With Joyce, I was able to pretend to isolate two words (*He war* or *yes, yes*); with Celan, one foreign word (*Shibboleth*); with Blanchot, one word and two homonyms (*pas*).[3] But I will never claim to have "read" or proposed a general reading of these works. I wrote a text, which in the face of the event of another's text, as it comes to me at a particular, quite singular, moment, tries to "respond" or to "counter-sign," in an idiom which turns out to be mine. But an idiom is never pure, its iterability opens it up to others. If my own "economy" could provoke other singular readings, I would be delighted. That it should produce "effects of generality" here or there, of relative generality, by exceeding singularity, is inscribed in the iterable structure of any language, but in order to talk about that seriously, it would be necessary to re-elaborate a whole "logic" of singularity, of the example, the counter-example, iterability, etc. That is what I try to do in another mode elsewhere, and often in the course of the readings I have just mentioned. They are all offered, simultaneously, as reflections on the signature, the proper name, singularity. All this to explain that I have given up on writing in the direction of Beckett—for the moment.

D.A.: "Aphorism Countertime" is an unusual text for you in that it presents a reading of a sixteenth-century work, *Romeo and Juliet*. Does a literary work as historically and culturally distant as this one pose any problems for your reading of it? And was your choice of this play largely by chance, as a result of an invitation, or do you feel that of Shakespeare's works this one merits special attention in terms of your interests and goals?

J.D.: As you have noticed, I did not read *Romeo and Juliet* as a sixteenth-century text, I was incapable of it. The title was, after all, "countertime." And also the aphorism, which means that I did not even claim to read the work itself as an ensemble. Not that I am only interested in modern texts, but I did not have the necessary competence to read this play "in its period." I should also remind you of the reasons, which are also the opportunities, for which I write these kinds of text. Spontaneously, I would never have had the audacity to write

3. EN See "Two Words for Joyce," "Ulysses Gramophone," *Shibboleth*, and *Parages*.

on *Romeo and Juliet* or anything at all of Shakespeare's. My respect for an oeuvre which is one of the "greatest" in the world for me is too intimidated, and I consider myself too incompetent. In this case, I was asked for a short, oblique text to accompany a production. In this sketch of a reading of *Romeo and Juliet*, I privileged the motifs of the contretemps and anachrony, which I was interested in anyway, and precisely in this place where they intersect with the question of the proper name. I would like all the same to say something about the historical problem, since you ask me: "Does a literary work as historically and culturally distant as this one pose any problem for your reading of it?"

Yes, lots of problems, and serious problems, of which I think I am reasonably aware. It would be necessary to reconstitute in the most informed and intelligible way, if necessary against the usual history of the historians, the historical element in a play like this—not just the historicity of its composition by Shakespeare, its inscription in a chain of works, etc. (I did at least indicate this dimension in my text and put the problem of structure that this raises), but also what is historical in the play itself: it's an enormous task, and one I think totally necessary. That doesn't mean that any reading which lets itself off this history— and up to a point that's the case with my modest reading in this little text (it's a tiny little text)—is thereby irrelevant. This brings us back to the question of the structure of a text in relation to history. Here the example of Shakespeare is magnificent. Who demonstrates better that texts fully conditioned by their history, loaded with history, and on historical themes, offer themselves so well for reading in historical contexts very distant from their time and place of origin, not only in the European twentieth century, but also in lending themselves to Japanese or Chinese productions and transpositions?

This has to do with the structure of a text, with what I will call, to cut corners, its iterability, which both puts down roots in the unity of a context and immediately opens this non-saturable context onto a recontextualization. All this is historical through and through. The iterability of the trace (unicity, identification, and alteration in repetition) is the condition of historicity—as too is the structure of anachrony and contretemps which I talk about in relation to *Romeo and Juliet*:

from this point of view my brief essay is not only "historical" in one or other of its dimensions, it is an essay on the very historicity of history, on the element in which "subjects" of history, just as much as the historians, whether or not they are "historicist," operate. To say that marks or texts are originally iterable is to say that without a simple origin, and so without a pure originarity, they divide and repeat themselves immediately. They thus become capable of being rooted out at the very place of their roots. Transplantable into a different context, they continue to have meaning and effectiveness.

Not that the text is thereby dehistoricized, but historicity is made of iterability. There is no history without iterability, and this iterability is also what lets the traces continue to function in the absence of the general context or some elements of the context. I give a somewhat better explanation of this in "Signature Event Context" and in "Limited Inc a b c . . ." Even if *Romeo and Juliet*'s historical context, even if its "external" borders or its internal social landscape are not altogether the ones in which I read it, the play can be read nowadays. We have available contextual elements of great stability (not natural, universal and immutable but fairly stable, and thus also destabilizable) which, through linguistic competence, through the experience of the proper name, of family structures which are still analogous ones, etc., allow reading, transformation, transposition, etc. There is a possible play, with regulated gaps and interpretative transformations. But this play would not be possible without the iterability which both repeats the same and—by repetition itself—introduces into it what we call in French the *jeu* ["play," "give,"], not simply in the sense of the ludic, but also in the sense of that which, by the spacing between the pieces of an apparatus, allows for movement and articulation—which is to say for history, for better or for worse. This play is sometimes what allows the machine to function normally, but sometimes the same word designates an articulation that is too loose, without rigor, the cause of an anomaly or a pathological malfunctioning. The question is always one of an economic evaluation: what makes the "best play"? How far does "good" play, which makes things work, risk giving rise to "bad" play which compromises working well? Why, in wanting at all costs to avoid play, because it could be bad, do we also risk depriving ourselves of "good" play, which is as much as to say of everything, at least of a minimal functioning or so-called "normal" functioning, in particular of writing, reading, history, etc.?

This is why, for all it is oblique, partial, modest, a reading like the one I attempt of *Romeo and Juliet* is perhaps not simply irrelevant or incompetent. Of course, I didn't reconstitute *all* the history. But who can claim to do that? And I said a couple of things about this "historico-anachronistic" situation in speaking of the singularity of the play and in the play by Shakespeare, of his proper name and proper names. I am certainly not claiming to make of this brief incursion an example or a model. It's something I felt like signing and even dating at a past moment in December, that year, at Verona (as it says at the end of the text). I wanted to remember this and say that I am very aware of this history of contretemps, of history as contretemps, of these laws which greatly exceed the case of *Romeo and Juliet*, since it is inscribed right on the structure of the name and the iterable mark. No one is obliged to be interested in what interests me. But if that did come about, then we would have to ask what is happening, on what conditions, etc. Which I often do, not always. I wanted to say that *Romeo and Juliet* is not the only example but that it's a very good example. Its singularity should not escape us even if, like any singularity, it is a singularity among others. And what only goes for one work, one proper name, evidently goes for any work, in other words for any singularity and any proper name. What is tragically and happily universal here is absolute singularity. How could one speak or write, otherwise? What would one have to say, otherwise? And all to say nothing, in fact? Nothing which absolutely touches on absolute singularity without straightaway missing it, while also never missing it? That's what I suggest in this little text and in a few others, especially *Shibboleth, Feu la cendre*, or "Che cos'è la poesia?" This tragedy, I mean this destiny without a strictly assignable destination, is also the tragedy of competence, relevance, truth, etc. There are many, but there has to be this play of iterability in the singularity of the idiom. And this play threatens what it makes possible. The threat cannot be separated from the chance, or the condition of possibility from what limits possibility. There is no pure singularity which affirms itself as such without instantly dividing itself, and so exiling itself.

You also asked me, "And was your choice of this play largely by chance, as a result of an invitation?" Yes, I did respond to an invitation which could have not come about. But I wouldn't have responded to it if the story of *Romeo and Juliet*—as for everyone—hadn't meant something to me which I wanted to talk about. And to "countersign" in a way. But there was the element of chance, of course, always the intersection of an old story, a timeless program, and apparent randomness. If the actor-producer Daniel Mesguich had not put the play on at that point (but why did he?), if he hadn't been interested in what I write (but why?—this opens up another chain of causality), he wouldn't have asked anything of me and I would never have written this text. That would have been no great loss. Especially since a certain content, a certain logic of this text is also to be found in some other texts of mine, in a form that is both similar and different. It's always the effect of the same a-logical "logic" of the singular and iterable mark. As to the question "Do you feel that of Shakespeare's works this one merits special attention in terms of your interests and goals?" No doubt this play lends itself in an "exemplary" way to what I wanted to say, to what I thought it necessary to think about the proper name, history, the contretemps, etc. But I tried to talk about all that specifically in relation to a text whose nontransposable singularity I respect. On the same "subject" I would write something completely different if I had to reply (responsibly, that's the point) to a different provocation or countersign a different singular work, signing but with a signature which countersigns and tries to respond in another way to the signature of the other (as I tried to do for the signatures and proper names of Blanchot, Genet, Artaud, Ponge, etc., but also for texts where the proper name was not linked in the same way to the patronym). My law, the one to which I try to devote myself or to respond, is *the text of the other*, its very singularity, its idiom, its appeal which precedes me. But I can only respond to it in a responsible way (and this goes for the law in general, ethics in particular) if I put in play, and in guarantee [*en gage*], my singularity, by signing, with another signature; for the countersignature signs by confirming the signature of the other, but also by signing in an absolutely new and inaugural way, both at once, like each time I confirm my own signature by signing once more: each time in the same way and each time differently, one more time, at another date.

Having said this, I would very much like to read and write in the space or heritage of Shakespeare, in relation to whom I have infinite admiration and gratitude; I would like to become (alas, it's pretty late) a "Shakespeare expert"; I know that everything is in Shakespeare: everything and the rest, so everything or nearly. But after all, everything is also in Celan, and in the same way, although differently, and in Plato or in Joyce, in the Bible, in Vico or in Kafka, not to mention those still living, everywhere, well, almost everywhere...

D.A.: One of the traditional claims of literary criticism is that it heightens or reveals the uniqueness, the singularity, of the text upon which it comments. Is traditional literary criticism capable of achieving this aim? To what extent is this a part of your aim in writing on literary texts? Is it possible to talk of the uniqueness of a text apart from this or that historical act of reading it?

J.D.: My response will once again be double and divided, apparently contradictory. But that has to do with what is called the experience of singularity. *On the one hand*, yes, I subscribe to the "traditional claims" and in this regard I share the most classical of concerns or desires: a work is always singular and is of interest only from this point of view. And that is why I like the word *oeuvre*, traditional as it is, which keeps this connotation (the English word *work* doesn't perhaps do this in the same way, generally). A work takes place just once, and far from going against history, this uniqueness of the institution, which is in no way natural and will never be replaced, seems to me historical through and through. It must be referred to as a proper name and whatever irreplaceable reference a proper name bears within it. Attention to history, context, and genre is necessitated, and not contradicted, by this singularity, by the date and the signature of the work: not the date and signature which might be inscribed on the *external* border of the work or *around* it, but the ones which constitute or institute the very body of the work, on the edge *between* the "inside" and the "outside." This edge, the place of reference, is both unique and divisible, whence the difficulty I was indicating. For *on the other hand*, while there is always *singularization*, absolute singularity is never given as a fact, an object or existing thing [*étant*] in itself, it is announced in a paradoxical experience. An absolute, absolutely pure singularity, if there were one, would not even show up, or at least would not be available for reading. To become readable, it has to be *divided*, to *participate* and *belong*. Then it is divided and takes *its part* in the genre, the type, the context, meaning, the conceptual generality of meaning, etc. It loses itself to offer itself. Singularity is never one-off [*ponctuelle*], never closed like a point or a fist [*poing*]. It is a mark [*trait*], a differential mark, and different from itself: different *with itself*. Singularity differs from itself, it is deferred [*se diffère*] so as to be what it is and to be repeated in its very singularity. There would be no reading of the work—nor any writing to start with—without this iterability. Here, it seems to me, are the paradoxical consequences to which the logic of the "traditional claims" should lead. To pick up the terms of your question, I would say that the "best" reading would consist in *giving oneself up to* the most idiomatic aspects of the work while also *taking account* of the historical context, of what is *shared* (in the sense of both participation and division, of continuity and the cut of separation), of what belongs to genre and type according to that clause or enclave of non-belonging which I analyzed in "The Law of Genre." And any work is singular in that it speaks singularly of both singularity and generality. Of iterability and the law of iterability.

This is what we were saying in relation to Kafka's "Before the Law," that text which, while it speaks in a general, powerful, formalizing and economical way of the generality of the law, remains absolutely unique among all the texts which speak of the same thing. What happens is always some *contamination*. The uniqueness of the event is this coming about of a singular relation between the unique and its repetition, its iterability. The event comes about, or promises itself initially, only by thus compromising itself by the singular contamination of the singular and what shares it. It comes about as impurity—and impurity here is chance.

Singularity "shared" in this way does not keep itself to the writing aspect, but also to the reading aspect and to what comes to sign, by countersigning, in reading. There is as it were a duel of singularities, a duel of writing and reading, in the course of which a countersignature comes both to confirm, repeat and respect the signature of the other, of the "original" work, and to *lead it off* elsewhere, so running the risk of *betraying* it, having to betray it in a certain way so as to respect it, through the invention of another signature just as singular. Thus redefined, the concept of countersignature gathers up the whole paradox: you have to give yourself over singularly to singularity, but singularity then does have to share itself out and so compromise itself, *promise to compromise itself*. In reality, I don't even think it is a matter of a *duel* here, in the way I just said a bit hastily: this experience always implies more than two signatures. No reading (and writing is also already a countersigning reading, looking at it from the work's side) would be, how can I put it, "new," "inaugural," "performative," without this multiplicity or proliferation of countersignatures. All these words, which usually tend to efface the axioms I am reminding us of here, need quotation marks (a countersignature cannot be simply, absolutely "new," "inaugural" or "performative" since it includes an element of "unproductive" repetition and of pre-convention, even if this is only the possibility of language use and the system of language [*du langage et de la langue*]).

Let's take any example at all. Although this play is taken up in a chain of other ones, *Romeo and Juliet* (which I mention in "Aphorism Countertime"), the *Romeo and Juliet* which bears Shakespeare's signature, takes place only once. This singularity is worked, in fact constituted, by the possibility of its own repetition (readings, indefinite number of productions, references, be they reproductive, citational, or transformative, to the work held to be original which, in its ideality, takes place just one single, first and last time). Reading must *give itself up* [*se rendre*] to this uniqueness, take it on board, keep it in mind, *take account* of it [*en rendre compte*]. But for that, for this "rendering" [*rendre*], you have to sign in your turn, write something else which *responds or corresponds* in an equally singular, which is to say irreducible, irreplaceable, "new" way: neither imitation, nor reproduction, nor metalanguage. This countersigning response, this countersignature which is responsible (for itself and for the other), says "yes" to the work, and again "yes, this work was there before me, without me, I testify," even if it begins by calling for the co-respondent countersignature; and even, then, if it turns out to have implied it from the very beginning, so as to presuppose the possibility of its birth, at the moment of giving a name. The countersignature of the other text is held under the law of the first, of its absolute pastness. But this absolute pastness was already the demand for the countersigning reading. The first only inaugurates from after, and as the expectation of, the second countersignature. What we have here is an incalculable scene, because we can't count 1, 2, 3, or the first before the second, a scene which never reveals itself, by definition, and whose phenomenality can only disappear, but a "scene" which must have programmed the "traditional claims" of all "literary criticism." It has doubtless produced the history of its theorems and its schools.

D.A.: On the subject of a "deconstructive literary criticism," Rodolphe Gasché has written as follows: "Derrida has, by reading literary writing itself, exhibited precisely those structures of textuality and 'literature' with which literary criticism is to enter into exchange. Still, the kind of infrastructures which underlie this exchange have not yet been developed as such" (*The Tain of the Mirror*, 269). Is "literature"—which Gasché is here distinguishing from what is commonly called literature—constituted by an infrastructure specific to it, that is, one which is clearly distinguishable from, for instance, *différance*, the arche-trace, supplementarity? Could you say anything—this is a massive topic which we can only broach here—about this possible specificity of "literature"?

J.D.: The word *infrastructure* troubles me a bit, even though I did once use it myself for pedagogical and analogical purposes, at the time of *Of Grammatology*, in a very specific rhetorical and demonstrative context, and even though I understand what justifies the strategic use of it proposed by Gasché (and I talked to him about it). In an analysis of "literary" writing, you do of course have to take account of the most "general" structures (I don't dare say "fundamental," "originary," "transcendental," "ontological," or "infra-structural," and I think it has to be avoided) of textuality in general. You were reminding us of them: *différance*, arche-trace, supplement, and everything I called "quasi-transcendental" in *Glas*. They are implicated in every literary text, but not all texts are literary—Gasché is right to remind us of this. Once you have situated the structure of textuality in general, you have to determine its becoming-literature, if I can put it like that, and then distinguish between fiction in general (not all fiction is literature, all literature is not strictly of the order of fiction), poetry and belles-lettres, the literature which has been called that for only a few centuries, etc. Also—and this is just what we're talking about here—you have to discern exactly the historically determined phenomenon of social conventions and the institutions which give rise, give its place, to literature. Gasché is right to point out that this historico-institutional structure is not a general "infrastructure" of the text. It is not the same level as what I won't call an infrastructure but rather the limitless generality of *différance*, the trace, the supplement, etc. Having said this, it is perhaps at this point that there could be a discussion with Gasché beyond the strategic choice of terminology, although literature is not the text in general, although not all arche-writing is "literary," I wonder whether literature is simply an example, one effect or region among others, of some general textuality. And I wonder if you can simply apply the classic question to it: what, on the basis of this general textuality, makes the specificity of literature, literariness?

I ask this question for two reasons. First of all, it is quite possible that literary writing in the modern period is more than one example among others, rather a privileged guiding thread for access to the general structure of textuality, to what Gasché calls the infrastructure. What literature "does" with language holds a revealing power which is certainly not unique, which it can share up to a point with law, for example with juridical language, but which in a given historical situation (precisely our own, and this is one more reason for feeling concerned, provoked, summoned by "the question of literature") teaches us more, and even the "essential," about writing in general, about the philosophical or scientific (for example linguistic) limits of the interpretation of writing. In short, this is one of the main reasons for my interest in literature and I am convinced that this motivates the interest of so many theorists of literature in deconstructive endeavors when these privilege writing.

Secondly, even if we should be relentlessly analyzing those historico-institutional matters, the politics and sociology of literature, this is not one institution among others or like the others. We have glimpsed more than once in the course of this conversation the paradoxical trait: it is an institution which consists in transgressing and transforming, thus in producing its constitutional law; or to put it better, in producing discursive forms, "works" and "events" in which the very possibility of a fundamental constitution is at least "fictionally" contested, threatened, deconstructed, presented in its very precariousness. Hence, while literature shares a certain power and a certain destiny with "jurisdiction," with the juridico-political production of institutional foundations, the constitutions of States, fundamental legislation, and even the theological-juridical performatives which occur at the origin of the law, at a certain point it can also exceed them, interrogate them, "fictionalize" them: with nothing, or almost nothing, in view, of course, and by producing events whose "reality" or duration is never assured, but which by that very fact are more thought-provoking, if that still means something.

D.A.: In "The Double Session" you use the formulation "there is no—or hardly any, ever so little—literature" (223). Could you elaborate on this comment?

J.D.: I don't remember the context in which I thought I could say—playing a bit, but believing in the necessity of the provocation—"there is ever so little literature." That certainly didn't mean that there are few texts I consider to be authentically literary, for example the ones I have been led to privilege, wrongly or rightly (those of Mallarmé or Joyce, Blanchot or Celan, Ponge or Genet). No—for the reasons we have just mentioned, I would rather emphasize that the existence of something like a *literary reality in itself* will always remain problematic. The literary event is perhaps more of an event (because less natural) than any other, but by the same token it becomes very "improbable," hard to verify. No *internal* criterion can guarantee the essential "literariness" of a text. There is no assured essence or existence of literature. If you proceed to analyze all the elements of a literary work, you will never come across literature itself, only some traits which it shares or borrows, which you can find elsewhere too, in other texts, be it a matter of the language, the meanings or the referents ("subjective" or "objective"). And even the convention which allows a community to come to an agreement about the literary status of this or that phenomenon remains precarious, unstable and always subject to revision. The "so little literature" was pointing in the direction of this convention, and so toward this fiction on the subject of an unfindable fiction inside a text, rather than toward a very small ideal library. But if it is not almost everything, it is anything but nothing—or, if it is nothing, it's a nothing which *counts*, which in my view counts a lot.

D.A.: You have expressed in the past a desire to write a text even less categorizable by generic conventions than *Glas* and *The Post Card*. If you were to succeed in this aim, what would be the relation of the text you wrote to existing traditions and institutions? Would it not only be neither philosophy nor literature, but not even a mutual contamination of philosophy and literature? Who would be able to read it?

J.D.: Still now, and more desperately than ever, I dream of a writing that would be neither philosophy nor literature, nor even contaminated by one or the other, while still keeping—I have no desire to abandon this—the memory of literature and philosophy. I am certainly not the only one to have this dream, the dream of a new institution to be precise, of an institution without precedent, without pre-institution. You will say, and quite rightly, that this is the dream of every literary work. Every literary work "betrays" the dream of a new institution of

73

literature. It betrays it first by revealing it: each work is unique and is a new institution unto itself. But it also betrays it in causing it to fail: insofar as it is unique, it appears in an institutional field designed so that it cuts itself up and abducts itself there: *Ulysses* arrives like one novel among others that you place on your bookshelf and inscribe in a genealogy. It has its ancestry and its descendants. But Joyce dreamt of a special institution for his oeuvre, inaugurated by it like a new order. And hasn't he achieved this, to some extent? When I spoke about this as I did in "Ulysses Gramophone," I did indeed have to understand and share his dream too: not only share it in making it mine, in recognizing mine in it, but that I share it in *belonging to the dream* of Joyce, in *taking a part* in it, in walking around in *his* space. Aren't we, today, people or characters in part constituted (as readers, writers, critics, teachers) *in* and *through* Joyce's dream? Aren't we Joyce's dream, his dream readers, the ones he dreamed of and whom we dream of being in our turn?

As to the question "Who would be able to read it?," there is no pre-given response. By definition the reader does not exist. Not before the work and as its straightforward "receiver." The dream we were talking about concerns what it is in the work which produces its reader, a reader who doesn't yet exist, whose competence cannot be identified, a reader who would be "formed," "trained," instructed, constructed, even engendered, let's say *invented* by the work. Invented, which is to say both found by chance and produced by research. The work then becomes an institution forming its own readers, giving them a competence which they did not possess before: a university, a seminar, a colloquium, a curriculum, a *course*. If we trusted the current distinction between competence and performance, we would say that the work's performance produces or institutes, forms or invents, a new competence for the reader or the addressee who thereby becomes a counter-signatory. It teaches him or her, *if s/he is willing*, to countersign. What is interesting here is thus the invention of the addressee capable of countersigning and saying "yes" in a committed and lucid way. But this "yes" is also an inaugural performance, and we recover the structure of iterability which would prevent us, at this point, from distinguishing rigorously between performance and competence, as between producer and receiver. As much as that between the addressee and the signatory or the writer and the reader. This is the space in which *The Post Card* is involved. It did so in a certain fashion, at the same time general and singular. Other ways are certainly possible—and yes, I would also like to involve myself in them.

2

" . . . THAT DANGEROUS SUPPLEMENT . . . "

ᏧᏏ Probably Derrida's best-known and most influential book, *Of Grammatology* is concerned with the status of *writing* in Western thought since Plato, though it takes as its major focus the works of Rousseau and, in particular, his short *Essay on the Origin of Languages*. Derrida argues that Rousseau—or, more strictly, the body of texts signed "Rousseau"—represents a moment of particular importance in the phase of philosophical history that stretches from Descartes to Hegel, in that a new model of presence, one based on the self-presence of a feeling subject, comes to the fore. Self-presence is founded on the experience of hearing oneself speak, and requires a particularly insistent rejection of writing and all that it represents. But Derrida is less interested in why Rousseau feels it is necessary to condemn writing than in the way he is forced, again and again, to rely on writing in order to make good the imperfections of the "perfect" speech he elevates. This structure of "supplementarity"—which undermines the logic of identity, of a clear distinction between A and not-A—can be traced in a number of oppositions in Rousseau's texts, all of them versions of his central opposition between Nature and its others (art, artifice, culture, education, language, technique, etc.).

One of the interesting features of Rousseau's writing is his use of literary forms and techniques; this sets him apart from the central philosophical tradition with its project of effacing the vehicle of meaning in order to allow the truth to be heard in all its purity. Rousseau is thus already engaged in a deconstruction of philosophical oppositions, and Derrida's reading attempts to draw out the deconstructive activity implicit in Rousseau's writing, though never explicitly articulated. In the chapter translated here (chapter 2 of part II, "Nature, Culture, Writing"), he considers Rousseau's shifting use of the word *supplément,* a word which can signal both the addition of something to an already complete entity and the making good of an insufficiency. It is in the realm of Rousseau's erotic life, as narrated in his autobiographical *Confessions,* that the strange contradictoriness of this term is most startlingly evident, producing a structure that matches exactly the contradictory relations of speech and writing in his more philosophically oriented work.

This section also includes an important methodological discussion, in which Derrida both makes clear the necessity for scrupulous commentary of the traditional sort and urges the kind of reading which he is undertaking—one that pays close attention to writing as writing, not as a mere window on some other, more "real," reality. The domain in which writing is allowed most significance is literature, yet, as Derrida points out, literature has usually been read in accordance with the model provided by philosophy: the reduction of the text to a context, a moral, a biographical or historical origin, a formal scheme, a psychoanalytic template, a political agenda. His claim goes further than the restoration of literature's rights, however; he argues that to read as he does is to activate the movements and relations (nonlogical, nonconceptual) upon which all these reductions depend. Following in the track of the wandering "supplement" in Rousseau's texts constitutes one such activation.

ᣔ *De la grammatologie* was first published in 1967 (Paris: Minuit); the English translation by Gayatri Chakravorty Spivak was published in 1976 (Baltimore: Johns Hopkins University Press). References to translations of Rousseau's texts are from the following editions: *Emile,* trans. Barbara Foxley (London: Dent, 1911); *The Confessions* (New York: Random House, 1945); *The Reveries of a Solitary,* trans. John Gould Fletcher (New York: Routledge, 1927). (The translations have occasionally been slightly modified.) French texts are cited from the Pléiade edition (see note 2). References to other works are given in the notes.

How people will cry out against me! I hear from afar the shouts of that false wisdom which is ever dragging us onwards, counting the present as nothing, and pursuing without a pause a future which flies as we pursue, that false wisdom which removes us from our place and never brings us to any other.
—*Emile*

All the papers which I have collected to fill the gaps in my memory and to guide me in my undertaking, having passed into other hands, will never return to mine.
—*Confessions*

I have implied it repeatedly: the praise of living speech, as it *preoccupies* Lévi-Strauss's discourse, is faithful to only one particular motif in Rousseau. This motif comes to terms with and is organized by its contrary: a perpetually reanimated mistrust with regard to so-called full speech. In the spoken address, presence is at once promised and refused. The speech that Rousseau raised above writing is speech as it should be or rather as it *should have been*. And we must pay attention to that mode, to that tense which relates us to presence within living colloquy. *In fact*, Rousseau had experienced the concealment within speech itself, in the mirage of its immediacy. He had recognized and analyzed it with incomparable acumen. We are dispossessed of the longed-for presence in the gesture of language by which we attempt to seize it. It is not only in the play of the mirror image which "captures his reflection and betrays his presence" that Jean-Jacques is subjected to the experience of the "robber robbed" that Starobinski admirably describes in *The Living Eye*.[1] It lies in wait for us from the first word. The speculary dispossession which at the same time institutes and deconstitutes me is also a law of language. It operates as a power of death in the heart of living speech: a power all the more redoubtable because it opens as much as it threatens the possibility of the spoken word.

Having in a certain way recognized this power which, inaugurating speech, dislocates the subject that it constructs, prevents it from being present to its signs, torments its language with a complete writing,

1. Jean Starobinski, *The Living Eye*, trans. Arthur Goldhammer (Cambridge, Mass.: Harvard University Press, 1990), 25.

Rousseau is nevertheless more pressed to exorcise it than to assume its necessity. That is why, straining toward the reconstruction of presence, he valorizes and disqualifies writing at the same time. At the same time; that is to say, in one divided but coherent movement. We must try not to lose sight of its strange unity. Rousseau condemns writing as destruction of presence and as disease of speech. He rehabilitates it to the extent that it promises the reappropriation of that of which speech allowed itself to be dispossessed. But by what, if not already a writing older than speech and already installed in that place?

The first movement of this desire is formulated as a theory of language. The other governs the experience of the writer. In the *Confessions,* when Jean-Jacques tries to explain how he became a writer, he describes the passage to writing as the restoration, by a certain absence and by a sort of calculated effacement, of presence disappointed of itself in speech. To write is indeed the only way of keeping or recapturing speech since speech denies itself as it gives itself. Thus an *economy of signs* is organized. It will be equally disappointing, closer yet to the very essence and to the necessity of disappointment. One cannot help wishing to master absence and yet we must always let go. Starobinski describes the profound law that commands the space within which Rousseau must move:

> How can he dispel the misunderstanding that prevents him from showing his true worth? How can he avoid the risks of improvised speech? What other mode of communication can he try? In what other way can he show himself? Jean-Jacques chooses to be *absent* and to *write.* Paradoxically, he will hide in order to make himself more visible and trust to the written word: "I would love society as much as any other man, were I not sure of showing myself there not only to my disadvantage but quite other than I really am. My decision to *write and to hide myself* was perfectly suited to me. With me present, no one would ever have known what I was worth" (*Confessions,* Pléiade I, 116). This confession is striking and deserves emphasis: Jean-Jacques breaks with society but only in order to present himself through the written word. He will polish his phrases at leisure, protected by solitude.[2]

2. Jean Starobinski, *Jean-Jacques Rousseau: Transparency and Obstruction,* trans. Arthur Goldhammer (Chicago: University of Chicago Press, 1988), 125. Naturally, I can cite Rousseau's interpreters only to indicate borrowings or to circumscribe a debate.

Let us note that the economy is perhaps indicated in the following: the operation that substitutes writing for speech also replaces presence by value: to the *I am* or to the *I am present* thus sacrificed, a *what* I am or a *what I am worth* is *preferred*. "With me present, no one would ever have known what I was worth." I renounce my present life, my present and concrete existence in order to make myself known in the ideality of truth and value. A well-known schema. The battle by which I wish to raise myself above my life even while I retain it, in order to enjoy recognition, is in this case within myself, and writing is indeed the phenomenon of this battle.

Such would be the writing lesson in Jean-Jacques's existence. The act of writing would be essentially—and here in an exemplary fashion—the greatest sacrifice aiming at the greatest symbolic reappropriation of presence. From this point of view, Rousseau knew that death is not the simple outside of life. Death by writing also inaugurates life. "I can certainly say that I never began to live, until I looked upon myself as a dead man" (*Confessions*, book 6, 236). As soon as one determines it within the system of this economy, does not the sacrifice— the "literary suicide"— vanish in the *appearance?* Is it anything but a symbolic reappropriation? Does it not renounce the *present* and the *proper* in order to master them better in their meaning, in the ideal form of truth, of the presence of the present and of the proximity or property of the proper?[3] We would be obliged to return a verdict of ruse and appearance if in fact we were to abide by these concepts (sacrifice, expenditure, renunciation, symbol, appearance, truth, etc.) which determine what we here call economy in terms of truth and appearance, starting from the opposition presence/absence.

But it goes without saying that every reader of Rousseau is guided by the admirable edition of the *Oeuvres complètes* now in progress at the Bibliothéque de la Pléiade (ed. Bernard Gagnebin and Marcel Raymond [Paris: Gallimard, 1959–69]), and by the masterful work of François Bouchardy, Pierre Burgelin, Jean-Daniel Candaux, Robert Derathé, Jean Fabre, Michel Foucault, Bernard Gagnebin, Henri Gouhier, Bernard Groethuysen, Bernard Guyon, Charly Guyot, Robert Osmont, Georges Poulet, Marcel Raymond, Sven Stelling-Michaud, and, here especially, Jean Starobinski.

3. EN The meanings of *propre* include all the connotations of the English "proper," including correctness, appropriateness, and ownership; *propriété* means both "property" and "correctness" (of stylistic choice). A further series of meanings revolves around "clean" and "cleanliness"; all these connotations are set to work in *Signsponge* (see the extract below, and note 4 to that extract).

But the work of writing and the economy of *différance* will not be dominated by this classical conceptuality, by this ontology or this epistemology.[4] On the contrary, these furnish its hidden premises. *Différance* does not *resist* appropriation, it does not impose an exterior limit upon it. *Différance* began by *broaching* alienation and it ends by leaving reappropriation *breached*. Until death. Death is the moment of *différance* to the extent that that movement is necessarily finite. This means that *différance* makes the opposition of presence and absence possible. Without the possibility of *différance,* the desire of presence as such would not find its breathing-space. That means by the same token that this desire carries in itself the destiny of its non-satisfaction. *Différance* produces what it forbids, makes possible the very thing that it makes impossible.

If *différance* is recognized as the obliterated origin of absence and presence, major forms of the disappearing and the appearing of the entity, it would still remain to be known if Being, before its determination into absence or presence, is already implicated in the thought of *différance*. And if *différance* as the project of the mastery of the entity should be understood with reference to the sense of Being. Can one not think the converse? Since the sense of Being is never produced as history outside of its determination as presence, has it not always already been caught within the history of metaphysics as the epoch of presence? This is perhaps what Nietzsche wanted to write and what resists the Heideggerian reading of Nietzsche; *différance* in its *active* movement—*what* is comprehended in the concept of *différance* without exhausting it—is what not only precedes metaphysics but also extends beyond the thought of Being. The latter speaks *nothing other than* metaphysics, even if it exceeds it and thinks it as what it is within its closure.

4. EN The term *différance* has been left in its original form. It is a Derridean coinage which brings together the senses of "deferring," "differing," "being deferred," and "being differentiated"; time and space, active and passive remain undecidable. For a full discussion, see Derrida's essay "Différance."

From/Of Blindness to the Supplement[5]

In terms of this problematical scheme, we must therefore think Rousseau's experience and his theory of writing together, the accord and the discord that, under the name of writing, relate Jean-Jacques to Rousseau, uniting and dividing his proper name. On the side of experience, a recourse to literature as reappropriation of presence, that is to say, as we shall see, of Nature; on the side of theory, an indictment against the negativity of the letter, in which must be read the degeneracy of culture and the disruption of the community.

If indeed one wishes to surround it with the entire constellation of concepts that shares its system, the word *supplement* seems to account for the strange unity of these two gestures.

In both cases, in fact, Rousseau considers writing as a dangerous means, a menacing aid, the critical response to a situation of distress. When Nature, as self-proximity, comes to be forbidden or interrupted, when speech fails to protect presence, writing becomes necessary. It must *be added* to the word urgently. I have identified in advance one of the forms of this *addition;* speech being natural or at least the natural expression of thought, the most natural form of institution or convention for signifying thought, writing is added to it, is adjoined, as an image or representation. In that sense, it is not natural. It diverts the immediate presence of thought to speech into representation and the imagination. This recourse is not only "bizarre," but dangerous. It is the addition of a technique, a sort of artificial and artful ruse to make speech present when it is actually absent. It is a violence done to the natural destiny of the language:

> Languages are made to be spoken, writing serves only as a supplement to speech. . . . Speech represents thought by conventional signs, and

5. EN *De l'aveuglement au supplément* means both "From blindness to the supplement" and "Of, concerning, blindness to the supplement." (Compare "*De la grammatologie.*")

writing represents speech in the same way. Thus the art of writing is nothing but a mediated representation of thought.[6]

Writing is dangerous from the moment that representation there claims to be presence and the sign of the thing itself. And there is a fatal necessity, inscribed in the very functioning of the sign, that the substitute make one forget the vicariousness of its own function and make itself pass for the plenitude of a speech whose deficiency and infirmity it nevertheless only *supplements*. For the concept of the supplement—which here determines that of the representative image—harbors within itself two significations whose cohabitation is as strange as it is necessary. The supplement adds itself, it is a surplus, a plenitude enriching another plenitude, the *fullest measure* of presence. It cumulates and accumulates presence. It is thus that art, *technē*, image, representation, convention, etc., come as supplements to nature and are rich with this entire cumulating function. This kind of supplementarity determines in a certain way all the conceptual oppositions within which Rousseau inscribes the notion of Nature to the extent that it *should* be self-sufficient.

But the supplement supplements. It adds only to replace. It intervenes or insinuates itself *in-the-place of;* if it fills, it is as one fills a void. If it represents and makes an image, it is by the anterior default of a presence. Compensatory [*suppléant*] and vicarious, the supplement is an adjunct, a subaltern instance which *takes-(the)-place* [*tient-lieu*]. As substitute, it is not simply added to the positivity of a presence, it produces no relief, its place is assigned in the structure by the mark of an emptiness. Somewhere, something can be filled up of *itself*, can accomplish itself, only by allowing itself to be filled through sign and proxy. The sign is always the supplement of the thing itself.

This second signification of the supplement cannot be separated from the first. We shall constantly have to confirm that both operate within Rousseau's texts. But the inflexion varies from moment to

6. EN Manuscript included in the Pléiade edition of Rousseau's works under the title *Pronunciation* (II, 1248).

moment. Each of the two significations is by turns effaced or becomes discreetly vague in the presence of the other. But their common function is shown in this: whether it adds or substitutes itself, the supplement is *exterior*, outside of the positivity to which it is super-added, alien to that which, in order to be replaced by it, must be other than it. Unlike the *complement*, dictionaries tell us, the supplement is an *"exterior addition"* (Robert's *French Dictionary*).

According to Rousseau, the negativity of evil will always have the form of supplementarity. Evil is exterior to nature, to what is by nature innocent and good. It supervenes upon nature. But always by way of compensation for [*sous l'espèce de la suppléance*] what *ought to* lack nothing at all in itself.

Thus presence, always natural, which for Rousseau more than for others means maternal, *ought to be* self-sufficient. Its *essence*, another name for presence, may be read through the grid of this ought to be [*ce conditionnel*]. Like Nature's love, "there is no substitute for a mother's love" [*la sollicitude maternelle ne se supplée point*], says *Emile* (13). It is in no way *supplemented*, that is to say it does not have to be supplemented, it suffices and is self-sufficient; but that also means that it is irreplaceable; what one would substitute for it would not equal it, would be only a mediocre makeshift. Finally it means that Nature does not supplement *itself* at all; Nature's supplement does not proceed from Nature, it is not only inferior to but other than Nature.

Yet all education, the keystone of Rousseauist thought, will be described or presented as a system of substitution [*suppléance*] destined to reconstitute Nature's edifice in the most natural way possible. The first chapter of *Emile* announces the function of this pedagogy. Although there is no substitute for a mother's love, "it is better that the child should suck the breast of a healthy nurse rather than of a petted mother, if he has any further evil to fear from her who has given him birth" (12). It is indeed culture or cultivation that must supplement a deficient Nature, a deficiency that cannot by definition be anything but an accident and a deviation from Nature. Culture or cultivation is here called habit; it is necessary and insufficient from the moment when the substitution of mothers is no longer envisaged "only from the physiological point of view":

Other women, or even animals, may give him the milk she denies him, but there is no substitute for a mother's love. The woman who nurses another's child in place of her own is a bad mother; how can she be a good nurse? She may become one in time; habit must overcome nature. (13)

Here the problems of natural right, of the relationship between Nature and Society, the concepts of alienation, alterity, and corruption, are adapted most spontaneously to the pedagogic problem of the substitution of mothers and children:

And this affection when developed has its drawbacks, which should make every sensible woman afraid to put her child out to nurse. Is she prepared to divide her mother's rights, or rather to abdicate them in favor of a stranger; to see her child loving another as much as and more than herself? (13)

If, premeditating the theme of writing, I begin by speaking of the substitution of mothers, it is because, as Rousseau will himself say, "more depends on this than you realize":

How emphatically would I speak if it were not so hopeless to keep struggling in vain on behalf of a real reform. More depends on this than you realize. Would you restore all men to their primal duties, begin with the mothers; the results will surprise you. Every evil follows in the train of this first sin; the whole moral order is disturbed, nature is quenched in every breast. (13)

Childhood is the first manifestation of the deficiency which, in Nature, calls for substitution [*suppléance*]. Pedagogy illuminates perhaps more crudely the paradoxes of the supplement. How is a natural weakness possible? How can Nature ask for forces that it does not furnish? How is a child possible in general?

First Maxim.—Far from being too strong, children are not strong enough for all the claims of nature. Give them full use of such strength as they have and which they will not abuse. *Second Maxim.*—Help them and supply what they lack, in intelligence or in strength, whenever the need is of the body. (35)

All the organization of, and all the time spent in, education will be regulated by this necessary evil: "supply [*suppléer*] what is lacking" and replace Nature. It must be done as little and as late as possible. "One of the best rules of good farming [*culture*] is to *keep things back* as much as possible" (193). "Give nature time to work before you *act in her place*" (71; italics added).

Without childhood, no supplement would ever appear in Nature. The supplement is here both humanity's good fortune and the origin of its perversion. The health of the human race:

> Plants are fashioned by cultivation, man by education. If man were born tall and strong, his size and strength would be of no good to him till he had learnt to use them; they would even harm him by preventing others coming to his aid; left to himself, he would die of want before he knew his needs. We lament the helplessness of infancy; we fail to perceive that the race would have perished had not man begun by being a child. (6)

The threat of perversion:

> While the Author of nature has given children the active principle, He takes care that it shall do little harm by giving them small power to use it. But as soon as they can think of people as tools that they are responsible for activating, they use them to carry out their wishes and to *supplement* their own weakness. This is how they become tiresome, masterful, imperious, naughty, and unmanageable; a development which does not spring from a natural love of power, but one which gives it to them, for it does not need much experience to realize how pleasant it is to act through the hands of others and to move the world by simply moving the tongue. (34; italics added)

The supplement will always be the moving of the tongue or acting through the hands of others. In it everything is brought together: progress as the possibility of perversion, regression toward an evil that is not natural and that adheres to the power of substitution that permits us to absent ourselves and act by proxy, through representation, through the hands of others. Through the written [*par écrit*]. This substitution always has the form of the sign. The scandal is that the sign, the image, or the representer, become forces and make "the world move."

This scandal is such, and its evil effects are sometimes so irreparable, that the world seems to turn the wrong way (and we shall see later what such a *catastrophe* can signify for Rousseau); then Nature becomes the supplement of art and society. It is the moment when evil seems incurable: "As the child does not know how to be cured, let him know how to be ill. The one art takes the place of [*supplée*] the other and is often more successful; it is the art of nature" (22). It is also the moment when maternal Nature, ceasing to be loved, as she ought to be, for herself and in an immediate proximity ("O Nature! O my mother! behold me under thy protection alone! Here there is no cunning or knavish mortal to thrust himself between me and thee." [*Confessions*, book 12, 669]), becomes the substitute for another love and for another attachment:

> The contemplation of Nature always had a very great attraction for his heart; he found there a supplement to the attachments that he needed; but he would have left the supplement for the thing, if he had had the choice, and he was reduced to conversing with the plants only after vain efforts to converse with human beings. (*Dialogues*, Pléiade I, 794)

That botany becomes the supplement of society is more than a catastrophe. It is the catastrophe of the catastrophe. For in Nature, the plant is the most *natural* thing. It is natural *life*. The mineral is distinguished from the vegetable in that it is a dead and useful Nature, servile to man's industry. When man has lost the sense and the taste of true natural riches—plants—he rummages in the entrails of his mother and risks his health:

> The Mineral Kingdom has nothing in itself either amiable or attractive; its riches, enclosed in the womb of the earth, seem to have been removed from the gaze of man in order not to tempt his cupidity; they are there like a reserve to serve one day as a *supplement* to the true wealth which is more within his grasp, and for which he loses taste according to the extent of his corruption. Then he is compelled to call in industry, to struggle, and to labor to alleviate his miseries; he searches the entrails of

earth; he goes seeking to its center, at the risk of his life and at the expense of his health, for imaginary goods in place of the real good which the earth offers of herself if he knew how to enjoy it. *He flies from the sun and the day, which he is no longer worthy to see.*[7] (*Reveries,* Seventh Promenade, 144–45; italics added)

Man has thus put out his eyes, he blinds himself by the desire to rummage in these entrails. Here is the horrible spectacle of the punishment that follows the crime, in sum a simple substitution:

He buries himself alive, and does well, not being worthy of living in the light of day. There quarries, pits, forges, furnaces, a battery of anvils, hammers, smoke and fire, succeed to the fair images of his rustic labors. The wan faces of the unhappy people who languish in the poisonous vapors of mines, of black forgemen, of hideous cyclops, are the spectacle which the working of the mine substitutes, in the womb of the earth, for that of green fields and flowers, the azure sky, amorous shepherds and robust laborers upon its surface.[8] (*Reveries,* 145)

Such is the scandal, such the catastrophe. The supplement is what neither Nature nor Reason can tolerate. Neither Nature, our "common mother" (*Reveries,* 143), nor the reason which is reasonable, if not reasoning.[9] And had they not done everything to avoid this catastrophe, to protect themselves from this violence and to guard and keep us from this fatal crime? "so that," says the second *Discourse* precisely of mines, "it looks as if nature had taken pains to keep the fatal secret from us."[10] And let us not forget that the violence that takes us toward

7. It may be objected that the animal represents a natural life even more animated than the plant, but one can only deal with it dead. "The study of animals is nothing without anatomy" (146).
8. Without looking for a principle of reading, I refer, out of curiosity and from among many other possible examples, to what Karl Abraham says of the Cyclops, of the fear of being blind, of the eye, of the sun, of masturbation, etc., in *Oeuvres complètes,* trans. Ilse Barande and E. Grin (Paris: Payot, 1965), II, 18f. Let us recall that in a sequence of Egyptian mythology, Seth, helper of Thoth (god of writing here considered as a brother of Osiris), kills Osiris by trickery (cf. Jacques Vandier, *La religion égyptienne* [Paris: P.U.F., 1944], 46). Writing, auxiliary and suppletory, kills the father and light in the same gesture.
9. See *De l'état de nature* [*Fragments politiques*], Pléiade III, 478.
10. Jean-Jacques Rousseau, *The Social Contract and Discourses,* trans. G. D. H. Cole (London: Dent, 1913), 200.

the entrails of the earth, the moment of mine-blindness, that is, of metallurgy, is the origin of society. For according to Rousseau, as we shall often confirm, agriculture, marking the organization of civil society, assumes the beginning of metallurgy. Blindness thus produces that which is born at the same time as society: the languages, the regulated substitution of signs for things, the order of the supplement. One goes *from blindness to the supplement*. But the blind person cannot see, in its origin, the very thing he produces to supplement his sight. *Blindness to the supplement* is the law. And especially blindness to its concept. Moreover, in order to *see* its meaning, it is not enough to locate its functioning. The supplement has no sense and is given to no intuition. We do not therefore make it emerge out of its strange penumbra. We speak its reserve.

Reason is incapable of thinking this double infringement upon Nature: that there is *lack* in Nature and that *because of that very fact* something *is added* to it. Yet one should not say that Reason is *powerless to think this;* it is constituted by that lack of power. It is the principle of identity. It is the thought of the self-identity of the natural being. It cannot even determine the supplement as its other, as the irrational and the non-natural, for the supplement comes *naturally* to put itself in Nature's place. The supplement is the image and the representation of Nature. The image is neither in nor out of Nature. The supplement is therefore equally dangerous for Reason, the natural health of Reason.

Dangerous supplement. These are the words that Rousseau uses in the *Confessions.* He uses them in a context which is only apparently different, and in order to explain, precisely, a "condition almost inconceivable to reason": "In a word, between myself and the most passionate lover there was only one, but that an essential, point of distinction, which makes my condition almost inconceivable to reason" (111).

If we lend to the text below a paradigmatic value, it is only provisional and does not prejudge what the discipline of a future reading might rigorously determine. No model of reading seems to me at the moment ready to measure up to this text—which I would like to read as a *text* and not as a document. Measure up to it fully and rigorously, that is, beyond what already makes the text more readable, and more readable, no doubt, than has been so far thought. My only ambition will be to draw out of it a signification which that presumed future reading will not be able to dispense with [*faire l'économie*]; the economy of a written text, circulating through other texts, referring to them constantly, conforming to the element of a language and to its regulated functioning. For example, what unites the word *supplement* to its concept was not invented by Rousseau and the originality of its functioning is neither fully mastered by Rousseau nor simply imposed by history and the language, by the history of the language. To speak of the writing of Rousseau is to try to recognize what escapes these categories of passivity and activity, blindness and responsibility. And one cannot abstract from the written text to rush to the signified it *would mean*,[11] since the signified is here writing itself. It is so little a matter of looking for a *truth signified* by these writings (metaphysical or psychological truth: Jean-Jacques's life behind his work) that if the texts that interest us *mean* [*veulent dire*] something, it is the engagement and the belonging that encompass existence and writing in the same *tissue,* the same *text.* The same is here called supplement, another name for *différance.*

Here is the irruption of the dangerous supplement in Nature, between nature and nature, between natural innocence as *virginity* and natural innocence as *pucelage:*[12] "In a word, between myself and the most passionate lover there was only one, but that an essential, point of distinction, which makes my condition almost inconceivable to reason." Here, the lineation should not hide the fact that the following paragraph is destined to explain the "only point of distinction" and the "condition almost inconceivable to reason." Rousseau elaborates:

> I had returned from Italy not quite the same as I had entered it, but as, perhaps, no one of my age has ever returned from it. I had brought back, not my virginity but my *pucelage.* I had felt the progress of years; my restless temperament had at last made itself felt, and its first outbreak,

11. EN The French *voudrait dire* literally means "would like to say"; *vouloir dire,* "to wish to say," is the normal French equivalent for the verb "to mean."

12. TN *Pucelage* is the more earthy French word for the actual physical fact of sexual intactness, in the female the membrane itself. Rousseau applies the word to his own case with some derision, contrasting it to the spiritual innocence of true "virginity."

quite involuntary, had caused me alarm about my health in a manner which shows better than anything else the innocence in which I had lived up to that time. Soon reassured, I learned that dangerous supplement which cheats Nature and saves up for young men of my temperament many forms of excess at the expense of their health, strength, and, sometimes, their life. (111)

We read in *Emile* (book IV): "If once he acquires this dangerous supplement he is ruined" (299). In the same book, it is also a question of "mak[ing] up ... by trading on ... inexperience" [*suppléer en gagnant de vitesse sur l'experience;* literally "supplementing by out-distancing experience"] (315), and of the "mind, which reinforces [*supplée*] ... the bodily strength" (129).

The experience of auto-eroticism is lived in anguish. Masturbation reassures ("soon reassured") only through that culpability traditionally attached to the practice, obliging children to take responsibility for the fault and to interiorize the threat of castration that always accompanies it. Pleasure is thus lived as the irremediable loss of the vital substance, as exposure to madness and death.[13] It is produced "at the expense of their health, strength, and, sometimes, their life." In the same way, the *Reveries* will say, the man who "searches the entrails of earth . . . goes seeking to its center, at the risk of his life and at the expense of his health, for imaginary goods in place of the real good which the earth offers of herself if he knew how to enjoy it [*en jouir*]." (145).

And indeed it is a question of the imaginary. The supplement that "cheats" maternal "nature" operates as writing, and as writing it is dangerous to life. This danger is that of the image. Just as writing opens the crisis of living speech in terms of its "image," its painting or its representation, so onanism announces the ruin of vitality in terms of imaginary seduction:

This vice, which shame and timidity find so convenient, possesses, besides, a great attraction for lively imaginations—that of being able to dispose of the whole sex as they desire, and to make the beauty which tempts

13. EN *La jouissance,* translated here by "pleasure," includes the meaning of "orgasm."

them minister to their pleasures, without being obliged to obtain its consent. (*Confessions*, 111)

The dangerous supplement, which Rousseau also calls a "fatal advantage," is properly *seductive;* it leads desire away from the good path, makes it err far from natural ways, guides it toward its loss or fall and therefore it is a sort of lapsus or scandal (*scandalon*). It thus destroys Nature. But the scandal of Reason is that nothing seems more natural than this destruction of Nature. It is myself who exerts myself to separate myself from the force that Nature has entrusted to me: "Seduced by this fatal advantage, I did my best to destroy the good constitution which Nature had restored to me, and which I had allowed time to strengthen itself." We know what importance *Emile* gives to time, to the slow maturation of natural forces. The entire art of pedagogy is a calculated patience, allowing the work of Nature time to come to fruition, respecting its rhythm and the order of its stages. The dangerous supplement destroys very quickly the forces that Nature has slowly constituted and accumulated. In "out-distancing" natural experience, it runs non-stop and consumes energy without possibility of recovery. As I shall confirm, like the sign it bypasses the presence of the thing and the duration of Being.

The dangerous supplement breaks with Nature. The entire description of this moving away from Nature has a *scene [théâtre]*. The *Confessions* stage the evocation of the dangerous supplement at the moment when it is a question of making visible a distancing which is neither the same nor an other; Nature draws away at the same time as the Mother, or rather "Mamma," who already signified the disappearance of the true mother and substituted herself for her in the ambiguous manner familiar to readers of the *Confessions*. It is therefore now a question of the distance between Mamma and the person she called "Little one."[14] As *Emile* says, all evil comes from the fact that "women

14. "'Little one' was my name; 'Mamma' was hers; and we always remained 'Little one' and 'Mamma,' even when advancing years had almost obliterated the difference between us. I find that these two names give a wonderfully good idea of the tone of our intercourse, of the simplicity of our manners, and, above all, of the mutual relation of our hearts. For me she was the tenderest of mothers, who never sought her own pleasure,

have ceased to be mothers, they do not and will not return to their duty" (14). A certain absence, then, of a certain sort of mother. And the experience of which we speak is such as to reduce that absence as much as to maintain it. A *furtive* experience, that of a thief who needs invisibility: that the mother be both invisible and not see. These lines are often quoted:

> I should never have done, if I were to enter into the details of all the follies which the remembrance of this dear mamma caused me to commit when I was no longer in her presence. How often have I kissed my bed, since she had slept in it; my curtains, all the furniture of my room, since they belonged to her, and her beautiful hand had touched them; even the floor, on which I prostrated myself, since she had walked upon it! Sometimes, even in her presence, I was guilty of extravagances, which only the most violent love seemed capable of inspiring. At table one day, just when she had put a piece of food into her mouth, I exclaimed that I saw a hair in it; she put back the morsel on her plate, and I eagerly seized and swallowed it.[15] In a word, between myself and the most passionate lover there was only one, but that an essential, point of distinction, which makes my condition almost inconceivable to reason. . . . [A little above, we read:] I only felt the full strength of my attachment when I no longer saw her. (111)

but always what was best for me; and if sensuality entered at all into her attachment for me, it did not alter its character, but only rendered it more enchanting, and intoxicated me with the delight of having a young and pretty mamma whom it was delightful to me to caress—I say caress in the strictest sense of the word, for it never occurred to her to be sparing of kisses and the tenderest caresses of a mother, and it certainly never entered my mind to abuse them. It will be objected that, in the end, we had relations of a different character; I admit it, but I must wait a little—I cannot say all at once" (106). Let us add this sentence from Georges Bataille: "I am myself the 'little one,' I have only a hidden place" (*Le petit*, 2d ed. [Paris: Pauvert, 1963], 9).

15. This passage is often cited, but has it ever been analyzed for itself? The Pléiade editors of the *Confessions*, Gagnebin and Raymond, are no doubt right in being cautious, as they are, systematically and inevitably, of what they call psychiatry (I, 1281*n;* this same note checks off very usefully all the texts where Rousseau recalls his "follies" or "extravagances"). But this caution is not legitimate, it seems to me, except to the extent that it concerns the abuse—which has hitherto no doubt been confounded with the use—of psychoanalytic reading, and where it does not prescribe the duplication of the usual commentary which has rendered this kind of text most often unreadable. [EN Some comments on specific examples of French psychoanalytic readings of Rousseau have been omitted here.]

The Chain of Supplements

The discovery of the dangerous supplement will be next cited *among* these "follies," but it will still retain a privilege; Rousseau evokes it after the others and as a sort of explanation of the state inconceivable to reason. For it is not a question of diverting total enjoyment [*jouissance*] toward a particular substitute, but now of experiencing it or miming it *directly and in its totality*. It is no longer a question of kissing the bed, the floor, the curtains, the furniture, etc., not even of "swallowing" the "piece [that] she had put into her mouth," but of "dispos[ing] of the whole sex as [one] desire[s]."

I remarked that the stage of this theater was not only a setting in the generally understood sense: an ensemble of accessories. The topographic disposition of the experience is not unimportant. Jean-Jacques is in the house of Madame de Warens; close enough to *Mamma* to see her and to nourish his imagination upon her but with the possibility of physical separation. It is at the moment when the mother disappears that substitution becomes possible and necessary. The play of maternal presence or absence, this alternation of perception and imagination must correspond to an organization of space; the text argues as follows:

> Add to this habit the circumstances of my position, living as I was with a beautiful woman, caressing her image in the bottom of my heart, seeing her continually throughout the day, surrounded in the evening by objects which reminded me of her, sleeping in the bed in which I knew she had slept! What causes for excitement! Many a reader, who reflects upon them, no doubt already considers me as half-dead! Quite the contrary; that which ought to have destroyed me was just the thing that saved me, at least for a time. Intoxicated with the charm of living with her, with the ardent desire of spending my life with her, I always saw in her, whether she were absent or present, a tender mother, a beloved sister, a delightful friend, and nothing more. . . . She was for me the only woman in the world; and the extreme sweetness of the feelings with which she inspired me did not allow my senses time to awake for others, and protected me against her and all her sex. (111–12)

This experience was not an event marking an archaic or adolescent period. It did not only construct or sustain a particular hidden foundation, an edifice of significations. It remained an active obsession whose "present" is constantly reactivated and constituted in its turn, until the end of Jean-Jacques Rousseau's "life" and "text." A little later, a little further on in the text of the *Confessions* (book 4), "a little incident, which I find some difficulty in relating," is related to us. The encounter with a man "addicted to the same vice." Terrified, Jean-Jacques runs away, "trembling as if" he had just "committed a crime." "The recollection of this incident cured me of it for a long time" (171).

For a long time? Rousseau will never stop having recourse to, and blaming himself for, this onanism that enables one to affect oneself by providing oneself with presences, by summoning absent beauties. In his eyes it will remain the model of vice and perversion. Affecting oneself by another presence, one *corrupts* oneself by oneself.[16] Rousseau neither wishes to think nor can think that this alteration does not simply happen to the self, that it is the self's very origin. He must consider it a contingent evil coming from without to affect the integrity of the subject. But he cannot give up what immediately restores to him the other desired presence; no more than one can give up language. This is why, in this respect as well, as he says in the *Dialogues* (Pléiade, I, 800), "to the end of his life he will remain an aged child."

The restitution of presence by language, restitution at the same time symbolic and immediate. This contradiction must be thought. Immediate experience of restitution because as experience, as consciousness or conscience, it *dispenses with passage through the world.* What is touching is touched, auto-affection gives itself as pure autarchy. If the presence that it then gives itself is the substitutive symbol of another presence, it has never been possible to desire that presence "in person" before this play of substitution and this symbolic experience of auto-affection. The thing itself does not appear outside of the symbolic system that does not exist without the possibility of auto-affection. Experience of *immediate* restitution, also because it *does not wait.* It is satisfied then and there and in the moment. If it waits, it is not because the other makes it wait. Pleasure [*La jouissance*] seems no longer to be deferred. "Why give oneself so much trouble in a hope

16. EN *On s'altère soi-même*, literally, "one makes oneself other."

remote from so poor and uncertain a success, when one can, from the very instant . . ." (*Dialogues*).

But what is no longer deferred is also absolutely deferred. The presence that is thus delivered to us in the present is a chimera. Auto-affection is a pure speculation. The sign, the image, the representation, which come to supplement the absent presence are the illusions that sidetrack us. To culpability, to the anguish of death and castration, is added or rather is assimilated the experience of frustration. *Donner le change* ["sidetracking" or "giving money"]: in whatever sense it is understood, this expression describes the recourse to the supplement admirably. In order to explain his "dislike" for "common prostitutes," Rousseau tells us that in Venice, at thirty-one, the "propensity which had modified all my passions" (*Confessions*, 35)[17] has not disappeared. "I had not lost the pernicious habit of satisfying my wants [*donner le change à mes besoins*]" (325).

The enjoyment of the *thing itself* is thus undermined, in its act and in its essence, by frustration. One cannot therefore say that it has an essence or an act (*eidos, ousia, energeia,* etc.). Something promises itself as it escapes, gives itself as it moves away, and strictly speaking it cannot even be called presence. Such is the constraint of the supplement, such, exceeding all the language of metaphysics, is this structure "almost inconceivable to reason." *Almost* inconceivable: simple irrationality, the opposite of reason, are less irritating and waylaying for classical logic. The supplement is maddening because it is neither presence nor absence and because it consequently breaches both our pleasure and our virginity. ". . . Abstinence and enjoyment, pleasure and prudence, equally escaped my grasp" (*Confessions*, 10).

Are things not complicated enough? The symbolic is the immediate,

---

17. In these celebrated pages of the first book of the *Confessions*, Rousseau compares the first experiences of reading ("secret and ill-chosen reading") to the first discoveries of auto-eroticism. Not that "filthy and licentious [books]" encouraged him in it. Quite the contrary. "Chance aided my modest disposition so well, that I was more than thirty years old before I set eyes upon any of those dangerous books which a fine lady finds inconvenient because, she says, they can only be read with one hand" (40). Without these "dangerous books," Jean-Jacques gives himself to other dangers. The following paragraph is well known; it closes thus: "It is sufficient for me to have defined the origin and first cause of a propensity which has modified all my passions, and which, restraining them by means of themselves, has always made me slow to act, owing to my excessive

presence is absence, the nondeferred is deferred, pleasure is the menace of death. But one stroke must still be added to this system, to this strange economy of the supplement. In a certain way, it was already legible. A terrifying menace, the supplement is also the first and surest protection: against that very menace. This is why it cannot be given up. And sexual auto-affection, that is auto-affection in general, neither begins nor ends with what one thinks can be circumscribed by the name of masturbation. The supplement has not only the power of *procuring* an absent presence through its image; procuring it for us through the proxy [*procuration*] of the sign, it holds it at a distance and masters it. For this presence is at the same time desired and feared. The supplement transgresses and at the same time respects the interdict. This is what also permits writing as the supplement of speech; but already also the spoken word as writing in general. Its economy exposes and protects us at the same time according to the play of forces and of the differences of forces. Thus, the supplement is dangerous in that it threatens us with death, but Rousseau thinks that it is not at all as dangerous as "cohabitation with women." Pleasure *itself,* without symbol or suppletory, that which would accord us (to) pure presence itself, if such a thing were possible, would be only another name for death. Rousseau says it:

> Enjoyment! [*Jouir!*] Does this ever fall to the lot of man? If I had ever, a single time in my life, tasted all the delights of love in their fullness, I do not believe that my frail existence would have endured it; I should have died on the spot. (*Confessions,* 226)

If one abides by the universal evidence, by the necessary and a priori value of this proposition in the form of a sigh, one must immediately recognize that "cohabitation with women," hetero-eroticism, can be lived (effectively, really, as we believe we can say) only through the ability to reserve within itself its own supplementary protection. In

impetuosity in desire" (41). The intention and the letter of this passage should be related to another page of the *Confessions* (459; cf. the Pléiade editors' note, I, 444), and to the page from which I quote these lines: "For I have always had a fancy for reading while eating, if I am alone; it supplies the want of society. I devour alternately a page and a morsel. It seems as if my book were dining with me" (278).

other words, between auto-eroticism and hetero-eroticism, there is not a frontier but an economic distribution. It is within this general rule that the differences are mapped out. This is Rousseau's general rule. And before trying—what I do not pretend to be doing here—to encompass the pure singularity of Rousseau's economy or his writing, we must carefully raise and articulate among them all the structural or essential necessities, at their different levels of generality.

It is from a certain determined representation of "cohabitation with women" that Rousseau had to have recourse throughout his life to that type of dangerous supplement that is called masturbation and that cannot be separated from his activity as a writer. To the end. Thérèse—the Thérèse of whom we can speak, Thérèse in the text, whose name and "life" belong to the writing we read—experienced it to her cost. In book 12 of the *Confessions,* at the moment when "I must speak without reserve," the "two reasons" for certain "resolutions" are confided to us:

> I must speak without reserve. I have never concealed either my poor mamma's faults or my own. I must not show greater favor to Thérèse either; and, pleased as I am to render honor to one who is so dear to me, neither do I wish to conceal her faults, if so be that an involuntary change in the heart's affections is really a fault. I had long since observed that her affection for me had cooled. . . . I was conscious again of an unpleasantness, the effects of which I had formerly felt when with mamma; and the effect was the same with Thérèse. Let us not look for perfections which are not to be found in nature; it would be the same with any other woman whatsoever. . . . My situation, however, was at that time the same, and even aggravated by the animosity of my enemies, who only sought to find me at fault. I was afraid of a repetition; and, not desiring to run the risk of it, I preferred to condemn myself to strict continence, than to expose Thérèse to the risk of finding herself in the same condition again. Besides, I had observed that intercourse with women distinctly aggravated my ill health. These two reasons combined caused me to form resolutions which I had sometimes been very inconsistent in keeping, but in which I had persevered with greater firmness for the last three or four years. (616–17)

In the *Manuscrit de Paris,* after "distinctly aggravated my ill health!" we read: "The corresponding vice, of which I have never been able to cure myself completely, appeared to me to produce less injurious results. These two reasons combined . . ."[18]

This perversion consists of preferring the sign and protects me from mortal expenditure. To be sure. But this apparently egotistical economy also functions within an entire system of moral representation. Egotism is redeemed by culpability, which determines auto-eroticism as a fatal waste and a wounding of the self by the self. But as I thus harm only myself, this perversion is not truly condemnable. Rousseau explains it in more than one letter. Thus: "With that exception and [the exception of] vices that have always done harm to me alone, I can expose to all eyes a life irreproachable in all the secrets of my heart" (to M. de Saint-Germain, 2-26-70). "I have great vices, but they have never harmed anyone but me" (to M. Le Noir, 1-15-72).[19]

Jean-Jacques could thus look for a supplement to Thérèse only on one condition: that the system of supplementarity in general be already open in its possibility, that the play of substitutions be already operative for a long time and that in *a certain way Thérèse herself be already a supplement*. As Mamma was already the supplement of an unknown mother, and as the "true mother" herself, at whom the known "psychoanalyses" of the case of Jean-Jacques Rousseau stop, was also in a certain way a supplement, from the first trace, and even if she had not "truly" died in giving birth. Here is the chain of supplements. The name *Mamma* already designates one.

Ah, my Thérèse! I am only too happy to possess you, modest and healthy, and not to find what I never looked for. [The question is of "maidenhood" *(pucelage)* which Thérèse has just confessed to have lost in innocence and by accident.] At first I had only sought amusement; I now saw that I had found more and gained a companion. A little intimacy with this excellent girl, a little reflection upon my situation, made me feel that, while thinking only of my pleasures, I had done much to promote my happiness. To

18. See editors' note, Pléiade edition, I, 1569. [TN The English translation incorporates, on p. 617, the sentence quoted in the Pléiade note.]

19. See also the editors' note, Pléiade edition, I, 109. [TN The letters quoted can be found in *Correspondence générale de J.-J. Rousseau*, ed. Théophile Dufour (Paris: Armand Colin, 1934), XIX, 242, and XX, 122, the latter actually addressed to M. de Sartine, lieutenant general of police.]

supply the place of my extinguished ambition, I needed a lively sentiment which should *fill* my heart. In a word, I needed a successor to mamma. As I should never live with her again, I wanted someone to live with her pupil, in whom I might find the simplicity and docility of heart which she had found in me. I felt it necessary that the gentle tranquillity of private and domestic life *should make up* to me for the loss of the brilliant career which I was renouncing. When I was quite alone, I felt a void in my heart, which it only needed another heart *to fill*. Destiny had deprived me of, or, at least in part, alienated me from, that heart for which Nature had formed me. From that moment I was alone; for *there has never been for me an intermediary between everything and nothing. I found in Thérèse the substitute [supplément] that I needed.*[20] (340–41; italics added)

Through this sequence of supplements a necessity is announced: that of an infinite chain, ineluctably multiplying the supplementary mediations that produce the sense of the very thing they defer: the mirage of the thing itself, of immediate presence, of originary perception. Immediacy is derived. That all begins through the intermediary is what is indeed "inconceivable to reason."

The Exorbitant Question of Method

"There has never been for me an intermediary between everything and nothing." The intermediary is the mid-point and the mediation, the middle term between total absence and the absolute plenitude of presence. It is clear that mediacy is the name of all that Rousseau wanted opinionatedly to efface. This wish is expressed in a deliberate, sharp, thematic way. It does not have to be deciphered. Jean-Jacques recalls it here at the very moment when he is spelling out the supplements that are linked together to replace a mother or a Nature. And here the supplement occupies the middle point between total absence and total presence. The play of substitution fills and marks a determined lack. But Rousseau argues as if the recourse to the supplement—here to Thérèse—was going to appease his impatience when confronted with the intermediary: "From that moment I was

20. Starobinski (*Jean-Jacques Rousseau: Transparency and Obstruction,* 179) and the editors of the *Confessions* (Pléiade I, 332n1) justly relate the use of the word *supplement* to what is made of it on p. 111 ("that dangerous supplement").

alone; for there has never been for me an intermediary between everything and nothing. I found in Thérèse the substitute that I needed."
The virulence of this concept is thus appeased, as if one were able to
arrest it, domesticate it, tame it.

This brings up the question of the usage of the word *supplement:* of
Rousseau's situation within the language and the logic that assures to
this word or this concept sufficiently *surprising* resources so that the
presumed subject of the sentence might always say, through using the
"supplement," more, less, or something other than what he *would
mean [voudrait dire].* This question is therefore not only of Rousseau's
writing but also of our reading. We should begin by taking rigorous
account of this *being held within [prise]* or this *surprise:* the writer
writes *in* a language and *in* a logic whose proper system, laws, and life
his discourse by definition cannot dominate absolutely. He uses them
only by letting himself, after a fashion and up to a point, be governed by
the system. And the reading must always aim at a certain relationship,
unperceived by the writer, between what he commands and what he
does not command of the patterns of the language that he uses. This
relationship is not a certain quantitative distribution of shadow and
light, of weakness or of force, but a signifying structure that critical
reading should *produce.*

What does "produce" mean here? In my attempt to explain that, I
would initiate a justification of my principles of reading. A justification,
as we shall see, entirely negative, outlining by exclusion a space of
reading that I shall not fill here: a task of reading.

To produce this signifying structure obviously cannot consist of
reproducing, by the effaced and respectful doubling of commentary,
the conscious, voluntary, intentional relationship that the writer institutes in his exchanges with the history to which he belongs thanks to
the element of language. This moment of doubling commentary should
no doubt have its place in a critical reading. To recognize and respect
all its classical exigencies is not easy and requires all the instruments of
traditional criticism. Without this recognition and this respect, critical
production would risk developing in any direction at all and authorize
itself to say almost anything. But this indispensable guardrail has
always only *protected,* it has never *opened,* a reading.

Yet if reading must not be content with doubling the text, it cannot legitimately transgress the text toward something other than it, toward a referent (a reality that is metaphysical, historical, psychobiographical, etc.) or toward a signified outside the text whose content could take place, could have taken place outside of language, that is to say, in the sense that we give here to that word, outside of writing in general. That is why the methodological considerations that we risk applying here to an example are closely dependent on general propositions that we have elaborated above; as regards the absence of the referent or the transcendental signified. *There is no outside-the-text.*[21] And that is neither because Jean-Jacques's life, or the existence of Mamma or Thérèse *themselves,* is not of prime interest to us, nor because we have access to their so-called "real" existence only in the text and we have no means of altering this, nor any right to neglect this limitation. All reasons of this type would already be sufficient, to be sure, but there are more radical reasons. What we have tried to show by following the guiding line of the "dangerous supplement" is that in what one calls the real life of these existences "of flesh and bone," beyond and behind what one believes can be circumscribed as Rousseau's text, there has never been anything but writing; there have never been anything but supplements, substitutive significations which could only come forth in a chain of differential references, the "real" supervening, and being added only while taking on meaning from a trace and from an invocation of the supplement, etc. And thus to infinity, for we have read, *in the text,* that the absolute present, Nature, that which words like "real mother" name, have always already escaped, have never existed; that what opens meaning and language is writing as the disappearance of natural presence.

Although it is not commentary, our reading must be intrinsic and remain within the text. That is why, in spite of certain appearances,

21. EN This is my literal translation of *Il n'y a pas de hors-texte,* one of Derrida's more notorious, and notoriously misunderstood, formulations. It does not mean "the things that we usually consider to be outside texts do not exist" but "there is nothing that completely escapes the general properties of textuality, *différance,* etc."—that is, as Derrida goes on to explain, no "natural presence" that can be known "in itself." But it is also true that there is no inside-the-text, since this would again imply an inside/outside boundary. See also the Introduction, note 21, above.

the locating of the word *supplement* is here not at all psychoanalytical, if by that we understand an interpretation that takes us outside of the writing toward a psychobiographical signified, or even toward a general psychological structure that could rightly be separated from the signifier. This method has occasionally been opposed to the traditional doubling commentary; it could be shown that it actually comes to terms with it quite easily. *The security with which the commentary considers the self-identity of the text, the confidence with which it carves out its contour, goes hand in hand with the tranquil assurance that leaps over the text toward its presumed content, in the direction of the pure signified.* And in effect, in Rousseau's case, psychoanalytical studies like those of Dr. Laforgue transgress the text only after having read it according to the most current methods. The reading of the literary "symptom" is the most banal, most academic, most naive reading. And once one has thus blinded oneself to the very tissue of the "symptom," to its proper texture, one cheerfully exceeds it toward a psychobiographical signified whose link with the literary signifier then becomes perfectly extrinsic and contingent. One recognizes the other aspect of the same gesture when, in general works on Rousseau, in a package of classical shape that gives itself out to be a synthesis that faithfully restores, through commentary and compilation of themes, the totality of the work and the thought, one encounters a chapter of biographical and psychoanalytical cast on the "problem of sexuality in Rousseau," with a reference in an appendix to the author's medical case history.

If it seems to us in principle impossible to separate, through interpretation or commentary, the signified from the signifier, and thus to destroy writing by the writing that reading still is, we nevertheless believe that this impossibility is historically articulated. It does not limit attempts at deciphering in the same way, to the same degree, and according to the same rules. Here we must take into account the history of the text in general. When we speak of the writer and of the encompassing power of the language to which he is subject, we are not only thinking of the writer in literature. The philosopher, the chronicler, the theoretician in general, and at the limit everyone writing, is thus taken by surprise. But, in each case, the person writing is inscribed in a determined textual system. Even if there is never a pure signified, there are different relationships as to that which, from the signifier, is *presented* as the irreducible stratum of the signified. For example, the philosophical text, although it is in fact always written, includes, precisely as its philosophical specificity, the project of effacing itself in the face of the signified content which it transports and in general teaches. Reading should be aware of this project, even if, in the last analysis, it intends to expose the project's failure. The entire history of texts, and within it the history of literary forms in the West, should be studied from this perspective. With the exception of a point of advance or a point of resistance which has only been very lately recognized as such, literary writing has, almost always and almost everywhere, in accordance with diverse fashions and across diverse ages, lent itself to that *transcendent* reading, that search for the signified which we here put in question, not to annul it but to understand it within a system to which such a reading is blind. Philosophical literature is only one example within this history but it is among the most significant. And it interests us particularly in the case of Rousseau, who at the same time and for profound reasons produced a philosophical literature to which belong *The Social Contract* and *La nouvelle Héloïse*, and chose to live by literary writing; by a writing which would not be exhausted by the message—philosophical or otherwise—which it could, so to speak, deliver. And what Rousseau has said, as philosopher or as psychologist, of writing in general, cannot be separated from the system of his own writing. This must be taken into account.

Which poses formidable problems. Problems of marking divisions in particular. Let me give three examples.

1. If the course I have followed in the reading of the "supplement" is not merely psychoanalytical, it is undoubtedly because the habitual psychoanalysis of literature begins by putting the literary signifier as such within parentheses. It is no doubt also because psychoanalytic theory itself is for me a collection of texts belonging to my history and my culture. To that extent, if it marks my reading and the writing of my interpretation, it does not do so as a principle or a truth that one could abstract from the textual system that I inhabit in order to illuminate it with complete neutrality. In a certain way, we are *within*

the history of psychoanalysis as we are *within* Rousseau's text. Just as Rousseau drew upon a language that was already there—and which is found to be somewhat our own, thus assuring us a certain minimal readability of French literature—in the same way we operate today within a certain network of significations marked by psychoanalytical theory, even if we do not master it and even if we are assured of never being able to master it perfectly.

But it is for another reason that this is not even a somewhat inarticulate psychoanalysis of Jean-Jacques Rousseau. Such a psychoanalysis would have to have already located all the structures of belonging that characterize Rousseau's text, all that is not unique in that it is—by reason of the encompassing power and the already-thereness of the language or of the culture—inhabited rather than produced by writing. Around the irreducible point of originality of this writing an immense series of structures, of historical totalities of all orders, are organized, enveloped, and blended. Supposing that psychoanalysis can by rights succeed in outlining them and their interpretations, supposing that it takes into account the entire history of metaphysics—the history of that Western metaphysics that entertains relationships of cohabitation with Rousseau's text, it would still be necessary for this psychoanalysis to elucidate the law of its own belonging to metaphysics and Western culture. Let us not pursue this any further. We have already measured the difficulty of the task and the element of frustration in our interpretation of the supplement. We are sure that something irreducibly Rousseauist is captured there but we have carried off, at the same time, a yet quite unformed mass of roots, soil, and sediments of all sorts.

2. Even supposing that Rousseau's text can be rigorously isolated and articulated within history in general, and then within the history of the sign *supplement*, one must still take into consideration many other possibilities. Following the appearances of the word *supplement* and of the corresponding concept or concepts, we traverse a certain path within Rousseau's text. To be sure, this particular path will assure us the economy of a synopsis. But are other paths not possible? And as long as the totality of paths is not effectively exhausted, how shall we justify this one?

3. In Rousseau's text, after having indicated—by anticipation and

as a prelude—the function of the sign *supplement*, I now prepare myself to give special privilege, in a manner that some might consider exorbitant, to certain texts like the *Essay on the Origin of Languages* and other fragments on the theory of language and writing.[22] By what right? And why these short texts, published for the most part after the author's death, difficult to classify, of uncertain date and inspiration?

To all these questions and within the logic of their system, there is no satisfying response. In a certain measure and in spite of the theoretical precautions that I formulate, my choice is in fact *exorbitant*.

But what is the exorbitant?

I wished to reach the point of a certain exteriority in relation to the totality of the age of logocentrism. Starting from this point of exteriority, a certain deconstruction of that totality which is also a traced path, of that orb (*orbis*) which is also orbitary (*orbita*), might be broached. The first gesture of this departure and this deconstruction, although subject to a certain historical necessity, cannot be given methodological or logical intraorbitary assurances. Within the closure, one can judge its style only in terms of the accepted oppositions. It may be said that this style is empiricist and in a certain way that would be correct.[23] The *departure* is radically empiricist. It proceeds like a wandering thought on the possibility of itinerary and of method. It is affected by nonknowledge as by its future and it *ventures out* deliberately. I have myself defined the form and the vulnerability of this empiricism. But here the very concept of empiricism destroys itself. To *exceed* the metaphysical orb is an attempt to get out of the orbit (*orbita*), to think the entirety of the classical conceptual oppositions, particularly the one within which the value of empiricism is held: the opposition of philosophy and nonphilosophy, another name for empiricism, for this incapability of sustaining on one's own and to the limit the coherence of one's discourse, for being produced as truth at the moment when the value of truth is shattered, for escaping the

22. EN The remaining chapters of *Of Grammatology* have as their focus Rousseau's *Essay on the Origin of Languages*.

23. EN *L'empirisme* in French has overtones of a nonsystematic, ad hoc manner of proceeding; hence it can function more obviously as an opposite of "philosophy" than the English term that translates it. See Marian Hobson, "Deconstruction, Empiricism, and the Postal Services," *French Studies* 36 (1982): 290–314.

internal contradictions of skepticism, etc. *The thought of this historical opposition between philosophy and empiricism is not simply empirical and it cannot be thus qualified without abuse and misunderstanding.*

Let us make the diagram more specific. What is exorbitant in the reading of Rousseau? No doubt Rousseau, as I have already suggested, has only a very relative privilege in the history that interests us. If we merely wished to situate him within this history, the attention that we accord him would be clearly disproportionate. But that is not our intention. We wish to identify a decisive articulation of the logocentric epoch. For purposes of this identification Rousseau seems to us to be most revealing. That obviously supposes that we have already prepared the exit, determined the repression of writing as the fundamental operation of the epoch, read a certain number of texts but not all of them, a certain number of Rousseau's texts but not all of them. This avowal of empiricism can sustain itself only by the strength of the question. The opening of the question, the departure from the closure of a self-evidence, the putting into doubt of a system of oppositions, all these movements necessarily have the form of empiricism and of errancy. At any rate, they cannot be described, *as to past norms,* except in this form. No other trace is available, and as these errant questions are not absolute beginnings in every way, they allow themselves to be effectively reached, on one entire surface of themselves, by this description which is also a criticism. We must begin *wherever we are*[24] and the thought of the trace, which cannot not take the scent into account, has already taught us that it was impossible to justify a point of departure absolutely. *Wherever we are:* in a text already where we believe ourselves to be.

Let us narrow the arguments down further. In certain respects, the theme of supplementarity is certainly no more than one theme among others. It is in a chain, carried by it. Perhaps one could substitute something else for it. *But it happens that this theme describes the chain itself, the being-chain of a textual chain, the structure of substitution, the articulation of desire and of language, the logic of all conceptual oppositions taken over by Rousseau,* and particularly the role and the

24. EN *Quelque part où nous sommes;* literally, "somewhere where we are."

function, in his system, of the concept of Nature. It tells us in a text what a text is, it tells us in writing what writing it, in Rousseau's writing it tells us Jean-Jacques's desire, etc. If we consider, according to the axial proposition of this essay, that there is nothing outside the text, our ultimate justification would be the following: the concept of the supplement and the theory of writing designate textuality itself in Rousseau's text, *en abyme*, to employ the current phrase. And we shall see that this abyss is not an accident, happy or unhappy. An entire theory of the structural necessity of the abyss will be gradually constituted in our reading; the indefinite process of supplementarity has always already *infiltrated* presence, always already inscribed there the space of repetition and the splitting of the self. Representation *in the abyss* of presence is not an accident of presence; the desire of presence is, on the contrary, born from the abyss of representation, from the representation of representation, etc. The supplement itself is quite exorbitant, in every sense of the word.

Thus Rousseau inscribes textuality in the text. But its operation is not simple. It tricks with a gesture of effacement, and the strategic relations like the relationships of force between the two movements form a complex design. This design seems to us to be represented in the handling of the concept of the supplement. Rousseau cannot utilize it at the same time in all the virtualities of its meaning. The way in which he determines the concept and, in so doing, lets himself be determined by that very thing that he excludes from it, the direction in which he bends it, here as addition, there as substitute, now as the positivity and exteriority of evil, now as a happy auxiliary, all this conveys neither a passivity nor an activity, neither an unconsciousness nor a lucidity on the part of the author. Reading should not only abandon these categories—which are also, let us recall in passing, the founding categories of metaphysics—but should produce the law of this relation to the concept of the supplement. It is certainly a production, because I do not simply duplicate what Rousseau thought of this relationship. The concept of the supplement is a sort of blind spot in Rousseau's text, the not-seen that opens and limits visibility. But the production, if it attempts to make the not-seen accessible to sight, does not leave the text. It has moreover only believed it was doing so by illusion. It is contained in the transformation of the language it designates, in the regulated exchanges between Rousseau and history. We know that these exchanges only take place by way of the language and the text, in the infrastructural sense that we now give to that word. And what we call production is necessarily a text, the system of a writing and of a reading which we know—a priori, but only now and with a knowledge that is not one at all—are ordered around their own blind spot.

3

MALLARMÉ

☙ This short discussion of Mallarmé's work was written for a volume in a series entitled *Tableau de la littérature française,* a collection of introductory essays on canonic French writers. Literally, the title of the series means "Picture of French Literature," and Derrida begins by questioning—in Mallarmé's name—the conception of literature that this phrase implies. Mallarmé's writing, both that which is classed as "literary" and that which is not, unsettles the traditional categories of literature and of literary criticism, including referent, book, theme, meaning, and form. But the model of the revolutionary writer single-handedly breaking with the past is inadequate; borrowing, as he so often does, from the texts he is reading, Derrida identifies the Mallarméan moment as one of *crisis,* simultaneously marking the end of literature as classically understood and the exposure of those aspects of literature which have always, potentially, threatened that classical understanding. Derrida emphasizes that this is not a matter of Mallarmé's taking to an extreme the exploitation of semantic richness that has been a critically foregrounded feature of poetry since the culture of ancient Greece, but his decomposition of the linguistic elements upon which such commentary depends, notably the *word.*

Especially important is Mallarmé's use of "spacing" as a way of drawing attention to the properties of language that are not reducible to meaning, intention, or reference. (*Espacement,* taken from the preface to Mallarmé's graphic poem *Un coup de dés,* can be nominal or verbal and can thus refer to an arrangement in space and/or an action in time.) All language, that is, can be understood in terms of "writing": the marks and white spaces on the page are only one realization of the articulations and systems of difference upon which the operations of signification rely, and which at the same time prevent signification from ever closing on itself or on the world. The unstable and undecidable relations between meanings, between meaning and form, between different grammatical categories, that Derrida traces in Mallarmé's texts are thus a revelation of the logic of language and not an aberrant distortion of it. For Derrida, the crisis that Mallarmé provokes and symptomatizes is both new—we are still developing critical methods adequate to it—and very old, at least as old as the rhetorical understanding of language and truth held by the sophists and driven to the margins of Western thought by Plato and Aristotle. This essay presents in brief compass some of the issues and examples discussed in detail in the second part of "The Double Session," not reprinted in this selection.

Ϩ▪ "Mallarmé" was published in *Tableau de la littérature française: De Madame de Staël à Rimbaud* (Paris: Gallimard, 1974); this is its first appearance in an English translation. All references to Mallarmé's texts are to the Pléiade edition of the *Oeuvres complètes,* ed. Henri Mondor and G. Jean-Aubry (Paris: Gallimard, 1945). Since much of Derrida's argument concerns untranslatable aspects of Mallarmé's language, the original French is given at many points, followed by a literal translation which makes no attempt to disambiguate and simplify the semantic uncertainties of the original. The translator, Christine Roulston, wishes to thank Claude Gillard for her invaluable knowledge, support, and sense of humor during the translation of this piece.

. . . I am inventing a language which necessarily must spring from a highly original poetics . . .
—Letter to Cazalis, 1864 (*Correspondance,* 137)

Is there *a place* for Mallarmé in a "history of literature"? Or, to begin with: does his text take place, take its place, in some overall picture of French literature? In a picture? of literature? of French literature? We have been reading him for close to a century now: we are only beginning to glimpse that something has been contrived (by Mallarmé? in any case in terms of what passes *through* him, what traverses him, as it were) in order to elude the categories of history and of literary classification, of literary criticism, and of all kinds of philosophies and hermeneutics. We are beginning to glimpse that the disruption of these categories is also the effect of what was written by Mallarmé.

We can no longer even talk here of an *event,* of the event of such a text; we can no longer question its *meaning* except by falling short of it, within the network of values which it has *in practice* put into question; the value of event on the one hand (presence, singularity without possible repetition, temporality, historicity),

> Once, and only once, for, because of an event which I shall explain, always, there is no Present, no—a present does not exist... For lack of a declaration by the crowd, for lack—of everything. The one who would call himself his own contemporary is misinformed, deserting, usurping, with equal impudence, when the past has ceased and a future is delayed or when the two are perplexingly mixed in order to mask the space between them. (*Quant au livre,* 372)

and, on the other hand, the value of meaning: Mallarmé never stopped tracking down signification wherever loss of meaning arose, in particular within the two alchemies of aesthetics and political economy.

> Everything is summed up in Aesthetics and in Political Economy. (*La musique et les lettres,* 656)

> Since, all in all, there are only two paths open to mental research, where our desire branches, aesthetics on the one hand, and on the other political economy: and alchemy was essentially the glorious, hasty and troubled precursor of the latter. Everything which by itself, pure, for lack of meaning, as it were, before the appearance, now of the crowd, must be restored to the social domain. The worthless stone, dreaming of gold, known as the philosopher's stone: but it announces, in financial terms, future credit, preceding capital or reducing it to the lowness of small change! ("Magie," 399–400)

The purity of the sign is *noticed* only at the point where the text, referring to nothing but itself, pointing to its inscription and its functioning while seeming, with no possible return, to refer to something other than itself, "loses even a meaning," like "specie" ("Or," 398). And if Mallarmé marks a rupture, it would still be in the form of repetition; for example, it would reveal the essence of past literature for what it is. One would have to discover, with the help of this text, through it, the new logic of this double operation; which moreover we could only attribute to Mallarmé by resorting to a naive and self-interested theory of the signature, the very one which Mallarmé, defining precisely what he called the "operation," never ceased derailing. A text is made to do without references; either to the thing itself, as we shall see, or to the author who consigns to it nothing except its disappearance. This disappearance is actively inscribed, it is not an accident of the text, it is rather its nature; it marks the signature of an unceasing omission. The book is often described as a tomb.

> The organization of a book of poems appears innate or everywhere, eliminating chance; and yet it is necessary, in order to omit the author . . . (*Crise de vers,* 366)

> The right to accomplish anything exceptional or different from the ordinary, is always paid for by the omission of the author and, as it were, by his death as such. (*Quant au livre,* 370)

Through the enigmatic *simul* of rupture and repetition we will define the *crisis,* the moment when simple *decision* is no longer possible, where the choice between opposing paths is suspended. A crisis, therefore, of criticism, which will always use judgment *to decide (krinein)* on value and meaning, to distinguish between what is and what is not, what has value and what has not, the true and the false, the beautiful and the ugly, all signification and its opposite. A crisis, equally, of rhetoric, which arms criticism with an entire hidden philosophy. A philosophy of *meaning,* of the *word,* of the *name.*

Has rhetoric ever been interested in anything other than the meaning of a text, that is to say, in its content? The substitutions which it defines are always from a full meaning to a full meaning; and even if one takes the place of the other, it is as meaning that it becomes a theme for rhetoric, even if this meaning is in the position of signifier or, in other words, of vehicle. But rhetoric, as such, does not deal with signifying forms (whether phonic or graphic) or with the effects of syntax, at least as far as semantic control does not dominate them. For rhetoric or criticism to have something to see or to do before a text, a meaning has to be *determinable*.

All of Mallarmé's text, however, is organized in such a way that at its strongest points, the meaning remains *undecidable*; from then on, the signifier no longer lets itself be traversed, it remains, resists, exists and draws attention to itself. The labor of writing is no longer a transparent ether. It catches our attention and forces us, since we are unable to go beyond it with a simple gesture in the direction of what it "means," to stop short in front of it or to work with it. We could borrow the formula for this permanent warning from a passage in *Les mots anglais:* "Reader, this is what you have before your eyes, a written work . . ." (902).

What suspends the decision is not the richness of meaning, the inexhaustible resources of a word, it is a certain play of the syntax ("I am profoundly and scrupulously a syntaxer")[1] In "Mimique," the word *hymen* is inscribed in such a place that it is impossible to decide whether it means the consummation of marriage or the veil of virginity.[2] The syntax of the short word *or* is sometimes calculated to prevent us from deciding whether it is the noun "gold," the logical conjunction "or," or the adverb of time, "now." Other such games have been identified: *continue* operates in the same utterance both as a verb or as an adjective:

> Mais sans or soupirer que cette vive nue
> L'ignition du feu toujours intérieur
> Originellement la seule continue

1. EN A comment made by Mallarmé to Maurice Guillemot, and recorded in the latter's *Villégiatures d'artistes* (1898); cited by Henri Mondor in *Vie de Mallarmé* (Paris: Gallimard, 1945), 507.
2. EN For a discussion of *hymen* in Mallarmé, see "The First Session" below.

Dans le joyau de l'oeil véridique ou rieur
("La chevelure," 53)

(But without gold wishing that this living cloud
The igniting of the fire always within
Originally the only one should continue/the only
 unremitting one
In the jewel of the truthful or laughing eye.)

Elsewhere, *offre* ("offer") acts as a verb and/or as a noun, *parjure* as a verb ("to perjure") and/or as a noun ("betrayal"), and/or as an adjective ("disloyal"). The mark of the "and/or" (and it is not fortuitous that this mark weighs down so many theoretical texts today) signs the most singular effects of Mallarméan writing.

This is why this crisis does not belong to symbolism, nor this text to its time. Here the undecidability is no longer attached to a multiplicity of meanings, to a metaphorical richness, to a system of correspondences. Something takes place, something "more" or "less," as one likes, in any case the angle of a certain *re-mark*, which prevents polysemy from having its horizon: the unity, the totality, the gathering of meaning. For example the sign *blanc* ("white," "blank," "space"), with all that is associated with it from one thing to the next, is a huge reservoir of meaning (snow, cold, death, marble, etc.; swan, wing, fan, etc.; virginity, purity, hymen, etc.; page, canvas, veil, gauze, milk, semen, Milky Way, star, etc.). It permeates Mallarmé's entire text, as if by symbolic magnetization. And yet, the white also marks, through the intermediary of the white page, the place of the writing of these "whites"; and first of all the spacing between the different significations (that of white among others), *the spacing of reading.* "The 'whites' indeed, assume primary importance" (*Un coup de dés,* 455). The white of the spacing has no determinate meaning, it does not simply belong to the plurivalence of all the other whites. More than or less than the polysemic series, a loss or an excess of meaning, it folds up the text toward itself, and at each moment points out the place (where "nothing will have taken place except the place" [*Un coup de dés,* 474–75]), the condition, the labor, the rhythm. As the page *folds in* upon itself, one will never be able to decide if *white* signifies something, or signifies only, or in addition, the space of writing itself. The use of the word *pli* ("fold") and its variations (*pliage, ploiement, repli, reploiement*, etc.), which is as frequent, produces the same effects.

Aristotle, whose *Poetics* and *Rhetoric* inaugurated the traditional praise of metaphor (in that it enunciates and makes known the same or the similar), also said that not to signify a single thing was to signify nothing. Mallarmé's text does not only break this rule, it eludes its false transgression, its symmetrical inversion: the polysemy which continues to *make a sign*—in the direction of the law.[3]

Is it a question here, as has often been said, of the power of the word, of the alchemy of the verb? Does not the name, the act of naming reach here its greatest efficacy, the one which has been recognized by poetics, rhetoric and philosophy from Aristotle to Hegel? Has not Mallarmé created his theme out of this idealizing power of the word which makes the existence of the thing appear and disappear by the simple declaration of its name? Let us read again

> I say: a flower! and beyond the oblivion to which my voice relegates any shape, insofar as it is something other than the calyx, there arises musically, as the suave idea itself, the one absent from every bouquet. (*Crise de vers*, 368)

The production and annihilation of the thing by means of the name; but first of all, by means of the verse-line or the play of the rhyme, the creation of the name itself:

> The verse-line which uses several vocables to recreate a whole, new word foreign to the language and, as it were, incantatory, completes this isolation of speech . . . (*Crise de vers*, 368)

And yet, by working on the unity of the word, the pacified harmony of a vocable and a meaning, Mallarmé has also, by disintegration, liberated its energy. The word, for him, is no longer the primary element of the language. The consequences of this are far-reaching.

---

3. TN The French *faire signe* means both to make a sign and to catch somebody's attention—in this case, the attention of the law.

Since we cannot follow them here, let us limit ourselves to a few examples.

Mallarmé knew that his "operation" on the word was also the dissection of a corpse; of a decomposable body each part of which could be of use *elsewhere:*

> Related to the whole of nature and in this way coming closer to the organism that possesses life, the Word presents itself, in its vowels and its diphthongs, like a piece of flesh, and, in its consonants, like a skeletal structure difficult to dissect. Etc., etc., etc. If life nourishes itself from its own past, or from a continual death, Science will trace this fact in language . . . (*Les mots anglais,* 901)

Already the identity of entire words disappears in a game which nevertheless seems to leave them intact. We are here between the homonym and the synonym: *elle* ("she") expresses all the *ailes* ("wings"), all the birds, all the dancers, all the fans, whether the two words are present in the rhyme—

> Car, comme la mouette, aux flots qu'elle a rasés
> Jette un écho joyeux, une plume de l'aile,
> Elle donna partout un doux souvenir d'elle!
>> ("Sa fosse est fermée," 8)

> (For, as the seagull, to the waters which it has
>> skimmed
> Gives a joyful echo, a feather from the wing,
> Everywhere she offered a gentle reminder of herself!)

—or whether one of the two words, by itself, summons the other *in absentia*—

> Une d'elles, avec un passé de ramages
> Sur ma robe blanchie en l'ivoire fermé
> Au ciel d'oiseaux . . .
>> (*Hérodiade,* 42)

(One of them, with a past of songs/branches
On my dress whitened in ivory closed
To the sky of birds . . .)

—or again:

Quand s'isole pour le regard un signe de l'éparse beauté générale, fleur,
onde, nuées et bijou, etc., si, chez nous, le moyen exclusif de le savoir
consiste à en juxtaposer l'aspect à notre nudité spirituelle afin qu'elle le
sente analogue et se l'adapte dans quelque confusion exquise d'elle avec
cette forme envolée—rien qu'au travers du rite, là, énoncé de l'Idée, est-
ce que ne paraît pas la danseuse . . . ? (*Crayonné au théâtre*, 295–96)

(When a sign of pervading general beauty manifests itself to the eye as a
flower, a wave, a cloud, a jewel, etc., if, for us, the only way to know it
consists in juxtaposing its appearance to our spiritual nakedness so that
our nakedness senses it to be analogous and adapts it in some exquisite
confusion between itself and this shape in flight—simply through the
ritual, there, a manifestation of the Idea, does not the dancer appear . . .?)

We could show that *aile* belongs to a more masculine chain of
significations (phallic, associated with the shape of the feather), even
as *elle* is propagated through more feminine significations. Anterior to
the word, L stands between the two and supports the entire Mallarméan suspense:

This letter would sometimes appear incapable of expressing by itself
anything other than an appetite with no result to follow . . . (*Les mots
anglais*, discussion of L, 957–58)

The I gives rise to games calculated with equal deliberateness and,
moreover, very closely related, whether they deal with the graphic form
of the stroke and the dot or with the acute sharpness of the phonic
form. It is the *fundamental I*, therefore, which enters into all kinds of
compositions: for example, with the L, in IL ("he," "it"), or conversely
LIT, LIS, each of these last two words leaving the way open for the
verbal function and/or for the nominal function (*le lit* ["the bed"], *il
lit* ["he reads"]; *le lis* ["the lily"], *lis!* ["read!"], *le livre* ["the book"]).

Le lis (*lilium virginal*) is also the page; one example among so many others, concerning "this principle accessory of Villiers de l'Isle-Adam, a manuscript":

> Delivered [*Livré*] up to the ignoble fact . . . several signs already readable [*lisibles*]. . . . He shared the existence of the underprivileged, precisely because of this light page interposed between the rest and himself! Then I think of family [*familiales*] arms and, notably that this paper, held like a lily [*lis*], would have ended up, in a legitimate, immaculate blossoming, as this hand on its "golden coat of arms . . ." (*Villiers de l'Isle-Adam*, 485–86)

And right next to the hymen and to the *la* (the musical note *A*, or the feminine definite article), here is the flower again, like an established order:

> Inerte, tout brûle dans l'heure fauve
> Sans marquer par quel art ensemble détala
> Trop d'hymen souhaité de qui cherche le *la:*
> Alors m'éveillerai-je à la ferveur première,
> Droit et seul, sous un flot antique de lumière,
> Lys! et l'un de vous tous pour l'ingénuité.
> ("L'après-midi d'ùn faune," 51)

> (Inert, all burns in the tawny hour
> Without showing by what art together ran off
> Too much hymen desired by the one who seeks the *la:*
> Then I shall awaken to the initial fervor,
> Upright and alone, under an ancient flood of light,
> Lilies! and one of you all for the sake of candor.)

Both writing and death lie down in the bed. The book is both the place of the hymen and the figure of the sepulchre. The "sepulchral door" [*porte sépulcrale*] is always close to a "heraldic clasp" [*fermoir héraldique*]. In *Hérodiade*, which includes an "empty bed" [*lit vide*]:

> Elle a chanté, parfois incohérente, signe
> Lamentable!
> le lit aux pages de vélin,

Tel, inutile et si claustral, n'est pas le lin!
Qui des rêves par plis n'a plus le cher grimoire,
Ni le dais sépulcral à la déserte moire,
Le parfum des cheveux endormis. L'avait-il?

(42–43)

(She sang, at times incoherent, a lamentable
Sign!
    the bed with vellum pages,
Such, useless and so monastic, is not linen!
Which no longer possesses the precious book of
    dreams by folds,
Nor the sepulchral dais with the abandoned watered
    silk,
The perfume of sleeping hair. Did it once?)

The "Prose pour des Esseintes" again sets up, not far from an "esoteric book" [*grimoire*] and an "iron-clad book" [*livre de fer vêtu*], between "a hundred irises" [*cent iris*], "of eternal parchments, / Before a sepulchre laughs" [*d'éternels parchemins, / Avant qu'un sépulcre ne rie*], and "too large a gladiolus" [*trop grand glaïeul*], the litigation and the stalk of the lily [*litige et la tige de lis*]:

Oh! sache l'Esprit de litige,
A cette heure où nous nous taisons,
Que de lis multiples la tige
Grandissait trop pour nos raisons . . .

(56)

(Oh! know, spirit of litigation,
At this hour when we are silent,
That from multiple lilies the stalk
Grew too much for our reasons . . .)

Let us not forget that these chains, which are infinitely vaster, more powerful and intertwined than is even possible to hint at here, are as if without support, always suspended. It is the Mallarméan doctrine of *suggestion*, of undecided allusion. Such indecision, which enables them to move alone and without end, cuts them off, in spite of appearances, from all meaning (signified theme) and from all referents (the thing itself, and the conscious or unconscious intention of the author). Which leads to numerous traps for criticism, and numerous new procedures and categories to be invented.

It remains, therefore, that the "word," the particles of its decomposition or of its reinscription, without ever being identifiable in their singular presence, finally refer only to their own game, and never really move toward anything else. The *thing* is included, as *the effect of the thing* in this long *citation* of the language. Simply, the signifier (which we refer to as such out of convenience, since strictly speaking it is no longer a question of the "sign" here), without ever being present for itself, is marked, in its place, in its powers and its values. We could always put it in quotation marks, for is not what Mallarmé writes, finally, the signifying resource of the language in the form of the I, the LIT, or the LIS, etc.? It is what we would call, among other things, the *re-mark*. "Reader, this is what you have before your eyes, a written work . . ."

"The eternal absence of the bed" [*L'absence éternelle de lit*], like the absence of the *lis* from every bouquet, also reminds us, whatever its effects of multiple meanings, that the *lit*, the thing itself or the theme are no more present to the text, or intended by it, than the word *lit* or *l'I* (the letter I), or the fragments of *enseve*li, *abo*li, etc. The "subject" of the text would be, if we could still talk of a subject here, this word, this letter, this syllable, the text which they already form in the tissue of their relations. Moreover, Mallarmé nearly always writes on a text—such is the referent—occasionally even on his own text in an earlier version. Let us take the example of the text entitled "Or" (398–99): it is a brilliant demonstration of a recourse to the homonym, to what Aristotle denounced as bad poetry, as an instrument of rhetoric for sophists. The first version *named* its referent, the event which was the pretext for it: the Panama scandal, the story of Ferdinand de Lesseps, etc., although it was in order to maintain them in the role of poetic opportunity:

> Apart from truths which the poet can extract and keep as his secret, outside of conversation, intending to produce them, at the opportune

moment in a transfigured form, nothing, in the glamor of this collapse of Panama, interests me. (1577)

In the final version, the extraction and condensation are such that only the sparkle of the gold is kept, and the referent is effaced: no more proper name. We could believe that this is in order to liberate a poetical meditation on the general meaning of or ("gold"). And gold is indeed, to a certain extent, the theme of this text, its "signified," as it were. On closer examination, however, we realize that it is only a question of writing, of dealing with the signifier "OR," and nothing more. An entire thematic configuration, and a very rich one, doubtless explores the vein of gold [la veine d'or] in all its senses, but it is primarily to bring attention to the signifier or; that is, gold [l'or], as it turns from its natural substance into a monetary sign, but also as a linguistic element, as letters, as a syllable, as a word. The act of naming, the direct relationship to the thing, is then suspended. "Specie, a tool of terrible precision, clear to consciences, loses even a meaning" (398). From then on [Dès lors] the crisis erupts, in the analogous fields of political economy and of language or of literary writing: "phantasma-gorical sunsets." All Mallarméan sunsets are moments of crisis, whose gilding [dorure] is continually evoked in the text by a dust of golden gleams [une poussière d'éclats d'or] (dehORs ["outside"], fantasma-gORiques ["phantasmagorical"], trésOR ["treasure"], hORizon ["ho-rizon"], majORe ["increase"], hORs ["outside"]) until the "efface-ment de l'or" ["disappearance of the gold"]; which loses itself in the numerous o's of this page, in the accumulated zeros which increase the value only to return it to the void: " . . . if a number increases [se majore] and recedes, toward the improbable, it inscribes more zeroes: which signifies that its totality is spiritually equivalent to nothing, almost" (398). About the void itself, nothing is decided.

This work on or is not limited to the page which carries this title. The sign or is re-marked everywhere. For example in these lines: "Fasse le ciel qu'il nous signe, or / Bravos et louange sonore" ("Triolets," 186) ("Have the sky give us a sign, now / Cheers and sonorous praises"). Or here is very close to sonore ("sonorous"): it frequently happens that Mallarmé places the noun or after the possessive adjective son—

son or. This is heard as *sonore;* it makes *son* hesitate between the form of the possessive adjective and that of the noun; it makes *or* quiver between the value of the noun and that of the determinative adjective: *son or* meaning "his gold," *le son or* meaning "the sound that is the color of gold" (for such is the fundamental color of music and of sunsets for Mallarmé), *le son or* meaning the empty phonic or graphic signifier *or.* Here are a few examples. The first will also bring attention to the play of *or* with *heure* ("hour"). We know that *or* and *ores,* the logical conjunction "whereas" and the adverb of time "now, already," have *hora,* hour, as their etymology. *Encore* is *hanc horam,* and here is what provides a certain reading of all the *encores* ("agains") and *alors* ("thens") of Mallarmé, who seems sometimes to be literally asserting the identity of *or* and of *heure:* ". . . *une éclipse, or, telle est l'heure*" (*La dernière mode,* 751) (". . . an eclipse, now, such is the hour"). *Igitur* is both a dismantling and a demonstration of this complicity between the goldsmith and the clockmaker. In the section called "Le Minuit"

> Certainement subsiste une présence de Minuit. L'heure n'a pas disparu par un miroir, ne s'est pas enfouie en tentures, évoquant un ameublement par sa vacante sonorité. Je me rappelle que son or allait feindre en l'absence un joyau nul de rêverie, riche et inutile survivance, sinon que sur la complexité marine et stellaire d'une orfèvrerie se lisait le hasard infini des conjonctions.
>
> Révélateur du Minuit, il n'a jamais alors indiqué pareille conjoncture, car voici l'unique heure. . . . J'étais l'heure qui doit me rendre pur. (435)

> (Certainly a presence of Midnight subsists. The hour has not disappeared through a mirror, has not buried itself in drapes, evoking a furnishing by its vacant sonority. I remember that its gold was going to feign in its absence a jewel void of reverie, rich and useless survival, except that upon the marine and stellar complexity of a goldsmith's work of art the infinite chance of conjunctions was to be read.
>
> Revealer of Midnight, he has never indicated such a conjunction, for here is the unique hour. . . . I was the hour which ought to make me pure.)

In the "Sonnet en -yx":

Sur les crédences, au salon vide: nul ptyx,
Aboli bibelot d'inanité sonore,
(Car le Maître est allé puiser des pleurs au Styx
Avec ce seul objet dont le Néant s'honore).

Mais proche la croisée au nord vacante, un or
Agonise selon peut-être le décor
Des licornes . . .

(68)

(On the credence tables, in the empty drawing-room:
  no ptyx,
Extinct curio of sonorous inanity,
(For the Master has gone to draw tears from the Styx
With that unique object on which the Void prides
  itself).

But near the vacant northern window, gold
Agonizes, perhaps according to the motif
Of unicorns . . .)

In "Mimique":

. . . un orchestre ne faisant avec son or, des frôlements de pensée et de soir, qu'en détailler la signification à l'égal d'une ode tue . . . (310)

(. . . an orchestra only marking with its gold, rustlings of thought and dusk, detailing its signification on a par with a silent ode . . .)

And the peculiar syntax to which this word is submitted only redoubles the semantic indecision ("*or, telle est l'heure* . . ." [*La dernière mode*, 751] ["now, such is the hour . . . "]; "*Apitoyé, le perpétuel suspens d'une larme qui ne peut jamais toute se former ni choir (encore le lustre) scintille en mille regards, or, un ambigu sourire dénoue la lèvre* . . ." [*Crayonné au théatre*, 296] ["Moved to pity, the permanent suspension of a tear which can never become fully formed or fall (the lustre once again) sparkles in a thousand gazes, whereas an ambiguous smile unties the lips . . . "]; "*Or—Le pliage est, vis-à-vis de la feuille imprimée grande, un indice* . . ." [*Quant au livre*, 379] ["Now—The fold is, with regard to the large printed sheet, a sign . . ."]).
  Gold, the color of sunsets, of moonrises ("*Ce lever de lune or* . . ."

[*Eventails*, 109] ["This rising of the golden moon . . . "]), of the ends of afternoons, the time of critical indecision, also connotes the tomb-book, the clasp ("*O fermoirs d'or des vieux missels! . . .*" [*Hérésies artistiques*, 257] ["O golden clasps of old missals! . . ."]; ". . . *à l'étin-celle d'or du fermoir héraldique*" [*Igitur*, 437] [". . . at the golden spark of the heraldic clasp"]).

Is *or*, here, one word or several words? The linguist—and the philosopher—will perhaps say that each time, since the meaning and function change, we should read a different word. And yet this diversity crosses itself and goes back to an appearance of identity which has to be taken into account. If what circulates in this way is not a family of synonyms, is it the simple mask of a homonymy? But there is no noun: the thing itself is (that which is) absent, nothing is simply named, the noun is also a conjunction or an adverb. No more word: the efficacy often comes from one syllable which scatters the word. There is, therefore, neither homonymy nor synonymy.

The classical rhetorician will be just as disarmed: we are not dealing here with any of the essentially semantic relations with which he is familiar. There is neither a metaphorical relation (there is no similarity between these instances of *or*); nor one of metonymy (besides the fact that the unities are not nouns, no identity is stable enough, of itself, to give rise to relationships of the whole and the part, of cause and effect, etc.).

Finally, why could not the critical treatment of a particular *or* play, at a distance, with its English homonym, or rather homogram, with the disjunctive *versus* which it enunciates? We know, and not only through his biography, that Mallarmé's language is always open to the influence of the English language, that there is a regular exchange between the two, and that the problem of this exchange is explicitly treated in *Les mots anglais*. For this reason alone, "Mallarmé" does not belong completely to "French literature."

How will one represent in a picture the historical displacement effected in this way, the opening and the repetition of a *memorable crisis* ("Here literature undergoes an exquisite and fundamental crisis" [*Crise de vers*, 360]), a reminder, in appearance, of the theological form of the great Book?

Quite rightly, this attempt has been likened to that of the great rhetoricians. Mallarmé is probably in greater historical complicity with them than with many of his "contemporaries," indeed of his "successors." But this is because he has broken with the protocols of rhetoric, that is, with the muted classical and philosophical representation that the rhetorical tradition has provided for itself, let us say since Plato and Aristotle. His text escapes the control of this representation, it demonstrates *in practice* its nonpertinence. If, on the contrary, the rhetor is not the one who submits his discourse to the correct rules of meaning, philosophy, philosophical dialectic, or truth, nor the one whom, in short, philosophical rhetoric accepts by imposing on him its rules of decorum, but if he is, instead, the one whom Plato, exasperated, wanted to drive out of the city like a sophist or an anti-philosopher, Mallarmé is then perhaps a very great rhetorician; a sophist, doubtless, but a sophist who is not deceived by the image of himself which philosophy has wanted to hand down to us by holding him in a Platonic speculum and at the same time, which is in no way contradictory, by making him an outlaw. We know that, like many readers of Mallarmé, Plato accompanied his active incomprehension with a declared admiration.

(One should probably also have spoken of Stéphane Mallarmé. One should have spoken of his work, of his thought, of his unconscious and of his themes, of what in short he seemed obstinately to want to say, of the game of necessity and chance, of being and non-being, of nature and literature, and other similar things. One should have spoken of influences, experienced or exercised; of his life, first of all, of his bereavements and his depressions, of his teaching, of his travels, of Anatole and Méry, of his friends, of the literary salons, etc. Until the final spasm of the glottis.)

4

THE FIRST SESSION

&. Since Plato first defined art in terms of the concept of *mimēsis*, and Aristotle developed this concept for the linguistic arts in the *Poetics*, Western literature and commentary on literature has been dominated by it. In this extract from "The Double Session," which comprises all of the "first session" except some introductory pages, Derrida shows how *mimēsis* has always been closely tied to a notion of *truth*, whether truth as *alētheia* (nature unveiling itself) or as *homoiōsis/adaequatio* (nature represented by an accurate imitation). By placing together an extract from Plato's *Philebus*, in which the internal contradictions of the notion of *mimēsis* are already evident (see in particular note 3), and Mallarmé's short prose-poem "Mimique," which stages those contradictions, Derrida is dramatizing the hold which this essentially philosophical notion—which he terms *mimetologism*—has had over literature since its beginnings, as well as literature's potential for suspending and questioning it, realized with particular force by Mallarmé.

In the introductory pages omitted here, Derrida sets the stage for his double session by raising, while suggesting the problematic nature of, the question "What is literature?" As we noted in the Introduction above, the philosophical question "What is . . . ?", the question of truth and essence, is one that literature resists—though this discussion of Mallarmé demonstrates that resisting here involves not opposing or ignoring but staging and exploiting. "Mimique" puts into play notions of mimesis, imitation, truth, representation, reference, and temporality, unsettling any absolute distinctions between that which is imitated and that which imitates, between truth and the representation of truth, between referent and reference, between present and past. It does this in many ways at once: in its concern with a mime who mimes nothing that pre-exists his mimicry, in its short-circuiting of temporal relations, in its situation as one term in a dizzying network of texts and performances which have no "origin," and in its exploitation of what Derrida calls the "between," the "antre," or the "hymen." Instead of abiding within the opposed domains of metaphysical concepts, clearly separated by a border that marks an inside and an outside, literature operates in a realm that undermines alternatives and the logic of identity. In Mallarmé's writing, Derrida locates this operation above all in a distinctive use of syntax, which often resists the reader's (philosophical) push toward a single, clear signified; but he finds it conveniently summed up in the term *entre* ("between") and its homophone *antre* ("cave"—translated here by the rare English word *antre,* which has the same meaning), and in the term *hymen,* which in French balances much more equivocally than its English counterpart between two opposed meanings, "marriage" and "maidenhead."

The first publication of "The Double Session" was accompanied by an editorial note explaining that the original presentation of this material took up two sessions of the *Groupe d'études théoriques* in 1969, and was untitled—the question of the title being one which Derrida, citing Mallarmé, raised himself, especially in the opening moments of the meeting (which included a brief mime performed by the lecturer). The editors therefore devised a title, which in French—*la double séance* (a phrase of Mallarmé's)—echoes *la double science,* the double science or double knowledge that is deconstruction, and alludes to *la double scène,* the double scene and staging of Mallarmé's "Mimique." The participants in the sessions were handed a sheet bearing a passage from Plato's *Philebus* (38e–39e) together with "Mimique" (Pléiade, 310). The layout and typography of that handout have been reproduced here.

The "second session," not reprinted here, is taken up largely with a wide-ranging reading of Mallarmé's texts in terms of their undecidability of meaning, their exploitation of phonetic networks, and their resistance to transcendent readings, as an alternative to the thematic interpretations which have dominated literary criticism. A shorter version of some of this material constitutes part of the essay on Mallarmé printed above.

&ngroup; "La Double Séance" was first published in *Tel quel* in 1970, and reprinted in *La dissémination* (Paris: Seuil, 1972); this section comprises pp. 201 and 208–55. The translation by Barbara Johnson was published in *Dissemination* (Chicago: University of Chicago Press, 1981). The translations of Mallarmé's writing are by Barbara Johnson, and the references are to the Pléiade edition of Mallarmé's *Oeuvres complètes,* ed. Henri Mondor and G. Jean-Aubry (Paris: Gallimard, 1945). Quotations from Plato's dialogues are taken from *The Collected Dialogues of Plato,* ed. Edith Hamilton and Huntington Cairns (Princeton: Princeton University Press, 1961).

On the page that each of you has, a short text by Mallarmé, "Mimique,"[1] is embedded in one corner, sharing or completing it, with a segment from the *Philebus,*[2] which, without actually naming *mimēsis,* illustrates the mimetic system and even defines it, let us say in anticipation, as a system of *illustration.*

What is the purpose of placing these two texts there, and of placing them in that way, at the opening of a question about what goes (on) or doesn't go (on) *between* [*entre*] literature and truth? That question will remain, like these two texts and like this mimodrama, a sort of epigraph to some future development, while the thing entitled surveys (from a great height) an event, of which we will still be obliged, at the end of the coming session, to point to the absence.

Because of a certain fold that we shall outline, these texts, and their commerce, definitively escape any exhaustive treatment. We can nevertheless begin to mark out, in a few rough strokes, a certain number of motifs. These strokes might be seen to form a sort of frame, the enclosure or borders of a history that would precisely be that of a certain play between literature and truth. The history of this relationship would be organized by—I won't say by *mimēsis,* a notion one should not be in a hurry to translate (especially by imitation), but by a certain interpretation of *mimēsis.* Such an interpretation has never

1. TN *Mimique:* 1. Adj. (a) Mimic. *Langage mimique,* (i) sign language, (ii) dumb show. (b) Z[oology]: Mimetic. 2. Subst. fem. (a) Mimic art; mimicry. (b) F[amiliar]: Dumb show." (*Mansion's Shorter French and English Dictionary.*)
2. TN *Philebus,* trans. R. Hackforth, in *The Collected Dialogues of Plato,* 1118–19. Translation slightly modified.

SOCRATES: And if he had someone with him, he would put what he said to himself into actual speech addressed to his companion, audibly uttering those same thoughts, so that what before we called opinion has now become assertion—PROTARCHUS: Of course—SOCRATES: Whereas if he is alone he continues thinking the same thing by himself, going on his way maybe for a considerable time with the thought in his mind.—PROTARCHUS: Undoubtedly.—SOCRATES: Well now, I wonder whether you share my view on these matters—PROTARCHUS: What is it?—SOCRATES: It seems to me that at such times our soul is like a book—PROTARCHUS: How so?—SOCRATES: It appears to me that the conjunction of memory with sensations, together with the feelings consequent upon memory and sensation, may be said as it were to write words in our souls. And when this experience writes what is true, the result is that true opinion and true assertions spring up in us, while when the internal scribe that I have suggested writes what is false we get the opposite sort of opinions and assertions.—PROTARCHUS: That certainly seems to me right, and I approve of the way you put it—SOCRATES: Then please give your approval to the presence of a second artist in our souls at such a time.—PROTARCHUS: Who is that?— SOCRATES: A painter, who comes after the writer and paints in the soul pictures of these assertions that we make.—PROTARCHUS: How do we make out that he in his turn acts, and when?—SOCRATES: When we have got those opinions and assertions clear of the act of sight, or other sense, and as it were see in ourselves pictures or images of what we previously opined or asserted. That does happen with us, doesn't it?— PROTARCHUS: Indeed it does.—SOCRATES: Then are the pictures of true opinions and assertions true, and the pictures of false ones false? PROTARCHUS: Unquestionably.—SOCRATES: Well, if we are right so far, here is one more point in this connection for us to consider.—PROTARCHUS: What is that?—SOCRATES: Does all this necessarily befall us in respect of the present and the past, but not in respect of the future?—PROTARCHUS: It applies equally to them all.—SOCRATES: We said previously, did we not, that pleasures and pains felt in the soul alone might precede those that come through the body? That must mean that we have anticipatory pleasures and anticipatory pains in regard to the future.—PROTARCHUS: Very true.—SOCRATES: Now do those writings and paintings, which a while ago we assumed to occur within ourselves, apply to past and present only, and not to the future?— PROTARCHUS: To the future especially.—SOCRATES: When you say "to the future, especially," do you mean that they are all expectations concerned with what is to come, and that we are full of expectations all our life long?—PROTARCHUS: Undoubtedly.—SOCRATES: Well now, as a supplement to all we have said, here is a further question for you to answer.

MIMIQUE

Silence, sole luxury after rhymes, an orchestra only marking with its gold, its brushes with thought and dusk, the detail of its signification on a par with a stilled ode and which it is up to the poet, roused by a date, to translate! the silence of afternoons of music; I find it, with contentment, also, before the ever original reappearance of Pierrot or of the poignant and elegant mime Paul Margueritte.

Such is this PIERROT MURDERER OF HIS WIFE composed and set down by himself, a mute soliloquy that the phantom, white as a yet unwritten page, holds in both face and gesture at full length to his soul. A whirlwind of naive or new reasons emanates, which it would be pleasing to seize upon with security: the esthetics of the genre situated closer to principles than any! (no)thing in this region of caprice foiling the direct simplifying instinct... This—"The scene illustrates but the idea, not any actual action, in a hymen (out of which flows Dream), tainted with vice yet sacred, between desire and fulfillment, perpetration and remembrance: here anticipating, there recalling, in the future, in the past, *under the false appearance of a present*. That is how the Mime operates, whose act is confined to a perpetual allusion without breaking the ice or the mirror: he thus sets up a medium, a pure medium, of fiction." Less than a thousand lines, the role, the one that reads, will instantly comprehend the rules as if placed before the stageboards, their humble depository. Surprise, accompanying the artifice of a notation of sentiments by unproffered sentences—that, in the sole case, perhaps, with authenticity, between the sheets and the eye there reigns a silence still, the condition and delight of reading.

been the act or the speculative decision of any one author at a given moment, but rather, if one reconstitutes the system, the whole of a history. Between Plato and Mallarmé—whose proper names, it should be understood, are not real references but indications for the sake of convenience and initial analysis—a whole history has taken place. This history was also a history of literature if one accepts the idea that literature was born in it and died of it, the certificate of its birth as such, the declaration of its name, having coincided with its disappearance, according to a logic that the hymen will help us define. And this history, if it has any meaning, is governed in its entirety by the value of truth and by a certain relation, inscribed in the hymen in question, *between* literature and truth. In saying "this history, if it has any meaning," one seems to be admitting that it might not. But if we were to go to the end of this analysis, we would see it confirmed not only that this history has a meaning, but that the very concept of history has lived only upon the possibility of meaning, upon the past, present, or promised presence of meaning and truth. Outside this system, it is impossible to resort to the concept of history without reinscribing it elsewhere, according to some specific systematic strategy.

True history, the history of meaning, is told in the *Philebus*. In rereading the scene you have before your eyes, you will have remarked four facets.

1. *The book is a dialogue or a dialectic.* At least it should be. The comparison of the soul to a book (*bibliōi*) comes up in such a way that the book appears only as a mode or instance of discourse (*logos*), namely, stilled, silent, internal discourse: not any "stilled ode" or "silence of afternoons of music," as in "Mimique," nor the "stilled voice," as in *Music and Letters,* but internalized speech. That is, in a word, thinking (*dianoia*) as it is defined in the *Theaetetus* and the *Sophist:* "Well, thinking and discourse are the same thing, except that what we call thinking is, precisely, the inward dialogue carried on by the mind with itself without spoken sound" (*Sophist, 263e*). " 'How do you describe that process of thinking (*dianoeisthai*)?' 'As a discourse that the mind carries on with itself about any subject it is considering. You must take this explanation as coming from an ignoramus, but I

have a notion that, when the mind is thinking, it is simply talking to itself, asking questions and answering them, and saying yes or no' " (*Theaetetus, 189e*). According to the reasoning of the *Philebus,* first there was the *doxa,* the opinion, feeling, or evaluation that sprang up spontaneously within me and pertained to an appearance or semblance of truth, prior to any communication or discourse. Then when I proffered that *doxa* aloud, addressing it to a present interlocutor, it became discourse (*logos*). But from the instant this *logos* can have been formed, when the possibility of dialogue has come into being, it might happen, through an accident of circumstance, that I wouldn't have a partner handy: alone, then, I address this discourse to myself, I converse with myself in a sort of inward commerce. What I then hold is still a discourse but it is soundless, aphonic, private—which also means deprived: of its mouthpiece, its voice. Now, it is in connection with this deficient *logos,* this blank voice, this amputated dialogue—amputated of its vocal organ as well as of its other—that Socrates resorts to the "metaphor" of the book. Our soul then resembles a book not only for the obvious reason that it is a kind of *logos* and dialogue (and the book is thus only a species within the genus "dialogue"), but particularly because this reduced or mumbled conversation remains a false dialogue, a minor interchange, equivalent to a loss of voice. In this dialogue that has run out of voice, the need for the book or for writing in the soul is only felt through lack of the presence of the other, through lack of any employment of the voice: the object is to reconstitute the presence of the other by substitution, and by the same token to repair the vocal apparatus. The metaphorical book thus has all the characteristics that, until Mallarmé, have always been assigned to the book, however these might or should have been belied by literary practice. The book, then, stands as a substitute for (so-called) living (so-called) dialogue.

2. *The truth of the book is decidable.* This false dialogue constituted by the book is not necessarily a dialogue that is false. The psychic *volumen,* the book within the soul, can be either true or false according as the writer in us (*par hēmin grammateus*) says and, as a direct consequence, writes down things that are true or false. The value of the book as flattened-out *logos* is a function of, in proportion to, in a

ratio (also *logos*) with, its truth. "When the internal scribe that I have suggested writes what is false we get the opposite sort of opinions and assertions." Psychic writing must in the last instance appear before the tribunal of dialectics and ontology. It is only worth its weight in truth, and truth is its sole standard of measurement. It is through recourse to the truth of that which is, of things as such, that one can always decide whether writing is or is not true, whether it is in conformity or in "opposition" to the true.

3. *The value of the book (true/false) is not intrinsic to it.* A span of writing is worth nothing in itself; it is neither good nor bad, neither true nor false. This proposal of neutrality (neither/nor), when exported outside the Platonic context, can have some surprising effects, as we shall see in a moment. But as for the Platonic book, its truth or falsity declares itself only at the moment when the writer transcribes an inner speech, when he copies into the book a discourse that has already taken place and stands in a certain relation of truth (of similarity) or falsity (dissimilarity) with things in themselves. If one steps outside the metaphorical instance of the book, one can say that the writer transcribes into the outer book, into the book in what is called its "proper" meaning, what he has previously engraved upon his psychic shell. It is with respect to that primary engraving that it is necessary to divide between the true and the false. The book, which copies, reproduces, imitates living discourse, is worth only as much as that discourse is worth. It can be worth less, to the extent that it is bereft of the *life* of *logos;* it can't be worth more. In this way, writing *in general* is interpreted as an imitation, a duplicate of the living voice or present *logos*. Writing in general is not, of course, literary writing. But elsewhere, in the *Republic*, for example, poets are judged and condemned only for being imitators, mimes that do not practice "simple diegesis." The specific place of the poet can as such be judged according to whether or not he makes use, and in this or that way, of mimetic form.[3] The

3. It is not possible for us to examine here the extremely complex system of Plato's concept of *mimēsis.* We will attempt elsewhere to reconstitute its network and its "logic" around three focal points.
   a. *The double parricide/The parricidal double.* Homer, toward whom Plato directs numerous signs of filial respect, admiration, and gratitude, is cast out of the city, like

every other mimetic poet, with all honors due to a being who is "holy and wondrous" (*hieron kai thaumaston*) (*Republic*, 398a), when he isn't being asked to "erase" from his text all the politically dangerous passages (386c). Homer, the blind old father, is condemned because he *practices* mimesis (or mimetic, rather than simple, diegesis). The other father, Parmenides, is condemned because he *neglects* mimesis. If violence must be done to *him*, it is because his *logos*, the "paternal thesis," would prohibit (one from accounting for) the proliferation of doubles ("idols, icons, likeness, semblances"). The necessity for this parricide, we are told in this very connection (*Sophist* 241d–e), ought to be plain enough for even the blind (*tuphlōi*) to see.

b. *The double inscription of mimēsis.* It is impossible to pin *mimēsis* down to a binary classification or, more precisely, to assign a single place to the *technē mimētikē* within the "division" set forth in the *Sophist* (at the point at which a method and a paradigm are being sought in an effort to hunt down the Sophist in an organized manner). The mimetic form is *both* one of the three forms of "productive or creative art" (*technē poiētikē*) *and*, on the other branch of the fork, a form or procedure belonging among the acquisitive arts (*ktētikē*) (nonproductive, nonpoetic) used by the Sophist in his hunt for rich young men (218d–233bff). As a "wizard and imitator," the Sophist is capable of "producing" "likenesses and homonyms" of everything that exists (234b–235a). The Sophist mimes the poetic, which nevertheless itself comprises the mimetic; he produces production's double. But just at the point of capture, the Sophist still eludes his pursuers through a supplementary division, extended toward a vanishing point, between two forms of the mimetic (235d): the making of likenesses (the *eikastic*) or faithful reproduction, and the making of semblances (the *fantastic*), which simulates the eikastic, pretending to simulate faithfully and deceiving the eye with a simulacrum (a phantasm), which constitutes "a very extensive class, in painting (*zōgraphia*) and in imitation of all sorts." This is an aporia (236e) for the philosophical hunter, who comes to a stop before this bifurcation, incapable of continuing to track down his quarry; it is an endless escape route for that quarry (who is also a hunter), who will turn up again, after a long detour, in the direction of Mallarmé's "Mimique." This mimodrama and the *double science* arising from it will have concerned only a certain obliterated history of the relations between philosophy and sophistics.

c. *Mimēsis, guilty or not guilty.* If we go back to *mimēsis* "prior" to the philosophical "decision," we find that Plato, far from linking the destiny of art and poetry to the structure of *mimēsis* (or rather to the structure of all of what people today often translate—in order to reject it—as re-presentation, imitation, expression, reproduction, etc.), disqualifies in *mimēsis* everything that "modernity" makes much of: the mask, the disappearance of the author, the simulacrum, anonymity, apocryphal textuality. This can be verified by rereading the passage in the *Republic* on simple narration and mimesis (393aff). What is important for our purposes here is this "internal" duplicity of the *mimeisthai* that Plato wants to cut in two, in order to separate good *mimēsis* (which reproduces faithfully and truly yet is already threatened by the simple fact of its duplication) from bad, which must be contained like madness (396a) and (harmful) play (396e).

Here is an outline of this "logic": 1. *Mimēsis* produces a thing's double. If the double is faithful and perfectly like, no qualitative difference separates it from the model. Three consequences of this: (a) The double—the imitator [*imitant;* i.e., that which imitates]—is nothing, is worth nothing in itself. (b) Since the imitator's value comes only from its model, it is good when the model is good, and bad when the model is bad. In itself it is neutral and transparent. (c) If *mimēsis* is nothing and is worth nothing in itself, then it is nothing in value and being—it is in itself negative. Therefore it is an evil: to imitate is bad in itself and not just when what is imitated is bad. 2. Whether like or unlike, the imitator is something, since *mimēsis* and likenesses do exist. Therefore this nonbeing does "exist" in some way (*The Sophist*). Hence: (a) in adding to the model, the imitator comes as a supplement and ceases to be a nothing or a nonvalue. (b) In adding to the "existing" model, the imitator is not the same thing, and even if the resemblance were absolute, the resemblance is never absolute (*Cratylus*). And hence never absolutely true.

kind of poetry whose case is thus being heard cannot, of course, be simply identified with what we call "literature." If, as we have precisely been tempted to think, literature is born/dead of a relatively recent break, it is nonetheless true that the whole history of the interpretation of the arts of letters has moved and been transformed within the diverse logical possibilities opened up by the concept of *mimēsis*. These are numerous, paradoxical, and disconcerting enough to have unleashed a rich system of combinations and permutations. Here is not the place for us to demonstrate this. Let us retain the schematic law that structures Plato's discourse: he is obliged sometimes to condemn *mimēsis* in itself as a process of duplication, wherever its model might be,[4] and sometimes to disqualify *mimēsis* only in function of the model that is "imitated," the mimetic operation in itself remaining neutral, or even advisable.[5] But in both cases, *mimēsis* is lined up alongside truth: either it hinders the unveiling of the thing itself by substituting a copy or double for what is; or else it works in the service of truth through the double's resemblance (*homoiōsis*). *Logos,* which is itself imitated by writing, only has value as truth; it is under this heading that Plato always interrogates it.

4.   And finally, a fourth trait, to finish out the frame of this text: the element of the thus characterized book is the *image* in general (the icon or phantasm), the imaginary or the *imaginal.* If Socrates is able to *compare* the silent relation between the soul and itself, in the "mute soliloquy" ("Mimique"), to a book, it is because the book imitates the soul or the soul imitates the book, because each is the image or *likeness* of the other ("image" has the same root as "*imitari*"). Both of these likenesses, even before resembling each other, were in themselves already reproductive, imitative, and pictorial (in the representative sense of the word) in essence. *Logos* must indeed be shaped according to the

(c) As a supplement that can take the model's place but never be its equal, the imitator is in essence inferior even at the moment it replaces the model and is thus "promoted." This schema (two propositions and six possible consequences) forms a kind of logical machine; it programs the prototypes of all the propositions inscribed in Plato's discourse as well as those of the whole tradition. According to a complex but implacable law, this machine deals out all the clichés of criticism to come.

4. *Republic,* 395*b–c* and passim.
5. *Republic,* 396*c–d.*

model of the *eidos*;[6] the book then reproduces the *logos,* and the whole is organized by this relation of repetition, resemblance (*homoiōsis*), doubling, duplication, this sort of specular process and play of reflections where things (*onta*), speech, and writing come to repeat and mirror each other.

As of this point, the appearance of the painter is prescribed and becomes absolutely ineluctable. The way is paved for it in the scene from the *Philebus*. This other "demiurge," the *zōgraphos,* comes *after* the *grammateus:* "a painter, who comes after the writer and paints in the soul pictures of these assertions that we make." This collusion between painting (*zōgraphia*) and writing is, of course, constant. Both in Plato and after him. But painting and writing can only be images of each other to the extent that they are both interpreted as images, reproductions, representations, or repetitions of something alive, of living speech in the one case, and of animal figures in the other (*zō-graphia*). Any discourse about the relationship between literature and truth always bumps up against the enigmatic possibility of repetition, within the framework of the *portrait.*

What, in fact, is the painter doing here? He too is painting metaphorically, of course, and in the soul, just like the *grammateus.* But he comes along after the latter, retraces his steps, follows his traces and his trail. And he *illustrates* a book that is already written when he appears on the scene. He "paints in the soul pictures of these assertions." Sketching, painting, the art of space, the practice of spacing, the inscription written inside the outside (the outwork [*hors-livre*]), all these are only things

6. After showing in the *Cratylus* that nomination excluded *mimēsis,* that the form of a word could not, mimelike, resemble the form of a thing (423aff), Socrates nevertheless maintains that, through another sort of resemblance, a non-sensible sort, the right name could be taken as an image of the thing in its "truth" (439aff). And this thesis is not carried away by the ironic oscillations of the *Cratylus.* The priority of what is, in its truth, over language, like the priority of a model over its image, is as unshakable as absolute certainty. "Let us suppose that to any extent you please you can learn things through the medium of names, and suppose also that you can learn them from the things themselves. Which is likely to be the nobler and clearer way—to learn of the image (*ek tēs eikonos*), whether the image and the truth of which the image is the expression have been rightly conceived, or to learn of the truth (*ek tēs alētheias*) whether the truth and the image of it have been duly executed? . . . We may admit so much, that the knowledge of things is not to be derived from names. No, they must be studied and investigated in themselves" (trans. B. Jowett).

that are added, for the sake of illustration, representation, or decoration, to the book of the discourse of inner thought. The painting that shapes the images is a portrait of the discourse; it is worth only as much as the discourse it fixes and freezes along its surface. And consequently, it is also worth only as much as the *logos* capable of interpreting it, of reading it, of saying what it is-trying-to-say [*veut-dire*] and what in truth it is being made to say through the reanimation that makes it speak.

But painting, that degenerate and somewhat superfluous expression, that supplementary frill of discursive thought, that ornament of *dianoia* and *logos*, also plays a role that seems to be just the opposite of this. It functions as a pure indicator of the essence of a thought or discourse defined as image, representation, repetition. If *logos* is first and foremost a faithful image of the *eidos* (the figure of intelligible visibility) of what is, then it arises as a sort of primary painting, profound and invisible. In that case painting in its usual sense, a painter's painting, is really only the painting of a painting. Hence it can reveal the essential picturality, the representativity, of *logos*. That is indeed the task assigned by Socrates to the *zōgraphos-dēmiourgos* in the *Philebus:* "How do we make out that he in his turn acts, and when?" asks Protarchus, and Socrates replies, "When we have got those opinions and assertions clear of the act of sight (*opseōs*), or other sense, and as it were see in ourselves pictures or images of what we previously opined or asserted." The painter who works after the writer, the worker who shapes his work after opinion and assertion, the artisan who follows the artist, is able, through an exercise of analysis, separation, and impoverishment, precisely to purify the pictorial, imitative, imaginal essence of thought. The painter, then, knows how to restore the naked image of the thing, the image as it presents itself to simple intuition, as it shows itself in its intelligible *eidos* or sensible *horaton*. He strips it of all that superadded language, of that legend that now has the status of a commentary, of an envelope around a kernel, of an epidermic canvas.

So that in psychic writing, between the *zōgraphia* and the *logos* (or *dianoia*) there exists a very strange relation: one is always the supplement of the other.[7] In the first part of the scene, the thought that directly fixed the essence of things did not essentially need the illustrative ornament that writing and painting constituted. The soul's thinking was only intimately linked to *logos* (and to the proffered or held-back voice). Inversely, a bit further on, painting (in the metaphorical sense of psychic painting, of course, just as a moment ago it was a question of psychic writing) is what gives us the image of the thing itself, what communicates to us the direct intuition, the immediate vision of the thing, freed from the discourse that accompanied it, or even encumbered it. Naturally, I would like to stress once more, it is always the *metaphors* of painting and writing that are linked in this way back and forth: we recall that, on another plane, outside these metaphors, Plato always asserts that in their literal sense painting and writing are totally incapable of any intuition of the thing itself, since they only deal in copies, and in copies of copies.

If discourse and inscription (writing-painting) thus appear alternately as useful complements or as useless supplements to each other, now useful, now useless, now in one sense, now in another, this is because they are forever intertwined together within the tissue of the following complicities or reversibilities:

1. They are both measured against the truth they are capable of.

2. They are images of each other and that is why one can replace [*suppléer*] the other when the other is lacking.

3. Their common structure makes them both partake of *mnēmē* ("memory") and *mimēsis*, of *mnēmē* precisely by dint of participating in *mimēsis*. Within the movement of the *mimeisthai*, the relation of the mime to the mimed, of the reproducer to the reproduced, is always a relation to a *past present*. The imitated comes before the imitator [*l'imitant*]. Whence the problem of time, which indeed does not fail to come up: Socrates wonders whether it would be out of the question to think that *grammata* and *zōgraphēmata* might have a relation to the future. The difficulty lies in conceiving that what is imitated could be still to come with respect to what imitates, that the image can precede

---

7. EN For a discussion of the "supplement," see " . . . That Dangerous Supplement . . ." above.

the model, that the double can come before the simple. The overtures of "hope" (elpis), anamnesis (the future as a past present due to return), the preface, the anterior future (future perfect), all come to arrange things.[8]

It is here that the value of mimēsis is most difficult to master. A certain movement effectively takes place in the Platonic text, a movement one should not be too quick to call contradictory. On the one hand, as we have just verified, it is hard to separate mnēmē from mimēsis. But on the other hand, while Plato often discredits mimēsis and almost always disqualifies the mimetic arts, he never separates the unveiling of truth, alētheia, from the movement of anamnesis (which is, as we have seen, to be distinguished from hupomnesis).[9]

What announces itself here is an internal division within mimēsis, a self-duplication of repetition itself; ad infinitum, since this movement feeds its own proliferation. Perhaps, then, there is always more than one kind of mimēsis; and perhaps it is in the strange mirror that reflects but also displaces and distorts one mimēsis into the other, as though it were itself destined to mime or mask itself, that history—the history of literature—is lodged, along with the whole of its interpretation. Everything would then be played out in the paradoxes of the supplementary double: the paradoxes of something that, added to the simple and the single, replaces and mimes them, both like and unlike, unlike

---

8. Nothing in the above-mentioned logical program was to change when, following Aristotle, and particularly during the "age of classicism," the models for imitation were to be found not simply in nature but in the works and writers of Antiquity that had known how to imitate nature. One could find a thousand examples up to the Romantics (including the Romantics and often those well after them). Diderot, who nevertheless so powerfully solicited the mimetological "machine," especially in Le paradoxe sur le comédien, confirms upon the analysis of what he calls the "ideal imagined model" (supposedly non-Platonic) that all manner of reversals are included in the program. And, as for the logic of the future perfect: "Antoine Coypel was certainly a man of wit when he recommended to his fellow artists: 'Let us paint, if we can, in such a way that the figures in our paintings will be the living models of the ancient statues rather than that those statues be the originals of the figures we paint.' The same advice could be given to literati" ("Pensées détachées sur la peinture," in Oeuvres esthétiques, ed. Paul Vernière [Paris: Garnier, 1968], 816).

9. EN Derrida discusses Plato's attempt to distinguish between a living memory (mnēmē) or knowledge as this kind of memory (alētheia, anamnesis) and the operation of being reminded by something external such as writing (hupomnēsis, hypomnesis) in "Plato's Pharmacy," Dissemination, 102–12, 135. This text also includes a discussion of Platonic mimēsis, 136–42.

because it is—in that it is—like, the same as and different from what it duplicates. Faced with all this, what does "Platonism" decide and maintain? ("Platonism" here standing more or less immediately for the whole history of Western philosophy, including the anti-Platonisms that regularly feed into it.) What is it that is decided and maintained in ontology or dialectics throughout all the mutations or revolutions that are entailed? It is precisely the *ontological:* the presumed possibility of a discourse about what is, the deciding and decidable *logos* of or about the *on* (being-present). That which is, the being-present (the matrix-form of substance, of reality, of the oppositions between matter and form, essence and existence, objectivity and subjectivity, etc.) is distinguished from the appearance, the image, the phenomenon, etc., that is, from anything that, presenting it *as* being-present, doubles it, re-presents it, and can therefore replace and de-present it. There is thus the 1 and the 2, the simple and the double. The double comes *after* the simple; it multiplies it as a *follow-up.* It follows, I apologize for repeating this, that the image *supervenes* upon reality, the representation upon the present in presentation, the imitation upon the thing, the imitator [*l'imitant*] upon the imitated. First there is what is, "reality," the thing itself, in flesh and blood as the phenomenologists say; then there is, imitating these, the painting, the portrait, the zographeme, the inscription or transcription of the thing itself. Discernibility, at least numerical discernibility, between the imitator and the imitated is what constitutes order. And obviously, according to "logic" itself, according to a profound synonymy, what is imitated is more real, more essential, more true, etc., than what imitates. It is anterior and superior to it. One should constantly bear in mind, henceforth, the clinical paradigm of *mimēsis,* the order of the three beds in the *Republic* X (596aff): the painter's, the carpenter's, and God's.

Doubtless this order will appear to be contested, even inverted, in the course of history, and on several occasions. But never have the absolute distinguishability between imitated and imitator, and the anteriority of the first over the second, been displaced by any metaphysical system. In the domain of "criticism" or poetics, it has been strongly stressed that art, as imitation (representation, description, expression, imagination, etc.), should not be "slavish" (this proposition scans twenty centuries of poetics) and that consequently, through the liberties it takes with nature, art can create or produce works that are more valuable than what they imitate. But all these derivative oppositions send us back to the same root. The extra-value or the extra-being makes art a richer kind of nature, freer, more pleasant, more creative: more natural. At the time of the great systematization of the classical doctrine of imitation, Desmarets, in his *Art of Poetry*, translates a then rather common notion:

> And Art enchants us more than nature does. . . .
> Not liking what is imitated, we yet love what imitates.

Whether one or the other is preferred (but it could easily be shown that because of the nature of the imitated/imitator relation, the *prefer-ence*, whatever one might say, can only go to the imitated), it is at bottom this order of appearance, the precedence [*pré-séance*] of the imitated, that governs the philosophical or critical interpretation of "literature," if not the operation of literary writing. This order of appearance is *the order of all appearance*, the very process of appearing in general. It is the order of truth. "Truth" has always meant two different things, the history of the essence of truth—the truth of truth—being only the gap and the articulation between the two interpretations or processes. To simplify the analyses made by Heidegger but without necessarily adopting the order of succession that he seems to recognize, one can retain the fact that the process of truth is *on the one hand* the unveiling of what lies concealed in oblivion (*alētheia*), the veil lifted or raised [*relevé*] from the thing itself, from that which *is* insofar as it is, presents itself, produces itself, and can even exist in the form of a determinable hole in Being; *on the other hand* (but this other process is prescribed in the first, in the ambiguity or duplicity of the presence of the present, of its *appearance*—that which appears *and* its ap-pearing—in the *fold* of the present participle),[10] truth is agreement (*homoiōsis* or *adaequatio*), a relation of resemblance or equality be-

---

10. Cf. Heidegger, "Moira," in *Early Greek Thinking*, trans. D. F. Krell and F. A. Capuzzi (New York: Harper & Row, 1975).

tween a re-presentation and a thing (unveiled present), even in the expression of a judgment.

Now, mimesis, all through the history of its interpretation, is always commanded by the process of truth:

1. either, even before it can be translated as imitation, *mimēsis* signifies the presentation of the thing itself, of nature, of the *phusis* that produces itself, engenders itself, and appears (to itself) as it really is, in the presence of its image, its visible aspect, its face: the theatrical mask, as one of the essential references of the *mimeisthai,* reveals as much as it hides. *Mimēsis* is then the movement of the *phusis,* a movement that is somehow natural (in the nonderivative sense of this word), through which the *phusis,* having no outside, no other, must be doubled in order to make its appearance, to appear (to itself), to produce (itself), to unveil (itself); in order to emerge from the crypt where it prefers itself; in order to shine in its *alētheia.* In this sense, *mnēmē* and *mimēsis* are on a par, since *mnēmē* too is an unveiling (an un-forgetting), *alētheia.*

2. or else *mimēsis* sets up a relation of *homoiōsis* or *adaequatio* between two (terms). In that case it can more readily be translated as imitation. This translation seeks to express (or rather historically produces) the thought of this relation. The two faces are separated and set face to face: the imitator and the imitated, the latter being none other than the thing or the meaning of the thing itself, its manifest presence. A good imitation will be one that is true, faithful, like or likely, adequate, in conformity with the *phusis* (essence or life) of what is imitated; it effaces itself of its own accord in the process of restoring freely, and hence in a living manner, the freedom of true presence.

In each case, *mimēsis* has to follow the process of truth. The presence of the present is its norm, its order, its law. It is in the name of truth, its only reference—*reference itself*—that *mimēsis* is judged, proscribed or prescribed according to a regular alternation.

The invariable feature of this reference sketches out the closure of metaphysics: not as a border enclosing some homogeneous space but according to a noncircular, entirely other, figure. Now, this reference is discreetly but absolutely displaced in the workings of a certain syntax, whenever any writing both marks and goes back over its mark with an undecidable stroke. This double mark escapes the pertinence or authority of truth: it does not overturn it but rather inscribes it within its play as one of its functions or parts. This displacement does not take place, has not taken place once, as an *event*. It does not occupy a simple place. It does not take place *in* writing. This dis-location (is what) writes/is written. This redoubling of the mark, which is at once a formal break and a formal generalization, *is exemplified by the text of Mallarmé, and singularly by the "sheet" you have before your eyes* (but obviously every word of this last proposition must by the same token be displaced or placed under suspicion).

Let us reread "Mimique." Near the center, there is a sentence in quotation marks. It is not a citation, as we shall see, but the simulacrum of a citation or explication:—"The scene illustrates but the idea, not any actual action . . ."

This is a trap: one might well be tempted to interpret this sentence and the sequence that follows from it in a very classical way, as an "idealist" reversal of traditional mimetology. One would then say: of course, the mime does not imitate any actual thing or action, any reality that is already given in the world, existing before and outside his own sphere; he doesn't have to conform, with an eye toward verisimilitude, to some real or external model, to some *nature,* in the most belated sense of the word. But the relation of imitation and the value of adequation remain intact since it is still necessary to imitate, represent, or "illustrate" the idea. But what is the idea? one would proceed to ask. What is the ideality of the idea? When it is no longer the *ontōs on* in the form of the thing itself, it is, to speak in a post-Cartesian manner, the copy inside me, the representation of the thing through thought, the ideality—*for* a subject—of what is. In this sense, whether one conceives it in its "Cartesian" or in its "Hegelian" modification, the idea is the presence of what is, and we haven't yet escaped from Platonism. It is still a matter of imitating (expressing, describing, representing, illustrating) an *eidos* or *idea,* whether it is a figure of the thing itself, as in Plato, a subjective representation, as in Descartes, or both, as in Hegel.

Of course. Mallarmé's text can be read this way and reduced to a brilliant literary idealism. The frequent use of the word *Idea*—often enlarged and hypostatized by a capital letter—and the story of the author's supposed Hegelianism tend to invite such a reading. And that invitation has rarely gone unanswered. But a reading here should no longer be carried out as a simple table of concepts or words, as a static or statistical sort of punctuation. One must reconstitute a chain in motion, the effects of a network and the play of a syntax. In that case "Mimique" can be read quite differently than as a neo-idealism or a neo-mimetologism. The system of *illustration* is altogether different there than in the *Philebus*. With the values that must be associated with it, the *lustre* is reinscribed in a completely other place.[11]

There is no imitation. The Mime imitates nothing. And to begin with, he doesn't imitate. There is nothing prior to the writing of his gestures. Nothing is prescribed for him. No present has preceded or supervised the tracing of his writing. His movements form a figure that no speech anticipates or accompanies. They are not linked with *logos* in any order of consequence. "Such is this PIERROT MURDERER OF HIS WIFE composed and set down by himself, a mute soliloquy . . ."

"Composed and set down by himself . . ." We here enter a textual labyrinth panelled with mirrors. The Mime *follows* no preestablished script, no program obtained elsewhere. Not that he improvises or lets himself go spontaneously: he simply does not obey any verbal order. His gestures, his gestural writing (and Mallarmé's insistence on describing the regulated gesture of dance or pantomime as a hieroglyphic inscription is legendary), are not dictated by any verbal discourse or imposed by any diction. The Mime inaugurates; he breaks into a white page: " . . . a mute soliloquy that the phantom, white as a yet unwritten page, holds in both face and gesture at full length to his soul."

The blank—the other face of this double session here declares its white color—extends between the candid virginity ("fragments of candor" . . . "nuptial proofs of the Idea") of the white (*candida*) page and the white paint of the pale Pierrot who, by simulacrum, writes in the paste of his own make-up, upon the page he is. Through all the surfaces superimposed white on white, between all the layers of Mallarméan

---

11. EN *Lustre,* an important Mallarméan word exploited by Derrida in this text, means, in English as well as in French, both "chandelier" and "brightness."

make-up, one comes across, every time, on analysis, the substance of some "drowned grease paint" ("The Chastised Clown" ["Le pitre châtié," 31]). One can read, each within the other, the Pierrot of "Mimique" and the "bad Hamlet" of the "Chastised Clown" ("Eyes, lakes with my simple intoxication of rebirth / Other than as the histrion who with a gesture evoked / As a quill the smoking lamps' ignoble soot, / I pierced a window in the canvas wall"). Pierrot is brother to all the Hamlets haunting the Mallarméan text. If one takes account of the crime, incest, or suicide in which they are all simultaneously engaged, then it is, in the form of an I or A, the ghost of a castrated point, quill, or stick that lies therein whetting its threats. To prove this, one must go through several relays, that of all signifiers containing -IQUE, for example, and this we shall not fail to do.[12]

The Mime is not subjected to the authority of any book: the fact that Mallarmé points this out is all the more strange since the text called "Mimique" is initially a reaction to a reading. Mallarmé had earlier had the booklet of the mimodrama in his hands, and it is this little work that he is at first commenting upon. We know this because Mallarmé had published the first version of this text, without its title, in the November 1886 issue of La revue indépendante. In place of what was to become the first paragraph of "Mimique," one could read this in particular: "A type of luxury not inferior to any gala seems to me to be, during the treacherous season all with its calls to go out, the setting aside, under the first lamp, of an evening at home for reading. The suggestive and truly rare booklet that opens in my hands is none other, in sum, than a pantomime booklet: Pierrot Murderer of His Wife . . ." (published by Calmann-Lévy, new edition, 1886).[13]

12. EN See the second part of "The Double Session," in Dissemination, especially 137–40.
13. The editors of the Pléiade edition of Mallarmé's works have not deemed it necessary to point out, in their "Notes et Variantes," that the text printed in La revue indépendante, which was part of a much longer sequence, did not carry the title "Mimique," and that the paragraph we have just quoted and broken off at the same point as the Pléiade editors was followed by a paragraph which, both in vocabulary and syntax, was quite different from the second paragraph of "Mimique." Contrary to the rule observed for other texts, those editors have not included the variants from the second version, published in Pages (Brussels, 1891) in the chapter called "Le Genre ou des Modernes," still without a title. "Mimique" is a third version, published under that title in Divagations (1897), in the series called Crayonné au théâtre. When the Pléiade editors,

after quoting two paragraphs from the *Revue indépendante* (up to *Pierrot Murderer of His Wife* . . .), go on to add: "These two paragraphs, in *Pages* (1891), were part (pp. 135–36) of the chapter 'le Genre ou des Modernes.' They also appeared in *Divagations*, p. 186," this description is both incomplete and inexact. If we have chosen to reproduce here the two earlier versions, it is because the transformation of each paragraph (in certain of its words, its syntax, its punctuation, its play of parentheses and italics, etc.) displays the economy of the "syntaxer" at work; and also because, at the proper moment, we will draw from them certain specific lessons.

a. *La revue indépendante* (1886) (immediately following the passage we have quoted in the body of the text). ". . . a pantomime booklet: *Pierrot Murderer of His Wife*, composed and set down by M. Paul Margueritte. A monomime, rather, I would say along with the author, before the tacit soliloquy that the phantom, white as a yet unwritten page, holds in both face and gesture at full length to himself. A whirlwind of delicate new thoughts emanates, which I would like to seize upon with security, and say. The entire esthetic of a genre situated closer to principles than any other! nothing in this region of fantasy being able to foil the direct simplifying instinct. Thus: "The scene illustrates but the idea, not any actual action, through a hymen out of which flows Dream, tainted with vice, yet sacred, between desire and fulfillment, perpetration and remembrance: here anticipating, there recalling, in the future, in the past, under the false appearance of a present. This is how the Mime operates, whose act is confined to a perpetual allusion: not otherwise does he set up a pure medium of fiction.' This marvelous bit of nothing, less than a thousand lines, whoever will read it as I have just done, will comprehend the eternal rules, just as though facing the stageboards, their humble depository. The surprise, which is also charming, caused by the artifice of a notation of sentiments by unproffered sentences, is that, in this sole case perhaps with authenticity, between the sheets and the eye silence is established, the delight of reading."

b. *Pages* (1891). "Silence, sole luxury after rhymes, an orchestra only marking with its gold, its brushes with dusk and cadence, the detail of its signification on a par with a stilled ode and which it is up to the poet, roused by a dare, to translate! the silence that I have sought ever since from afternoons of music, I have also found with contentment before the reappearance, always as original as himself, of Pierrot, that is, of the bright and sagacious mime, Paul Legrand. [This paragraph can now be found in *Crayonné au théâtre*, in *Oeuvres complètes*, 340.]

"Such is this *Pierrot Murder of His Wife* composed and set down by M. Paul Margueritte, a tacit soliloquy that the phantom, white as a yet unwritten page, holds in both face and gesture at full length to himself. A whirlwind of naïve or new thoughts emanates, which it would be pleasing to seize upon with security, and say. The entire esthetic of a genre situated closer to principles than any other! nothing in this region of fantasy being able to foil the direct simplifying spirit. Thus: "The scene illustrates but the idea, not any actual action, through a hymen (out of which flows Dream), tainted with vice yet sacred, between desire and fulfillment, perpetration and remembrance: here anticipating, there recalling, in the future, in the past, *under the false appearance of a present*. That is how the Mime operates, whose act is confined to a perpetual allusion: not otherwise does he set up a pure medium of fiction.' This role, less than a thousand lines, whoever reads it will comprehend the rules as if placed before the stageboards, their humble depository. The surprise, too, accompanying the artifice of a notation of sentiments by unproffered sentences, is that, in this sole case perhaps with authenticity, between the sheets and the eye is established this silence, the delight of reading."

On comparing these three versions, we can draw a first conclusion: the sentence in quotation marks is indeed a simulacrum of a citation—an expli-citation, rather—an impersonal, concise, solemn statement, a kind of illustrious rule, an anonymous axiom or law of unknown origin. Aside from the fact that such a "citation" is nowhere to be found (particularly among the different booklets, prefaces, and notes), the fact that it changes slightly in the course of the three versions would suffice to prove that we are dealing with a Mallarméan fiction. Its syntax should already have suggested as much.

It is thus in a booklet, upon a page, that Mallarmé must have read the effacement of the booklet before the gestural initiative of the Mime. That, in fact, is a structural necessity, marked in the text of "Mimique." Whether Mallarmé ever did actually go to *see* the "spectacle" *too* is not only hard to verify but irrelevant to the organization of the text. What Mallarmé *read,* then, in this little book is a prescription that *effaces itself through its very existence,* the order given to the Mime to imitate nothing that in any way preexists his operation: neither an act "the scene illustrates but the idea, not any actual action") nor a word ("stilled ode ... mute soliloquy that the phantom, white as a yet

It is not impossible that, several years earlier, Mallarmé had *also* attended a performance by this *Pierrot.* The second edition, the "rare booklet" to which "Mimique" is responding, was indeed accompanied by the following Notice, signed by Paul Margueritte himself: "In 1881, the amusement afforded by a theatrical performance in the country, an unexpected success in the role of Pierrot, beneath the white mask and in Deburau's costume, made me suddenly become enamoured of pantomime, and write and act out, among other scenarios, this one: PIERROT MURDERER OF HIS WIFE. Having never seen a mime, Paul Legrand or Rouff, or read anything concerning this special art, I was ignorant of all traditions. I thus came up with a personal Pierrot, in conformity with my innermost esthetic self. As I sensed him and translated him, it seems, he was a modern being, neurotic, tragic, and ghostly. For lack of the proper sideshow stage, I was prevented from going on with this eccentric vocation, this veritable artistic madness that had gripped me, to which I owed certain singular personality-sheddings, strange nervous sensations, and, on the mornings after, some cerebral intoxications like those one gets from hashish. Unknown, a beginner in the world of letters, without any supporting cast or Columbine, I modestly performed a few monomimes in drawing-rooms and for the general public. Poets and artists judged my attempts curious and new: MM. Léon Cladel, Stéphane Mallarmé, J. K. Huysmans, and M. Théodore de Banville, who, in a letter sparkling with wit, tried to dissuade me, alleging that the worldly public was too... witty, and that the heyday of pantomime had passed. *Amen.* If anything is left of my mimic efforts, it is the literary conception of a modern, suggestive Pierrot, donning at will the flowing classical costume or the tight black suit, and moving about in uneasiness and fear. This idea, set down in a little pantomime,* was one I later developed in a novel,** and I intend to use it again in two volumes that will be: a study of artistic sensations, and a collection of pantomimes. *Henceforth I should be allowed to emphasize the dates of my works.* My cup is small, but I drink it all. It would be unjust if my forthcoming books should seem to be inspired by someone else, and if I should be accused of imitation or plagiarism. Ideas belong to everyone. I am convinced that it is by mere coincidence that following PIERROT MURDERER OF HIS WIFE there should have appeared a work with a similar title and that after the character of Paul Violas in ALL FOUR there should follow a Pierrot reminiscent of him. I am just affirming my priority and reserving it for the future. This granted, the affection I feel toward the pretty art of pantomime, for Pierrots—Willette's Album, Huysmans's *Skeptical Pierrot,* and Hennique—induces me to applaud any effort that will resuscitate, on stage or in a book, our friend Pierrot." (*Pierrot Murderer of His Wife,* 1882, Schmidt, printer. **All Four,* a novel, 1885, ed. Giraud.)

This lengthy quotation is also of interest in that it marks the historical complexity of the textual network in which we are already engaged and in which Margueritte declares his claim to originality.

unwritten page, holds in both face and gesture at full length to his soul").

In the beginning of this mime was neither the deed nor the word. It is prescribed (we will define this word in a moment) to the Mime that he not let anything be prescribed to him but his own writing, that he not reproduce by imitation any action (*pragma:* affair, thing, act) or any speech (*logos:* word, voice, discourse). The Mime ought only to write himself on the white page he is; he must *himself* inscribe *himself* through gestures and plays of facial expressions. At once page and quill, Pierrot is both passive and active, matter and form, the author, the means, and the raw material of his mimodrama. The histrion produces himself here. Right here—"A veracious histrion was I of myself!" (495).

Before we investigate this proposition, let us consider what Mallarmé is *doing* in "Mimique." We read "Mimique." Mallarmé (he who fills the function of "author") writes upon a white page on the basis of a text he is reading in which it is written that one must write upon a white page. One could nevertheless point out that while the referent indicated by Mallarmé is not a spectacle he actually perceived, it is at least a "real" object called a booklet, which Mallarmé could see, the brochure he has before his eyes or in his hands (since he says so!: "The suggestive and truly rare booklet that opens in my hands"), which is firmly maintained in its self-identity.

Let us see, since we must see, this little book. What Mallarmé has in his hands is a second edition, issued four years after the first, five years after the performance itself. The author's Note has replaced the Preface by a certain Fernand Beissier. The latter had described what he had *seen:* in the barn of an old farm, in the midst of a crowd of workers and peasants, a *mimodrama*—with no entry fee—of which he gives an outline after having described the setting at length. An inebriated Pierrot, "white, long, emaciated," enters with an undertaker. "And the drama began. For it truly was a drama we attended, a brutal, bizarre drama that burned the brain like one of Hoffmann's fantastic tales, atrocious at times, making one suffer like a veritable nightmare. Pierrot, who remains alone, tells how he has killed Columbine who had been unfaithful to him. He has just buried her, and no one will ever know of his crime. He had tied her to the bed while she was asleep, and he had tickled her feet until a horrible, ghastly death burst upon her amongst those atrocious bursts of laughter. Only this long white Pierrot with his cadaverous face could have come up with the idea of this torture fit for the damned. And, miming the action, he represented before us the whole scene, simulating the victim and the murderer by turns."

Beissier describes the reaction of the audience and wonders what sort of reception Paris would give this "bizarre, tormented, bony Pierrot who seems to be slightly neurotic" ("This destroyed all my ideas about that legendary Pierrot who once made me laugh so hard . . .") The next day, he tells us, he meets the Mime who has "become a man of the world again": it is Paul Margueritte, the brother of Victor Margueritte, the son of the general, Mallarmé's cousin. He asks Beissier to write a preface to the booklet of *Pierrot Murderer of His Wife* which he, Paul Margueritte, intends to write and publish. That is exactly what has happened. The Preface is dated "Valvins [where Mallarmé had a vacation house.—Trans.], September 15, 1882": it is thus not improbable that Mallarmé, linked to the enterprise in all these ways, might have attended the performance and read the first edition of the booklet.

The temporal and textual structure of the "thing" (what shall we call it?) presents itself, for the time being, thus: a mimodrama "takes place," as a gestural writing preceded by no booklet; a preface is planned and then written *after* the "event" to precede a booklet written *after the fact,* reflecting the mimodrama rather than programming it. This Preface is replaced four years later by a note written by the "author" himself, a sort of floating outwork [*hors-livre*].

Such is the object that is supposed to have served as Mallarmé's supposed "referent." What was it, then, that he had in his hands, before his eyes? At what point? in what now? along what line?

We have not yet opened the booklet "itself." The textual machination derives its complexity first of all from the fact that this little book, a verbal text aligning words and sentences, describes retrospectively a purely gestural, silent sequence, the inauguration of a writing of the body. This discrepancy or heterogeneity in the signifier is remarked upon by Margueritte in an N.B. After the physical presentation of

Pierrot in which white predominates ("in a white surtout..." "... with head and hands as white as plaster . . ." "... a white kerchief . . ." "... hands of plaster, too . . ."): "N.B.—Pierrot seems to speak?—A pure literary fiction!—Pierrot is *mute,* and the drama is, from one end to the other, *mimed."* These words—"pure," "fiction," "mute"—will be picked up again by Mallarmé.

Within this literary fiction whose verbal writing supervenes after the occurrence [*coup*] of a different sort of writing, the latter—the gestural act of the mimodrama—is described as anamnesis. It is already the memory of a certain past. The crime has already taken place at the moment Pierrot mimes it. And he mimes—"in the present"—*"under the false appearance of a present,"* the perpetrated crime. But in miming the past in the present, he reconstitutes, in the said "present," the deliberations through which he prepared the murder, when, examining all possible means to be used, he was still dealing with a crime to come, a death to give. Pierrot has sent the undertaker away; he stares at Columbine's portrait and "points at it with a mysterious finger." "I remember... let's close the curtains! I don't dare... (He backs up and, without looking behind him, pulls the drapes shut. His mouth trembles and then an invincible force wrenches from him the secret that has risen to his lips. The MUSIC stops, listens).

Here [italics, large letters, the discourse of the mute mime]:

Columbine, my charming wife, the Columbine in the portrait, was sleeping. She slept over there, in the big bed: I killed her. Why?... Ah, here is why! My gold, she filched; my best wine, she drank; my back, she beat, and hard, too: as for my forehead, she decorated it. A cuckold, yes, that's what she made me, and exorbitantly, but what does that matter? I killed her—because I felt like it, I am the master, what can anyone say? To kill her, yes... that pleases me. But how shall I go about it? (For Pierrot, like a sleepwalker, reproduces his crime, and in his hallucination, the *past* becomes *present.*) [a sleepwalker: all this is happening, if one can still say, between sleep and wakefulness, perception and dream; the words *"past"* and *"present"* are underlined by the author; we encounter them again, underlined differently, in "Mimique." Thus, in the apparent present of his writing, the author of the booklet, who is none other than the Mime, describes in words the past-present of a mimodrama which itself, in its apparent present, silently mimed an event—the crime—in the past-present but of which the present has never occupied the stage, has never been perceived by anyone, nor even, as we shall see, ever really been committed. Never, anywhere, not even in the theatrical fiction. The booklet reminds us that the mime "is reproducing his crime," miming what he remembers, and in so doing is obliged to begin by miming, in the present, the past deliberations over a crime yet to be committed]. Of course, there's the rope—pull it tight and blam! it's done! yes, but then the tongue hanging out, the horrible face? no— the knife? or a saber, a long saber? zap! in the heart... yes, but then the blood flows out in torrents, streaming.—Ugh! what a devil of a... Poison? a little tiny vial, quaff it and then... yes! then the cramps, the runs, the pains, the tortures, ah! how awful (it would be discovered, anyway). Of course, there's the gun, bam! but bam! would be heard.— Nothing, I can think of nothing. (He paces gravely back and forth, deep in thought. By accident, he trips). Ow! that hurts! (He strokes his foot.) Oof! that hurts! It's not serious, it's better already. (He keeps on stroking and tickling his foot.) Ha! ha! that's funny! Ha! Ha! No, it makes me laugh. Ah! (He abruptly lets go of his foot. He slaps himself on the head.) I've got it! (Slyly:) I've got it! I'm going to tickle my wife to death. There!"

Pierrot then mimes all the way to the "supreme spasm" the rising of ecstatic hilarity. The crime, the orgasm, is mimed doubly: the Mime plays the roles of both Pierrot and Columbine alternately. Here, simply, is the descriptive passage (in parentheses and in roman letters) in which the crime and the orgasm (what Bataille calls dying laughing and laughing [at] dying) take place such that in the final analysis what happens is nothing, no violence, no stigmata, no traces; the perfect crime in that it can be confused only with the heights of pleasure [jouissance] obtainable from a certain speculation. The author indeed disappears since Pierrot also is (plays) Columbine and since at the end of the scene he dies, too, before the spectacle of Columbine, who suddenly comes to life and, inside her portrait, bursts out laughing. Here, then, is the apparent production of the spasm or, let us already hazard the word, of the hymen: "And now, let's tickle: Columbine, it's you that will pay for this." (And he tickles wild, he tickles fierce, he tickles again, he tickles without mercy, then throws himself on the bed and becomes Columbine. She [he] writhes in horrible gaiety. One of the arms gets loose and frees the other arm, and these two crazed arms start fulminating against Pierrot. She [he] bursts out in a true, strident, mortal laugh; sits bolt upright; tries to jump out of bed; and still her [his] feet are dancing, tickled, tortured, epileptic. It is the death throes. She [he] rises up once or twice—supreme spasm!—opens her [his] mouth for one last curse, and throws back, out of the bed, her [his] drooping head and arms. Pierrot becomes Pierrot again. At the foot of the bed, he is still scratching, worn out, gasping, but victorious...)

After congratulating him(her)self for having, through this nonviolent crime, through this sort of masturbatory suicide, saved his (her) head from the "chopper's blow [*coup de couperet*]" of the guillotine ("I wash my hands of it, you understand"), the androgynous mime is overtaken, incoercibly, by "Columbine's tickle, like a contagious, avenging ill." He tries to escape it by what he calls a "remedy": the bottle with which another erotic scene concludes in a "spasm" and a "swoon." After the second lapse, a hallucination presents him with a Columbine who has become animate in her portrait, bursting out in laughter. Pierrot is again overcome by trepidation and tickling, and finally he dies at the feet of his "painted victim laughing still."

With all its false bottoms, its abysses, its *trompe-l'oeil*, such an arrangement of writings could not be a simple pretextual referent for Mallarmé's "Mimique." But despite the (structural, temporal, textual) complexity of this booklet-object, one might have been tempted to consider it a system closed upon itself, folded back over the relation, which is certainly very tangled, between, let us say, the "act" of the mimodrama (the one Mallarmé says writes itself upon a white page) and the retrospectiveness [*l'après-coup*] of the booklet. In this case, Mallarmé's textual play of reference would be checked by a definite safety-catch.

But such is not the case. A writing that refers back only to itself carries us *at the same time,* indefinitely and systematically, to some other writing. At the same time: this is what we must account for. A writing that refers only to itself and a writing that refers indefinitely to some other writing might appear noncontradictory: the reflecting screen never captures anything but writing, indefinitely, stopping no-where, and each reference still confines us within the element of reflection. Of course. But the difficulty arises in the relation between the medium of writing and the determination of each textual unit. It is necessary that while referring each time to another text, to another determinate system, each organism refer only to *itself* as a determinate structure; a structure that is open and closed *at the same time*.

Letting itself be read for itself, doing without any external pretext, "Mimique" is also haunted by the ghost or grafted onto the arborescence of another text. Concerning which, "Mimique" explains that that text describes a gestural writing dictated by nothing and pointing only toward its own initiality, etc. Margueritte's booklet is thus, for "Mimique," both a sort of epigraph, an hors d'oeuvre, and a seed, a seminal infiltration: indeed both at once, which only the operation of the *graft* can no doubt represent. One ought to explore systematically not only what appears to be a simple etymological coincidence uniting the graft and the graph (both from *graphion:* writing implement, stylus), but also the analogy between the forms of textual grafting and so-called vegetal grafting, or even, more and more commonly today, animal grafting. It would not be enough to compose an encyclopedic catalogue of grafts (approach grafting, detached scion grafting; whip grafts, splice grafts, saddle grafts, cleft grafts, bark grafts; bridge grafting, inarching, repair grafting, bracing; T-budding, shield budding, etc.); one must elaborate a systematic treatise on the textual graft. Among other things, this would help us understand the functioning of footnotes, for example, or epigraphs, and in what way, to the one who knows how to read, these are sometimes more important than the so-called principal or capital text. And when the capital title itself becomes a scion, one can no longer choose between the presence or absence of the title.[14]

14. For the reasons being set forth here, this concept of the textual graft would be hard to confine simply to the field of a "human psychology" of the imagination, as Bachelard defines it in the following beautifully written passage from *L'eau et les rêves* [*Water and Dreams*] (Paris: Corti, 1948): "What we love above all in man is what can be written about him. Does what can't be written deserve to be lived? We have thus been obliged to content ourselves with the *grafted* material imagination, and we have almost always confined ourselves to the study of the different branches of the materializing imagination found *above the graft* whenever any culture has put its mark on any nature.

"Moreover, this is not, for us, a simple metaphor. On the contrary, the *graft* appears to us to be a concept essential to the understanding of human psychology. It is, in our view, the human sign as such, the necessary sign for specifying human imagination. For us, humanity imagining is something that lies beyond nature naturing. It is the graft that can really give the material imagination the exuberance of forms. It is the graft that can transmit the variety and density of matter to the formal imagination. It forces the seedling

We have pointed out just about all the structural elements of Margueritte's book. We know what its theme and title are. What is left?
On the title page, between the author's proper name and the title on
the one hand, and the name of the writer of the preface on the other
hand, there is an *epigraph* and a third proper name. It is a quotation
from Théophile Gautier:

> The story of Pierrot who tickled his wife,
> And thus made her laughingly give up her life.

Now we know. This whole mimodrama refers back one more step,
through the incision marked by the epigraph, to another text. At least
one, and whatever Margueritte may have said in his Note. An eye graft,
a text extending far out of sight.

Out of sight—you are here slowly coming back to the hymen and
dissemination—for there would be a certain imprudence in believing
that one could, at last, stop at a textual seed or principle of life referring
only to itself in the form of Gautier's *Pierrot Posthume*.[15] A notch is
marked there, one that again opens onto another text and practices
another reading. The analysis of all this would be infinite. Harlequin

to flower and gives matter to the flower. In a completely nonmetaphorical sense, the
production of a poetic work requires that there be a union between a dreaming activity
and an ideating activity. Art is grafted nature" (14–15; original emphasis). These statements are disputed, from a "psychocritical" point of view, by Charles Mauron, *Des
métaphores obsédantes au mythe personnel* [*From Obsessive Metaphors to Personal
Myth*] (Paris: Corti, 1963), 26–27.

15. A Harlequinade in one act and in verse (done in collaboration with P. Siraudin),
first performed on the Vaudeville stage on October 4, 1847. Margueritte was much later
to write: "The perusal of a tragic tale by Commander Rivière along with two lines by
Gautier, 'The story of Pierrot who tickled his wife, And thus made her laughingly give
up her life,' determined my Satanic, ultraromantic and yet very modern conception: a
refined, neurotic, cruel yet ingenuous Pierrot in whom all possible contrasts were alloyed,
a veritable psychic Proteus, a bit sadistic, quite willingly a lush, and a perfect scoundrel.
Thus it is that with *Pierrot Murderer of His Wife*—a tragic nightmare *à la* Hoffmann
or Edgar Allan Poe, in which Pierrot makes his wife die laughing by tickling the bottoms
of her feet—I was a precursor in the revival of pantomime back in 1881; I might even
say *the* precursor" (*Nos Tréteaux* [*Our Stage*], 1910). Margueritte seems not to be
familiar with all the back corridors and genealogies of this scene. For example, death by
foot tickling occurs in *Les roueries de Trialph, Notre contemporain avant son suicide*
[*Trialph's Tricks: Our Contemporary prior to His Suicide*] by Lassailly (1833); tickling
to death is already found in *The White Devil* by Webster (1612): "He tickles you to
death, makes you die laughing" (V, iii), the whole time, of course, in the interval and
already, so to speak, in the English language.

offers a mouse to Columbine under the pretext that "A woman's cat holding us in her claws; / A mouse is the right gift to place in her paws." To which Columbine replies: "A jewel-box is nicer than thirty mousetraps." All this at the moment that Pierrot's death in Algiers is being announced by Harlequin ("Bah! nothing's surer: his obituary, / On the opening pages of each dictionary, / Is visibly written with paraphs profuse, / Just under Pierrot attached to a noose."). Pierrot returns, and is summoned to testify to his own death: "I can rejoice no longer in seeing myself," and he wanders about like a phantom. Mistakenly, he drinks a philter of resurrection and swallows the mouse Harlequin has surreptitiously introduced into the bottle. He begins to wiggle and laugh, "mad and wild-eyed" ("If I only could slip down a tomcat inside!"), and finally decides to kill himself. And in the course of a soliloquy, as he deliberates over the various ways of putting an end to his life, *he remembers something he has read:* "Let's go commit suicide once and for all. / Hm, what about rope? No, that's no solution: / Hemp doesn't go with my soul's constitution... / Jump off a bridge? cold water's too chilling... / Smother myself in a bed with down filling? / Fi! I'm too white to be aping Othello... / Not feathers, nor water, nor rope for this fellow... / . . . I have it: I've read in an old-fashioned story / The tale of a husband who tickled his wife, / And thus made her laughingly give up her life... / . . . He tickles himself. Ha! ha! I shall soon leap about like a calf / If I don't... Let's go on... How this does make me laugh! / I'm bursting! and now to move down to the feet. / I'm fainting, I'm crawling, I'm in a fire's heat! / How the universe opens before my dazed eyes! / Ho! ho! I am fainting and cannot arise." *Columbine:* "Who's this idiot pinching himself just for fun?" *Pierrot:* "A ghost who is dying." *Columbine:* "Say that again?"

After a number of other episodes (scenes of poisoning, Pierrot as a vampire figure, etc.), Pierrot turns to address the audience. This time we do not have a Mime-librettist attributing fictional status to a booklet of words being substituted for a mute mimic. We have a Pierrot who, while speaking upon the stage, begs forgiveness for having done so, the entire thing being enclosed within the writing of a booklet: "Pardon Pierrot for speaking, please. Most of the time / I play my part only through grimace and mime. / I silently move like a phantom in white, /

Always fooled, always beaten, and trembling with fright, / Through all the imbroglios traced out in bold / Brush-strokes by the Comedy dreamed up of old. / *Comedia dell'arte* was once this art's name, / Where actors embroidered their role as it came."

One could go on at great length in order to find out where this Pierrot had read the exemplary story of this husband who tickled his wife and thus made her laughingly give up her life. With all the threads provided by the *comedia dell'arte,* one would find oneself caught in an interminable network.[16] Bibliographical research, source studies, the archeology of all Pierrots would be at once endless and useless, at least as far as what interests us here is concerned, since the process of cross-referencing and grafting is *remarked inside* Mallarmé's text, which thereby has no more "inside" than it can properly be said to be *by* Mallarmé.

The moment at which we appeared to take leave of that text was marked by the proposition I shall here recall: setting down and composing by himself his soliloquy, tracing it upon the white page he himself is, the Mime does not allow his text to be dictated to him from any other place. He represents nothing, imitates nothing, does not have to conform to any prior referent with the aim of achieving adequation or verisimilitude. One can here foresee an objection: since the mime imitates nothing, reproduces nothing, opens up in its origin the very thing he is tracing out, presenting, or producing, he must be the very movement of truth. Not, of course, truth in the form of adequation

16. Among other intersections, one would encounter a *Pierrot Dead and Alive,* a *Pierrot Valet of Death* (with a review by Nerval, who had combed all of Europe in order to study pantomime), a *Pierrot Hanged* (by Champfleury) in punishment for the theft of a book, a Pierrot disguised as a mattress on which his Columbine more or less makes love with Harlequin, after which they make a hole in the mattress cover and card the wool, which prompts Théophile Gautier to write: "A moment later some woolcarders appear and subject Pierrot to a painful quarter-hour [*quart d'heure* ~ *cardeur* (carder)]; to be carded, what a fate! it's enough to take your breath [*l'haleine* ~ *la laine* (wool)] away. Please excuse these puns, which cannot occur in pantomime, which proves the superiority of those sorts of works over all others." Elsewhere, Gautier notes that "the origin of Pierrot," "the symbol of the proletarian," is just as "interesting" as those enigmas "that have aroused the curiosity of the . . . Father Kirchers, the Champollions, etc." This is a lead to follow. I would like to thank Paule Thévenin for helping me in this library of Pierrots, who are all, including Margueritte's, at once living and dead, living more dead than alive, *between* life and death, taking into consideration those effects of specular doubling which the abundant literature of the time associates with Hoffmann, Nerval, and even Poe.

between the representation and the present of the thing itself, or between the imitator and the imitated, but truth as the present unveiling
of the present: monstration, manifestation, production, *alētheia*. The
mime produces, that is to say makes appear *in praesentia*, manifests
the very meaning of what he is presently writing: of what he *performs*.
He enables the thing to be perceived in person, in its true face. If one
followed the thread of this objection, one would go back, beyond
imitation, toward a more "originary" sense of *alētheia* and of *mimeisthai*. One would thus come up with one of the most typical and
tempting metaphysical reappropriations of writing, one that can always crop up in the most divergent contexts.

One could indeed push Mallarmé back into the most "originary"
metaphysics of truth if all mimicry [*mimique*] had indeed disappeared,
if it had effaced itself in the scriptural production of truth.

But such is not the case. *There is* mimicry. Mallarmé sets great store
by it, along with simulacrum (and along with pantomime, theater, and
dance; all these motifs intersect in particular in *Richard Wagner, rêverie
d'un poète français,* which we are holding and commenting upon here
behind the scenes). We are faced then with mimicry imitating nothing;
faced, so to speak, with a double that doubles no simple, a double that
nothing anticipates, nothing at least that is not itself already double.
There is no simple reference. It is in this that the mime's operation does
allude, but alludes to nothing, alludes without breaking the mirror,
without reaching beyond the looking-glass. "That is how the Mime
operates, whose act is confined to a perpetual allusion without breaking
the ice or the mirror." This speculum reflects no reality; it produces
mere "reality-effects." For this double that often makes one think of
Hoffmann (mentioned by Beissier in his Preface), reality, indeed, is
death. It will prove to be inaccessible, otherwise than by simulacrum,
just like the dreamed-of *simplicity* of the supreme spasm or of the
hymen. In this speculum with no reality, in this mirror of a mirror, a
difference or dyad does exist, since there are mimes and phantoms. But
it is a difference without reference, or rather a reference without a
referent, without any first or last unit, a ghost that is the phantom of
no flesh, wandering about without a past, without any death, birth, or
presence.

Mallarmé thus preserves the differential structure of mimicry or *mimēsis*, but without its Platonic or metaphysical interpretation, which implies that somewhere the being of something that *is*, is being imitated. Mallarmé even maintains (and maintains himself in) the structure of the *phantasma* as it is defined by Plato: the simulacrum as the copy of a copy. With the exception that there is no longer any model, and hence, no copy, and that this structure (which encompasses Plato's text, including his attempt to escape it) is no longer being referred back to any ontology or even to any dialectic. Any attempt to reverse mimetologism or escape it in one fell swoop by leaping out of it *with both feet* would only amount to an inevitable and immediate fall back into its system: in suppressing the double or making it dialectical, one is back in the perception of the thing itself, the production of its presence, its truth, as idea, form, or matter. In comparison with Platonic or Hegelian idealism, the displacement we are here for the sake of convenience calling "Mallarméan" is more subtle and patient, more discreet and efficient. It is a simulacrum of Platonism or Hegelianism, which is separated from what it simulates only by a barely perceptible veil, about which one can just as well say that it already runs—unnoticed—between Platonism and itself, between Hegelianism and itself. Between Mallarmé's text and itself. It is thus not simply false to say that Mallarmé is a Platonist or a Hegelian. But it is above all not true.[17]

17. Just as the motif of neutrality, in its negative form, paves the way for the most classical and suspect attempts at reappropriation, it would be imprudent just to cancel out the pairs of metaphysical oppositions, simply to *mark off* from them any text (assuming this to be possible). The strategic analysis must be constantly readjusted. For example, the deconstruction of the pairs of metaphysical oppositions could end up defusing and neutralizing Mallarmé's text and would thus serve the interests invested in its prevailing traditional interpretation, which up to now has been massively idealist. It is in and against this context that one can and should emphasize the "materialism of the idea." We have borrowed this definition from Jean Hyppolite (". . . within this materialism of the idea he imagines the diverse possibilities for reading the text . . ." "Le coup de dés de Stéphane Mallarmé et le message," in *Les études philosophiques*, 1958, no. 4). This is an example of that *strategic dissymmetry* that must ceaselessly counterbalance the neutralizing moments of any deconstruction. This dissymmetry has to be minutely calculated, taking into account all the analyzable differences within the topography of the field in which it operates. It will in any case be noted that the "logic of the hymen" we are deciphering here is not a logic of negative neutrality, nor even of neutrality at all. Let us also stress that this "materialism of the idea" does not designate the content of some projected "philosophical" doctrine proposed by Mallarmé (we are indeed in the process of determining in what way there *is* no "philosophy" in his text, or rather that that text is calculated in such a way as no longer to be situated *in* philosophy), but

And vice versa.

What interests us here is less these propositions of a philosophical type than the mode of their reinscription in the text of "Mimique." What is marked there is the fact that, this imitator having in the last instance no imitated, this signifier having in the last instance no signified, this sign having in the last instance no referent, their operation is no longer comprehended within the process of truth but on the contrary comprehends *it,* the motif of the last instance being inseparable for metaphysics as the search for the *archē,* the *eschaton,* and the *telos.*[18]

If all this leaves its mark upon "Mimique," it is not only in the chiseled precision of the writing, its extraordinary formal or syntactical felicity; it is also in what seems to be described as the thematic content or mimed event, and which in the final analysis, despite its effect of content, is nothing other than the space of writing: in this "event"—hymen, crime, suicide, spasm (of laughter or pleasure)—in which nothing happens, in which the simulacrum is a transgression and the transgression a simulacrum, everything describes the very structure of the text and effectuates its possibility. That, at least, is what we now must demonstrate.

The operation, which no longer belongs to the system of truth, does not manifest, produce, or unveil any presence; nor does it constitute any conformity, resemblance, or adequation between a presence and a representation. And yet this operation is not a unified entity but the manifold play of a scene that, illustrating nothing—neither word nor deed—beyond itself, illustrates nothing. Nothing but the many-faceted multiplicity of a lustre which itself is nothing beyond its own fragmented light. Nothing but the idea which is nothing. The ideality of the idea is here for Mallarmé the still metaphysical name that is still necessary in order to mark nonbeing, the nonreal, the nonpresent. This mark points, alludes without breaking the glass, to the beyond of

precisely the form of what is at stake in the operation of writing and "Reading—That practice—," in the inscription of the "diverse possibilities for reading the text."

18. For the reasons indicated in the preceding note, the simple erasing of the metaphysical concept of last instance would run the risk of defusing the necessary critique it permits in certain determinate contexts. To take this double inscription of concepts into account is to practice a *double science,* a bifid, *dissymmetrical* writing. Whose "general economy," defined elsewhere, does indeed constitute, in a displaced sense of the words, the last instance.

beingness, toward the *epekeina tēs ousias:* a hymen (a closeness and a veil) between Plato's sun and Mallarmé's lustre. This "materialism of the idea" is nothing other than the staging, the theater, the visibility of nothing or of the self. It is a dramatization which *illustrates nothing,* which illustrates *the nothing,* lights up a space, re-marks a spacing as a nothing, a blank: white as a yet unwritten page, blank as a difference between two lines. "I am for—no illustration . . ."[19]

This chain of terms, Theater-Idea-Mime-Drama, can be found sketched out in one of the fragments from the unpublished plans for the *Book:*

> "*The summary of the theater*
> *as Idea and hymn*
> *whence theater* = *Idea*"

And, a bit further on, off to one side:

> "*Theater*   V   *Idea*
>   *Drama*
> *Hero*   *Hymn*
> *mime*   *dance*"

The stage [*scène*] thus illustrates but the stage, the scene only the scene; there is only the equivalence between *theater* and *idea,* that is (as these two names indicate), the visibility (which remains outside) of the visible that is being effectuated. The scene illustrates, in the text of a hymen—which is more than an anagram of "hymn" [*hymne*]—"in a hymen (out of which flows Dream), tainted with vice yet sacred, between desire and fulfillment, perpetration and remembrance: here

---

19. The context of this quotation should here be restituted and related back to what was said, at the start of this session, concerning the book, the extra-text [*hors-livre*], the image, and the illustration; then it should be related forward to what will be set in motion, in the following session, between the book and the movement of the stage. Mallarmé is responding to a survey: "I am for—no illustration; everything a book evokes should happen in the reader's mind: but, if you replace photography, why not go straight to cinematography, whose successive unrolling will replace, in both pictures and text, many a volume, advantageously" (878).

anticipating, there recalling, in the future, in the past, *under the false appearance of a present."*

"Hymen" (a word, indeed the only word, that reminds us that what is in question is a "supreme spasm") is first of all a sign of fusion, the consummation of a marriage, the identification of two beings, the confusion between two. *Between* the two, there is no longer difference but identity. Within this fusion, there is no longer any distance between desire (the awaiting of a full presence designed to fulfill it, to carry it out) and the fulfillment of presence, between distance and non-distance; there is no longer any difference between desire and satisfaction. It is not only the difference (between desire and fulfillment) that is abolished, but also the difference between difference and nondifference. Nonpresence, the gaping void of desire, and presence, the fullness of enjoyment, amount to the same. By the same token [*du même coup*], there is no longer any textual difference between the image and the thing, the empty signifier and the full signified, the imitator and the imitated, etc. But it does not follow, by virtue of this hymen of confusion, that there is now only one term, a single one of the differents.[20] It does not follow that what remains is thus the fullness of the signified, the imitated, or the thing itself, simply present in person. It is the difference between the two terms that is no longer functional. The confusion or consummation of this hymen eliminates the spatial heterogeneity of the two poles of the "supreme spasm," the moment of dying laughing. By the same token, it eliminates the exteriority or anteriority, the independence, of the imitated, the signified, or the thing. Fulfillment is summed up within desire; desire is (ahead of) fulfillment, which, still mimed, remains desire, "without breaking the mirror."

What is lifted, then, is not difference but the different, the differents, the decidable exteriority of differing terms. Thanks to the confusion and continuity of the hymen, and not in spite of it, a (pure and impure) difference inscribes itself without any decidable poles, without any independent, irreversible terms. Such difference without presence ap-

20. EN Derrida uses the unusual term *différents* here; I have altered the original translation's "differends" to "differents," since the former term (*différend* in French) suggests an irresolvable dispute, and has in recent years been made widely familiar in translations of the work of J.-F. Lyotard.

pears, or rather baffles the process of appearing, by dislocating any orderly time at the center of the present. The present is no longer a mother-form around which are gathered and differentiated the future (present) and the past (present). What is marked in this hymen between the future (desire) and the present (fulfillment), between the past (remembrance) and the present (perpetration), between the capacity and the act, etc., is only a series of temporal differences without any central present, without a present of which the past and future would be but modifications. Can we then go on speaking about *time, tenses,* and *temporal* differences?

The center of presence is supposed to offer itself to what is called perception or, generally, intuition. In "Mimique," however, there is no perception, no reality offering itself up, in the present, to be perceived. The plays of facial expression and the gestural tracings are not present in themselves since they always refer, perpetually allude or represent. But they don't represent anything that has ever been or can ever become present: nothing that comes before or after the mimodrama, and, within the mimodrama, an orgasm-crime that has never been committed and yet nevertheless turns into a suicide without striking or suffering a blow, etc. The signifying allusion does not go through the looking-glass: "a perpetual allusion without breaking the ice or the mirror," the cold, transparent, reflective window ("without breaking the ice or the mirror" is added in the third version of the text), without piercing the veil or the canvas, without tearing the moire. The antre of Mallarmé, the theater of his glossary: it lies in this suspension, the "center of vibratory suspense," the repercussions of words between the walls of the grotto, or of the glottis, sounded among others by the rhymes *hoir* ("heir"), *soir* ("evening"), *noire* ("black"), *miroir* ("mirror"), *grimoire* ("wizard's black book,") *ivoire* ("ivory"), *armoire* ("wardrobe"), etc.

What does the hymen that illustrates the suspension of differents remain, other than Dream? The capital letter marks what is new in a concept no longer enclosed in the old opposition: Dream, being at once perception, remembrance, and anticipation (desire), each within the others, is really none of these. It declares the "fiction," the "medium, the pure medium, of fiction" (the commas in *"milieu, pur, de fiction"* also make their appearance in the third version), a presence both perceived and not perceived, at once image and model, and hence image without model, neither image nor model, a medium (medium in the sense of middle, neither/nor, what is between extremes, and medium in the sense of element, ether, matrix, means). When we have rounded a certain corner in our reading, we will place ourselves on that side of the lustre where the "medium" is shining. The referent is lifted, but reference remains: what is left is only the writing of dreams, a fiction that is not imaginary, mimicry without imitation, without verisimilitude, without truth or falsity, a miming of appearance without concealed reality, without any world behind it, and hence without appearance: *"false appearance . . ."* There remain only traces, announcements and souvenirs, foreplays and aftereffects [*avant-coups et après-coups*] which no present will have preceded or followed and which cannot be arranged on a line around a point, traces "here anticipating, there recalling, in the future, in the past, *under the false appearance of a present.*" It is Mallarmé who underlines (as of the second version, in *Pages*) and thus marks the ricochet of the moment of mimed deliberation from Margueritte's *Pierrot:* at that point—in the past—where the question is raised of what to do in the future ("But how shall I go about it?"), the author of the booklet speaks to *you* in parentheses, in the "present": ("For Pierrot, like a sleepwalker, reproduces his crime, and in his hallucination, the *past* becomes *present.*") (Underlined by the author.) The historical ambiguity of the word *appearance* (at once the appearing or apparition of the being-present *and* the masking of the being-present behind its appearance) impresses its indefinite fold on this sequence, which is neither synthetic nor redundant: *"under the false appearance of a present."* What is to be re-marked in the underlining of this circumstantial complement is the displacement without reversal of Platonism and its heritage. This displacement is always an effect of language or writing, of syntax, and never simply the dialectical overturning of a concept (signified). The very motif of dialectics, which marks the beginning and end of philosophy, however that motif might be determined and despite the resources it entertains within philosophy against philosophy, is doubtless what Mallarmé has marked with his syntax at the point of its sterility, or rather, at the point that will soon, provisionally, analogically, be called the undecidable.

Or *hymen.*

The virginity of the "yet unwritten page" opens up that space. There are still a few words that have not been illustrated: the opposition *vicious/sacred* ("hymen (out of which flows Dream), tainted with vice yet sacred"; the parentheses intervene in the second version to make it clear that the adjectives modify "hymen"), the opposition *desire/ perpetration,* and most importantly the syncategorem *between [entre].*

To repeat: the hymen, the confusion between the present and the nonpresent, along with all the indifferences it entails within the whole series of opposites (perception/nonperception, memory/image, memory/desire, etc.), produces the effect of a medium (a medium as element enveloping both terms at once; a medium located between the two terms). It is an operation that *both* sows confusion *between* opposites *and* stands *between* the opposites "at once." What counts here is the *between,* the in-between-ness of the hymen. The hymen "takes place" in the "inter-," in the spacing between desire and fulfillment, between perpetration and its recollection. But this medium of the *entre* has nothing to do with a center.

The hymen enters into the antre. *Entre* can just as easily be written with an *a.* Indeed, are these two *(e)(a)ntres* not really the same? Littré: "ANTRE, s.m. 1. Cave, natural grotto, deep dark cavern. 'These antres, these braziers that offer us oracles,' *Voltaire, Oedipe* II, 5.2. Fig. The antres of the police, of the Inquisition. 3. *Anatomy:* name given to certain bone cavities.—*Syn: Antre, cave, grotto. Cave,* an empty, hollow, concave space in the form of a vault, is the generic term; *antre* is a deep, dark, black cave; *grotto* is a picturesque cave created by nature or by man. *Etym.* Antrum, ἄντρον; Sanscrit, *antara,* cleft, cave. *Antara* properly signifies 'interval' and is thus related to the Latin preposition *inter* (see *entre*). Provenc. *antre;* Span. and Ital. *antro.*" And the entry for ENTRER ["to enter"] ends with the same etymological reference. The *interval* of the *entre,* the in-between of the hymen: one might be tempted to visualize these as the hollow or bed of a valley (*vallis*) without which there would be no mountains, like the sacred vale between the two flanks of the Parnassus, the dwelling-place of the

Muses and the site of Poetry; but *intervallum* is composed of *inter* (between) and *vallus* (pole), which gives us not the pole in between, but the space between two palisades. According to Littré.

We are thus moving from the logic of the palisade, which is always, in a sense, "full," to the logic of the hymen. The hymen, the consummation of differents, the continuity and confusion of the coitus, merges with what it seems to be derived from: the hymen as protective screen, the jewel box of virginity, the vaginal partition, the fine, invisible veil which, in front of the hystera, stands *between* the inside and the outside of a woman, and consequently between desire and fulfillment. It is neither desire nor pleasure but in between the two. Neither future nor present, but between the two. It is the hymen that desire dreams of piercing, of bursting, in an act of violence that is (at the same time or between) love and murder. If either one *did* take place, there would be no hymen. But neither would there simply be a hymen in (case events go) *no* place. With all the undecidability of its meaning, the hymen only takes place when it doesn't take place, when nothing *truly* happens, when there is consummation without violence, or a violence without blows, or a blow without marks, a mark without a mark (a margin), etc., when the veil is, *without being,* torn, for example when one is made to die or come laughing.

Ὑμήν [*humēn*] designates a fine, filmy membrane enveloping certain bodily organs; for example, says Aristotle, the heart or the intestines. It is also the cartilage in certain fish, the wings of certain insects (bees, wasps, and ants, which are called hymenoptera), the foot membranes in certain birds (the hymenopoda), a white pellicle over the eyes of certain birds, the sheath encasing the seed or bean of plants. A tissue on which so many bodily metaphors are written.

There exist treatises on membranes or *hymenologies;* descriptions of membranes or *hymenographies.* Rightly or wrongly, the etymology of "hymen" is often traced to a root *u* that can be found in the Latin *suo, suere* (to sew) and in *huphos* (tissue). *Hymen* might then mean a little stitch (*syuman*) (*syuntah,* sewn, *siula,* needle; *schuh,* sew; *suo*). The same hypothesis, while sometimes contested, is put forth for *hymn,* which would thus not be a merely accidental anagram of *hymen* [*hymne/hymen*]. Both words would have a relation with *huphainō* (to weave, spin—the spider web—machinate), with *huphos* (textile, spider web, net, the text of a work—Longinus), and with *humnos* (a weave, later the weave of a song, by extension a wedding song or song of mourning). Littré: ". . . according to Curtius, ὕμνος has the same root as ὑφάω, to weave, ὑφή, ὕφος, textile; in that long ago era when writing was unknown, most of the words used to designate a poetic composition were borrowed from the art of the weaver, the builder, etc."

The hymen is thus a sort of textile. Its threads should be interwoven with all the veils, gauzes, canvases, fabrics, moires, wings, feathers, all the curtains and fans that hold within their folds all—almost—of the Mallarméan corpus. We could spend a night doing that. The text of "Mimique" is not the only place where the word *hymen* occurs. It appears, with the same syntactical resources of undecidability, handled more or less systematically, in the "Cantate pour la première communion" ["Cantata for the First Communion"] composed by Mallarmé at the age of sixteen ("in this mysterious hymen / Between strength and weakness"), in "L'après-midi d'un faune" ["The Afternoon of a Faun"] ("Too much hymen hoped for by him who seeks the *la*"), in the "Offrandes à divers du faune" ["Gifts of the Faun to a Few"] ("The Faun would dream of hymen and of a chaste ring"), and especially in *Richard Wagner, rêverie d'un poète français,* where all the elements of the constellation are named over two pages (543–5): the Mime, the hymen, the virgin, the occult, the penetration and the envelope, the theater, the hymn, the "folds of a tissue," the touch that transforms nothing, the "song, spurting out of a rift," the "fusion of these disparate forms of pleasure."

A folding back, once more: the hymen, "a medium, a pure medium, of fiction," is located between present acts that don't take place. What takes place is only the *entre,* the place, the spacing, which is nothing, the ideality (as nothingness) of the idea. No act, then, is *perpetrated* ("hymen . . . between perpetration and remembrance"); no act is committed as a crime. There is only the memory of a crime that has never been committed, not only because on the stage we have never seen it in the present (the Mime is recalling it), but also because no violence has been exerted (someone has been made to die of laughter, and then the "criminal"—bursting with hilarity—is absolved by his own death), and because this crime is its opposite: an act of love. Which itself has not taken place. To perpetrate, as its calculated consonance with "penetrate" suggests, is to pierce, but fictively, the hymen, the threshold never crossed. Even when he takes that step, Pierrot remains, before the doors, the "solitary captive of the threshold" ("Pour votre chère morte" ["For Your Dear Departed"]).

To pierce the hymen or to pierce one's eyelid (which in some birds is called a hymen), to lose one's sight or one's life, no longer to see the light of day, is the fate of all Pierrots. Gautier's *Pierrot Posthume* succumbs to it, prior to Margueritte's. It is the fate of the simulacrum. He applies the procedure to himself and pretends to die, after swallowing the mouse, then by tickling himself, in the supreme spasm of infinite masturbation. This Pierrot's hymen was perhaps not quite so subtly transparent, so invisibly lacking in consistency, as Mallarmé's. But it is also because his hymen (marriage) remains precarious and uncertain that he kills himself or passes himself off as dead. Thinking that, if he is already dead in others' eyes, he would be incapable of rising to the necessary hymen, the *true* hymen, between Columbine and himself, this posthumous Pierrot simulates suicide: "I'll beat up on Harlequin, take back my wife... / But how? and with what? my soul's all my life, / I'm a being of reason, I'm all immaterial. / A hymen needs palpable things, not ethereal... / What a puzzle! to settle these doubts, let's not stall: / Let's go commit suicide once and for all."[21] But suicide being still another species of the genus "hymen," he will never have finished killing himself, the "once and for all" expressing precisely that which the hymen always makes a mockery of, that before which we shall always burst out laughing.

21. The word *Hymen*, sometimes allegorized by a capital H, is of course part of the vocabulary of "Pierrots" ("Harlequin and Polichinelle both aspire to a glorious hymen with Columbine," Gautier), just as it is included in the "symbolist" code. It nevertheless remains—and is significant—that Mallarmé with his syntactic play remarks the undecidable ambivalence. The "event" (the historical event, if you wish) has the form of a repetition, the mark—readable because doubled—of a quasi-tearing, a *dehiscence*. "DE-HISCENCE: s.f. Botanical term. The action through which the distinct parts of a closed organ open up, without tearing, along a seam. A regular predetermined splitting that, at a certain moment in the cycle, is undergone by the closed organs so that what they contain can come out ... E. Lat. *Dehiscere*, to open slightly, from *de* and *hiscere*, the frequentative of *hiare* (see *hiatus*)." Littré.

Quant au livre [*As for the Book*]: The structures of the hymen, suicide, and time are closely linked together. "Suicide or abstention, to do nothing, why? Only time in the world, for, due to an event that I shall explain, always, there is no Present, no—a present does not exist... For lack of the Crowd's declaration, for lack—of all. Ill-informed is he who would pronounce himself his own contemporary, deserting, usurping, with equal impudence, when some past has ceased and a future is slow in coming or else both are perplexedly mixed with a view to masking the gap" (372).

A masked gap, impalpable and insubstantial, interposed, slipped between, the *entre* of the hymen is reflected in the screen without penetrating it. The hymen remains in the hymen. The one—the veil of virginity where nothing has yet taken place—remains in the other—consummation, release, and penetration of the antre.

And vice versa.

The mirror is never passed through and the ice never broken. At the edge of being.

At the edge of being, the medium of the hymen never becomes a mere mediation or work of the negative; it outwits and undoes all ontologies, all philosophemes, all manner of dialectics. It outwits them and—as a cloth, a tissue, a medium again—it envelops them, turns them over, and inscribes them. This nonpenetration, this nonperpetration (which is not simply negative but stands between the two), this suspense in the antre of perpenetration, is, says Mallarmé, "perpetual": "This is how the Mime operates, whose act is confined to a perpetual allusion without breaking the ice or the mirror: he thus sets up a medium, a pure medium, of fiction." (The play of the commas [*virgulae*] only appears, in all its multiplicity, in the last version, inserting a series of cuts marking pauses and cadence, spacing and shortness of breath, within the continuum of the sequence).[22] Hymen in perpetual motion: one can't get out of Mallarmé's antre as one can out of Plato's cave. Never min(e)d

22. "... I prefer, as being more to my taste, upon a white page, a carefully spaced pattern of commas and periods and their secondary combinations, imitating, naked, the melody—over the text, advantageously suggested if, even though sublime, it were not punctuated" (407).

[*mine de rien*];[23] it requires an entirely different kind of speleology which no longer searches behind the lustrous appearance, outside the "beyond," "agent," "motor," "principal part or nothing" of the "literary mechanism" (*Music and Letters*, 647).

" . . . as much as it takes to illustrate one of the aspects and this lode of language" (406).

"That is how the Mime operates": every time Mallarmé uses the word *operation*, nothing happens that could be grasped as a present event, a reality, an activity, etc. The Mime doesn't *do* anything; there is no act (neither murderous nor sexual), no acting agent and hence no patient. Nothing *is*. The word *is* does not appear in "Mimique," which is nevertheless conjugated in the *present*, within and upon the "*false appearance of a present*," with one exception, and even then in a form that is not that of a declaration of existence and barely that of a predicative copula ("It is up to the poet, roused by a dare, to translate!"). Indeed, the constant ellipsis of the verb "to be" by Mallarmé has already been noted.[24] This ellipsis is complementary to the frequency of the word *jeu* [play, game, act]; the practice of "play" in Mallarmé's writing is in collusion with the casting aside of "being." The *casting aside* [*mise à l'écart*] of being defines itself and literally (im)prints itself in dissemination, *as* dissemination.

The play of the hymen is *at once* vicious and sacred, "tainted with vice yet sacred." And so, too, is it neither the one nor the other since nothing happens and the hymen remains suspended *entre*, outside and inside the antre. Nothing is more vicious than this suspense, this distance played at; nothing is more perverse than this rending penetration that leaves a virgin womb intact. But nothing is more marked by the sacred, like so many Mallarméan veils, more folded, intangible, sealed, untouched. Here we ought to grasp fully the analogy between "Mimique"'s "scenario" and the one that is spottily sketched out in the fragments of the *Book* [*Le "Livre" de Mallarmé*, ed. Jacques Scherer (Paris: Gallimard, 1978)]. Among them, these:

23. TN In French, *mine de rien* means, in its colloquial sense, "as though it were of no importance," but literally it can mean "a mine full of nothing."

24. Cf. Jacques Scherer, *L'expression littéraire dans l'oeuvre de Mallarmé* (Paris: Nizet, 1947), 142ff.

19A

On the other side, both future
and past

Such is what takes place
visible
with him omitted

(one arm, another,
raised, posture of
a dancer

20A

to open onto[1] medium (solitary
within the self—[2] this extends
to the mysterious fore-stage, like the
ground—preparation for the festival
=   intermission*

confusion of the two

with <u>interruption</u> of the open ground   or = **
the action in
the background
—taking up where
one leaves off

=   *intermission
before alone
and growing
with the medium

(recall the festival (regrets, etc.)

and   the curtain rises—falls   the "house"
and backdrop
corresponds to <u>ground</u>   the beyond

and mysterious <u>fore-stage</u>—corresponds to
what hides the <u>background</u> (canvas, etc.) makes its
mystery—

background = the "house"   ** with lustres

1. onto a second ground
2. solitary festival in the self—festival

21A

        the electrical arabesque
   lights up behind—and the two
veils

   —a sort of sacred rending of the
veil, written there—or rends—

   and two beings at once bird
and scent—like the two in a
      pulpit
high (balcony) com

---

   the egg   church

22A

   . . . .
   . . . .
   There, that is all the echo says—
double, lying, questioned
by the <u>wandering spirit</u> (of the wind)

24A

   . . . .
   . . . .
   —During that time—the curtain
of the diorama deepened—shadow
more and more pronounced, as though hollowed
out by it—by the mystery—

   The blinds have rendered themselves null . . . .
   . . . .

169A   [in the corner of a page]

   Operation*
   crime   oath?
   *which is neither. nor.
   . . . .

50B

   5 years. the lustre

The Mime is *acting* from the moment he is ruled by no actual action and aims toward no form of verisimilitude. The act always plays out a difference without reference, or rather without a referent, without any absolute exteriority, and hence, without any inside. The Mime mimes reference. He is not an imitator; he mimes imitation. The hymen interposes itself between mimicry and *mimēsis* or rather between *mimē-sis* and *mimēsis*. A copy of a copy, a simulacrum that simulates the Platonic simulacrum—the Platonic copy of a copy as well as the Hegelian curtain[25] have lost here the lure of the present referent and thus find themselves lost for dialectics and ontology, lost for absolute knowledge. Which is also, as Bataille would literally have it, "mimed." In this perpetual allusion being performed in the background of the *entre* that has no ground, one can never know what the allusion alludes to, unless it is to itself in the process of alluding, weaving its hymen and manufacturing its text. Wherein illusion becomes a game conforming only to its own formal rules. As its name indicates, allusion *plays*. But that this play should in the last instance be independent of truth does not mean that it is false, an error, appearance, or illusion. Mallarmé writes "allusion," not "illusion." Allusion, or "suggestion" as Mallarmé says elsewhere, is indeed that operation we are here *by analogy* calling undecidable. An undecidable proposition, as Gödel demon-

25. As for the hymen between Hegel and Mallarmé, one can analyze, for example, in the *Phenomenology of Spirit*, a certain curtain-raising observed from the singular standpoint of the *we*, the philosophic consciousness, the subject of absolute knowing: "The two extremes . . ., the one, of the pure inner world, the other, that of the inner being gazing into this pure inner world, have now coincided, and just as they, *qua* extremes, have vanished, so too the middle term, as something other than these extremes, has also vanished. This curtain [*Vorhang*] hanging before the inner world is therefore drawn away, and we have the inner being . . . gazing into the inner world—the vision of the undifferentiated selfsame being, which repels itself from itself, posits itself as an inner being containing different moments, but for which equally these moments are immediately *not* different—*self-consciousness*. It is manifest that behind the so-called curtain which is supposed to conceal the inner world, there is nothing to be seen unless *we* go behind it ourselves, as much in order that we may see, as that there may be something behind there which can be seen. But at the same time it is evident that we cannot without more ado go straightway behind appearance" [trans. Miller, 103]. I would like to thank A. Boutruche for recalling this text to my attention.

strated in 1931, is a proposition which, given a system of axioms governing a multiplicity, is neither an analytical nor deductive consequence of those axioms, nor in contradiction with them, neither true nor false with respect to those axioms. *Tertium datur*, without synthesis.

"Undecidability" is not caused here by some enigmatic equivocality, some inexhaustible ambivalence of a word in a "natural" language, and still less by some *"Gegensinn der Urworte"* [26] ("antithetical sense of primal words") (Abel). In dealing here with *hymen*, it is not a matter of repeating what Hegel undertook to do with German words like *Aufhebung, Urteil, Meinen, Beispiel,* etc., marveling over that lucky accident that installs a natural language within the element of speculative dialectics. What counts here is not the lexical richness, the semantic infiniteness of a word or concept, its depth or breadth, the sedimentation that has produced inside it two contradictory layers of signification (continuity and discontinuity, inside and outside, identity and difference, etc.). What counts here is the formal or syntactical *praxis* that composes and decomposes it. We have indeed been making believe that everything could be traced to the word *hymen*. But the irreplaceable character of this signifier, which everything seemed to grant it, was laid out like a trap. This word, this syllepsis,[27] is not indispensable; philology and etymology interest us only secondarily, and the loss of the "hymen" would not be irreparable for "Mimique." It produces its effect first and foremost through the syntax, which disposes the *entre*

---

26. We are referring less to the text in which Freud is directly inspired by Abel (1910) than to *Das Unheimliche* (1919), of which we are here, in sum, proposing a rereading. We find ourselves constantly being brought back to that text by the paradoxes of the double and of repetition, the blurring of the boundary lines between "imagination" and "reality," between the "symbol" and the "thing it symbolizes" ("The Uncanny," trans. Alix Strachey, in *On Creativity and the Unconscious* [New York: Harper & Row, 1958], 152), the references to Hoffmann and the literature of the fantastic, the considerations on the *double meaning* of words: "Thus *heimlich* is a word the meaning of which develops towards an ambivalence, until it finally coincides with its opposite, *unheimlich*. *Unheimlich* is in some way or other a sub-species of *heimlich*" (131) (to be continued).

27. "The mixed tropes called *Syllepses* consist of taking one and the same word in two different senses, one of which is, or is supposed to be, the original, or at least the *literal*, meaning; the other, the *figurative*, or supposedly figurative, even if it is not so in reality. This can be done by *metonymy, synecdoche,* or *metaphor*" (P. Fontanier, *Les figures du discours*, introduction by G. Genette [Paris: Flammarion, 1968], 105). [TN This figure is more commonly called *zeugma* in English.]

in such a way that the suspense is due only to the placement and not to the content of words. Through the "hymen" one can remark only what the place of the word *entre* already marks and would mark even if the word "hymen" were not there. If we replaced "hymen" by "marriage" or "crime," "identity" or "difference," etc., the effect would be the same, the only loss being a certain economic condensation or accumulation, which has not gone unnoticed. It is the "between," whether it names fusion or separation, that thus carries all the force of the operation. The hymen must be determined through the *entre* and not the other way around. The hymen in the text (crime, sexual act, incest, suicide, simulacrum) is inscribed at the very tip of this indecision. This tip advances according to the irreducible excess of the syntactic over the semantic. The word "between" has no full meaning of its own. *Inter* acting[28] forms a syntactical plug; not a categorem, but a syncategorem: what philosophers from the Middle Ages to Husserl's *Logical Investigations* have called an incomplete signification. What holds for "hymen" also holds, *mutatis mutandis,* for all other signs which, like *pharmakon, supplément, différance,*[29] and others, have a double, contradictory, undecidable value that always derives from their syntax, whether the latter is in a sense "internal," articulating and combining under the same yoke, *huph'hen* ["under one," the Greek etymology of *hyphen*], two incompatible meanings, or "external," dependent on the code in which the word is made to function. But the syntactical composition and decomposition of a sign renders this alternative between internal and external inoperative. One is simply dealing with greater or lesser syntactical units at work, and with economic differences in condensation. Without reducing all these to the same, quite the contrary, it is possible to recognize a certain serial law in these points of indefinite pivoting: they mark the spots of what can never be mediated, mastered, sublated, or dialecticized through any *Erinnerung* or *Aufhebung.* Is it by chance that all these play effects, these "words" that escape philosophical mastery, should have, in

___

28. EN The original is "Entre *ouvert*": "*between* open" (or "open *between*"), and, understood as *entr'ouvert,* "half-open."

29. EN For *pharmakon* see "Plato's Pharmacy"; for *supplément* see "...That Dangerous Supplement ..." above; for *différance,* see "Différance."

widely differing historical contexts, a very singular relation to writing? These "words" admit into their games both contradiction and noncontradiction (and the contradiction and noncontradiction *between* contradiction and noncontradiction). Without any dialectical *Aufhebung,* without any time off, they belong in a sense both to consciousness and to the unconscious, which Freud tells us can tolerate or remain insensitive to contradiction. Insofar as the text depends upon them, *bends* to them [*s'y plie*], it thus plays a *double scene* upon a double stage. It operates in two absolutely different places at once, even if these are only separated by a veil, which is both traversed and not traversed, *inter*sected [*entr'ouvert*]. Because of this indecision and instability, Plato would have conferred upon the double science arising from these two theaters the name *doxa* rather than *epistēmē*. *Pierrot Murderer of His Wife* would have reminded him of the riddle of the bat struck by the eunuch.[30]

Everything is played out, everything and all the rest—that is to say, the game—is played out in the *entre,* about which the author of the *Essai sur la connaissance approchée,* who also knew all about caves,[31] says that it is "a mathematical concept" (32). When this undecidability is marked and re-marked in *writing,* it has a greater power of formaliza-

---

30. "And again, do the many double things appear any the less halves than doubles?— None the less.—And likewise of the great and the small things, the light and the heavy things—will they admit these predicates any more than their opposites?—No, he said, each of them will always hold of, partake of, both.—Then each *is* each of these multiples rather than it *is not* that which one affirms it to be?—They are like those jesters who palter with us in a double sense at banquets, he replied, and resemble the children's riddle about the eunuch and his hitting of the bat—with what and as it sat on what they signify that he struck it.* For these things too equivocate, and it is impossible to conceive firmly any one of them to be or not to be or both or neither. . . . But we agreed in advance that if anything of that sort should be discovered, it must be denominated opinable, not knowable, the wanderer between being caught by the faculty that is betwixt and between" (*Republic* V, 479 *b, c, d,* trans. Paul Shorey, p. 719). [*TN Francis M. Cornford, in his edition of the *Republic* (New York: Oxford University Press, 1945), glosses the riddle as follows (188): "A man who was not a man (eunuch), seeing and not seeing (seeing imperfectly) a bird that was not a bird (bat) perched on a bough that was not a bough (a reed), pelted and did not pelt it (aimed at it and missed) with a stone that was not a stone (pumice-stone.)"]

31. The chapter of *La terre et les rêveries du repos* [*Earth and Dreams of Rest*] which deals with *caves* does not, however, mention Mallarmé's in its rich survey of various "caves in literature." If this fact is not simply insignificant, the reason for it may perhaps appear later in the course of our discussion of Mallarmé's "imaginary." [EN These texts are by Gaston Bachelard; *Essai sur la connaissance approchée* (Paris: Vrin, 1927), *La terre et les rêveries du repos* (Paris: Corti, 1948).]

tion, even if it is "literary" in appearance, or appears to be attributable to a natural language, than when it occurs as a proposition in logico-mathematical form, which would not go as far as the former type of mark. If one supposes that the distinction, still a metaphysical one, between natural language and artificial language be rigorous (and we no doubt here reach the limit of its pertinence), one can say that there are texts in so-called natural languages whose power of formalization would be superior to that attributed to certain apparently formal notations.

One no longer even has the authority to say that "between" is a purely syntactic function. Through the re-marking of its semantic void, it in fact begins to signify.[32] Its semantic void *signifies*, but it signifies spacing and articulation; it has as its meaning the possibility of syntax; it orders the play of meaning. *Neither purely syntactic nor purely semantic*, it marks the articulated opening of that opposition.

The whole of this dehiscence, finally, is repeated and partially opened up in a certain "lit" ["bed," "reads"], which "Mimique" has painstakingly set up. Toward the end of the text, the syntagm "le lit" reproduces the strategem of the hymen.

Before we come to that, I would like to recall the fact that in this "Mimique," which is cannily interposed between two silences that are breached or broached thereby ("Silence, sole luxury after rimes . . . there reigns a silence still, the condition and delight of reading."), as a "gambol" or "debate" of "language," it has never been a question of anything other than reading and writing. This text could be read as a sort of handbook of literature. Not only because the metaphor of writing comes up so often ("a phantom . . . white as a yet unwritten

---

32. From that point on, the syncategorem "between" contains as its meaning a semantic quasi-emptiness; it signifies the spacing relation, the articulation, the interval, etc. It can be nominalized, turn into a quasi-categorem, receive a definite article, or even be made plural. We have spoken of "betweens," and this plural is in some sense primary. *One* "between" does not exist. In Hebrew, *entre* can be made plural: "In truth this plural expresses not the relation between one individual thing and another, but rather the intervals between things (*loca aliis intermedia*)—in this connection see chapter 10, verse 2, of Ezekiel—or else, as I said before, this plural represents preposition or relation abstractly conceived." (Spinoza, *Abrégé de grammaire hébraique* [Paris: Vrin, 1968], 108).

page")—which is also the case in the *Philebus*—but because the necessity of that metaphor, which *nothing* escapes, makes it something other than a particular figure among others. What is produced is an absolute extension of the concepts of writing and reading, of text, of hymen, to the point where nothing of what *is* can lie beyond them. "Mimique" describes a scene of writing within a scene of writing and so on without end, through a structural necessity that is marked in the text. The mime, as "corporeal writing" (*Ballets*), mimes a kind of writing (hymen) and is himself written in a kind of writing. Everything is reflected in the medium or speculum of reading-writing, "without breaking the mirror." There is writing without a book, in which, each time, at every moment, the marking tip proceeds without a past upon the virgin sheet; but there is also, *simultaneously,* an infinite number of booklets enclosing and fitting inside other booklets, which are only able to issue forth by grafting, sampling, quotations, epigraphs, references, etc. Literature voids itself in its limitlessness. If this handbook of literature meant to *say* something, which we now have some reason to doubt, it would proclaim first of all that there is no—or hardly any, ever so little—literature; that in any event there is no essence of literature, no truth of literature, no literary-being or being-literary of literature. And that the fascination exerted by the "is," or the "what is" in the question "what is literature" is worth what the hymen is worth—that is, not exactly nothing—when for example it causes one to die laughing. All this, of course, should not prevent us—on the contrary—from attempting to find out what has been represented and determined under that name—"literature"—and why.

Mallarmé *reads.* He writes while reading; while reading the text written by the Mime, who himself reads in order to write, reading for example the *Pierrot posthume* so as to write with his gestures a mimic that owes that book nothing, since he reads the mimic he thus creates in order to write after the fact the booklet that Mallarmé is reading.

But does the Mime read his role in order to write his mimic or his booklet? Is the initiative of reading his? Is he the acting subject who knows how to read what he has to write? One could indeed believe that although he is passive in reading, he at least has the active freedom to choose to begin to read, and that the same is true of Mallarmé; or even that you, dear everyreader, retain the initiative of reading all these texts, including Mallarmé's, and hence, to that extent, in that place, you are indeed attending it, deciding on it, mastering it.

Nothing could be less certain. The syntax of "Mimique" imprints a movement of (non-Platonic) simulacrum in which the function of *le lit* ["the bed," "reads it," "reads him"] complicates itself to the point of admitting a multitude of subjects among whom you yourself are not necessarily included. Plato's clinical paradigm is no longer operative.

The question of the text is—(for whom are) / (for whoever reads) these sheets.[33]

Among diverse possibilities, let us take this: the Mime does not read his role; he is also read by it. Or at least he is both read and reading, written and writing, between the two, in the suspense of the hymen, at once screen and mirror. As soon as a mirror is interposed in some way, the simple opposition between activity and passivity, between production and the product, or between all concepts in -er and all concepts in -ed (*imitator/imitated, signifier/signified*, structure/structured, etc.), becomes impracticable and too formally weak to encompass the graphics of the hymen, its spider web, and the play of its eyelids.

This impossibility of identifying the path *proper* to the letter of a text, of assigning a unique place to the subject, of locating a simple origin, is here consigned, plotted by the machinations of the one who calls himself "profoundly and scrupulously a syntaxer." In the sentence that follows, the syntax—and the carefully calculated punctuation— prevent us from ever deciding whether the subject of "reads" is the role ("less than a thousand lines, the role, the one that reads . . .") or some anonymous reader ("the role, the one that reads, will instantly comprehend the rules as if placed before the stageboards . . .") Who is "the one"? "The one" [*qui*] may of course be the indefinite pronoun meaning "whoever," here in its function as a subject. This is the easiest reading; the role—whoever reads it will instantly understand its rules.

33. TN *La question du texte est—pour qui le lit:* both "The question of the text is for the one who reads it (or him)" and "The question of the text is: whom is the bed for?"

Empirical statistics would show that the so-called "linguistic sense" would most often give this reading.

But nothing in the grammatical code would render the sentence incorrect if, without changing a thing, one were to read "the one" (subject of "reads") as a pronoun whose antecedent was "role." Out of this reading would spring a series of syntactic and semantic transformations in the function of the words "role," le [it or him]," "placed," and in the meaning of the word "comprehend." Thus: "Less than a thousand lines, the role [subject, not object], the one [referring back to "role"] that reads [the one that reads "him," not "it", referring to the Mime, the subject of the preceding sentence], will instantly comprehend [embrace, contain, rule, organize: read] the rules as if placed before the stageboards [the role is placed facing the stage, either as the author-composer, or as the spectator-reader, in the position of the "whoever" in the first hypothesis], their humble depository."

This reading is possible. It is "normal" both from the syntactic and from the semantic point of view. But what a laborious artifice! Do you really believe, goes the objection, that Mallarmé consciously parceled out his sentence so that it could be read two different ways, with each object capable of changing into a subject and vice versa, without our being able to arrest this movement? Without our being able, faced with this "alternative sail," to decide whether the text is "listing to one side or the other" (A Throw of Dice). The two poles of the reading are not equally obvious: but the syntax at any rate has produced an effect of indefinite fluctuation between two possibilities.

Whatever might have been going on in Mallarmé's head, in his consciousness or in his unconscious, does not matter to us here; the reader should now know why. That, in any event, does not hold the least interest for a reading of the text. Everything in the text is interwoven, as we have seen, so as to do without references, so as to cut them short. Nevertheless, for those who are interested in Stéphane Mallarmé and would like to know what he was thinking and meant to do by writing in this way, we shall merely ask the following question. But we are asking it on the basis of texts, and published texts at that: how is one to explain the fact that the syntactic alternative frees itself only in the third version of the text? How is one to explain the fact that, some words being moved, others left out, a tense transformed, a comma added, then and only then does the one-way reading, the only reading possible in the first two versions, come to shift, to waver, henceforth without rest? and without identifiable reference? Why is it that, when one has written, without any possible ambiguity, this: "This marvelous bit of nothing, less than a thousand lines, whoever will read it as I have just done, will comprehend the eternal rules, just as though facing the stageboards, their humble depository" (1886),

and then this: "This role, less than a thousand lines, whoever reads it will comprehend the rules as if placed before the stageboards, their humble depository" (1891),

one should finally write this, with all possible ambiguity: "Less than a thousand lines, the role, the one that reads, will instantly comprehend the rules as if placed before the stageboards, their humble depository" (1897)?

Perhaps he didn't know what he was doing? Perhaps he wasn't conscious of it? Perhaps, then, he wasn't completely the author of what was being written? The burst of laughter that echoes deep inside the antre, in "Mimique," is a reply to all these questions. They can have been formulated only through recourse to certain oppositions, by presupposing possibilities of decision whose pertinence was rigorously swept away by the very text they were supposed to question. Swept away by that hymen, the text always calculates and suspends some supplementary "surprise" and "delight." "Surprise, accompanying the artifice of a notation of sentiments by unproffered sentences—that, in the sole case, perhaps, with authenticity, between the sheets and the eye there reigns a silence still, the condition and delight of reading." Supplement, principle, and bounty. The baffling economy of seduction.

enter . . . between . . . a silence

> "Each session or play being a game, a fragmentary
> show, but sufficient at that unto itself . . ."
> (Le "Livre," [The "Book"] 93 (A))

5

BEFORE THE LAW

&. The self-questioning question "What is literature?" is taken up again in this extended reading of Kafka's short parable *Before the Law*, which appears as part of *The Trial* but was published as a separate text in Kafka's lifetime. Derrida focuses on the institutional, ethical, and juridical implications of any such question: what is the law according to which a text can be classified as "literary" or "nonliterary," and who is entitled (and by what legal authority) to make such a decision? Literature, that is, is seen as a historical (and relatively recent) institution, brought into being and governed by laws; but the texts which come under its aegis have the peculiar attribute of being able to stage and suspend all the presuppositions upon which any such institution rests—among them the operation of laws, the property of belonging to a category, the function of proper names. Crucial to the literary text are such features as its external boundaries, its uniqueness, its authorship, its title, and its acts of reference, yet equally crucial is the way in which these features are put into question as stable properties or concepts. Kafka's text stages this simultaneous assertion and undermining of the institution of literature in a remarkably condensed and striking fashion, and Derrida is as interested in its unique qualities as a literary act as he is in the more general issues it raises. Indeed, it is this problematic relation between the singular and the general (the basis of Kafka's story) which provides one of the main motifs of Derrida's essay, and which could be reapplied to the essay itself as a unique intervention in the debate about literature and law.

The title of Derrida's text is identical to that of Kafka's fable, although—as he points out in his opening comments—this identity also necessarily involves a difference, as does the identity between the title and the opening words of Kafka's story. Neither text specifies the type of law in question; moral law, judicial law, and natural law are all implicated in the dramatization and discussion of the condition of being "before the law," subject to an imperative to which unmediated access is impossible. The strict notion of the law is predicated upon its absolute separability from anything like fiction, narrative, history, or literature; yet, as Derrida shows in his reading of Kafka's fiction, this separation cannot be sustained. Not only does literature simultaneously depend on and interrogate laws, but the law—the continual subject of narratives—can only be understood as self-contradictory, lacking in pure essence, and structurally related to what Derrida terms *différance* or, in its nonmetaphysical sense, "literature." Being before the law is therefore not wholly distinguishable from being before the literary text; and in both cases, as Kafka's parable suggests, the intangibility of that which we confront stems not from some concealed essence but from its very accessibility.

This essay may be fruitfully read in conjunction with the following one, "The Law of Genre," which, starting from a different literary text, engages with the question of obligation to the law and its representatives, and the importance of literature in approaching that question.

ɬ "Before the Law" was first given as a lecture to the Royal Philosophical Society in London in 1982. Part of the French text was published as "Devant la loi" in *Philosophy and Literature,* ed. A. Phillips Griffiths (Cambridge: Cambridge University Press, 1984). This lecture was then combined with additional material on the work of J.-F Lyotard and presented at the 1982 Colloque de Cerisy on Lyotard; the extended text was published as "Préjugés: Devant la loi" in the conference volume (Derrida et al., *La faculté de juger* [Paris: Minuit, 1985], 87–139). An English translation by Avital Ronell of most of the original version was published as "Devant la loi" in *Kafka and the Contemporary Critical Performance: Centenary Readings,* ed. Alan Udoff (Bloomington: Indiana University Press, 1987). The following text, based on Ronell's translation, is that of the complete original version, which has not hitherto been published in French or in English. Additional material has been translated by Christine Roulston, who also assisted in the editing of the entire piece and provided the translator's footnotes.

.... : science does likewise (and even our law, it is said, has legitimate
fictions on which it bases the truth of its justice) . . .
                                        —Montaigne, *Essays* II, 12

A title occasionally resonates like the citation of another title. But
as soon as it names something else, it no longer simply cites, it diverts
the other title under cover of a homonym. All of this could never occur
without some degree of prejudice or usurpation.

I shall try to do justice to these possibilities by beginning to read—
and reading here amounts to citing—Kafka's story entitled *Vor dem
Gesetz* or, in English, *Before the Law*. While the translation of the title
may appear problematical, in three words it sums up in advance and
formalizes what is at stake.

BEFORE THE LAW

Before the Law stands a doorkeeper. To this doorkeeper there comes a
countryman and prays for admittance to the Law. But the doorkeeper
says that he cannot grant admittance at the moment. The man thinks it
over and then asks if he will be allowed in later. "It is possible," says the
doorkeeper, "but not at the moment." Since the gate stands open, as
usual, and the doorkeeper steps to one side, the man stoops to peer
through the gateway into the interior. Observing that, the doorkeeper
laughs and says: "If you are so drawn to it, just try to go in despite my
veto. But take note: I am powerful. And I am only the least of the
doorkeepers. From hall to hall there is one doorkeeper after another, each
more powerful than the last. The third doorkeeper is already so terrible
that even I cannot bear to look at him." These are difficulties the countryman has not expected; the Law, he thinks, should surely be accessible at
all times and to everyone, but as he now takes a closer look at the
doorkeeper in his fur coat, with his big sharp nose and long, thin, black
Tartar beard, he decides that it is better to wait until he gets permission
to enter. The doorkeeper gives him a stool and lets him sit down at one
side of the door. There he sits for days and years. He makes many attempts
to be admitted, and wearies the doorkeeper by his importunity. The
doorkeeper frequently has little interviews with him, asking him questions
about his home and many other things, but the questions are put indiffer-
ently, as great lords put them, and always finish with the statement that
he cannot be let in yet. The man, who has furnished himself with many

things for his journey, sacrifices all he has, however valuable, to bribe the doorkeeper. That official accepts everything, but always with the remark: "I am only taking it to keep you from thinking you have omitted anything." During these many years the man fixes his attention almost continuously on the doorkeeper. He forgets the other doorkeepers, and this first one seems to him the sole obstacle preventing access to the Law. He curses his bad luck, in his early years boldly and loudly, later, as he grows old, he only grumbles to himself. He becomes childish, and since in his years-long contemplation of the doorkeeper he has come to know even the fleas in his fur collar, he begs the fleas as well to help him and to change the doorkeeper's mind. At length his eyesight begins to fail, and he does not know whether the world is really darker or whether his eyes are only deceiving him. Yet in his darkness he is now aware of a radiance that streams inextinguishably from the gateway of the Law. Now he has not very long to live. Before he dies, all his experiences in these long years gather themselves in his head to one point, a question he has not yet asked the doorkeeper. He waves him nearer, since he can no longer raise his stiffening body. The doorkeeper has to bend low towards him, for the difference in height between them has altered much to the countryman's disadvantage. "What do you want to know now?" asks the doorkeeper. "You are insatiable." "Everyone strives to reach the Law," says the man, "so how does it happen that for all these many years no one but myself has ever begged for admittance?" The doorkeeper recognizes that the man has reached his end, and to let his failing senses catch the words roars in his ear: "No one else could ever be admitted here, since this gate was made only for you. I am now going to shut it."[1]

I shall underline somewhat heavily a few axiomatic trivialities or presuppositions. I have every reason to suppose that we shall readily agree upon them at first, even if I mean later to undermine the conditions of such a consensus. In appealing to this agreement among us I am referring, a little rashly perhaps, to our community of subjects participating on the whole in the same culture and subscribing, in a given context, to the same system of conventions. What are they?

The first axiomatic belief is our recognition that the text I have just read has its own identity, singularity and unity. We consider these, a priori, inviolable, however enigmatic the conditions of this self-iden-

---

1. TN Franz Kafka, "Before the Law" in *Wedding Preparations in the Country and Other Stories,* trans. Willa. and Edwin Muir (Harmondsworth: Penguin, 1978).

tity, this singularity, and this unity actually remain. There is a beginning and an end to this story whose boundaries or limits seem guaranteed by a certain number of established *criteria*—established, that is, by positive rules and conventions. We presuppose this text, which we hold to be unique and self-identical, to exist as an original version incorporated in its birthplace within the German language. According to the most widespread beliefs in our domains, we generally allow that such a so-called original version constitutes the ultimate reference for what might be called the legal personality of the text, its identity, its unicity, its rights, and so on. All this is now guaranteed by law, by a set of legal acts which have their own history, even if the discourse that justifies them tends most often to claim that they are rooted in natural law.

The second element of this axiomatic consensus, essentially inseparable from the first, is that the text has an author. The existence of its signatory is not fictitious, in contrast with the characters in the story. Again, it is the law which requires and guarantees that the difference between the *presumed* reality of the author, bearing the name of Franz Kafka, whose civil status is registered by authority of the state, be one thing, while the fictitious characters within the story be another. This difference implies a system of laws and conventions without which the consensus to which I am presently referring, within a context that to a certain extent we share, would never have the chance of appearing— whether it is well founded or not. Now, we can know at least the apparent history of this system of laws, the judicial events that have articulated its evolution into the form of positive law. This history of conventions is very recent, and everything it guarantees remains essentially unstable, as fragile as an artifice. As you know, among the works we have inherited there are those in which unity, identity, and completion remain problematic because nothing can allow us to decide for certain whether the unfinished state of the work is a real accident or a pretence, a deliberately contrived simulacrum by one or several authors of our time or before. There are and have been works in which one or several authors are staged as characters without leaving us signs or strict criteria for distinguishing between their two functions or values. The *Conte du Graal* (*Story of the Grail*), for example, still raises such problems (complete or incomplete, real or feigned incompletion, the inscription of authors within the story, pen names and literary rights).[2] Without wishing to cancel the differences and historical mutations here, one can be sure that, according to modalities which are each time original, these problems arise in every period and for every work.

Our third axiom or presupposition is that in this text, bearing the title *Before the Law,* events are related,[3] and the relation belongs to what we call literature. There is something of a relation or a narrative form in this text; the narration carries everything along in its train; it determines each atom of the text, even if not everything figures directly as part of the narration. Leaving aside the question of whether this narrativity is the genre, mode, or type of the text,[4] let me simply note in a preliminary way that this narrativity, in this particular case, belongs, in our view, to literature. To this end, I appeal once more to the same prior consensus which we share. Without yet touching upon the contextual presuppositions of our consensus, I take it that we are dealing with what seems to be a literary relation [*récit*] (the word *récit* also raises problems of translation which I shall keep in reserve). Does all this remain too obvious or trivial to merit our attention? I think not. Certain relations do not belong to literature, historical chronicles, for example, or accounts that we encounter daily. Thus, I might tell you that I have appeared before the law for a traffic violation after somebody photographed me at night while I was driving home at an excessive speed. Or that I was to appear before the law in Prague, accused of drug trafficking. It is therefore not as narrative that we define *Before the Law* as a literary phenomenon, nor is it as fictional, allegorical, mythical, symbolic, parabolic narrative, and so on. There are fictions, allegories, myths, symbols, or parables that are not specifi-

2. On all these questions (truly or deceptively incomplete, multiple authorship: "literary property, a problem that seems not, or hardly, to have existed in the Middle Ages" [52]) see Roger Dragonetti, *La vie de la lettre au Moyen Age (Le conte du Graal)* (Paris: Seuil, 1980).

3. TN *Il y a du récit,* literally "there is *récit*" or "there is some *récit*." In this translation, *récit* is usually rendered as "story" or "relation," depending on context, though the former suggests fiction, and the latter non-fiction, rather too strongly. See also "The Law of Genre," note 3, below.

4. Cf. Gérard Genette, "Genres, 'types,' modes," *Poétique* 32 (November 1977): 389–421; republished with some changes as *Introduction à l'architexte* (Paris: Seuil, 1979).

cally literary. What then decides that *Before the Law* belongs to what we think we understand under the name of literature? And who decides? Who judges? To focus these two questions (what and who), I ought to stress that neither of them will be privileged and that they concern literature rather than belles-lettres, poetry or discursive art in general, although these distinctions remain highly problematical.[5]

The double question, then, would be as follows: "Who decides, who judges, and according to what criteria, that this relation belongs to literature?"

I shall say without further delay that I cannot give nor am I withholding an answer to such a question. Perhaps you will think that I am leading you toward a purely aporetic conclusion or in any case toward a problematic overstatement; one would thus claim that the question was badly phrased or that when it comes to literature we cannot speak of a work belonging to a field or class, that there is no such thing as a literary essence or a specifically literary domain strictly identifiable as such; or, indeed, that this name of literature perhaps is destined to remain improper, with no criteria, or assured concept or reference, so that "literature" has something to do with the drama of naming, the law of the name and the name of the law. You would doubtless not be wrong. However, I am less interested in the generality of these laws or these problematical conclusions than in the singularity of a proceeding which, in the course of a unique drama, summons them before an irreplaceable corpus, before this very text, before *Before the Law*. There is a singularity about relationship to the law, a law of singularity which must come into contact with the general or universal essence of the law without ever being able to do so. Now this text, this singular text, as you will already have noted, names or relates in its way this conflict without encounter between law and singularity, this *paradox* or *enigma* of being-before-the-law; and *ainigma*, in Greek, is often a relation, a story, the obscure words of a fable: "These are difficulties the countryman has not expected; the Law, he thinks, should surely be accessible at all times and to everyone. . . ." The answer, if we can

---

5. EN See Derrida's discussion of the distinction between "literature" and "poetry" in the interview above, pp. 40–41; and see also the Introduction, note 30.

still call it that, comes at the end of the story, which also marks the end of the man: "The doorkeeper recognizes that the man has reached his end, and to let his failing senses catch the words roars in his ear: 'No one else could ever be admitted here, since this gate was made only for you. I am now going to shut it.' "

My only ambition, therefore, without offering an answer, will be to focus, at the risk of deforming, this double question (who decides, who judges, and with what entitlement, what belongs to literature?) and, above all, to summon before the law the utterance [*énoncé*] itself of this double question, indeed, as is commonly said in France today, the subject of its enunciation [*énonciation*]. Such a subject would claim to read and understand the text entitled *Before the Law* as a story and would classify it conventionally as literature; s/he would believe that s/he knew what literature was and would merely wonder, being so well armed: what authorizes me to determine this relation as a literary phenomenon? Or to judge it under the category of "literature"?

It is a matter, then, of summoning this question, the subject of the question and the subject's system of axioms or conventions "before the law," before *Before the Law*. What would this mean?

We cannot reduce the singularity of the idiom. To appear before the law means in the German, French, or English idiom to come or to be brought before judges, the representatives or guardians of the law, for the purpose, in the course of a trial, of giving evidence or being judged. The trial, the judgment (*Urteil*), this is the place, the site, the setting— this is what is needed for such an event to take place: "to appear before the law."

Here, "Before the Law," an expression I put in quotation marks, is the title of a story. This is the fourth axiomatic presupposition to be added to our list. We think we know what a title is, notably the title of a work. It is placed in a specific position, highly determined and regulated by conventional laws: at the beginning of and at a set distance above the body of a text, but in any case *before* it. The title is generally chosen by the author or by his or her editorial representatives whose property it is. The title names and guarantees the identity, the unity and the boundaries of the original work which it entitles. It is self-evident that the power and import of a title have an essential relationship with something like the law, regardless of whether we are dealing with titles in general or with the specific title of a work, literary or not. A sort of intrigue is already apparent in a title which names the law (*Before the Law*), a little as if the law had entitled itself or as if the word "title" had insidiously inserted itself into the title. Let us suspend this intrigue.

Let us emphasize the topology. Another intriguing aspect is that the sense of the title announces a topological indication, *before the law*. The same utterance, the same name (for the title is a name), or in any case the same group of words, would not have the value of a title were they to appear elsewhere, in places not prescribed by convention, for example in a different context or in a different place within the same context. In this case, for instance, the expression "*Vor dem Gesetz*" occurs a first or, if you like, a second time, as the beginning of the story, it is part of the first sentence, "*Vor dem Gesetz steht ein Tür-hüter*," "Before the Law stands a doorkeeper." Although we can assume that the same meaning underlies these two occurrences of the same expression, they are homonyms rather than synonyms, for they do not name the same thing; they do not have the same reference or the same value. On either side of the invisible line that separates title from text, the first names the text in its entirety, of which it is in sum the proper name and title, the second designates a situation, the site where the character is localized within the internal geography of the story. The former, the title, is *before* the text and remains external if not to the fiction then at least to the content of the fictional narration. The latter is also at the head of the text, before it, but already in it; this is a first internal element of the narration's fictive content. And yet, although it is outside the fictional narrative or the story that is being told, the title (*Before the Law*) remains a fiction that likewise bears the signature of the author or a representative of the author. We would say that the title belongs to literature even if its belonging has neither the structure nor the status of that which it entitles, to which it remains essentially heterogeneous. That the title belongs to literature does not prevent it from having legal authority. For example, the title of a book allows us to classify it in a library, to attribute to it rights of authorship, as well as the trials and judgments which can follow, and the like. However, this function does not operate like the title of a nonliterary work, say a textbook of physics or law.

The reading of *Before the Law* which I shall now attempt will be colored by a seminar during which, last year, I thought I had teased out this story of Kafka's. In truth, it was Kafka's story which laid siege to my attempt at a discourse on moral law and respect for law in Kant's doctrine of practical reason, and on Heidegger's and Freud's views on moral law and respect in the Kantian sense of the term. The details of this struggle would be out of place here; but to point out the principal titles and *topoi,* let me indicate that the first question concerned the strange status of the example, the symbol, and the type in Kant's doctrine. Kant speaks of a *typology* and not a schematism of practical reason; of a *symbolic* presentation of moral good (the beautiful as a symbol of morality; *Critique of Judgment,* 59); and finally, of a respect which, though never addressed to things, is nevertheless aimed at persons only insofar as they offer an *example* of the moral law: this respect is due only to the moral law, which never shows itself but is the only cause of that respect. Further, I was concerned with the "as if" (*als ob*) in the second formulation of the categorical imperative: "Act as if the maxim of your action were by your will to turn into a universal law of nature." This "as if" enables us to reconcile practical reason with an historical teleology and with the possibility of unlimited progress. I tried to show how it almost introduces narrativity and fiction into the very core of legal thought, at the moment when the latter begins to speak and to question the moral subject. Though the authority of the law seems to exclude all historicity and empirical narrativity, and this at the moment when its rationality seems alien to all fiction and imagination—even the transcendental imagination— it still seems *a priori* to shelter these parasites.[6] Two other motifs among those pointing to Kafka's story caught my attention: the motif of height and the sublime that plays an essential role in it,

6. It is at this point that the seminar examined Heidegger's interpretation of "respect" as related to the transcendental imagination. Cf. *Kant and the Problem of Metaphysics,* chapter 30 in particular.

and the motif of guarding and the guardian.[7] This, in broad outline, served as the context in which I read *Before the Law*. A space, then, in which it is difficult to say whether Kafka's story proposes a powerful, philosophic ellipsis or whether pure, practical reason contains an element of the fantastic or of narrative fiction. One of the questions could be phrased as follows; what if the law, without being itself transfixed by literature, shared the conditions of its possibility with the literary object?

In order to formulate this question in the briefest manner, I will speak of an *appearance,* in the legal sense, of the story and the law, which appear together and find themselves summoned one before the other: the story, as a certain type of *relation,* is linked to the law that it relates, appearing, in so doing, before that law, which appears before it. And yet, as we shall read, nothing really presents itself in this appearance; and just because this is given to us to be read does not mean that we shall have proof or experience of it.

It seems that the law as such should never give rise to any story. To be invested with its categorical authority, the law must be without history, genesis, or any possible derivation. That would be *the law of the law.* Pure morality has no history: as Kant seems at first to remind us, no intrinsic history. And when one tells stories on this subject, they can concern only circumstances, events external to the law and, at best, the modes of its revelation. Like the man from the country in Kafka's story, narrative accounts would try to approach the law and make it present, to enter into a relation with it, indeed, to enter it and become *intrinsic* to it, but none of these things can be accomplished. The story of these maneuvers would be merely an account of that which escapes the story and which remains finally inaccessible to it. However, the inaccessible incites from its place of hiding. One cannot be concerned with the law, or with the law of laws, either at close range or at a distance, without asking where it has its place and whence it comes. I say "the law of laws" because in Kafka's story one does not know

7. Among other examples: at the end of the *Critique of Practical Reason,* philosophy is presented as the guardian (*Aufbewahrerin*) of the pure science of morals; it is also the "narrow gate" (*enge Pforte*) leading to the doctrine of wisdom.

what kind of law is at issue—moral, judicial, political, natural, etc. What remains concealed and invisible in each law is thus presumably the law itself, that which makes laws of these laws, the being-law of these laws. The question and the quest are ineluctable, rendering irresistible the journey toward the place and the origin of law. The law yields by withholding itself, without imparting its provenance and its site. This silence and discontinuity constitute the phenomenon of the law. To enter into relations with the law which says "you must" and "you must not" is to act as if it had no history or at any rate as if it no longer depended on its historical presentation. At the same time, it is to let oneself be enticed, provoked, and hailed by the history of this non-history. It is to let oneself be tempted by the impossible: a theory of the origin of law, and therefore of its non-origin, for example, of moral law. Freud (whom Kafka is known to have read, although this Austro-Hungarian law of the early 1900s is not important here) invented the concept if not the word "repression" as an answer to the question of the origin of moral law. This was before Kafka wrote *Vor dem Gesetz* (1919), though this relation is of little interest to us, and more than twenty-five years before the second topography and the theory of the superego. From the time of the letters to Fliess, he gives the account of his presentiments and premonitions, with a kind of unsettled fervor, as though he were on the verge of a revelation: "Another presentiment tells me *as though I already knew* [my emphasis, J.D.]—but I know nothing at all—that I shall very soon uncover the source of morality" (May 31, 1897; 249).[8] There follow some accounts of dreams, and four months later another letter announces "the certain insight that there are no indications of reality in the unconscious, so that one cannot distinguish between truth and fiction that has been cathected with affect" (September 21, 1897; 264). Some weeks later still, there is another letter, from which I quote the following lines:

> ... after the frightful labor pains of the last few weeks, I gave birth to a new piece of knowledge. Not entirely new, to tell the truth; it had repeat-

8. TN *The Complete Letters of Sigmund Freud to Wilhelm Fliess, 1881–1904*, trans. and ed. J. M. Masson (Cambridge, Mass.: Harvard University Press, 1985).

edly shown itself and withdrawn again; but this time it stayed and looked upon the light of day. Strangely enough, I had had a presentiment of such events a good while beforehand. For instance, I wrote to you once in the summer that I was going to find the source of normal sexual repression (morality, shame, and so forth) and then for a long time failed to find it. Before the vacation trip I told you that the most important patient for me was myself; and then, after I came back from vacation, my self-analysis, of which there was at the time no sign, suddenly started. A few weeks ago came my wish that repression might be replaced by my knowledge of the essential thing *lying behind it* [my emphasis, J.D.]; and that is what I am concerned with now. (November 14, 1897; 278–79)

Freud goes on to consider the concept of repression, the hypothesis that it is organic in origin and linked with the upright position, that is, to a certain *elevation*.[9] The passage to the upright position raises man, thus distancing his nose from the sexual zones, anal or genital. This distance ennobles his height and leaves its traces by delaying his action. Delay, difference, ennobling elevation, diversion of the olfactory sense from the sexual stench, repression—here the origins of morality:

To put it crudely, the memory actually stinks just as in the present the object stinks; and in the same manner as we turn away our sense organ (the head and nose) in disgust, the preconscious and the sense of consciousness turn away from the memory. This is *repression*.

What, now, does normal repression furnish us with? Something which, free, can lead to anxiety; if psychically bound, to rejection—that is to say, the affective basis for a multitude of intellectual processes of development, such as morality, shame, and the like. Thus the whole of this arises at the expense of extinct (virtual) sexuality. (November 14, 1897; 280)

Whatever the initial poverty of this notion of repression, the only example of "intellectual processes" that Freud gives of it is the moral law or sense of decency. The scheme of elevation, the upward movement, everything that is marked by the prefix *super* (*über*) is here as decisive as the schema of purification, of the turning away from impurity, from the zones of the body that are malodorous and must not be

---

9. This argument should be linked with what Freud later says about Kant, the categorical imperative, the moral law within us, and the starry sky above us.

touched. The turning away is an upward movement. The high (and therefore the great) and the pure, are what repression produces as origin of morality, they are what *is better* absolutely, they are the origin of value and of the judgment of value. This is further defined in the *Outline of a Scientific Psychology* and later in other references to the categorical imperative, the starry sky above us and so on.

From the outset, therefore, Freud, like others, wanted to write a history of the law. He was following its traces and told Fliess his own history (his auto-analysis, as he put it), the history of the trail he followed in tracking the law. He smelled out the origin of law, and for that he had to smell out the sense of smell. He thus set in motion a great narrative, an interminable auto-analysis, in order to relate, to give an account of, the origin of the law, in other words the origin of what, by breaking away from its origin, interrupts the genealogical story. The law, intolerant of its own history, intervenes as an absolutely emergent order, absolute and detached from any origin. It appears as something that does not appear as such in the course of a history. At all events, it cannot be constituted by some history that might give rise to any story. If there were any history, it would be neither presentable nor relatable: the history of that which never took place.

Freud scented it, he had a nose for this sort of thing, he even had, as he says, a "presentiment." And he told Fliess of this, with whom an incredible story of noses was unfolding, lasting until the end of their friendship, which was marked by the sending of a last postcard of two lines.[10] Had we pursued this track, we should also have had to speak of the shape of the nose, which is pointed and prominent. This has given rise to all manner of discussion in psychoanalytic circles, but perhaps there has not been enough attention paid to the hairs which do not always hide themselves decently inside the nostrils, to the point where they sometimes have to be cut.

---

10. In 1897, Fliess published a work on the *Relations Between Nose and Female Genitals.* An ear, nose, and throat specialist, he greatly valued his speculations on the nose and bisexuality, on the analogy between nasal and genital mucous membranes as much in men as in women, and on the swelling of nasal mucous membranes and the rhythm of menstruation.

If, without taking into account any relation between Freud and Kafka, you now place yourself before "Before the Law," and before the doorkeeper (the *Türhüter*), and if, settling before him, like the man from the country, you observe him, what do you see? What feature captivates you to the point that you isolate and fixate upon it? Clearly the abundance of the hair, whether natural or artificial, around pointed shapes, and to begin with the nasal protuberance. All this is very black, and the nose comes to symbolize that genital zone which is represented in these dark colors even though it is not always somber. Given his situation, the man from the country does not know the law which is always the city's law, the law of cities and edifices protected by gates and boundaries, of spaces shut by doors. He is therefore astonished by the doorkeeper of the law, a man of the town, and he stares at him. "These are difficulties the countryman has not expected; the Law, he thinks, should surely be accessible at all times and to everyone, but as he now takes a closer [*genauer*] look at the doorkeeper in his fur coat [*in seinem Pelzmantel*] [the artificial hair, that of the town and the law, which will be added to the natural hairiness], with his big sharp nose and long, thin, black Tartar beard, he decides that it is better to wait [literally: *entschliesst er sich, doch lieber zu warten, bis er die Erlaubnis zum Eintritt bekommt*, he decides to prefer to wait] until he gets permission to enter."

The sequence scans neatly. Even if it looks as though there is a simple narrative and chronological juxtaposition, the contiguity and selection of details lead to a logical inference. The grammatical structure of the sentence implies the following: as soon as (*als*, at the moment when) the man from the country sees the doorkeeper with his big, pointed nose and his abundant black hair, he decides to wait, he judges that it is better to wait. It is at the sight of this hairy promontory, before this abundance of dark forest surrounding a headland, a nasal point or protuberance, that, through a strange and at the same time a completely natural consequence (we might say uncanny, *unheimlich*), the man makes a resolution, a decision. Does he decide to renounce entry after appearing determined to enter? Not in the least: he decides to put off deciding, he decides not to decide, he delays and adjourns while he waits. But waits for what? For "permission to enter," as it is written? But you will have noticed that such permission was refused him only in the form of an adjournment: "It's possible, but not now."

Let us be patient too. But don't go thinking that I am stressing this story to mislead you, or to make you wait in the anteroom of literature or fiction for a properly philosophic treatment of the question of law and the respect before it, or of the categorical imperative. Is not what holds us in check before the law, like the man from the country, also what paralyzes and detains us when confronted with a story: is it not its possibility and its impossibility, its readability and unreadability, its necessity and prohibition, and the questions of relation, of repetition and of history?

This seems at first sight to be due to the essentially inaccessible character of the law, to the fact that a "first sight" of it is always refused, as the doublet of the title and the incipit already suggest. In a certain way, Vor dem Gesetz is the story of this inaccessibility, of this inaccessibility to the story, the history of this impossible history, the map of this forbidden path: no itinerary, no method, no path to accede to the law, to what would happen there, to the topos of its occurrence. Such inaccessibility puzzles the man from the country, beginning with the moment he looks carefully at the doorkeeper, who is himself the observer, overseer, and sentry, the very figure of vigilance, or we might say of conscience. What the man from the country asks for is the way in: is not the law defined precisely in terms of its accessibility; is it not or must it not be so "at all times and to everyone"? This could give rise to the problem of exemplarity, particularly in Kant's notion of "respect": this is only the effect of the law, Kant emphasizes, it is due only to the law and appears to answer a summons only before the law, it addresses persons only insofar as they give the example of the fact that a law can be respected. Thus one never accedes directly either to the law or to persons, one is never immediately before any of these authorities; as for the detour, it may be infinite: the very universality of the law exceeds all finite boundaries and thus carries this risk. But let us leave it at that, for fear that we too might be diverted from our story.

The law, thinks the man from the country, should be accessible at all times and to everyone. It should be universal. By the same token, no one, we maintain in French, is supposed to be ignorant of the law,[11] that is to say, of positive law; provided s/he is not illiterate and can read the text or delegate this task and skill to a lawyer, to the representation of a man of law. Unless being able to read makes the law less accessible still. Reading a text might indeed reveal that it is untouchable, literally intangible, *precisely because it is readable,* and for the same reason unreadable to the extent to which the presence within it of a clear and graspable sense remains as hidden as its origin. Unreadability thus no longer opposes itself to readability. Perhaps man is the man from the country as long as he cannot read; or, if knowing how to read, he is still bound up in unreadability within that very thing which appears to yield itself to be read. He wants to see or touch the law, he wants to approach and "enter" it, because perhaps he does not know that the law is not to be seen or touched but deciphered. This is perhaps the first sign of the law's inaccessibility, or of the delay it imposes upon the man from the country. The gate is not shut, it is "open as usual" (says the text), but the law remains inaccessible; and if this forbids or bars the gate to genealogical history, it also fuels desire for the origin and genealogical drive, which wear themselves out as much before the process of the law's engenderment as before parental generation. Historical research leads the *relation* toward an impossible exhibition of a site and an event, of a taking-place where law originates as prohibition.

The law as prohibition: let us abandon this formula, suspend it for a while.

When Freud goes beyond his initial schema for the origin of morality and names the categorical imperative in Kant's sense, he does so within a seemingly historical framework. A story [*récit*] refers back to the unique historicity of an event, namely the murder of the primeval father, as clearly stated at the end of *Totem and Taboo* (1912):

> The earliest moral precepts and restrictions in primitive society have been explained by us as reactions to a deed which gave those who performed

11. TN *Nul n'est censé ignorer la loi;* in other words, "Ignorance of the law is no excuse."

it the concept of "crime." They felt remorse [but how and why, if this is *before* morality, *before* law? J.D.] for the deed and decided that it should never be repeated and that its performance should bring no advantage. This creative sense of guilt still persists among us. We find it operating in an asocial manner in neurotics, and producing new moral precepts and persistent restrictions, as an atonement for crimes that have been committed and as a precaution against the committing of new ones.[12]

Speaking of the totemic meal and "mankind's earliest festival" (203) to commemorate the murder of the father and the origin of morality, Freud emphasizes the sons' ambivalence toward the father; in a movement that I shall call, precisely, repentance, he himself appends a note. This note is important for me. It explains the excess of tenderness by the increase of horror conferred upon the crime by its total uselessness: "Not one of the sons had in fact been able to put his original wish— of taking his father's place—into effect" (204). The murder fails because the dead father holds even more power. Is not the best way of killing him to keep him alive (and finite)—and is not the best way of keeping him alive to murder him? Now, failure, Freud specifies, is conducive to moral reaction. Thus morality arises from a useless crime which in fact kills nobody, which comes too soon or too late and does not put an end to any power; in fact, it inaugurates nothing since repentance and morality had to be possible *before* the crime. Freud appears to cling to the reality of an event, but this event is a sort of non-event, an event of nothing or a quasi-event which both calls for and annuls a narrative account. For this "deed" or "misdeed" to be effective, it must be somehow spun from fiction. Everything happens *as if.* The guilt is none the less effective and painful for all that: "The dead father became stronger than the living one had been—for events took the course we so often see them follow in human affairs to this day" (204). Since the father dead is more powerful than he was when alive, since he lives better from his death and, very logically, he would have been dead while he was alive, more dead alive than *post mortem,*

12. TN *Totem and Taboo,* trans. James Strachey, in *The Origins of Religion,* Pelican Freud Library, vol. 13 (Harmondsworth: Penguin, 1985), 222. Further references are given in the text.

the murder of the father is not an event in the ordinary sense of the word. Nor is the origin of moral law. Nobody would have encountered it in its proper place of happening, nobody would have faced it in its taking place. Event without event, pure event where nothing happens, the eventiality of an event which both demands and annuls the relation in its fiction. Nothing new happens and yet this nothing new would instate the law, the two fundamental prohibitions of totemism, namely murder and incest. However, this pure and purely presumed event nevertheless marks an invisible rent in history. It resembles a fiction, a myth, or a fable, and its relation is so structured that all questions as to Freud's intentions are at once inevitable and pointless ("Did he believe in it or not? did he maintain that it came down to a real and historical murder?" and so on). The structure of this event is such that one is compelled neither to believe nor disbelieve it. Like the question of belief, that of the reality of its historical referent is, if not annulled, at least irremediably fissured. Demanding and denying the story, this quasi-event bears the mark of fictive narrativity (fiction *of* narration as well as fiction as narration: fictive narration as the simulacrum of narration and not only as the narration of an imaginary history). It is the origin of literature at the same time as the origin of law—like the dead father, a story told, a spreading rumor, without author or end, but an ineluctable and unforgettable story. Whether or not it is fantastic, whether or not it has arisen from the imagination, even the transcendental imagination, and whether it states or silences the origin of the fantasy, this in no way diminishes the imperious necessity of what it tells, its law. This law is even more frightening and fantastic, *unheimlich* or uncanny, than if it emanated from pure reason, unless precisely the latter be linked to an unconscious fantastic. As of 1897, let me repeat, Freud stated his "certain insight that there are no indications of reality in the unconscious, so that one cannot distinguish between truth and fiction that has been cathected with affect."

If the law is fantastic, if its original site and occurrence are endowed with the qualities of a fable, we can see that *das Gesetz* remains essentially inaccessible even when it, the law, presents or promises itself. In terms of a quest to reach the law, in order to stand before it, face to face and with respect, or to introduce oneself to it and into it, the story becomes the impossible story of the impossible. The story of prohibition is a prohibited story.

Did the man from the country wish to enter the law or merely the place where law is safeguarded? We cannot tell, and perhaps there is no genuine choice, since the law figures itself as a kind of place, a *topos* and a taking place. At all events, the man from the country, who is also a man existing *before the law*,[13] as nature exists before the city, does not want to stay before the law, in the situation of the doorkeeper. The latter also stands *before the law*. This may mean that he respects it: to stand or appear before the law is to submit to it and respect it, the more so as respect keeps one at a distance, *on the other side,* forbidding contact or penetration. But this could mean that, standing before the law, the doorkeeper enforces respect for it. In charge of surveillance, he does guard duty *before the law* by turning his back to it, without facing up to it, as it were, and thus not "in front" of it; he is a sentry guarding the entry to the edifice and holding at a respectful distance visitors who *present themselves* before the castle. The inscription "before the law" is therefore divided once more: according to its textual place, it was in a certain sense twofold already, as title or *incipit*. It further redoubles itself in what it says or describes: namely, a division of territory and an absolute opposition in the situation with regard to the law. The two characters in the story, the doorkeeper and the man from the country, are both before the law, but since in order to speak they face each other, their position "before the law" is an opposition. One of them, the doorkeeper, turns his back on the law and yet stands before it (*Vor dem Gesetz steht ein Türhüter*). The man from the country, on the other hand, is also before the law but in a contrary position, insofar as one can suppose that, being ready to enter, he faces it. The two protagonists are both attendant before the law but in opposition to one another, being on either side of a line of inversion whose mark in the text is precisely the separation of the title from the narrative body. The double inscription of "*Vor dem Gesetz*" flanks an

13. TN The French is *un homme d'avant la loi*. The double meaning of "before" (and *vor* in German)—spatial and temporal—does not occur in French; *devant* refers exclusively to a spatial relationship, and *avant* is used for time.

invisible line that divides, separates and of itself renders divisible a unique expression. It splits the line.

This can happen only with the rise of an entitling authority, in its topical and juridical function. That explains my interest in the story entitled in this way rather than in an all but identical passage in *The Trial* that appears of course without a title. In German as in French and English, the expression "before the law" commonly describes the position of a subject who respectfully and submissively comes before the representatives or guardians of the law. S/he presents himself or herself before representatives: the law in person, so to speak, is never present, even though the expression "before the law" seems to signify "in the presence of the law." The man is therefore in front of the law without ever facing it; while he may be in front of it, he thus never confronts it. The first words of the incipit are snatched up by a sentence whose interrupted version might be the title (*"Vor dem Gesetz," "Vor dem Gesetz steht ein Türhüter"*); these words come to signify something else entirely, perhaps even the opposite of the title that nevertheless reproduces them, just as often some poems receive as their title the beginning of a first line. I repeat here that the structure and function of the two occurrences, of the two events of the same mark, are certainly heterogeneous, but as these two different yet identical events are not linked in narrative sequence or logical consequence, we cannot say that one *precedes* the other in any order. Both come first in their order, and neither of the two homonyms or perhaps synonyms cites the other. The entitling event confers upon the text its law and its name, but this is a *coup de force,* for example with respect to *The Trial,* from which the story is torn to become another institution. Without rehearsing the narrative sequence, the event opens a scene, giving rise to a topographical system of law that prescribes the two inverse and adverse positions, the antagonisms of two characters equally concerned with it. The entitling sentence describes the one who turns his back to the law (to turn one's back also means to ignore, neglect, or even transgress)—not in order that the law present itself or that one be present to it but, on the contrary, in order to prohibit all presentation. The other, who faces the law, sees no more than the one who turns his back to it. Neither is in the presence of the law. The only two characters in the story are blind and separated from one another, and from the law. Such is the modality of this rapport, of this relation, of this narration: blindness and separation, a kind of non-rapport. For we must not forget that the doorkeeper too is separated from the law by other doorkeepers "each more powerful than the last" (*einer mächtiger als der andere*): "But take note: I am powerful. And I am only the least of the doorkeepers [the lowest in the hierarchy, *der unterste*]. From hall to hall there is one doorkeeper after another, each more powerful than the last. The third doorkeeper is already so terrible that even I cannot bear to look at him" (*den Anblick . . . ertragen*). The lowest of doorkeepers is the first to see the man from the country. The first in the order of the narration is the last in the order of the law and in the hierarchy of its representatives. And this first-last doorkeeper never sees the law: he cannot even bear the sight of the doorkeepers who are *before* him, prior to and above him. This is inscribed in his title of doorkeeper. He is in full view, observed even by the man who, *in his view*, decides not to decide or judges that he does not have to stop his judging. I use "man" here for the man from the country, as sometimes in the story which suggests that the doorkeeper is perhaps no longer just a man, and that the "man" is both Man and anybody, the anonymous subject of the law. The latter thus decides that he would "rather wait," at the very moment when his attention is caught by the pilosity and the pointed nose of the doorkeeper. His resolution of nonresolution brings the story into being and sustains it. Yet permission had never been denied him: it had merely been delayed, adjourned, deferred.[14] It is all a question of time, and it is the time of the story; however, time itself does not appear until this adjournment of the presentation, until the law of delay or the advance of the law, according to the anachrony of the relation.

The present prohibition of the law is not a prohibition in the sense

---

14. EN Compare the following fragment from Kafka's notebooks: "I ran past the first watchman. Then I was horrified, ran back again and said to the watchman: 'I ran through here while you were looking the other way.' The watchman gazed ahead of him and said nothing. 'I suppose I really oughtn't to have done it,' I said. The watchman still said nothing. 'Does your silence indicate permission to pass?'..." (*Wedding Preparations in the Country and Other Posthumous Prose Writings*, trans. Ernst Kaiser and Eithne Wilkins [London: Secker & Warburg, 1954], 354–55).

of an imperative constraint; it is a *différance*.[15] For after having said to him "later," the doorkeeper specifies: "If you are so drawn to it, just try to go in despite my veto." Earlier he had said merely "not at the moment." He then simply steps aside and lets the man stoop to look inside through the door, which always remains open, marking a limit without itself posing an obstacle or barrier. It is a mark, but it is nothing firm, opaque, or uncrossable. It lets the inside (*das Innere*) come into view—not the law itself, perhaps, but interior spaces that appear empty and provisionally forbidden. The door is physically open, the doorkeeper does not bar the way by force. It is his discourse, rather, that operates at the limit, not to prohibit directly, but to interrupt and defer the passage, to withhold the pass. The man has the natural, physical freedom to penetrate spaces, if not the law. We are therefore compelled to admit that he must forbid himself from entering. He must force himself, give himself an order, not to obey the law but rather to *not gain access*[16] to the law, which in fact tells him or lets him know: do not come to me. I order you not to come yet to me. It is there and in this that I am law and that you will accede to my demand, without gaining access to me.

For the law is prohibition/prohibited [*interdit*]. Noun and attribute. Such would be the terrifying double-bind of its own taking-place. It is prohibition: this does not mean that it prohibits, but that it is itself prohibited, a prohibited place. It forbids itself and contradicts itself by placing the man in its own contradiction:[17] one cannot reach the law, and in order to have a *rapport* of respect with it, *one must not*[18] have

---

15. EN See ". . . That Dangerous Supplement . . .," note 4, above.

16. TN The French *accéder à* means both "accede to" and "gain access to."

17. This contradiction probably is not simply that of a law, which in itself supposes and therefore produces transgression, the active or actual relationship to sin, to the fault. *Before the Law* perhaps gives rise to, in a kind of movement or trembling between the Old and the New Testament, a text which is both archived and altered, such as the Epistle to the Romans 7. More time needs to be devoted to the relationship between these two texts. Paul reminds his brothers, "people who know the law," that "the law exercises its power over man as long as he lives." And the death of Christ would be the death of this old law by which we "know" sin: dead along with Christ, we are released, absolved from this law, we are dead to this law, to the great age of its "letter," in any case, and we serve it in a new "spirit." And Paul adds that when he was without law, he lived; and when, along with the law, the commandment came, he died.

18. TN The original is *il faut ne pas, il ne faut pas*, literally, "*it must be that one does not, it must not be that one does.*"

a rapport with the law, *one must interrupt the relation.* One must *enter into relation* only with the law's representatives, its examples, its guardians. And these are interrupters as well as messengers. We must remain ignorant of who or what or where the law is, we must not know who it is or what it is, where and how it presents itself, whence it comes and whence it speaks. This is what *must* be before the *must* of the law. [*Voilà ce qu'*il faut *au* il faut *de la loi*]. *Ci falt,* as used to be written in the Middle Ages at the end of a story.[19]

This, then, is the trial and judgment, the process and the *Urteil,* the originary division of the law. The law is prohibited. But this contradictory self-prohibition allows man the freedom of self-determination, even though this freedom cancels itself through the self-prohibition of entering the law. Before the law, the man is a subject of the law in appearing before it. This is obvious, but since he is *before* it because he cannot enter it, he is also *outside the law* (an outlaw). He is neither under the law nor in the law. He is both a subject of the law and an outlaw. Since he stoops to view the inside, we are led to suppose that, for the time being, he is taller than the open door—and this question of size will have to be dealt with. On observing the doorkeeper more carefully, he decides to await a permission simultaneously given and deferred, although the first doorkeeper's hint suggests that the delay will be indefinite. After the first guardian there are an undefined number of others, perhaps they are innumerable, and progressively more powerful and therefore more prohibitive, endowed with greater power of delay. Their potency is *différance,* an interminable *différance,* since it lasts for days and "years," indeed, up to the end of (the) man. *Différance* till death, and for death, without end because ended. As the doorkeeper represents it, the discourse of the law does not say "no" but "not yet," indefinitely. That is why the story is both perfectly ended and yet brutally, one could say primally, cut short, interrupted.

19. *Ci falt:* this terminal sign, by which the medieval writer marks the end of his work before giving its title or his own name, rightly does not occur in the *Story of the Grail,* the unfinished romance by Chrétien de Troyes. Derived from Latin *fallere,* giving *faillir* ("to fall" and "to deceive") and *falloir* ("to lack"), the verb *falt* (or *faut*), in the Old French formula *ci falt,* takes the meaning of "here ends" without losing the idea of "lack" and "failure." "Thus the work ends at the point where it begins to be lacking" (Dragonetti, *op. cit.,* 9). Dragonetti's thesis in this book is that "the *Story of the Grail* was quite complete" (ibid).

What is delayed is not this or that experience, the access to some enjoyment or to some supreme good, the possession or penetration of something or somebody. What is deferred forever till death is entry into the law itself, which is nothing other than that which dictates the delay. The law prohibits by interfering with and deferring the "ference" ["*férance*"], the reference, the rapport, the relation. What *must not* and cannot be approached is the origin of *différance:* it must not be presented or represented and above all not penetrated. That is the law of the law, the process of a law of whose subject we can never say, "There it is," it is here or there. It is neither natural nor institutional; one can never reach it, and it never reaches the depths of its original and proper taking-place. It is even more "sophisticated," so to speak, than the convention of conventionalism which is conventionally attributed to the sophists. It is always cryptic; that is, it is a secret which a caste—for example, the nobility of which Kafka speaks in *Zur Frage der Gesetze*[20]—pretends to possess by delegation. The secret is nothing—and this is the secret that has to be kept well, nothing either present or presentable, but this nothing must be well kept. To this task of keeping, the nobility is delegated. The nobility is nothing but this, and, as *The Problem of Our Laws* suggests, the people would be taking many risks in depriving themselves of it. They would understand nothing of the essence of the law. If the nobility is necessary, it is because this essence has no essence, it can neither be nor be there. It is both obscene and unpresentable—and the nobles must be left to take charge of it. One has to be a noble for this. Unless one is God.

In fact, here is a situation where it is never a question of trial or judgment, nor of verdict or sentence, which is all the more terrifying. There is some law, some law which *is not there but which exists.* The judgment, however, does not arrive. In this other sense, the man of nature is not only a subject of the law outside the law, he is also, in both an infinite and a finite way, the prejudged; not so much as a

---

20. EN *The Problem of Our Laws* (*The Great Wall of China: Stories and Reflections*, trans. Willa and Edwin Muir [New York: Schocken Books, 1946], 254–57) is a short parable describing a class-divided society in which the laws are completely unknown to the people, giving rise to two schools of thought: that the ancient laws are scrupulously, though secretly, administered by the nobles, and that there is no law, except what the nobles do.

prejudged subject but as a subject before a judgment which is always in preparation and always being deferred. Prejudged as having to be judged, arriving in advance of the law which only signifies "later."

And if this concerns the essence of the law, it is that the latter has no essence. It eludes this essence of being which would be presence. Its "truth" is this non-truth which Heidegger calls the truth of truth. As such, as truth without truth, it *guards itself*, it guards itself without doing so, guarded by a doorkeeper who guards nothing, the door remaining open—and open on nothing. Like truth, the law would be the guarding itself (*Wahrheit*), only the guarding. And this singular look between the guardian and the man.

But, beyond a look, beyond beings (the law is nothing that is present), the law calls in silence. Even before moral conscience as such, it forces an answer, it calls for responsibility and guarding. It puts into motion both the guardian and the man, this odd couple, attracting them to it and stopping them before it. It determines the being-for-death before it. Another minute displacement and the guardian of the law (*Hüter*) would resemble the shepherd of Being (*Hirt*). I believe in the need for this "*rapprochement*," as we say, but under the proximity, or perhaps the metonymy (law, another name for Being, Being, another name for law; in both cases, the "transcendent," as Heidegger says of Being), there is perhaps still hidden or guarded the abyss of a difference.

The story (of what never happens) does not tell us what kind of law manifests itself in its non-manifestation: natural, moral, judicial, political? As to gender, the German is neuter, *das Gesetz*, neither feminine nor masculine. In French, the feminine determines a semantic contagion that we cannot forget,[21] any more than we can ignore language as the elementary medium of the law. In Maurice Blanchot's *The Madness of the Day*, we can speak of an apparition of the Law, and it is a feminine "silhouette," neither a man nor a woman, but a feminine silhouette come as companion to the quasi-narrator of a forbidden or impossible narration (that is the whole story of this non-story).[22] The narrative "I" frightens the Law. It is the Law who seems to be afraid

21. TN "The Law" is *la loi* and *elle* throughout; the English translation necessarily elides this submerged potential for genderization.
22. EN See "The Law of Genre" below.

and to beat a retreat. As for the narrator, in another analogy without rapport to *Before the Law,* he recounts his appearance before the law's representatives (policemen, judges, doctors), men who demanded from him an account which he could not give, although it is the very one he puts forward in order to relate the impossible.

Here, we know neither *who* nor *what* is the law, *das Gesetz.* This, perhaps, is where literature begins. A text of philosophy, science, or history, a text of knowledge or information, would not abandon a name to a state of not-knowing, or at least it would do so only by accident and not in an essential or constitutive way. Here one does not know the law, one has no cognitive rapport with it; it is neither a subject nor an object *before* which one could take a position. Nothing holds before the law. It is not a woman or a feminine figure, even if man—*homo* and *vir*—wants to enter or penetrate it (that, precisely, is its trap). Nor yet is the law a man; it is neutral, beyond sexual and grammatical gender, and remains thus indifferent, impassive, little concerned to answer *yes* or *no.* It lets the man freely determine himself, it lets him wait, it abandons him. It is neuter, neither feminine nor masculine, indifferent because we do not know whether it is a (respectable) person or a thing, who or what. The law is produced (without showing itself, thus without producing itself) in the space of this non-knowledge. The doorkeeper watches over this theater of the invisible, and the man wishes to look in *by stooping.* Is the law then low, lower than he, or does he respectfully bow before what the author of *The Madness of the Day* calls the "knee" of the Law? Unless indeed the law is lying down, or as we say of justice and its representatives, "seated." The law then would not stand up, which is perhaps again why it would be difficult to place oneself *before* it. In fact, the whole scenography of the story would be a drama of standing and sitting. At the beginning, at the origin of the story, the doorkeeper and the man are up, standing, and face to face. At the end of the text, at the interminable but interrupted end of the story and of history, at the end of man, the end of this man's life, the doorkeeper is much taller than his interlocutor and has to bend down in his turn from an *overhanging* height; and the story of the law marks the looming dominance or difference in height (*Grössenunterschied*), which gradually alters itself to the man's disadvantage and seems to measure the time of the story. In the interval, in mid-text, which is also the middle of the man's life after he decides to wait, the doorkeeper gives him a footstool and makes him sit down. The man stays there, "sitting for days and years," all his life. In the end, he sinks back into childhood, as we say. The difference in height may also point to the relationship between generations. The child dies old like a small child (on four, two, and finally three legs—and take into account the footstool) before a doorkeeper who grows, standing and over-seeing.

The law is silent, and of it nothing is said to us. Nothing, only its name, its common name and nothing else. In German it is capitalized, like a proper name. We do not know what it is, who it is, where it is. Is it a thing, a person, a discourse, a voice, a document, or simply a nothing that incessantly defers access to itself, thus forbidding *itself* in order thereby to become something or someone?

The elderly child finally becomes almost blind but hardly knows it: "He does not know whether the world is really darker or whether his eyes are only deceiving him. Yet in his darkness he is now aware of a radiance that streams inextinguishably from the gateway of the Law." This is the most religious moment of the writing.

There is an analogy with Judaic law here. Hegel narrates a story about Pompey, interpreting it in his own way. Curious to know what was behind the doors of the tabernacle that housed the holy of holies, the triumvir approached the innermost part of the Temple, the center (*Mittelpunkt*) of worship. There, says Hegel, he sought "a being, an essence offered to his meditation, something meaningful (*sinnvolles*) to command his respect; and when he thought he was entering into the secret (*Geheimnis*), before the ultimate spectacle, he felt mystified, disappointed, deceived (*getauscht*). He found what he sought in 'an empty space' and concluded from this that the genuine secret was itself entirely extraneous to them, the Jews; it was unseen and unfelt (*ungesehen und ungefühlt*)."

Guardian after guardian. This differantial topology [*topique différantielle*] adjourns, guardian after guardian, within the polarity of high and low, far and near (*fort/da*), now and later. The same topology without its own place, the same atopology [*atopique*], the same madness defers the law as the nothing that forbids itself and the neuter that annuls oppositions. The atopology annuls that which takes place, the event itself. This nullification gives birth to the law, before as before and before as behind. That is why there is and is not place for a story. The differantial atopology pushes the repetition of the story *before the law*. It confers on it that which it takes away, its title of story. This applies both to the text signed by Kafka and entitled *Before the Law* and to the passage of *The Trial* that seems to recount almost the same story, condensing the whole of *The Trial* in the scene of *Before the Law*.

It would be tempting, beyond the limits of this reading, to reconstitute this story without story within the elliptic envelope of Kant's *Critique of Practical Reason* or Freud's *Totem and Taboo*, but however far we might go in this direction, we could never explain the parable of a relation called "literary" with the help of semantic contents originating in philosophy or psychoanalysis, or drawing on some other source of knowledge. We have seen why this must be so: the fictitious nature of this ultimate story which robs us of every event, of this pure story, or story without story, has as much to do with philosophy, science, or psychoanalysis as with literature.

I conclude. These are the doorkeeper's last words: "I am now going to shut it," I close the door, I conclude (*Ich gehe jetzt und schliesse ihn*).

In the terms of a certain medical code, the expression *ante portas* refers to the place of premature ejaculation, of which Freud claims to have given the clinical description, the symptomatology and the aetiology. In the text or before the text entitled *Vor dem Gesetz* (*vor* being the preposition inscribed, *in the first place,* in the title set in place "before the law"), what happens or does not happen, its place and non-place *ante portas*, is this not precisely the hymen with the law, the entry (*Eintritt*) into the law? The adjournment until the death of the elderly child, the *little old man,* can be interpreted as non-penetration by premature ejaculation or by non-ejaculation. The result, namely, the judgment and conclusion, is the same. The tabernacle remains empty and dissemination fatal. Relation to the law remains interrupted, a without-relation that one should not attempt to grasp too precipitously in terms of the sexual or genital paradigm of *coitus interruptus,* of impotence and the neuroses that Freud deciphers in it. Is this not the place [*n'y a-t-il pas lieu*] to question what we calmly call sexual relations in the context of the storyless story of the law? One can be quite sure that the so-called normal pleasures [*jouissances*] would not escape this enquiry.

N'y a-t-il pas lieu, I said in French, in a barely translatable way. This implied: "it must" be questioned. The French idiom that established law here also pronounces the law: *il y a lieu de* means *il faut*, "it is prescribed, opportune, or necessary to . . . " It is commanded by law.

Is this not in fact what the doorkeeper says? Is it not "there is place for you here . . ." ["*il y a lieu pour toi, ici*"]. There is a place for you? For what, we do not know, but there is a place. You must. *Il y a lieu*. The doorkeeper is not *ante portas* but *ante portam*. Prohibiting nothing, he does not guard the doors but the door. And he insists upon the uniqueness of this singular door. The law is neither manifold nor, as some believe, a universal generality. It is always an idiom, and this is the sophistication of Kant's thought. Its door concerns only you, *dich*, *toi*—a door that is unique and specifically destined and determined for you (*nur für dich bestimmt*). At the moment when the man comes to his end, just before his death, the doorkeeper points out to him that he will not reach his destination, or that it will not reach him. The man comes to his end without reaching his end. The entrance is destined for and awaits him alone; he arrives there but cannot arrive at entering; he cannot arrive at arriving.[23] Thus runs the account of an event which arrives *at* not arriving, which manages not to happen. The doorkeeper, recognizing that the man is near the end, shouts out to reach his failing ear: "No one else could ever be admitted here, since this gate was made only for you. I am now going to shut it."

And this is the final word, the conclusion or closure of the story.

The text would be the door, the entrance (*Eingang*), what the doorkeeper has just closed. And to conclude, I shall start from this judgment,[24] with this conclusion of the doorkeeper. As he closes the object, he closes the text. Which, however, closes on nothing. The story *Before*

---

23. TN *Arriver à* can mean "to arrive at," "to achieve," "to succeed in," "to happen to."

24. TN In the original, *je partirai de cette sentence (arrêt ou jugement)*: *sentence* means "verdict" or "maxim"; *arrêt* means "halt" or "legal judgment."

the Law does not tell or describe anything but itself as text. It does only this or does also this. Not within an assured specular reflection of some self-referential transparency—and I must stress this point— but in the unreadability of the text, if one understands by this the impossibility of acceding to its proper significance and its possibly inconsistent content, which it jealously keeps back. The text guards itself, maintains itself—like the law, speaking only of itself, that is to say, of its non-identity with itself. It neither arrives nor lets anyone arrive. It is the law, makes the law and leaves the reader before the law.

To be precise. We are *before* this text that, saying nothing definite and presenting no identifiable content beyond the story itself, except for an endless *différance*, till death, nonetheless remains strictly intangible. Intangible: by this I understand inaccessible to contact, impregnable, and ultimately ungraspable, incomprehensible—but also that which we have not the *right* to touch. This is an "original" text, as we say; it is forbidden or illicit to change or disfigure it, or to touch its form. Despite the non-identity in itself of its sense or destination, despite its essential unreadability, its "form" presents and performs itself as a kind of personal identity entitled to absolute respect. If someone were to change one word or alter a single sentence, a judge could always declare him or her to have infringed upon, violated, or disfigured the text. A bad translation will always be summoned to stand before the original, which supposedly acts as a *point of reference*, being authorized by its author or his or her legal representatives and identified by its title, which according to civil status is its proper name, and framed between its first and last word. Anyone impairing the original identity of this text may have to appear before the law. This may happen to any reader in the presence of the text, to critic, publisher, translator, heirs, or professors. All these are then at the same time doorkeepers and men from the country. On both sides of the frontier.

The title and the initial words, I said; these are "Before the Law," precisely, and again, "Before the law." The last words are "I am now going to shut it." This "I" of the doorkeeper is also that of the text or of the law, announcing the identity with itself of a bequeathed corpus, of a heritage that pronounces non-identity with itself. Neither identity nor non-identity is natural, but rather the effect of a juridical performative. This (and it is no doubt what we call the writing, the act and signature of the "writer") *poses before* us, preposes or proposes a text that lays down the law, and in the first place with respect to itself. In its very act, the text produces and pronounces the law that protects it and renders it intangible. It does and says, saying what it does by doing what it says. This possibility is implicit in any text, even if it does not take as obviously a self-referential form as in this case. At once allegorical and tautological, Kafka's story operates across the naively referential framework of its narration which leads us past a portal that it comports, an internal boundary opening on nothing, before nothing, the object of no possible experience.

Devant la loi, dit le titre. *Vor dem Gesetz,* the title says.

Devant la loi, dit le titre. *Vor dem Gesetz,* says the title.[25]

The text bears its title and bears upon it. Would not its proper object, if it had one, be the effect produced by the play of the title? To show and to veil in an ellipsis the powerful operation of the given title?

The door furthermore severs the title from itself. It is interposed between the expression "Before the Law" as title or proper name and the same expression as incipit, and thus splits the origin. As we saw, the incipit belongs to the text and has neither the same value nor the same referent as the title, but *qua* incipit its relationship to the body of the text is unique. It marks the boundary that guarantees the identity of the corpus. Between the two events of "Before the Law," within the repetition itself, there passes a line separating two boundaries. It splits the boundary by dividing its line. The homonymy remains impassive, however, as if nothing had happened. It is as if nothing had come to pass.

I conclude. Here I interrupt this type of analysis, which could be carried to much greater length, and return to my initial question.

What would allow us to judge that this text belongs to "literature"; and, anyway, what is literature? No answer will be forthcoming, I fear; does not the question once more betray the rustic simplicity of a man

25. TN These two lines are reproduced unchanged from the original.

from the country? That in itself would not be enough to disqualify it, for (the) man's reason imperturbably claims its rights; it is indefatigable at any age.

If we subtract from this text all the elements which could belong to another register (everyday information, history, knowledge, philosophy, fiction, and so forth—anything that is not necessarily affiliated with literature), we vaguely feel that what is *at work* in this text retains an essential rapport with the play of framing and the paradoxical logic of boundaries, which introduces a kind of perturbation in the "normal" system of reference, while simultaneously *revealing* an essential structure of referentiality. It is an obscure revelation of referentiality which does not make reference, which does not refer, any more than the eventness of the event is itself an event.

That this nevertheless makes up a work is perhaps a gesture toward literature. An insufficient gesture, perhaps, but a necessary one: there is no literature without a work, without an absolutely singular performance, and this necessary irreplaceability again recalls what the man from the country asks when the singular crosses the universal, when the categorical engages the idiomatic, as a literature always must. The man from the country had difficulty in grasping that an entrance was singular or unique when it should have been universal, as in truth it was. He had difficulty with literature.

How can we check the subtraction just mentioned? *The Trial* itself proposes a counterproof. We find there the same *content* differently framed, with a different system of boundaries and above all without a proper title, except that of a volume of several hundred pages. From the point of view of literature, the same content gives rise to an entirely different work. What differs from one work to the other is not the *content,* nor is it the *form* (the signifying expression, the phenomena of language or rhetoric). It is the movements of framing and referentiality.

These two works become, along the lines of their strange filiation, a metonymic interpretation of each other, each becoming a part that is absolutely independent of the other and each time greater than the whole; the title of the other. This is not yet enough. If framing, title, and referential structure are necessary for the literary work as such to emerge, these conditions of possibility still remain too general and hold for other texts to which we would hardly ascribe literary value. These possibilities give the text the power to *make the law,* beginning with its own. However, this is on condition that the text itself can appear *before the law* of another, more powerful text protected by more powerful guardians. Indeed, the text (for example the so-called "literary" text and particularly this story by Kafka) before which we the readers appear as before the law, this text protected by its guardians (author, publisher, critics, academics, archivists, librarians, lawyers, and so on) cannot establish law unless a more powerful system of laws ("a more powerful guardian") guarantees it, in particular the set of laws and social conventions that legitimates all these things.

If Kafka's text says all this about literature, the powerful ellipsis it gives us does not entirely belong to literature. The place from which it tells us *about* the laws of literature, the law without which no literary specificity would take shape or substance, this place cannot be simply *interior* to literature.

It is necessary to think [*il y a lieu de penser*] *together,* no doubt, a certain historicity of law and a certain historicity of literature. If I speak of "literature" rather than of poetry or belles-lettres, it is to emphasize the hypothesis that the relatively modern specificity of literature as such retains a close and essential rapport to a period in legal history. In a different culture, or in Europe at a different period of the history of positive law, of explicit or implied legislation on the ownership of works, for example in the Middle Ages or earlier, the identity of this text, its play with the title, with signatures, and with its boundaries or those of other texts, this whole framing system would function differently and under different conventional guarantees. Not that during the Middle Ages it would have been without institutional protection and supervision.[26] But that protection had quite a different way of regulating the identity of works, which were more readily delivered to the transformative initiatives of copyists or other "guardians," to the graftings practiced by inheritors or other "authors" (whether anonymous or not, whether masked by pseudonyms or not, or whether more-

26. Dragonetti, *op. cit.,* 52ff. Cf. also the works of Ernst Kantorowicz, especially his article "Sovereignty of the Artist," republished in *Selected Studies* (Locust Valley, N.Y.: J. J. Augustin, 1965).

or-less identifiable individuals or groups). But, whatever the structure of the juridical and therefore political institution that protects the work, the latter always is and remains *before the law*. Only under the conditions of law does the work have an existence and a substance, and it becomes "literature" only at a certain period of the law that regulates problems involving property rights over works, the identity of corpora, the value of signatures, the difference between creating, producing, and reproducing, and so on. Roughly speaking, this law became established between the late seventeenth and early nineteenth centuries in Europe. Still, the concept of literature that upholds this law remains vague. The positive laws here referred to pertain to other arts as well and shed no critical light on their own conceptual presuppositions. What matters here is that these obscure presuppositions are also the lot of "guardians," critics, academics, literary theorists, writers, and philosophers. They all have to appeal to a law and appear before it, at once to watch over it and be watched by it. They all interrogate it naively on the singular and the universal, and none receives an answer that does not involve *différance:* (no) more law and (no) more literature [*plus de loi et plus de littérature*].

In this sense, Kafka's text tells us perhaps of the being-before-the-law of any text. It does so by ellipsis, at once advancing and retracting it. It belongs not only to the literature of a given period, inasmuch as it is itself before the law (which it articulates), before a certain type of law. The text also points obliquely to literature, speaking of itself as a literary effect—and thereby exceeding the literature of which it speaks.

But is it not necessary for all literature to exceed literature? [*Mais n'y a-t-il pas lieu, pour toute littérature, de déborder la littérature?*] What would be a literature that would be only what it is, literature? It would no longer be itself if it were itself. This is also part of the ellipsis of "Before the Law." Surely one could not speak of "literariness" as a *belonging to* literature, as of the inclusion of a phenomenon or object, even a work, within a field, a domain, a region whose frontiers would be pure and whose titles indivisible. The work, the opus, does not belong to the field, it is the transformer of the field.

Perhaps literature has come to occupy, under historical conditions that are not merely linguistic, a position that is always open to a kind of subversive juridicity. It would have occupied this place for some time, without itself being wholly subversive, indeed often the contrary. This subversive juridicity requires that self-identity never be assured, nor reassuring; and it supposes also a power to produce performatively the statements of the law, of the law that literature can be, and not just of the law to which literature submits. Thus literature itself makes law, emerging in that place where the law is made. Therefore, under certain determined conditions, it can exercise the legislative power of linguistic performativity to sidestep existing laws from which, however, it derives protection and receives its conditions of emergence. This is owing to the referential equivocation of certain linguistic structures. Under these conditions literature can *play the law,*[27] repeating it while diverting or circumventing it. These conditions, which are also the conventional conditions of any performative, are doubtless not purely linguistic, although any convention can give rise in its turn to a definition or contract of a linguistic nature. We touch here on one of the most difficult points of this whole problematic: when we must recover language without language, language beyond language, this interplay of forces which are mute but already haunted by writing, where the conditions of a performative are established, as are the rules of the game and the limits of subversion.

In the fleeting moment when it plays the law, a literature passes literature. It is on both sides of the line that separates law from the outlaw, it splits the being-before-the-law, it is at once, like the man from the country, "before the law" and "prior to the law" ["*devant la loi*" et "*avant la loi*"]. Prior to the being-before-the-law which is also that of the doorkeeper. But within so unlikely a site, would it have taken place? Would it have been appropriate to [*y aura-t-il lieu de*] name literature?

This has hardly been a scene of categorical reading. I have ventured glosses, multiplied interpretations, asked and diverted questions, abandoned decipherings in mid-course, left enigmas intact; I have accused, acquitted, defended, praised, subpoenaed. This scene of reading seemed

---

27. TN *Jouer la loi* implies both "playing at being the law" and "deceiving the law" as well as "playing the law."

to be concentrated around an insular story. However, besides all the metonymical hand-to-hand engagements which it could have had with *The Problem of Our Laws* or with Paul's Epistle to the Romans 7, this exegetical dramatization is perhaps, and primarily, a piece or a moment, a fragment of *The Trial*. The latter would therefore have already set up a *mise-en-abyme* of everything you have just heard, unless *Before the Law* does the same thing through a more powerful ellipsis which itself would engulf *The Trial,* and us along with it. Chronology is of little relevance here, even if, as we know, it is only *Before the Law* that Kafka will have published, under this title, during his lifetime. The structural possibility of this *contre-abyme* opens a challenge to this order.

In *The Trial* (chap. 9, "In the Cathedral"), the text which forms the whole of *Before the Law,* with, naturally, the exception of the title, is related *in quotation marks* by a priest. This priest is not only a narrator, he is someone who cites or who tells a story. He cites a work which does not belong to the text of the law in the Scriptures, but, he says, to " 'the writings which preface the Law' ": " 'You are deluding yourself about the Court,' said the priest [to K.]. 'In the writings which preface the Law that particular delusion is described thus: before the Law stands . . . ,' " etc.[28] This entire chapter is a prodigious scene of Talmudic exegesis, concerning *Before the Law,* between the priest and K. It would take hours to study the grain of it, its ins and outs. The general law of this scene is that the text (the short story in quotation marks, *Before the Law,* if you like), which seems to be the object of the hermeneutical dialogue between the priest and K., is also the program, down to its very detail, of the exegetical altercation to which it gives rise; the priest and K. being in turn the doorkeeper and the man from the country, exchanging their place before the law, miming one another, going toward one another. Not a single detail is missing, and we could verify this, if you wished, in the course of another session of patient reading. I don't want to keep you here until the end of the day or of your days, even though you are seated and seated not at the door

28. TN *The Penguin Complete Novels of Franz Kafka,* trans. Willa and Edwin Muir (Harmondsworth: Penguin Books, 1983), 161. All further references will be to this edition.

but in the castle itself. I shall simply cite a few places in the chapter to conclude, a little like the white pebbles which one drops on a path, or those on the tomb of the rabbi Loew which I saw again at Prague a few months ago, just before an arrest and an investigation without trial during which the representatives of the law asked me, among other things, whether the philosopher whom I was going to visit was a "Kafkologue" (I had said that I had come to Prague *also* to follow the tracks of Kafka); my officially appointed lawyer had told me: "You must feel that you are living a story by Kafka"; and upon leaving me: "Don't take this too tragically, live it as a literary experience." And when I said that I had never seen the drugs that were supposed to have been discovered in my suitcase before the customs officers themselves saw them, the prosecutor replied: "That's what all drug traffickers say."

Here, then, are the little white pebbles. It is a question of prejudgment and prejudice.

"But I am not guilty," said K.; "it's a misunderstanding. And if it comes to that, how can any man be called guilty? We are all simply men here, one as much as the other." "That is true," said the priest, "but that's how all guilty men talk." "Are you prejudiced against me too?" asked K. "I have no prejudices against you," said the priest. "I thank you," said K.; "but all the others who are concerned in these proceedings are prejudiced against me. They are influencing even outsiders. My position is becoming more and more difficult." "You are misinterpreting the facts of the case," said the priest. "The verdict is not so suddenly arrived at, the proceedings only gradually merge into the verdict." (159–60)

After the priest has told K. the story without a title—the story of "before the law" taken from the works which *precede* the law, K. concludes that "the doorkeeper deluded the man." To which the priest—to a certain extent identifying himself with the doorkeeper—takes up a defense of the latter during a long lesson in Talmudic style which begins, "You have not enough respect for the written word and you are altering the story . . . " During this lesson, among other things particularly destined to read *Before the Law* in its very unreadability, he warns, "The commentators note in this connection: 'The right perception of any matter and a misunderstanding of the same matter do not wholly exclude each other' " (164).

The second stage: he convinces K., who then identifies himself with the doorkeeper and justifies him. Immediately the priest reverses the interpretation and changes the places of identification:

"You have studied the story more exactly and for a longer time than I have," said K. They were both silent for a little while. Then K. said: "So you think the man was not deluded?" "Don't misunderstand me," said the priest, "I am only showing you the various opinions concerning that point. You must not pay too much attention to them. The scriptures are unalterable and the comments often enough merely express the commentator's bewilderment. In this case there even exists an interpretation which claims that the deluded person is really the doorkeeper." "That's a far-fetched interpretation," said K. "On what is it based?" (164)

So we get a second exegetico-Talmudic wave from the priest, who is both, in some way, an abbot and a rabbi, a kind of Saint Paul, the Paul of the Epistle to the Romans who speaks according to the law, of the law and against the law, "whose letter has aged"; he is also the one who says that "apart from the law sin lies dead": "I was once alive apart from the law, but when the commandment came, sin revived and I died . . . " (Romans 7).

" '[This interpretation] is based,' answered the priest, 'on the simple-mindedness of the doorkeeper. The argument is that he does not know the Law from inside, he knows only the way that leads to it, where he patrols up and down. His ideas of the interior are assumed to be childish, and it is supposed that he himself is afraid of the other guardians whom he holds up as bogies before the man. Indeed, he fears them more than the man does . . . '" (164–65).

I leave you to read the rest of an incredible scene, where the priest-rabbi goes on and on dissecting—or de-fleaing—this story whose decipherment searches out even this little creature.[29]

Everything includes without including [*tout y comprend, sans comprendre*], *en abyme, Before the Law,* for example the quasi-tabernacu-

29. TN *Cherche jusqu'à la petite bête* is also a colloquial phrase for "splitting hairs."

lar glow ("The lamp in his hand had long since gone out. The silver image of some saint once glimmered into sight immediately before him, by the sheen of its own silver, and was instantaneously lost in the darkness again [Saint Paul, perhaps]. To keep himself from being utterly dependent on the priest, K. asked: 'Aren't we near the main doorway now?' 'No,' said the priest, 'we're a long way from it. Do you want to leave already?' " (167), or again, in the same *contre-abyme* as *Before the Law*, it is K. who asks the abbot to wait and this same request even entails asking the priest-interpreter to ask a question himself. It is K. who asks him to ask (" 'Please wait a moment.' 'I am waiting,' said the priest. 'Don't you want anything more to do with me?' asked K. 'No,' said the priest." [167]). Let us not forget that the abbot, like the doorkeeper of the story, is a representative of the law, a doorkeeper as well, since he is the chaplain of prisons. And he reminds K., not of who he is, the doorkeeper or priest of prisons, but that K. must first understand and say himself who he, the priest, is. These are the last words of the chapter:

> "You must first see that I can't help being what I am," said the priest. "You are the prison chaplain," said K., groping his way nearer to the priest again; his immediate return to the Bank was not so necessary as he had made out, he could quite well stay longer. "That means I belong to the Court," said the priest. "So why should I make any claims upon you? The court makes no claims upon you. *Das Gericht will nichts von dir. Es nimmt dich auf, wenn du kommst, und es entlässt dich, wenn du gehst.* It receives you when you come and it relinquishes you when you go." (168)

6

The Law of Genre

༚ The question of *genre*—literary genre but also gender, genus, and taxonomy more generally—brings with it the question of law, since it implies an institutionalized classification, an enforceable principle of non-contamination and non-contradiction. But genre always potentially exceeds the boundaries that bring it into being, for a member of a genre always signals its membership by an explicit or implicit mark; its relation to the generic field is, in the terminology of speech-act theory, a matter of *mention* as well as *use*. Derrida sees this not as an occasional and optional possibility but as a constitutive property of genre; and the crucial feature of any such mention, or possibility-of-mention, is that it cannot be said to belong to the genre it mentions. Derrida calls this re-marking, this being inside and outside at the same time, "the law of the law of genre."

The text which raises these issues for Derrida is Maurice Blanchot's short fiction *The Madness of the Day*. It's a text which stages an encounter between the narrating "I" and the law—or rather two encounters, since the law appears in a double guise, both as that which is enforced by its representatives (here medical experts) and as a mysterious, apparently female, figure. Derrida does not minimize the baffling quality of Blanchot's writing; in his introduction to *Parages* (a collection of his essays on Blanchot) he says of his relation to the works one can call "literary," as distinct from those that are more obviously critical or philosophical:

> The fictions remained inaccessible to me, as if immersed in a fog from which there came to me only fascinating gleams, and occasionally, but at irregular intervals, the flare of an invisible lighthouse on the coast. I will not say that here they have now emerged from this reserve; on the

contrary. But in their very dissimulation, in the distancing of the inaccessible *as such*, because they give onto it in the act of giving it names, they have presented themselves to me afresh. With a force that is now ineluctable, the most discreet yet the most provocative force, the force of obsession and conviction, the injunction of a truth without truth, always beyond the fascination of which people speak in connection with them. They do not *exercise* this fascination. They traverse it, describe it, they yield it up to thought, rather than making use of it or playing at it. (11)

Among the fascinating topics touched on in *The Madness of the Day* are law (and in this respect the piece is continuous with "Before the Law," reprinted above), gender, affirmation, madness, narrative, and, as the above quotation suggests, fascination. But the story is of particular interest to Derrida because it is not merely a representation of a certain content; if so, it could be rephrased philosophically. Blanchot's text (in its various versions) itself enacts the displacements and overrunnings that concern the narrative—not, it might be noted, in some satisfying achievement of organic form, but in a way that challenges the initial separation of content and form that a theory of organic union presupposes. In particular, the use, or rather mention, of a generic designation, and the refusal of the narrative to obey the linearity and closure of the genre, make the experience of reading *The Madness of the Day*—and Derrida's response to it—one which brings home (beyond any discursive explanation) the inability of a law of genre to maintain absolute purity, and the productiveness of this apparent failure of the literary institution.

ॐ "La loi du genre" was originally given as a lecture at an international colloquium on *Genre* held in July 1979 in Strasbourg. The first version of the text was published in *Glyph* 7 (1980) together with an English translation by Avital Ronell (the volume also contains other contributions to the same colloquium). Ronell's translation is given here with some editorial modifications made in the light of the revised version published in 1986 in *Parages* ([Paris: Galilée], 249–87), which contains three other essays that relate to Blanchot's fictions: "Pas," "Survivre" (translated as "Living On/Borderlines"), and "Titre à préciser" (translated as "Title [to be specified]").

Genres are not to be mixed.[1]

I will not mix genres.

I repeat: genres are not to be mixed. I will not mix them.

Now suppose I let these utterances resonate all by themselves. Suppose: I abandon them to their fate, I set free their random virtualities and turn them over to your hearing, to whatever mobility they retain and you bestow upon them to engender effects of all kinds without my having to stand behind them.

I merely said, and then repeated: genres are not to be mixed; I will not mix them.

As long as I release these utterances (which others might call speech acts) in a form yet scarcely determined, given the open context out of which I have just let them be grasped from "my" language—as long as I do this, you may find it difficult to choose among several interpretative options. They are legion, as I could demonstrate. They form an open and essentially unpredictable series. But you may be tempted by *at least* two types of hearing, two modes of interpretation, or, if you prefer to give these words more of a chance, two different genres of hypothesis. Which ones?

On the one hand, it could be a matter of a fragmentary discourse whose propositions would be of the descriptive, constative, and neutral genre. In such a case, I would have named the operation which consists of "not mixing genres." I would have designated this operation in a neutral fashion without evaluating it, without recommending or advising against it, certainly without binding anyone to it. Without claiming to lay down the law or to make this an act of law, I merely would have summoned up, in a fragmentary utterance, the sense of a practice, an act or event, as you wish: which is what sometimes happens when it is a matter of "not mixing genres." With reference to the same case, and to a hypothesis of the same type, same mode, same genre—or same order: when I said, "I will not mix genres," you may have discerned a foreshadowing description—I am not saying a prescription—the descriptive designation telling in advance what will transpire, pre-

---

1. EN *Ne pas mêler les genres;* literally, "not to mix genres"—the French phrase can be either a pure infinitive or an imperative, and Derrida draws on this undecidability in the discussion that follows. An English equivalent would be "No mixing of genres."

dicting it in the constative mode or genre, i.e. it will happen thus. I will not mix genres. The future tense describes, then, what will surely take place, as you yourselves can judge; but for my part it does not constitute a commitment. I am not making you a promise here, nor am I issuing myself an order or invoking the authority of some law to which I am resolved to submit myself. In this case, the future tense does not set the time of a performative speech act of a promising or ordering type.

But another hypothesis, another type of hearing, and another interpretation would have been no less legitimate. "Genres are not to be mixed" could strike you as a sharp order. You might have heard it resound the elliptical but all the more authoritarian summons to a law of "do" or "do not" which, as everyone knows, occupies the concept or constitutes the value of *genre*. As soon as the word *genre* is sounded, as soon as it is heard, as soon as one attempts to conceive it, a limit is drawn. And when a limit is established, norms and interdictions are not far behind: "Do," "Do not," says "genre," the word *genre*, the figure, the voice, or the law of genre. And this can be said of all genres of genre, be it a question of a generic or a general determination of what one calls "nature" or *phusis* (for example, a biological *genre*, or the human *genre*, a genre of all that is in general), or be it a question of a typology, designated as non-natural and depending on laws or orders which were once held to be opposed to *phusis* according to those values associated with *technē, thesis, nomos* (for example, an artistic, poetic or literary genre).[2] But the whole enigma of genre springs perhaps most closely from within this limit between the two genres of genre which, neither separable nor inseparable, form an odd couple of one without the other in which each evenly serves the other a citation to appear in the figure of the other, simultaneously and indiscernibly saying "I" and "we," me the genre, we genres, without it being possible to think that the "I" is a species of the genre "we." For who would have us believe that we, we two for example, would form a genre or belong to one? Thus, as soon as genre announces itself, one must respect a norm, one must not cross a line of demarcation, one must

2. EN *Genre* in French carries the general sense of "genus," "kind," or "type" (*le genre humain* means "the human race"); the sense of artistic or literary genre; and the sense of "gender," especially grammatical gender.

not risk impurity, anomaly or monstrosity. And so it goes in all cases, whether or not this law of genre be interpreted as a determination or perhaps even as a destination of *phusis*, and regardless of the weight or range imputed to *phusis*. If a genre is what it is, or if it is supposed to be what it is destined to be by virtue of its *telos*, then "genres are not to be mixed"; one should not mix genres, one owes it to oneself not to get mixed up in mixing genres. Or, more rigorously, genres should not intermix. And if it should happen that they do intermix, by accident or through transgression, by mistake or through a lapse, then this should confirm, since, after all, we are speaking of "mixing," the essential purity of their identity. This purity belongs to the typical axiom: it is a law of the law of genre, whether or not the law is, as it is considered justifiable to say, "natural." This normative position and this evaluation are inscribed and prescribed even at the threshold of the "thing itself," if something of the genre "genre" can be so named. And so it follows that you might have taken the second sentence in the first person, "I will not mix genres," as a vow of obedience, as a docile response to the injunction emanating from the law of genre. In place of a constative description, you would then hear a promise, an oath; you would grasp the following respectful commitment: I promise you that I will not mix genres, and, through this act of pledging faithfulness to my commitment, I will be faithful to the law of genre, since of itself, it invites and commits me in advance not to mix genres. By publishing my response to the imperious call of the law, I would correspondingly commit myself to be responsible.

Unless, of course, I were actually implicated in a wager, a challenge, an impossible bet—in short, a situation that would exceed the matter of merely engaging a commitment from me. And suppose for a moment that it were impossible not to mix genres. What if there were, lodged within the heart of the law itself, a law of impurity or a principle of contamination? And suppose the condition for the possibility of the law were the *a priori* of a counter-law, an axiom of impossibility that would confound its sense, order and reason?

I have just proposed an alternative between two interpretations. I did not do so, as you can imagine, in order to leave it at that. The line or trait that seemed to separate the two bodies of interpretation is affected *straight away* by an essential disruption that, for the time being, I shall let you name or qualify in any way you care to: as internal division of the trait, impurity, corruption, contamination, decomposition, perversion, deformation, even cancerization, generous proliferation or degenerescence. All these disruptive "anomalies" are engendered—and this is their common law, the lot or site they share—by *repetition*. One might even say by citation or re-citation [*ré-cit*], provided that the restricted use of these two words is not a call to strict generic order. A citation in the strict sense implies all sorts of contextual conventions, precautions and protocols in the mode of reiteration, of coded signs such as quotation marks or other typographical devices used for writing a citation. The same holds no doubt for the *récit* as a form, mode, or genre of discourse, even—and I shall return to this— as a literary type.[3] And yet the law that protects the usage, in *stricto sensu*, of the words *citation* and *récit*, is threatened intimately and in advance by a counterlaw that constitutes this very law, renders it possible, conditions it and thereby makes itself—for reasons of edges on which we shall run aground in just a moment—impossible to edge through, to edge away from or to hedge around. The law and the counter-law serve each other citations summoning each other to appear, and each re-cites the other in these proceedings. There would be no cause for concern if one were rigorously assured of being able to distinguish with rigor between a citation and a non-citation, a *récit* and a non-*récit* or a repetition within the form of one or the other.

I shall not undertake to demonstrate, assuming it is still possible, why you were unable to decide whether the sentences with which I opened this presentation and marked this context were or were not repetitions of a citational type; or whether they were or were not of the performative type; or certainly whether they were, both of them, together—and each time together—the one or the other. For perhaps

---

3. EN The translator's use of the French *récit* has been retained here, and continued throughout the essay, because the argument hinges on the complex of meanings possessed by this term in Blanchot's text; most importantly for this text they include both the sense of a completely fictional narration and the sense of an account of real events which the speaker witnessed or was involved in. See also "Before the Law" above, note 3 and *passim*.

someone has noticed that, from one repetition to the next, a change insinuated itself into the relationship between the two initial utterances. The punctuation was slightly modified, as was the content of the second independent clause. This barely noticeable shift could theoretically have created a mutual independency between the interpretative alternatives that might have tempted you to opt for one or the other, or for one *and* the other of these two decisions. A particularly rich combinatory of possibilities would thus ensue, which, in order not to exceed my time limit and out of respect for the law of genre and of the audience, I shall abstain from recounting. I am simply going to assume a certain relationship between what has just now happened and the origin of literature, as well as its aborigine or its abortion, to quote Philippe Lacoue-Labarthe.

Provisionally claiming for myself the authority of such an assumption, I shall let our field of vision contract as I limit myself to a sort of species of the genre "genre." I shall focus on this genre of genre which is generally supposed, and always a bit too rashly, not to be part of nature, of *phusis,* but rather of *technē,* of the arts, still more narrowly of poetry, and most particularly of literature. But at the same time, I take the liberty to think that, while limiting myself thus, I exclude nothing, at least in principle and *de jure*—the relationships here no longer being those of extension, from exemplary individual to species, from species to genre as genus or from the genre to genre in general; rather, as we shall see, these relationships are a whole order apart. What is at stake, in effect, is exemplarity and the whole *enigma*—in other words, as the word *enigma* indicates, the *récit*—which works through the logic of the example.

Before going about putting a certain example to the test, I shall attempt to formulate, in a manner as elliptical, economical, and formal as possible, what I shall call the law of the law of genre. It is precisely a principle of contamination, a law of impurity, a parasitical economy. In the code of set theories, if I may use it at least figuratively, I would speak of a sort of participation without belonging—a taking part in without being part of, without having membership in a set. The trait that marks membership inevitably divides, the boundary of the set comes to form, by invagination, an internal pocket larger than the whole; and the consequences of this division and of this overflowing remain as singular as they are limitless.[4]

The *récit* which I will discuss presently makes the impossibility of the *récit* its theme, its impossible theme or content at once inaccessible, indeterminable, interminable and inexhaustible; and it makes the word *"récit"* its titleless title, the mentionless mention of its genre. This text, as I shall try to demonstrate, seems to be made, among other things, *to make light* [*se jouer*] of all the tranquil categories of genre-theory and history in order to upset their taxonomic certainties, the distribution of their classes, and the presumed stability of their classical nomenclatures. It is a text destined, at the same time, to summon up these classes by conducting their proceeding, by proceeding from the proceeding to the law of genre. For if the juridical code has frequently thrust itself upon me in order to hear this case, it has done so to call as witness a (possibly) exemplary text, and because I am convinced rights and the law are bound up in all of this.

Here now, very quickly, is the law of overflowing, of *excess*, the law of participation without membership, which I mentioned earlier. It will seem meager to you, and even of staggering abstractness. It does not particularly concern either genres, or types, or modes or any form in the strict sense of its concept. I therefore do not know under what title the field or object submitted to this law should be placed. It is perhaps the limitless field of general textuality. I can take each word of the series (genre, type, mode, form) and decide that it will hold for all the others (all genres of genres, types, modes, forms; all types of types, genres, modes, forms; all forms of forms, etc.). The trait common to these classes of classes is precisely the identifiable recurrence of a common trait by which one recognizes, or should recognize, a membership in a class. There should be a trait upon which one could rely in order to decide that a given textual event, a given "work," corresponds

4. EN Some paragraphs have been omitted here; they discuss an essay by Gérard Genette, "Genres, 'types,' modes" (*Poétique* 32 [November 1977]: 389–421; revised and reissued as *Introduction à l'architexte* [Paris: Seuil, 1979]). Derrida is particularly interested in Genette's insistence on the distinction between *modes* (which are formal and linguistic categories) and *genres* (which are determined by content). The *récit*, for Genette, is a mode.

to a given class (genre, type, mode, form, etc.). And there should be a code enabling one to decide questions of class-membership on the basis of this trait. For example—a very humble axiom, but, by the same token, hardly contestable—if a genre exists (let us say the novel, since no one seems to contest its generic quality), then a code should provide an identifiable trait and one which is identical to itself, authorizing us to adjudicate whether a given text belongs to this genre or perhaps to that genre. Likewise, outside of literature or art, if one is bent on classifying, one should consult a set of identifiable and codifiable traits to determine whether this or that, such a thing or such an event, belongs to this set or that class. This may seem trivial. Such a distinctive trait *qua* mark is however always *a priori remarkable*. It is always possible that a set—I have compelling reasons for calling this a text, whether it be written or oral—re-marks on this distinctive trait within itself. This can occur in texts that do not, at a given moment, assert themselves to be literary or poetic. A defense speech or newspaper editorial can indicate by means of a mark, even if it is not explicitly designated as such, "Voilà! I belong, as anyone may remark, to the type of text called a defense speech or an article of the genre newspaper-editorial." The possibility is always there. This does not constitute a text *ipso facto* as "literature," even though such a possibility, always left open and therefore eternally remarkable, situates perhaps in every text the possibility of its becoming literature. But this does not interest me at the moment. What interests me is that this re-mark—ever possible for every text, for every corpus of traces—is absolutely necessary for and constitutive of what we call art, poetry or literature. It underwrites the eruption of *technē,* which is never long in coming. I submit this axiomatic question for your consideration: can one identify a work of art, of whatever sort, but especially a work of discursive art, if it does not bear the mark of a genre, if it does not signal or mention it or make it remarkable in any way? Let me clarify two points on this subject. First, it is possible to have several genres, an intermixing of genres or a total genre, the genre "genre" or the poetic or literary genre as genre of genres. Second, this re-mark can take on a great number of forms and can itself pertain to highly diverse types. It need not be a "mention" of the type found beneath the title of certain books (novel, *récit,* drama).

The remark of belonging need not pass through the consciousness of the author or the reader, although it often does so. It can also refute this consciousness or render the explicit "mention" mendacious, false, inadequate or ironic according to all sorts of overdetermined figures. Finally, this remarking-trait need be neither a theme nor a thematic component of the work—although of course this instance of belonging to one or several genres, not to mention all the traits that mark this belonging, often have been treated as theme, even before the advent of what we call "modernism." If I am not mistaken in saying that such a trait is remarkable in every aesthetic, poetic or literary corpus, then consider this paradox, consider the irony (which is not reducible to a consciousness or an attitude): this supplementary and distinctive trait, a mark of belonging or inclusion, does not properly pertain to any genre or class. The re-mark of belonging does not belong. It belongs without belonging, and the "without" (or the suffix "-less") which relates belonging to non-belonging appears only in the timeless time of the blink of an eye. The eyelid closes, but barely, an instant among instants, and what it closes is verily the eye, the view, the light of day. But without the respite or interval of a blink, nothing would come to light. To formulate it in the scantiest manner—the simplest but most apodictic—I submit for your consideration the following hypothesis: a text would not *belong* to any genre. Every text *participates* in one or several genres, there is no genreless text, there is always a genre and genres, yet such participation never amounts to belonging. And not because of an abundant overflowing or a free, anarchic and unclassifiable productivity, but because of the *trait* of participation itself, because of the effect of the code and of the generic mark. In marking itself generically, a text unmarks itself [*se démarque*]. If remarks of belonging belong without belonging, participate without belonging, then *genre-designations cannot be simply part of the corpus.* Let us take the designation "novel" as an example. This should be marked in one way or another, even if it does not appear in the explicit form of a subtitled designation, and even if it proves deceptive or ironic. This designation is not novelistic; it does not, in whole or in part, take part in the corpus whose denomination it nonetheless imparts. Nor is it simply extraneous to the corpus. But this singular *topos* places within and without the work, along its boundary, an inclusion and exclusion with regard to genre in general, as to an identifiable class in general. It gathers together the corpus and, at the same time, in the same blinking of an eye, keeps it from closing, from identifying itself with itself. This axiom of non-closure or non-fulfillment enfolds within itself the condition for the possibility and the impossibility of taxonomy. This inclusion and this exclusion do not remain exterior to one another; they do not exclude each other. But neither are they immanent or identical to each other. They are neither one nor two. They form what I shall call the *genre-clause*, a clause stating at once the juridical utterance, the designation that makes precedent and law-text, but also the closure, the closing that excludes itself from what it includes (one could also speak, without winking, of a floodgate [*écluse*] of genre). The clause or floodgate of genre declasses what it allows to be classed. It tolls the knell of genealogy or of genericity, which it however also brings forth to the light of day. Putting to death the very thing that it engenders, it cuts a strange figure; a formless form, it remains nearly invisible, it neither sees the day nor brings itself to light. Without it, neither genre nor literature come to light, but as soon as there is this blinking of an eye, this clause or this floodgate of genre, at the very moment that a genre or a literature is broached, at that very moment, degenerescence has begun, the end begins.

The end begins, this is a citation. Maybe a citation. I might have taken it from that text which seems to me to bring itself forth as an example, as an example of this unfigurable figure of clusion.

What I shall try to convey to you now will not be called by its generic or modal name. I shall not say this drama, this epic, this novel, this novella or this *récit*, certainly not this *récit*. All of these generic or modal names would be equally valid or equally invalid for something which is not even quite a book, but which was published in 1973 in the form of a small volume of thirty-two pages under the title *La folie du jour*.[5] The author's name: Maurice Blanchot. In order to speak

5. EN For a bilingual edition, see Maurice Blanchot, *The Madness of the Day*, trans. Lydia Davis (Barrytown, N.Y.: Station Hill Press, 1981). The page references given here are to this volume, though the quotations have been translated by Avital Ronell.

about it, I shall call this thing "La folie du jour," its given name which it bears legally and which gives us the right, as of its publication date, to identify and classify it in our copyright records at the Bibliothèque Nationale. One could fashion a nonfinite number of readings from *La folie du jour*. I have attempted a few myself, and shall do so again elsewhere, from another point of view. The *topos* of view, sight, blindness, *point of view* is, moreover, inscribed and traversed in *La folie du jour* according to a sort of permanent revolution that engenders and virtually brings to the light of day points of view, twists, versions and reversions of which the sum remains necessarily uncountable and the account impossible. The deductions, rationalizations, and warnings that I must inevitably propose will arise, then, from an act of unjustifiable violence. A brutal and mercilessly depleting selectivity will obtrude upon me, upon us, in the name of a law that *La folie du jour* has, in its turn, already reviewed, and with the foresight that a certain kind of police brutality is perhaps an inevitable accomplice to our concern for professional competence.

What will I ask of *La folie du jour?* To answer, to testify, to say what it has to say with respect to the law of mode or the law of genre, and more precisely, with respect to the law of the *récit*.

On the cover, below the title, we find no mention of genre. In this most peculiar place that belongs neither to the title nor to the subtitle, nor even simply to the corpus of the work, the author did not affix, although he has often done so elsewhere, the designation "*récit*" or "novel." About this designation which figures elsewhere and which appears to be absent here, I shall say only two things.

1.   On the one hand it commits one to nothing. Neither reader nor critic nor author are bound to believe that the text preceded by this designation conforms readily to the strict, normal, normed or normative definition of the genre, to the law of the genre or of the mode. Confusion, irony, the shift in conventions toward a new definition (in what name could it be prohibited?), the search for a supplementary effect, any of these things could prompt one to entitle as *novel* or *récit* what in truth or according to yesterday's truth would be neither one nor the other. All the more so if the words *récit, novel, ciné-roman, complete dramatic works* or, for all I know, *literature* are no longer in

the place which conventionally mentions genre but, as has happened and will happen again (shortly), they are found to be holding the position and function of the title itself, of the work's given name.

2. Blanchot has often had occasion to modify the genre-designation from one version of his work to the next, or from one edition to the next. Since I am unable to cover the entire spectrum of this problem, I shall simply cite the example of the designation *"récit"* effaced between one version and the next of *L'arrêt de mort* at the same time as a certain epilogue is removed from the end of the double *récit* which, in a manner of speaking, constitutes this book.[6] This effacement of *"récit,"* leaving a trace that, inscribed and filed away, remains as an effect of supplementary relief which is not easily accounted for in all of its facets. I cannot arrest the course of my lecture here, no more than I can pause to consider the very scrupulous and minutely differentiated distribution of the designations *"récit"* and *"novel"* from one narrative work to the next, no more than I can question whether Blanchot distinguished the genre and mode designations, no more than I can discuss Blanchot's entire discourse on the difference between the narratorial voice and the narrative voice which is, to be sure, something other than a mode. I would point out only one thing: at the very moment the first version of *L'arrêt de mort* appears, bearing mention as it does of *"récit,"* the first version of *La folie du jour* is published with another title about which I shall momentarily speak.

La folie du jour, then, makes no mention of genre or mode. But the word *"récit"* appears at least five times in the last two pages in order to name the theme of *La folie du jour,* its sense or its story, its content or part of its content—in any case, its decisive proceedings and stakes. It is a *récit* without a theme and without a cause entering from the outside; yet it is without interiority. It is the *récit* of an impossible *récit* whose "production" occasions what happens, or rather, what remains; but the *récit* does not relate it, nor relate to it as to an outside reference, even if everything remains foreign to it and out of bounds. It is even less feasible for me to relate to you the story of *La folie du jour* which

6. EN *L'arrêt de mort* has been translated by Lydia Davis as *Death Sentence* (Barrytown, N.Y.: Station Hill Press, 1978). For an extended reading of this fiction, see Derrida's "Living On/Borderlines."

is staked precisely on the possibility and the impossibility of relating a story. Nonetheless, in order to create the greatest possible clarity, in the name of daylight itself, that is to say (as will become clear), in the name of the law, I shall take the calculated risk of flattening out the unfolding or coiling up of this text, its permanent revolution whose rounds are made to resist any kind of flattening. And this is why the one who says "I," the one who after all speaks to us, who "recites" for us, this one who says "I" tells his inquisitors that he cannot manage to constitute himself as narrator (in the sense of the term that is not necessarily literary), and tells them that he cannot manage to identify with himself sufficiently, or to remember himself well enough to gather the story and *récit* that are demanded of him—which the representatives of society and the law require of him. The one who says "I" (who does not manage to say "I") seems to relate what has happened to him, or rather, what has nearly happened to him after presenting himself in a mode that defies all norms of self-presentation: he nearly lost his sight following a traumatic event—probably an assault. I say "probably" because *La folie du jour* wholly upsets, in a discreet but terribly efficient manner, all the certainties upon which so much of discourse is constructed: the value of an event, first of all, of reality, of fiction, of appearance and so on, all this being carried away by the disseminal and mad polysemy of "day," of the word *day,* which, once again, I cannot dwell upon here. Having nearly lost his sight, having been taken in by a kind of medico-social institution, he now resides under the watchful eye of doctors, handed over to the authority of these specialists who are representatives of the law as well, legist doctors who demand that he testify—and in his own interest, or so it seems at first—about what happened to him so that remedial justice may be dispensed. His faithful *récit* of events should render justice unto the law. The law demands a *récit.*

Pronounced five times in the last three paragraphs of *La folie du jour,* the word "*récit*" does not seem to designate a literary genre, but rather a certain type or mode of discourse. That is, in effect, the appearance of it. Everything seems to happen as if the *récit*—the question of or rather the demand for the *récit,* the response and the nonresponse to the demand—found itself staged and figured as one of the themes, objects, stakes in a more bountiful text, *La folie du jour,* whose genre would be of another order and would in any case overstep the boundaries of the *récit* with all of its generality and all of its genericity. The *récit* itself would not cover this generic generality of the literary corpus named *La folie du jour.* Now we might already feel inclined to consider this appearance suspect and be jolted from our certainties by an allusion that "I" makes at a certain moment: the one who says "I," who is not by force of necessity a narrator, nor necessarily always the same, notes that the representatives of the law, those who demand of him a *récit* in the name of the law, consider and treat him, in his personal and civil identity, not only as an "educated" man—and an educated man, they often tell him, ought to be able to speak and recount; as a competent subject, he ought to know how to piece together a story by saying "I" and "exactly" how things happened to him—they regard him not only as an "educated" man, but also as a writer. He is writer and reader, a creature of "libraries," *the* reader of this *récit.* This is not sufficient cause, but it is, in any case, a first clue and one whose impact incites us to think that the required *récit* does not simply remain in an extraneous relationship to literature or even to a literary genre. Lest we not be content with this suspicion, let us weigh the possibility of the inclusion of a modal structure within a vaster, more general corpus, whether literary or not and whether or not related to the genre. Such an inclusion raises questions concerning edge, borderline, boundary, and overflowing which do not arise without a fold.

What sort of a fold? According to which fold and which figure of folding?

Here are the three final paragraphs; they are of unequal length, with the last of them comprising approximately one line:

They demanded: Tell us "exactly" how things happened.—A *récit?* I began: I am neither learned nor ignorant. I have known some joy. This is saying too little. I related the story in its entirety, to which they listened, it seems, with great interest—at least initially. But the end was a surprise for us all. "After that beginning," they said "you should proceed to the facts." How so? The *récit* was over.

I should have realized that I was incapable of composing a *récit* of these events. I had lost the sense of the story; this happens in a good many illnesses. But this explanation only made them more demanding. Then I remarked, for the first time, that they were two and that this infringement on their traditional method—even though it can be explained away by the fact that one of them was an eye doctor, the other a specialist in mental illnesses—increasingly gave our conversation the character of an authoritarian interrogation, overseen and controlled by a strict set of rules. To be sure, neither of them was the chief of police. But being two, due to that, they were three, and this third one remained firmly convinced, I am sure, that a writer, a man who speaks and reasons with distinction, is always capable of recounting the facts which he remembers.

A *récit?* No, no *récit,* never again. (18)

In the first of the three paragraphs that I have just cited, he claims that something is to begin after the word *"récit"* punctuated by a question mark ("A *recit?"*—herein implied: they want a *récit,* is it then a *récit* that they want? "I began . . . "). This something is nothing other than the first line on the first page of *La folie du jour.* These are the same words, in the same order, but this is not a citation in the strict sense for, stripped of quotation marks, these words commence or recommence a quasi-*récit* that will engender anew the entire sequence including this new point of departure. In this way, the first words ("I am neither learned nor ignorant . . . ") that come after the word *"récit"* and its question mark, that broach the beginning of the account extorted by the law's representatives—these first words mark a collapse that is unthinkable, unrepresentable, unsituable within a linear order of succession, within a spatial or temporal sequentiality, within an objectifiable topology or chronology. One sees, without seeing, one reads the crumbling of an upper boundary or of the initial edge in *La folie du jour,* uncoiled according to the "normal" order, the one regulated by common law, editorial convention, positive law, the regime of competency in our logo-alphabetical culture, etc. Suddenly, this upper or initial boundary, which is commonly called the first line of a book, is forming a pocket inside the corpus. It is taking the form of an *invagination* through which the trait of the first line, the borderline, splits while remaining the same and traverses yet also bounds the corpus. The *"récit"* which he claims is beginning at the end, and by legal requisition, is none other than the one that has begun from the beginning of *La folie du jour* and in which, therefore, he gets around to saying that he begins, etc. And it is without beginning, or end, without content and without edge. There is only content without edge—without boundary or frame—and there is only edge without content. The inclusion (or the occlusion, the inocclusive invagination) is interminable, it is an analysis of the *récit* that can only turn in circles in an unarrestable, inenarrable and insatiably recurring manner—but one terrible for those who, in the name of the law, require that order reign in the *récit*, for those who want to know, with all the required competence, "exactly" how this happens. For if "I" or "he" continued to tell what he has told, he would end up endlessly returning to this point and once more beginning to begin, that is to say, to begin with an end that precedes the beginning. And from the viewpoint of objective space and time, the point at which he stops is absolutely unascertainable ("I have told them the entire story . . . "), for there is no "entire" story except for the one that interrupts itself in this way.

A lower edge of invagination will, if one can say so, respond to this "first" invagination of the upper edge by intersecting it. The "final line" resumes the question posed *before* the "I began" ("A *récit?*") and tells of the resolution or the promise, the commitment made never again to produce a *récit*. As if he had already given one! And yet, yes (yes and no), a *récit* has taken place. Hence the last word: "A *récit?* No, no *récit*, never again." It has been impossible to decide whether the recounted event and the event of the *récit* itself ever took place. Impossible to decide whether there was a *récit*, for the one who barely manages to say "I" and to constitute himself as narrator recounts that he has not been able to recount—but what, exactly? Well, everything, including the demand for a *récit*. And if an assured and guaranteed decision is impossible, this is because there is nothing more to be done than to decide without guardrail, without limits, to commit oneself, to perform, to wager, to allow chance its chance. It is also impossible to decide whether the promise "No, no *récit*, never again" is a part of or apart from the *récit*. Legally speaking, it is party to *La folie du jour*, but not necessarily to the *récit* or to the simulacrum of the *récit*. Its trait splits again into an internal and external edge. It repeats—without citing—the question apparently posed above (A *récit?*), of which it can be said that, in this permanent revolution of order, it follows, doubles or reiterates it in advance. Thus another lip or invaginating loop takes shape here. This time the lower edge creates a pocket in order to come back into the corpus and to rise again on this side of the upper or initial line's line of invagination. This would form a *double chiasmatic invagination of edges:*

> A. "I am neither learned nor ignorant . . . "
> B. "A *récit?* I began:
> A'. I am neither learned nor ignorant . . . "
> B'. "A *récit?* No, no *récit,* never again . . . "

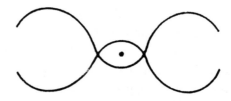

The *I* of "I began" appears to carry the full responsibility of the *récit,* at least of the *récit* that could be seen as *included* and which nevertheless also becomes larger than what appears to include it. *I* represents the beginning, the very act of beginning, reminding us by the same token that it is *en archē,* in the beginning, the first word of the book: "I am neither learned nor ignorant." It is required of him or her, of me, of *I* both to begin and to repeat, to give an account of the facts. And, in short, to assume one's responsibilities. But in order to give an account of the facts, a relation begins which relates another relation in which the *I* is included. Moreover, represented here in the sketch I have just drawn as a point, an eye, a point of view, the *I* seems not to belong to the lineage of the two *récits* which are forever intertwined and intersected. The inaugural decision to answer the demand and to "begin" the *récit* does not belong to the *récit,* any more than does the "No, no *récit,* never again" at the end of the book, an inverse resolution which seems not to cite anything either. "I began" and "No, no *récit*, never again" could therefore resemble *quasi-transcendental* commitments on the part of the *récit*, the modes of which are different, but which are equally exterior to the actual content of the narration. The first describes or notes, in the past tense, a kind of performative: I begin, I began. The other enunciates, in a more manifestly performative mode, in the present tense, a decision engaging the future. It is the decision to begin and then to interrupt the relation for good, to take some kind of responsibility in answer to the demand for a *récit*, which would tear the canvas of a narrative text even as it tends to envelop itself indefinitely within itself. It was inevitable that I begin and that I end, even if I begin with the end, and if "the end begins."

Could it be this simple? and this reassuring? as the purity of a transcendental or a performative, in the end, can always be? Certainly, the two resolutions appear to be inaugural, and the final one itself has the form of an inaugural decision having come spontaneously to interrupt any possible sequence. But these two resolutions immediately become once again *moments of passage*, within the general *récit* entitled *La folie du jour*. If, after "I began: I am neither learned nor ignorant . . . " the simulacrum of repetition continued according to its own logic and the internal necessity of its movement, turning endlessly upon itself, the "I began" and the "No, no *récit*, never again" would be unmistakably inscribed and bound there, taken up in the general fabric, in the citation and the narration, in the madness of a fiction that no decidability can safely interrupt. "I began . . . " and "No, no *récit*, never again" belong to the sequel, to the *consequence* of the text that *I* begin(s) to cite. One could say that they are *implicitly cited,* reimplicated within this singular continuum. No tearing, never again between A, B, A', B', not even within B and B', between the question and the answer.

It is thus impossible to decide whether an event, *récit, récit* of event or event of *récit* took place. Impossible to settle upon the simple borderlines of this corpus, of this ellipsis unremittingly canceling itself within its own expansion. When we fall back on the poetic consequences enfolding within this dilemma, we find that it becomes difficult indeed to speak here with conviction about a *récit* as a determined mode included within a more general corpus or one simply related, in its determination, to other modes, or, quite simply, to something other than itself. All is *récit* and nothing is; the exit out of the *récit* remains *within* the *récit* in a *noninclusive* mode, and this structure is itself related so remotely to a dialectical structure that it even inscribes dialectics in the ellipsis of the *récit*. All is *récit,* nothing is: and we shall not know whether the relationship between these two propositions— the strange conjunction of the *récit* and the *récit*-less—belongs to the *récit* itself. What indeed happens when the edge pronounces a sentence?

Faced with this type of difficulty—the consequences or implications of which cannot be deployed here—one might be tempted to have recourse to the law or the rights which govern published texts. One might be tempted to argue as follows: all these insoluble problems of delimitation are raised "on the inside" of a book classified as a work of literature or literary fiction. Pursuant to these juridical norms, this book has a beginning and an end that leave no opening for indecision. This book has a determinable beginning and end, a title, an author, a publisher. It is called *La folie du jour.* At this place, where I am pointing, on this page, right here, you can see its first word; here, its final period, perfectly situable in objective space. And all the sophisticated transgressions, all the infinitesimal subversions that may captivate you are not possible except within this enclosure for which these transgressions and subversions moreover maintain an essential need in order to take place. Furthermore, on the inside of this normed space, the word "*récit*" does not name a literary operation or genre, but a current mode of discourse, and it does so regardless of the formidable problems of structure, edge, set theory, the part and whole, etc., that it raises in this "literary" corpus.

That is all well and good. But in its very relevance, this objection cannot be sustained—for example, it cannot save the modal determination of the *récit*—except by referring to extra-literary and even extra-linguistic juridical norms. The objection appeals to the law and calls to mind the fact that the subversion of *La folie du jour* needs the law in order to take place. Whereby the objection reproduces and accomplishes the demonstration staged within *La folie du jour:* the *récit,* mandated and prescribed by law but also, as we shall see, commanding, requiring, and producing law in turn. In short, the whole critical scene of competence in which we are engaged is *party* to and *part* of *La folie du jour,* in whole and in part, the whole is a part.

The whole does nothing but begin. I could have begun with what resembles the absolute beginning, within the juridico-historical order of this publication. What has been lightly termed the first version of *La folie du jour* was not a book. Published in the journal *Empédocle* (May 2, 1949), it bore another title—indeed, several other titles. On the journal's cover, here it is, one reads:

Maurice Blanchot
Un récit?

Later the question mark disappears twice. First, when the title is reproduced within the journal in the table of contents:

Maurice Blanchot
Un récit

then below the first line:

Un récit
par
Maurice Blanchot

Could you tell whether these titles, written earlier and filed away in the archives, make up a single title, titles of the same text, titles of the *récit* (which of course figures as an impracticable mode in the book), or the title of a genre? Even if the latter were to cause some confusion, it would be of the sort that releases questions already implemented and enacted by *La folie du jour.* This enactment enables in turn the denaturalization and deconstitution of the opposition nature/history and mode/genre.

What could the words "A *récit*" refer to in their manifold occurrences and diverse punctuations? And precisely how does reference function here? In one case, the question mark can *also* serve as a supplementary remark indicating the necessity of all these questions as the insolvent character of indecision: is this a *récit?* Is it a *récit* that I entitle? asks the title in entitling. But also, announcing outside the inside of the story: is it a *récit* that they want? What entitles them? Is it a *récit* as discursive mode or as literary operation, or perhaps even as literary genre or fiction on the theme of mode and genre? Likewise, the title could excerpt, as does a metonymy, a fragment of the *récit* without a *récit* (to wit, the words "a *récit*" with and without a question mark), but such an iterative excerpting is not citational. For the title, guaranteed and protected by law but also making law, retains a referential structure which differs radically from the one underlying other occurrences of the "same" words in the text. Whatever the issue—title, reference, or mode and genre—the case before us always involves the law and, in particular, the relations formed around and to law. All the questions which we have just addressed can be traced to an enormous matrix that generates the nonthematizable thematic power of a simulated *récit:* it is this inexhaustible writing which recounts without telling, and which speaks without recounting.

Récit of a *récit* without *récit,* a *récit* without edge or boundary, *récit* all of whose visible space is but some border of itself without "self," consisting of the framing edge without content, without modal or generic boundaries—such is the law of this textual event. This text also speaks the law, its own and that of the other as reader. And speaking the law, it also imposes itself as a law text, as the text of the law. What is, then, the law of the genre of this singular text? It is law, it is the figure of the law which will also be the invisible center, the themeless theme of *La folie du jour,* or, as I am now entitled to say, of "A *récit?*"

But this law, as law of genre, is not exclusively binding on genre understood as category of art and literature. Paradoxically, and just as impossibly, the law of genre is also binding on that which draws genre into engendering, generations, genealogy, and degenerescence. You have already witnessed its approach often enough, with all the figures of this degenerescent self-engendering of a *récit,* with this figure of the law which, like the day that it is, challenges the opposition between the law of nature and the law of symbolic history. The remarks that have just been made on the double chiasmatic invagination of edges should suffice to exclude any notion that these complications are matters of pure form or that they could be formalized outside the content. The question of the literary genre is not a formal one: it covers the motif of the law in general, of generation in the natural and symbolic senses, of birth in the natural and symbolic senses, of the generation difference, sexual difference between the feminine and masculine gender, of the hymen between the two, of a relationless relation between the two, of an identity and difference between the feminine and masculine. The word *hymen* not only points toward a paradoxical logic that is inscribed without being formalized under this name;[7] it also reminds us of everything that Philippe Lacoue-Labarthe and Jean-Luc Nancy tell us in *The Literary Absolute* about the relationship between genre (*Gattung*) and marriage, as well as the whole series *gattieren* (to mix, to classify), *gatten* (to couple), *Gatte/Gattin* (husband/wife), and so forth.[8]

Once articulated within the precinct of Blanchot's entire discourse on the neuter, the most elliptical question would inevitably have to assume this form: what about a neutral genre/gender? Or one whose neutrality would not be *negative* (neither . . . nor), nor dialectical, but affirmative, and doubly affirmative (or . . . or)?

Here again, due to time limitations but also to more essential reasons concerning the structure of the text, I shall have to excerpt some isolated fragments. This will not occur without a supplement of violence and pain.

First word and most important word of *La folie du jour*, "I" presents itself as self [*moi*], me, a man. Grammatical law leaves no doubt about this subject. The first sentence, phrased in French in the masculine ("*Je ne suis ni savant ni ignorant*" and not "*je ne suis ni savante ni ignorante*") says, with regard to knowledge, nothing but a double negation (*neither . . . nor*). Thus, no glint of *self-presentation*. But the double negation gives passage to a double affirmation (yes, yes) that enters

7. EN For a discussion of the *hymen* as an undecidable term, see "The First Session" above, especially pp. 160–175.

8. Philippe Lacoue-Labarthe and Jean-Luc Nancy, *The Literary Absolute*, trans. Philip Barnard and Cheryl Lester (Albany: State University of New York Press, 1988), 91.

into alignment or alliance with itself. Forging an alliance or marriage-bond ("hymen") with itself, this boundless double affirmation utters a measureless, excessive, immense *yes:* both to life and to death:

> I am neither learned nor ignorant. I have known some joy. This is saying too little: I am living, and this life gives me the greatest pleasure. And death? When I die (perhaps soon), I shall know an immense pleasure. I am not speaking of the foretaste of death, which is bland and often disagreeable. Suffering is debilitating. But this is the remarkable truth of which I am sure: I feel a boundless pleasure in living and shall be bound-lessly content to die. (5)

Now, seven paragraphs further along, the chance and probability of such an affirmation (one that is double and therefore boundless, lim-itless) is granted to woman. It returns to woman. Rather, not to woman or even to the feminine, to the female gender [*genre feminin*], or to the generality of the feminine gender but—and this is why I spoke of chance and probability—"usually" to women. It is "usually" women who say *yes, yes.* To life to death. This "usually" avoids treating the feminine as a general and generic force; it makes an opening for the event, the performance, the uncertain contingencies, the encounter. And it is indeed from the contingent experience of the encounter that "I" will speak here. In the passage that I am about to cite, the expression "men" occurs twice. The second occurrence names the sexual genre, the sexual difference (*aner, vir*—but sexual difference does not occur between a species and a genre); in the first occurrence, "men" comes into play in an indecisive manner in order to name the human race (named "species" in the text) or sexual difference:

> Men would like to escape death, bizarre *species* that they are. And some cry out, "die, die," because they would like to escape life. "What a life! I'll kill myself, I'll surrender!" This is pitiful and strange; it is in error.
> But I have encountered *beings* who never told life to be quiet or death to go away—usually women, beautiful creatures. As for men, terror besieges them . . . (7; italics added)

What has thus far transpired in these seven paragraphs? Usually women, beautiful creatures, relates "I." As it happens, encounter, chance, affirmation of chance do not always manage to happen. There is no natural or symbolic law, universal law, or law of a genre/gender here. Only usually, usually women, (comma of apposition) beautiful creatures. Through its highly calculated logic, the comma of apposition leaves open the possibility of thinking that these women are not, on the one hand, beautiful and then, on the other hand, as it happens, capable of saying *yes, yes* to life to death, of not saying *be quiet, go away* to life to death. The comma of apposition lets us think they are beautiful, women and beauties, these creatures, insofar as they affirm both life and death. Beauty, the feminine beauty of these "beings," would be bound up with this double affirmation.

Now I myself, who "am neither learned nor ignorant," "I feel a boundless pleasure in living and shall be boundlessly content to die." In this random claim that links affirmation usually to women, beautiful ones, it is then more than probable that, as long as I say *yes, yes,* I am a woman and beautiful. I am a woman, and beautiful. Grammatical sex (or anatomical as well, in any case, sex submitted to the law of objectivity): the masculine gender [*genre*] is thus affected by the affirmation through a random drift that could always render it other. A sort of secret coupling would take place here, forming an odd marriage ("hymen"), an odd couple, for none of this can be regulated by objective, natural, or civil law. The "usually" is a mark of this secret and odd hymen, of this coupling that is also perhaps a mixing of genders/genres. The genders/genres pass into each other. And we will not be barred from thinking that this mixing of genders, viewed in light of the madness of sexual difference, may bear some relation to the mixing of literary genres.

"I," then, keep alive the chance of being a female or of changing sex. Transsexuality permits me, in a more than metaphorical and transferential way, to engender. "I" can give birth, and many other signs which I cannot mention here bear this out, among other things the fact that on several occasions I "bring something forth to the light of day." In the rhetoric of *La folie du jour,* the idiomatic expression "to bring forth to the light of day" [*donner le jour*] is one of the players in an exceedingly powerful polysemic and disseminal game that I shall not attempt to reproduce here. I only retain its standard and dominant meaning which the spirit of linguistics gives it: *donner le jour* is to give birth—a verb whose subject is usually maternal, that is to say, generally female. At the center, closely hugging an invisible center, a primal scene could have alerted us, if we had had the time, to the *point of view* of *La folie du jour* and to *A Primal Scene*.[9] This is also called a "short scene."

"I" can bring forth to light, can give birth. To what? Well, precisely to law, or more exactly, to begin with, to the representatives of law, to those who wield authority—and let us also understand by this the authority of the author, the rights of authorship—simply by virtue of possessing an overseer's right, the right to see, the right to have everything in sight. This panoptic, this synopsis, they demand nothing else, but nothing less. Now herein lies the essential paradox: from where and from whom do they derive this power, this right-to-sight that permits them to have "me" at their disposal? Well, from "me," rather, from the subject who is subjected to them. It is the "I"-less "I" of the narrative voice, the "I" "stripped" of itself, the one that does not take place, it is he who brings them to light, who engenders these lawmen in giving them insight into what regards them and what should not regard them.

I liked the doctors well enough. I did not feel belittled by their doubts. The bother was that their authority grew with every hour. One isn't initially aware of it, but these men are kings. Showing me my rooms they said: Everything here belongs to us. They threw themselves upon the parings of my mind: This is ours. They interpellated my story: Speak! and it placed itself at their service. In haste, I stripped myself of myself. I distributed my blood, my privacy among them, I offered them the universe, I brought them forth to the light of day. Under their unblinking gaze, I became a water drop, an ink blot. I was shrinking into them, I was held entirely in their view and when, finally, I no longer had anything but my perfect nullity present and no longer had anything to see, they, too, ceased to see me, most annoyed, they rose shouting: Well, where are you? Where are you hiding? Hiding is prohibited, it is a misdeed, etc. (14)

9. Maurice Blanchot, *Une scène primitive*—initially published separately (in *Première livraison*, 1976), the text thus entitled was reinscribed in *L'écriture du désastre* (1980). [EN This work has been translated by Ann Smock as *The Writing of the Disaster* (Lincoln: University of Nebraska Press, 1986).]

Law, day. It is generally believed that one can oppose law to affirmation, and particularly to unlimited affirmation, to the immensity of *yes, yes*. Law—we often figure it as an instance of the interdictory limit, of the binding obligation, as the negativity of a boundary not to be crossed. Now the mightiest and most divided trait of *La folie du jour* or of "A *récit?*" is the one relating the birth of the law, its genealogy, engenderment, generation, or genre, the very genre of the law, to the process of the double affirmation. The excessiveness of *yes, yes* is no stranger to the genesis of law (nor to genesis itself, as could be easily shown, for there is also at stake here a *récit* of Genesis in "the light of seven days" [11]). The double affirmation is not foreign to the genre, genius or spirit of the law. No affirmation, and certainly no *double* affirmation without the law sighting the light of day and the daylight becoming law. Such is the madness of the day, such is a *récit* in its "remarkable" truth, in its truthless truth.

Now the feminine, the almost always affirmative gender/genre ("usually women"), is also the gender of this figure of law, not of its representatives, but of the law herself who, throughout a *récit*, forms a couple with me, with the "I" of the narrative voice.

The law is in the feminine.

She is not a woman (it is only a figure, a "silhouette," and not a representative of the law) but she, *la loi*, is in the feminine, declined in the feminine; not only as a grammatical gender in my language; elsewhere Blanchot will have brought this gender into play for speech ["*la parole*"] and for thought ["*la* pensée"]. No, she is described as a "female element," which does not signify a female person. And the affirmative "I," the narrative voice, who has brought forth the representatives of the law to the light of day, claims to find the law seductive—sexually seductive. The law appeals to him: "The truth is that she appealed to me. In this milieu overpopulated with men, she was the only female element. One time she had me touch her knee: a bizarre impression. I declared to her: I am not the kind of man who contents himself with a knee. Her response: that would be revolting!" (16–17). She pleases him and he would not like to content himself with the knee that she "had (him) touch." This contact with the knee [*genou*], as my student and friend Pierre-François Berger brought to my notice, recalls the inflectional contiguity of the I and the we, the *je* and the *nous*, of an I/we couple of whom we shall speak again in a moment.

The law's female element has thus always attracted: me, I, he, we. The law attracts: "The law attracted me. . . . In order to tempt her, I called softly to the law: 'Approach, so I can see you face to face' (I wanted to take her aside for a moment). Impudent appeal; what would I have done had she responded?" (9).

He is perhaps subjected to law, but he neither attempts to escape her, nor does he shrink before her: he wishes to seduce the law to whom he gives birth (there is a hint of incest in this) and especially— this is one of the most striking and singular traits of this scene—he inspires fear in the law. He not only troubles the representatives of the law, the lawmen who are medical experts and the "psy" 's—who demand of him, but are unable to obtain, an organized account, a testimony oriented by a sense of history or his history, ordained and ordered by reason, and by the unity of an *I think,* or of an *originally synthetic apperception accompanying all representations.* That the "I" here does not always accompany itself is by no means borne lightly by the lawmen; in fact, he alarms thus the lawmen, he radically persecutes them, and, in his manner, conceals from them without altercation the truth they demand and without which they are nothing. But he not only alarms the lawmen, he alarms the law; one would be tempted to say the law herself, if she did not remain here a silhouette and an effect of the *récit.* And what is more, this law whom the "I" frightens is none other than "me," than the "I," effect of his desire, child of his affirmation, of the genre "I" clasped in a specular couple with "me." They are inseparable (*je/nous* and *genou, je/toi* and *je/toit*), and so she tells him, once more, as truth: "The truth is that we can no longer be separated. I shall follow you everywhere, I shall dwell under your roof (*toit*), we shall have the same sleep" (15). We see the law, whose silhouette stands behind her representatives, frightened by "me," by "him"; she is inclined toward and declined by *je/nous,* I/we, in front of "me," in front of him, her knees marking perhaps the articulation of a gait [*pas*], the flexion of the couple and sexual difference, but also the contiguity without contact of the hymen and the "mixing of genres."

Behind their backs, I perceived the silhouette of the law. Not the familiar law, who is strict and not terribly agreeable: this one was different. Far from falling prey to her menace, I was the one who seemed to frighten her. According to her, my glance was lightning and my hands, grounds on which to perish. Moreover, she ridiculously attributed to me all kinds of power, she declared herself perpetually at my knees. But she let me demand nothing, and when she granted me the right to be in all places, that meant that I hadn't a place anywhere. When she placed me above the authorities, that meant: you are authorized to do nothing. (14–15)

"I hadn't a place anywhere," at the same time as she granted me the right to be in all places. It's in this way that Blanchot elsewhere designates the non-place and the topological or hypertopological mobility of the narrative voice.

What game is the law, a law of this genre, playing? What is she playing at when she has her knee touched? For if *La folie du jour* plays down the law, plays at law, plays with law, it is also because the law herself plays. The law, in its female element, is a silhouette that plays. At what? At being born, at being born *like anybody or nobody*.[10] She plays upon her generation and her genre, she plays out her nature and her history, and she makes a plaything of a *récit*. In mock-playing herself she recites; and she is born of the one for whom she becomes the law. She is born of him himself, one could even say of her herself, since her gender can reverse itself *in the affirmation; he* or *she* is the narrative voice, *him, her, I, we,* the neuter gender that lets itself be captivated by the law, subjects itself to her and escapes her, whom she escapes and whom she loves, etc. She lets herself be put in motion, she lets herself be *cited* by him when, in the midst of her game, she says, pursuing an idiom that her disseminal polysemy conveys to the abyss, "I see day":

Here is one of her games. [He has just recalled that she "once had [him] touch her knee."] She showed me a section of the space between the top of the window and the ceiling: "You are there," she said. I looked at this

10. TN *Naître comme personne;* this phrases releases a number of interpretations: it lets us hear *naître* (to be born) as *n'être* (not to be), and *personne* as a person and its opposite, nobody.

point with intensity. "Are you there?" I looked at it with all my power. "Well?" I felt the scars of my gaze leap, my sight became a wound, my head, a gap, a gutted bull. Suddenly she cried out: "Oh! I see day! Oh God!" etc. I protested that this game tired me enormously, but she was insatiable for my glory. (17)

For the law to see the day is her madness, is what she loves madly like glory, the sunlit illustration, the day of the writer, of the author who says "I," and who brings forth law to the light of day. He says that she is insaturable, insatiable for his glory—he who is, too, author of the law to which he submits himself, he who engenders her, he, her mother who no longer knows how to say "I" or to keep memory intact. I am the mother of law, behold my daughter's madness. It is also the madness of the day, for day, the word *day* in its disseminal abyss, is law, the law of the law. My daughter's madness is to want to be born— like anybody and nobody [*comme personne*]. Whereas she remains a "silhouette," a shadow, a profile, her face never in view. He had said to her, to the law, in order to "tempt her": "Approach, so I can see you face to face."

Such would be the "remarkable truth" that clears an opening for the madness of day—and that appeals, like law, like madness, to the one who says "I" or "I/we." Let us be attentive to this syntax of truth. She, the law, says: "The truth is that we can no longer be separated. I shall follow you everywhere, I shall live under your roof . . ." He: "The truth is that she appealed to me . . . ," she, law, but also—and this is always the principal theme of these sentences—she, truth [*La vérité, c'est qu'elle me plaisait*]. One cannot conceive truth without the madness of the law.

I have let myself be commanded by the law of our encounter, by the convention of our subject, notably genre, the law of genre. This law, articulated as an I/we which is more or less autonomous in its movements, assigned us places and limits. Even though I have launched an appeal against this law, it was she who turned my appeal into a confirmation of her own glory. But she also desires ours insatiably.

Submitting myself to the subject of our colloquim, as well as to its law, I have sifted "A *récit*," *La folie du jour*. I have isolated a type, if not a genre, of reading from an infinite series of trajectories or possible courses. I have pointed out the generative principle of these courses, beginnings, and new beginnings in every sense: but from a certain point of view. Elsewhere—in accordance with other subjects, other colloquia and lectures, other I/we drawn together in one place—other trajectories could have come to light.

Nonetheless, it would be folly to draw any sort of general conclusion here. I could not say what exactly has happened in this scene, nor in my discourse or my account. What was perhaps seen, in the time of a blink, is a madness of law—and, therefore, of order, reason, sense and meaning, of day: "But often," (said "I") "I was dying without saying a thing. In time, I became convinced that I was seeing the madness of day face to face; such was the truth: light became mad, clarity took leave of her senses; she assailed me unreasonably, without a set of rules, without a goal. This discovery was like jaws clutching at my life."

I am woman, and beautiful; my daughter, the law, is mad about me. I speculate on my daughter. My daughter is mad about me; this is law.

The law is mad, she is mad about "me." And across the madness of this day, I keep this in sight.[11] There, this will have been my self-portrait of the genre.

The law is mad. The law is mad, is madness; but madness is not the predicate of law. There is no madness without the law; madness cannot be conceived before its relation to law. This is the law, the law is a madness.

There is a general trait here: the madness of the law mad for me, the day madly in love with me, the silhouette of my daughter mad about me, her mother, etc. But *La folie du jour*, "A *récit*?" without *récit*, carrying and miscarrying its titles, is not at all exemplary of this general trait. Not at all, not of the whole [*Pas du tout*]. This is not an example of a general or generic whole. Not of the whole, not at all. Of the

---

11. EN Several meanings are possible for *ça me regarde* in this context: "this is of concern to me," "it watches me," even "the id watches me."

whole, which begins by finishing and never finishes beginning apart from itself, of the whole that stays at the edgeless boundary of itself, of the whole greater and less than a whole and nothing. "A *récit?*" will not have been exemplary. Rather, with regard to the whole, it will have been wholly counter-exemplary.

The genre has always in all genres been able to play the role of order's principle: resemblance, analogy, identity and difference, taxonomic classification, organization and genealogical tree, order of reason, order of reasons, sense of sense, truth of truth, natural light and sense of history. Now, the test of "A *récit?*" brought to light the madness of genre. Madness has given birth to, thrown light on genre in the most dazzling, most blinding sense of the word. And in the writing of "A *récit?*", in literature, satirically practicing all genres, imbibing them but never allowing herself to be saturated with a catalogue of genres, she, madness, has started spinning Peterson's genre-disc like a demented sun.[12] And she does not only do so *in* literature, for in concealing the boundaries that sunder mode and genre, she has also inundated *and* divided the borders between literature and its others.

There, that is the whole of it, it is only what "I," so they say, here kneeling at the edge of literature, see. In sum, the law. The law summoning. [*La loi en somme.*] What "I" sees and what "I" says that I see in a *récit* where I/we are, where I summon us [*où je/nous somme*].

12. EN Julius Peterson was a German aesthetician of the first part of the twentieth century who devised a schema encompassing all literary genres, laid out in the form of a wheel. See Genette, *Introduction à l'architexte,* 56–60.

7

ULYSSES GRAMOPHONE

HEAR SAY YES IN JOYCE

When Derrida was invited to deliver the opening address at the Ninth International James Joyce Symposium in Frankfurt in 1984, he had already on a number of occasions made clear the importance of Joyce's writing to his own work, and in the one essay on Joyce he had published at that time, "Two Words for Joyce" (which devotes most attention to *Finnegans Wake*), he had given some account of this continuing importance. But few people in the audience could have been prepared for the long, detailed, circuitous, always unpredictable, frequently comic exploration of *Ulysses* that developed out of the apparently innocuous opening, "Oui, oui, vous m'entendez bien, ce sont des mots français."

The essay's wandering path, as it weaves together the story of its own composition, fragments of the text of *Ulysses,* and a number of the issues which Derrida has addressed at length elsewhere, mimes both Joyce's novel (together with its Homeric predecessor) and a crucial aspect of its argument: the necessary connection between chance and necessity. What must have seemed to most of its first audience a haphazard trajectory becomes, with greater familiarity, an intricately plotted itinerary, a series of circular movements that keep returning to themselves and at the same time opening themselves beyond previously established limits. And one of Derrida's points—broached also in "Aphorism Countertime"—is that what we call "chance events" are made possible only by the pre-existence of a network of codes and connections; hence one of his deployments of the figure of Elijah in *Ulysses,* as the mega-switchboard operator. But the emphasis runs the other way as well; Elijah is *also* a figure for the unexpected, the unpredictability built into any highly complex program (and Derrida associates himself, the outsider to the Joyce establishment, with this figure).

Joyce's oeuvre, in the thematics of this lecture, stands for the most comprehensive synthesis of the modern university's fields of knowledge, containing within itself all that can be written about itself. Approached in this light, the laughter it evokes is a derisive mockery of the efforts of those who analyze and systematize, who try to say something *new*. Yet it is precisely the overdetermined complexity of this textual program that makes *possible* the new, the advent of the completely other, the chance collocation that results in a new invention. And so the laughter of Joyce's writings has another modality, a positive, if fleeting, affirmation, which we might compare with the fleeting appearance of "literature" suggested by Mallarmé's "Mimique" (see p. 177 above). Both of these responses are necessary, and both are evident in Derrida's dealings with *Ulysses:* his painstaking counting of the *yes*es in the text, and his relishing of the coincidences that stud the history of his writing on the text, during an odyssey that takes him from Ohio to Tokyo, from Tokyo to Paris.

It is the *yes* in *Ulysses* that provides the connection between many of the diverse sequences of the lecture. The apparent simplicity of the word quickly gives way to a sense of its capacity to upset all the conventional, "philosophical" categorizations of linguistics. In Derrida's hands it starts to show its affinity with a number of other terms— *différance*, supplement, trace, re-mark, hymen, etc.—that open onto the unnameable preconditions of all naming and categorizing. Every utterance involves a kind of minimal "yes," an "I am here" (Derrida finds a number of telephones in *Ulysses* that help him to make this point); an affirmation that "precedes" (not temporally or logically) even the utterance "I," whether vocalized or silent. But the other crucial feature of "yes" is that it is always a *response*, strikingly dramatized in the words of Molly Bloom that bring *Ulysses* to a close, and this remains true even if it is a response to oneself; that is to say, it always involves a relay through an other. (*Oui dire*—saying yes—is always *ouï dire*—hearsay.) "Yes" breaches time as well as space, as it always involves a commitment, a willingness to say "yes" again. With this relay, this differing and deferring, this necessary failure of total self-identity, comes spacing (space *and* time), gramophoning (writing *and* speech), memory, recording, computers, and ultimately the whole Joyce mega-machine. In other words, the very possibility of a Joyce industry—the acme and splendid caricature of contemporary humanistic studies—stems from the distance established within the apparently simple "yes"; it is this that provides it with its tools (which are essentially those of the Western philosophical tradition) and its materials. At the same time, because its projects—totalization, theorization, formalization, explication, archeology, instrumentalization—all demand the abolition of that self-difference and spacing, it is the "yes" that renders its task uncompletable, and the notion of a "competent" scholar in Joyce studies impossible. It is this ultimate impossibility that gives Joyce studies its chance, if it will take the risk (for instance, by inviting outsiders to its symposia); since if it were not for the incalculable self-difference of the "yes," the answers would already, in principle, be known, and the mocking modality of Joycean laughter would be the only one.

As always, Derrida is responding to what seems to him at a given moment to be the singularity of Joyce's text: its encyclopedic ambitions (one might even say that Derrida *imagines* a text that fulfills these ambitions more totally than Joyce was able to do), its simultaneous foregrounding of complex connectedness and chance collocations, its double-edged comedy (we might recall how the tradition of *Ulysses* criticism has frequently divided between those who see it as essentially satiric and those who see it as life-enhancingly affirmative), its involvement with communications networks (in both technological and more general senses), its concern with the relation of the self to itself (notably in interior monologues), and its extraordinary capacity to generate an international industry, of which the biennial James Joyce Symposia are the most remarkable manifestation. (We might note, however, that the "play of the signifier"—often taken to be the major affinity between Joyce and Derrida—is not of great importance here.) In order to sketch some kind of response to this singularity, to countersign Joyce's signature with his own (both signatures being, like all signatures, at once unique and programmable; and, like all signatures, involving a "yes," just as all *yes*es involve a signature), Derrida exploits an assortment of examples from *Ulysses,* often examples which thematize the issues under discussion—though he makes it clear that the requirements of exposition always necessitate a certain violence in excerpting from a text. Most notable, of course, are the occurrences of "yes": it becomes clear that even if *Ulysses* did not contain a single actualized "yes," the argument would be no different—but the number and variety of instances of the word, and in particular its function in the last chapter, allow Derrida to focus very precisely his powerful response to Joyce's achievement.

&. Derrida's two essays on Joyce have been published together in French under the title *Ulysse gramophone: Deux mots pour Joyce*

(Paris: Galilée, 1987); the English translation of the first version of "Ulysse gramophone: Ouï-dire de Joyce" was published in the Proceedings of the Ninth International James Joyce Symposium, *James Joyce: The Augmented Ninth*, ed. Bernard Benstock (Syracuse, N.Y.: Syracuse University Press, 1988). The text was translated by Tina Kendall and revised by Shari Benstock; translator's notes are by Shari Benstock. The translation has been editorially modified in the light of the published French text. The text of *Ulysses* to which Derrida refers is that of the Penguin edition (Harmondsworth, 1968).

———————————

Oui, oui, you are receiving me, these are French words.[1] To be sure, and I do not even need to reinforce my message with another phrase, all you need is to have heard the first word, *oui,* to know, that is if you understand enough French, that, thanks to the authorization graciously bestowed on me by the organizers of this James Joyce Symposium, I shall address you, more or less, in the language presumed to be mine [*ma langue supposée*], though the last expression can be almost seen as an anglicism.

But can *oui* be quoted or translated? This is one of the questions I intend to pose during this talk. How can the sentences that I have just thrown out at you be translated? The one I began with, just as Molly begins and ends what is too lightly referred to as her monologue, that is, the repetition of a *oui,* is not content just to *mention,* it *uses* in its own way these two *ouis,* the ones that I now quote. In my opening, you could not decide, and you are still incapable of deciding, if I was saying *oui* to you or if I was quoting, or shall we say more generally, if I was mentioning the word *oui* twice, as a reminder, and I quote, that these are indeed French words.

In the first case, I affirm, acquiesce, subscribe to, approve, reply, or make a promise; at any rate, I commit myself and I sign: to take up

1. TN The French verb *entendre* includes in its range of meanings "to hear" and "to understand," both of which are implied in the translation "receiving."

again the old speech act theory distinction, which is useful up to a certain point, between *use* and *mention,* the use of *oui* is always implicated in the moment of a signature.

In the second case, I would, rather, have quoted or mentioned the *oui, oui.* Now if the act of quoting or mentioning also undoubtedly presupposes some signature, some confirmation of the act of mentioning, this remains implicit and the implicit *oui* is not to be confused with the quoted or mentioned *oui.*

So you still do not know what I wanted to *say* or *do* when I began with this sentence, "*Oui, oui,* you are receiving me, these are French words." In fact you are not receiving me loud and clear at all.

I repeat the question: how will the sentences that I have just thrown out at you be translated? Insofar as they mention or quote *oui,* they repeat the French word, and translation is, in principle, absurd or illegitimate: *yes, yes,* these are not French words. When at the end of the *Discours de la méthode,* Descartes explains why he had decided to write in the language of his country, the Latin translation of the *Discours* simply omits this paragraph. What is the sense of writing a sentence in Latin, the gist of which is: the following reasons illustrate why I am now writing in French? It is true that the Latin translation was the only one violently to erase this affirmation of the French language. For it was not just one translation among many; it claimed, according to the laws of the philosophical society of the time, to bring the *Discours de la méthode* back to what should have been the true original in its true language. But we'll leave that for another lecture.[2] I simply wanted to mark that the affirmation of a language through itself is untranslatable. An act which in one language *remarks* the language itself, and which in this way affirms doubly, once by speaking it and once by saying that it has thus been spoken, opens up the space for a *re-marking,* which, at the same time and in the same double way, defies and calls for translation. According to a distinction I have hazarded elsewhere concerning history and the name of Babel,[3] what remains *untranslatable* is at bottom the only thing *to translate,* the

---

2. See "Languages and Institutions of Philosophy," lectures I and II.
3. EN See "Des tours de Babel" and "Two Words for Joyce."

only thing *translatable*. What must be translated of that which is translatable can only be the untranslatable.

You have already realized that I have been preparing the ground to speak to you about the *oui,* the *yes,* or at the very least, about some of the modalities of *oui,* and I shall now be more explicit, in the form of an initial sketch focusing on some of the sequences in *Ulysses.*

To put an end, without further ado, to circulation or to an interminable circumnavigation, to avoid the aporia with a view to a better beginning, I threw myself in the water, as we say in French, and I decided to open myself, together with you, to a chance encounter. With Joyce, luck is always taken in hand by the law, by meaning, by the program, according to the overdetermination of figures and ruses. And yet the chance nature of meetings, the randomness of coincidences lends itself to being affirmed, accepted, yes, even approved in all their fallings-out.[4] In all their fallings-out, that is to say, in all the genealogical chances that set adrift the notion of legitimate filiation in *Ulysses* and no doubt elsewhere. This is all too clear in the encounter between Bloom and Stephen, to which I shall return shortly.

To throw oneself in the water, I was saying. I was, to be specific, thinking of the water of a lake. But, knowing Joyce's word, you may have thought that I was referring to the bottle in the sea. But lakes were not so foreign to him, as I shall presently demonstrate.

The throw of the dice to which I said *oui,* deciding in the same gesture to subject *you* to it too: I give it the proper name—Tokyo.

Tokyo: does this city lie on the western circle that leads back to Dublin or to Ithaca?

An aimless wandering, a random trek, led me one day to the passage ("Eumaeus," The Shelter, 1 a.m.) in the course of which Bloom names "the coincidence of meeting, discussion, dance, row, old salt, of the here today and gone tomorrow type, night loafers, the whole galaxy of events, all went to make up a miniature cameo of the world we live in" (*U,* 567). The "galaxy of events" was translated into French by

4. EN "Fallings-out" here does duty for *échéances,* which combines the sense of necessity (*l'échéance* is the falling due of a bill) and chance (*le cas échéant* means "if it should happen"). With regard to the next sentence, it is worth citing part of the etymology of *échéance* given in *Robert:* "17th cent.: inheritance by collateral line."

"gerbe ['sheaf'] *des évenéments,"* which omits the milk and therefore the milky tea that runs through *Ulysses,* turning it into a milky way or "galaxy." Allow me one more slight detour, a parenthesis: we were wondering what happens to the *yes* when it is repeated in a "mention" or in a quotation. But what happens when it becomes a trademark, a kind of nontransferable commercial license? And since we are spinning in the milk here, what happens when *yes* becomes, yes, a brand, or a brandname, of yoghurt? I shall come back to Ohio, this place marked in *Ulysses.* Now in Ohio there exists a type of Dannon yoghurt which is simply called YES. Underneath the YES to be read on the lid, we find the slogan: "Bet You Can't Say No to Yes."

"Coincidence of meeting" declares the passage I was in the middle of quoting. A little later the name *Tokyo* crops up: suddenly, like a telegram or the heading of a page in a newspaper, *The Telegraph,* which is to be found under Bloom's elbow, "as luck would have it"— as it says at the beginning of the paragraph.

The name *Tokyo* is associated with a battle. "Great battle Tokio." It is not Troy, but Tokyo, in 1904; the battle with Russia. Now, I was in Tokyo just over a month ago, and that is where I began writing this lecture—or rather, I began to dictate the main ideas into a pocket cassette recorder.

I decided to date it like this—and dating is signing—on the morning of 11 May when I was looking for postcards in a sort of news agency in the basement of the Okura Hotel. I was looking for postcards that would show Japanese lakes, or let's call them inland seas. It had crossed my mind to follow the edges of lakes in *Ulysses,* to venture out on a grand lakeside tour between the lake of life which is the Mediterranean Sea and the *Lacus Mortis* referred to in the hospital scene, as it happens, and dominated by the symbol of the mother: ". . . they came trooping to the sunken sea, *Lacus Mortis.* . . . Onward to the dead sea they tramp to drink . . ." (*U,* 411). This is, in fact, what I had initially thought of for this lecture on *Ulysses,* to *address,* as you say in English, the postcard scene, to some extent the inverse of what I did in *La carte postale,* where I tried to restage the babelization of the postal system in *Finnegans Wake.* You will no doubt know better than I that the whole pack of postcards perhaps hints at the hypothesis that the geography of Ulysses' trips around the Mediterranean lake could have the structure of a postcard or a cartography of postal dispatches. This will gradually be illustrated, but for the moment I should like to take up a remark made by J. J. in which he speaks of the equivalence of a postcard and a publication. Any public piece of writing, any open text, is also offered like the exhibited surface, in no way private, of an open letter, and therefore of a postcard with its address incorporated in the message and hereafter open to doubt, and with its coded and at the same time stereotyped language, trivialized by the very code and number. Conversely, any postcard is a public document, deprived of all privacy and, moreover, in this way laying itself open to the law. This is indeed what J. J. says: "—And moreover, says J. J. [they are not just any initials], a postcard is publication. It was held to be sufficient evidence of malice in the testcase Sadgrove *v* Hole. In my opinion an action might lie" (U, 320). Translated: there would be cause for a certain action to be pursued before the law, to sue, but also that the action itself might tell an untruth. In the beginning, the speech act...

The trace, the relay, of the postcard that we are following can be found in Mr. Reggy Wylie's postcard, "his silly postcard" that Gerty could tear "into a dozen pieces" (U, 360). Among others, there is also the "postcard to Flynn" on which Bloom remembers, furthermore, having forgotten to write the address, which underlies the nature of anonymous publicity: a postcard has no proper addressee, apart from the person who acknowledges having received it with some inimitable signature. *Ulysses,* an immense postcard. "Mrs. Marion. Did I forget to write the address on that letter like the postcard I sent to Flynn?" (U, 367). I lift these postcards from a discursive path, or more precisely, a narrative path, which I cannot reconstitute each time. Here there is an ineluctable problem of method to which I shall return in a moment. The postcard without an address does not let itself be forgotten; it recalls itself to Bloom's memory just when he is looking for a misplaced letter: "Where did I put the letter? Yes, all right" (U, 365). We can assume that the reassuring "yes" accompanies and confirms the return of memory: the letter's place has been found. A little further, after Reggy's "silly postcard," there is the "silly letter": "Damned glad I didn't do it in the bath this morning over her silly I will punish you letter" (*U, 366*). Let us leave enough time for the fragrance of this bath and the revenge of this letter to reach us. You could pursue the intensification of derision up to Molly's sarcastic remarks about Breen: "now [he's] going about in his slippers to look for £1000 for a postcard up up O Sweetheart May" (*U, 665*).

So I was in the middle of buying postcards in Tokyo, in an underground passage in the Hotel Okura. Now the sequence which, in telegraphic style, mentions the "Great battle Tokio," after having recalled the "coincidence of meeting," the illegitimate genealogy and erratic seed that links Stephen to Bloom, "the galaxy of events," and so on, is a passage from another postcard. Not this time a postcard without an address but a postcard without a message. So one could say a postcard without a text, which could be reduced to the mere association of a picture and an address. Now it so happens that here the address is fictitious too. The addressee of this messageless card is a sort of fictitious reader. Before returning to this question, let us complete a circle by way of the "Tokyo" sequence, which I must quote. It follows closely upon the extraordinary exchange between Bloom and Stephen on the subject of *belonging:* "You suspect, Stephen retorted with a sort of half laugh, that I may be important because I belong to the *Faubourg Saint Patrice* called Ireland for short" (*U, 565*).

"I would go a step farther, Mr. Bloom insinuated" (the French translation, which renders "a step farther" as *un peu plus loin,* and which met the approval of J. J., who cosigned it, lacks among other things the association "stepfather," which superimposes at the heart of all these genealogical fantasies, with their generic crossovers and chance disseminations, a dream of legitimation through adoption and the return of the son, or through marriage with the daughter. But we can never tell who belongs to whom, what to whom, what to what, who to what. There is no subject of belonging, no more than there is an owner of the postcard: it remains without any assigned addressee.)

—But I suspect, Stephen interrupted, that Ireland must be important because it belongs to me.

—What belongs? queried Bloom, bending, fancying he was perhaps under some misapprehension. Excuse me. Unfortunately I didn't catch the latter portion. What was it you?...

Stephen speeds things up: "We can't change the country. Let us change the subject" (*U*, 565–66).

But going to Tokyo is not enough to change the country, let alone the language.

A little later, then; the return of the messageless postcard made out to a fictitious addressee. Bloom thinks of the aleatory encounters, the galaxy of events, and he dreams of writing, as I am doing here, of what happens to him, his story, "my experiences," as he puts it, and he wants to keep some kind of chronicle of this, a diary within a newspaper, by making free associations without constraint. So here it is, we are drawing close to the postcard in the vicinity of Tokyo: "The coincidence of meeting . . . the whole galaxy of events. . . . To improve the shining hour he wondered whether he might meet with anything approaching the same *luck* [my italics] as Mr. Philip Beaufoy if taken down in writing. Supposing he were to pen something out of the common groove (as he fully intended doing) at the rate of one guinea per column, *My Experiences*, let us say, *in a Cabman's Shelter*" (*U*, 567).

My Experiences is both my "phenomenology of mind" in the Hegelian sense of a "science of the experience of consciousness" and the great circular return, the autobiographic-encyclopedic circumnavigation of Ulysses: there has often been talk of the Odyssey of the phenomenology of mind. Here the phenomenology of mind would have the form of a diary of the conscious and the unconscious in the chance form of letters, telegrams, newspapers called, for example, *The Telegraph* (long-distance writing), and also of postcards whose only text, sometimes, taken out of a sailor's pocket, exhibits nothing but a phantom address.

Bloom has just spoken of "My Experiences":

The pink edition, extra sporting, of the *Telegraph*, tell a graphic lie, lay, as luck would have it, beside his elbow and as he was just puzzling again, far from satisfied, over a country belonging to him and the preceding rebus the vessel came from Bridgwater and the postcard was addressed to A. Boudin, find the captain's age, his *eyes* [my emphasis on the word *eyes*, to which we shall return] went aimlessly over the respective captions which came under his special province, the allembracing give us this day our daily press. First he got a bit of a start but it turned out to be only something about somebody named H. du Boyes, agent for typewriters or something like that. Great battle Tokio. Lovemaking in Irish £200 damages. (*U, 567*)

I am not going to analyze here the stratigraphy of this "battle Tokio" field: experts can do that ad infinitum; the limitations of a lecture permit me only to recount to you, like a postcard cast to sea, *my experiences in Tokyo,* and then to pose the question in passing of the *yes,* of chance, and of Joycean experience as expertise: what is an expert, a Ph.D. scholar in things Joycean? What of the Joycean institution and what should I think of the hospitality with which it honors me today in Frankfurt?

Bloom juxtaposes the allusion to the postcard and something that already offers a pure associative juxtaposition, the contiguity of which is apparently insignificant and yet this insignificance is underlined: it is the question of the captain's age, which we should guess rather than calculate, after the presentation of a series of facts, the figures of a *rebus,* with no evident connection to the question in hand. Nevertheless, always understood in the joke is the fact that the captain is the captain of a ship. Now the postcard is in fact the very same one the sailor spoke about, a sea-traveler, a captain who, like Ulysses, returns one day from a long circular voyage around the Mediterranean lake. A few pages earlier, same place, same time: "—Why, the sailor answered, upon reflection upon it, I've circumnavigated a bit since I first joined on. I was in the Red Sea. I was in China and North America and South America. I seen icebergs plenty, growlers. I was in Stockholm and the Black Sea, the Dardanelles, under Captain Dalton the best bloody man that ever scuttled a ship. I seen Russia. . . . I seen maneaters in Peru..." (*U, 545–46*).

He has been everywhere except Japan, I said to myself. And here he is taking a messageless postcard out of his pocket. As for the address, it is fictitious, as fictitious as *Ulysses,* and it is the only thing that this Ulysses has in his pocket:

He fumbled out a picture postcard from his inside pocket, which seemed to be in its way a species of repository, and pushed it along the table. The printed matter on it stated: *Choza de Indios. Beni, Bolivia.*

All focused their attention on the scene exhibited, at a group of savage women in striped loincloths. . . .

His postcard proved a centre of attraction for Messrs the greenhorns for several minutes, if not more. . . .

Mr. Bloom, without evincing surprise, unostentatiously turned over the card to peruse the partially obliterated address and postmark. It ran as follows: *Tarjeta Postal. Señor A. Boudin, Galeria Becche, Santiago, Chile.* There was no message evidently, as he took particular notice. Though not an implicit believer in the lurid story narrated . . . , having detected a discrepancy between his name (assuming he was the person he represented himself to be and not sailing under false colours after having boxed the compass on the strict q.t. somewhere) and the fictitious addressee of the missive which made him nourish some suspicions of our friend's *bona fides,* nevertheless . . . (*U,* 546–47)

So I am in the process of buying postcards in Tokyo, pictures of lakes, and apprehensive about the intimidating talk to be given before the "Joyce scholars" on the subject of *yes* in *Ulysses,* and on the institution of Joyce Studies when, in the shop in which I find myself quite by chance, in the basement of the Hotel Okura, I fall upon— "coincidence of meeting"—a book entitled *16 Ways to Avoid Saying No* by Massaki Imai. It was, I believe, a book of commercial diplomacy. It is said that out of courtesy the Japanese avoid, as far as possible, saying no, even when they mean no. How can you make *no* heard, when you mean it without saying it? How can *no* be translated by *yes,* and what does translation mean when dealing with the odd pair yes/ no; this is, then, a question that awaits us.[5] Next to this book, on the

---

5. The way this question is dealt with would be heavily overdetermined by the Irish idiom which silently and broadly weighs over the whole text. In its own way, Irish also avoids "yes" and "no" in their direct form. To the question, "Are you ill?", it replies neither "yes" nor "no," using instead the form "I am" or "I am not." "Was he sick?" would elicit "He was" or "He was not," and so on. The manner in which the word *hoc* came to take on the meaning of "yes" is not at all alien to this process. *Oïl (hoc illud)* and *oc* served then to designate languages by the way people said "yes" in them. [EN *Langue d'oïl* was the language of northern France which became modern French; *langue d'oc* was the southern language.] Italian was sometimes called the *si* language. Yes, the name of a language.

same shelf and by the same author, there was another book, again in the English translation: *Never Take Yes for an Answer*. Now if it is difficult to say something very definite, and certainly metalinguistic, on this odd word, *yes*, which names nothing, describes nothing, whose grammatical and semantic status is most enigmatic, it seems at least possible to affirm the following: it must be taken for an answer. It is always in the form of an answer. It occurs after the other, to answer a request or a question, at least implicit, of the other, even if this is the other in me, the representation in me of another speech. *Yes* implies, as Bloom would say, an "implicit believer" in some summons of the other. *Yes* always has the meaning, the function, the mission of an *answer*, even if this answer, as we shall also see, sometimes has the force of an originary and unconditional commitment. Now our Japanese author advises us never to take "yes for an answer." Which may mean two things: *yes* can mean "no," or *yes* is not an answer. Outside the diplomatic-commercial context in which it is situated, such prudence could take us further.

But I am continuing the chronicle of *my experiences*. Just as I was jotting down these titles, an American tourist of the most typical variety leaned over my shoulder and sighed: "So many books! What is the definitive one? Is there any?" It was an extremely small bookshop, a news agency. I almost replied, "Yes, there are two of them, *Ulysses* and *Finnegans Wake*," but I kept this *yes* to myself and smiled inanely like someone who does not understand the language.

Up until now I have been speaking to you about letters in *Ulysses*, and postcards, about typewriters and telegraphs, but the telephone is missing, and I must relate to you a telephonic experience. For a long time, I have thought—and this is still true today—that I would never be ready to give a talk on Joyce to an audience of Joyce experts. But when it comes to Joyce, what is an expert? that's my question. Still just as intimidated and behind schedule, I felt highly embarrassed when, in March, my friend Jean-Michel Rabaté telephoned me to ask for a title. I didn't have one. I only knew that I wanted to discuss *yes* in *Ulysses*.

I had even tried casually counting them; more than 222 *yeses* in the so-called original version (and we know better than ever what precautions we must take when we use this expression). I came up with this no doubt approximate figure after an initial counting up, which took into consideration only the *yeses* in their explicit form.[6] I mean the word *yes,* since there are other examples of *yes* without the word *yes,* and indeed, the number of *yeses* is not the same in translation, which is a major problem; the French version adds quite a few. More than a quarter of these *yeses* are to be found in what is so ingenuously termed Molly's monologue: from the moment there is *yes,* a break will have been made in the monologue, the other is hooked up somewhere on the telephone.

When Jean-Michel Rabaté phoned me, I had, then, already decided to interrogate, if we can put it like that, the *yeses* of *Ulysses* as well as the institution of Joycean experts, and also to question what happens when the word *yes* is written, quoted, repeated, archived, recorded, gramophoned, or is the subject of translation or transfer. But I still had no title, only a statistic and a few notes on a single sheet. I asked Rabaté to wait a second, went up to my room, cast a glance at the page of

6. In the week following this lecture, a student and friend whom I met in Toronto was to draw my attention to another counting up of *yeses.* This calculation arrived at a far higher figure, having no doubt included all the *ayes,* which, I note in passing, are pronounced like the word *I* and pose a problem to which I shall return. Here is the other estimation, that of Noel Riley Fitch in *Sylvia Beach and the Lost Generation: A History of Literary Paris in the Twenties and Thirties* (New York: Norton; London: Penguin, 1983). If I quote the whole paragraph, it is because it seems to me to go beyond the mere arithmeticality of the *yes:* "One consultation with Joyce concerned Benoist-Méchin's translation of the final words of *Ulysses:* 'and his heart was going like mad and yes I said Yes I will.' The young man wanted the novel to conclude with a final 'yes' following the 'I will.' Earlier Joyce had considered using 'yes' (which appears 354 times in the novel) as his final word, but had written 'I will' in the draft that Benoist-Méchin was translating. There followed a day of discussion in which they dragged in all the world's greatest philosophers. Benoist-Méchin, who argued that in French the '*oui*' is stronger and smoother, was more persuasive in the philosophical discussion. 'I will' sounds authoritative and Luciferian. 'Yes,' he argued, is optimistic, an affirmation to the world beyond oneself. Joyce, who may have changed his mind earlier in the discussion, conceded hours later, 'yes,' the young man was right, the book would end with 'the most positive word in the language' " (109–10). [EN The computer which controlled the typesetting of the 1984 critical edition of *Ulysses* prepared by Hans Walter Gabler, and unveiled at the Frankfurt Symposium, made its own count of the *yeses* in the text, and came up with the figure of 359 (not including any *ayes*); see Wolfhard Steppe with Hans Walter Gabler, *A Handlist to James Joyce's "Ulysses"* (New York: Garland, 1985). But this is clearly not the "*n*th generation computer" envisaged by Derrida later in this essay.]

notes and a title crossed my mind with a kind of irresistible brevity, the authority of a telegraphic order: *hear say yes in Joyce* [*l'oui dire de Joyce.*] So, you are receiving me, Joyce's saying *yes* but also the saying or the *yes* that is heard, the *saying yes* that travels round like a quotation or a rumor circulating, circumnavigating via the ear's labyrinth, that which we know only by hearsay [*ouï-dire*]. The play on "hear say yes," *l'oui-dire* and *l'ouï-dire*, can be fully effective only in French, which exploits the obscure, babelian homonymy of *oui* with just a dotted "i," and *ouï* with a diaresis. The untranslatable homonymy can be heard (by hearsay, that is) rather than read *with the eyes*—the last word, *eyes*, let us note in passing, giving itself to a reading of the grapheme *yes* rather than a hearing of it. *Yes* in *Ulysses* can only be a mark at once written and spoken, vocalized as a grapheme and written as a phoneme, yes, *in a word, gramophoned.*

So the *ouï dire* seemed to me to be a good title, sufficiently untranslatable and potentially capable of captioning what I wanted to say about the *yeses* in Joyce. Rabaté said "yes" to me on the telephone, that this title was fine. A few days, less than a week, later, I received Rabaté's admirable book, *Joyce, portrait de l'auteur en autre lecteur* [*James Joyce, Authorized Reader*], whose fourth chapter is entitled *Molly: ouï-dire* (with a diaresis). "Curious coincidence, Mr. Bloom confided to Stephen unobtrusively," just when the sailor admits that he already knows Simon Dedalus; "coincidence of meeting" says Bloom a little later when he bumps into Stephen. So I decided to keep this title as a subtitle to commemorate the coincidence, convinced as I was that the same title did not serve quite the same story.

But as Jean-Michel Rabaté can confirm, it was during another such chance meeting—I was driving along with my mother and I leapt out of my car in a Paris street at the sight of Jean-Michel Rabaté—that we later said, on my return from Japan, that this coincidence must have been "telephoned" in some way by some rigorous program for which the prerecorded necessity, like an answering service, even though it passed through a great number of wires, must have come together in some telephone exchange and worked on us, separately, the one with or on the other, the one before the other without any legitimate belonging being able to be assigned. But this tale of correspondence and telephones does not stop here. Rabaté had to pass on by telephone the title of my talk to someone: this did not fail to produce some specifically Joycean and programmed deformations at the expert exchange, as I received one day from Klaus Reichert a letter on Ninth International James Joyce Symposium letterhead from which I shall just quote this paragraph: "I am very curious to know about your Lui/Oui's which could be spelt Louis as well I suppose. And the Louis' have not yet been detected in Joyce as far as I know. Thus it sounds promising from every angle."

There is at least one major difference between Rabaté, Reichert, and myself, as there is between all of you and myself, and that is the difference of competence. All of you are experts, you belong to one of the most remarkable of institutions. It bears the name of a man who did everything, and admitted it, to make this institution indispensable, to keep it busy for centuries, as though on some new Tower of Babel to "make a name" again. The institution can be seen as a powerful reading machine, a signature and countersignature machine in the service of his name, of his "patent." But as with God and the Tower of Babel, it is an institution which he did everything he could to make impossible and improbable in its very principle, to deconstruct it in advance, even going as far as to undermine the very concept of competence, upon which one day an institutional legitimacy might be founded, whether we are dealing with a competence of knowledge or know-how.

Before returning to this question, that is, of what you and I are doing here, as an exemplification of competence and incompetence, I shall hang on to the telephone for a little longer, before breaking off a more or less telepathic communication with Jean-Michel Rabaté. Up until now we have amassed letters, postcards, telegrams, typewriters, et cetera. We should remember that if *Finnegans Wake* is the sublime babelization of a *penman* and *postman,* the motif of postal difference, of remote control and telecommunication, is already powerfully at work in *Ulysses*. And this is *remarked,* as always, *en abyme.* For example, in "THE WEARER OF THE CROWN": "Under the porch of the general post office shoeblacks called and polished. Parked in North Prince's street, His Majesty's vermilion mailcars, bearing on their sides the royal initials, E. R., received loudly flung sacks of letters, postcards, lettercards, parcels, insured and paid, for local, provincial, British and overseas delivery" (*U*, 118). This *remote control* technology, as we say of television, is not an external element of the context; it affects the inside of meaning in the most elementary sense, even so far as the statement or the inscription of practically the shortest word, the gramophony of *yes*. This is why the wandering circumnavigation of a postcard, letter, or a telegram shifts designations only in the perpetual buzzing of a telephonic obsession, or again, if you take into account a gramophone or answering machine, a telegramophonic obsession.

If I am not mistaken, the first phone call sounds with Bloom's words: "Better phone him up first" in the section entitled "AND IT WAS THE FEAST OF THE PASSOVER" (*U*, 124). A little before, he had somewhat mechanically, like a record, repeated this prayer, the most serious of all prayers for a Jew, the one that should never be allowed to become mechanical, to be gramophoned: *Shema Israel Adonai Elohenu*. If, more or less legitimately (for everything and nothing is legitimate when we lift out some segment on the basis of narrative metonymy) we take out this element from the most manifest thread of the story, then we can speak of the telephonic *Shema Israel* between God, who is infinitely removed (a long-distance call, a collect call from or to the "collector of prepuces") and Israel. *Shema Israel* means, as you know, call to Israel, listen Israel, hello Israel, to the address of the name of Israel, a person-to-person call.[7] The "Better phone him up first" scene takes

---

7. Elsewhere, in the brothel, it is the circumcised who say the "Shema Israel," and there is also the *Lacus Mortis*, the Dead Sea: "THE CIRCUMCISED: (*In a dark guttural chant as they cast dead sea fruit upon him, no flowers*) *Shema Israel Adonai Elohenu Adonai Echad*" (*U*, 496).

And while we are speaking of Ulysses, the Dead Sea, the gramophone, and soon laughter, here is *Remembrance of Things Past:* "He stopped laughing; I should have liked to recognize my friend, but, like Ulysses in the *Odyssey* when he rushes forward to embrace his dead mother, like the spiritualist who tries in vain to elicit from a ghost an answer which will reveal its identity, like the visitor at an exhibition of electricity who cannot believe that the voice which the gramophone restores unaltered to life is not a voice spontaneously emitted by a human being, I was obliged to give up the attempt." A little higher up: "The familiar voice seemed to be emitted by a gramophone more perfect than any I had ever heard." *The Past Recaptured*, trans. Andreas Mayor (New York: Vintage, 1971), 188–89. Biographies: "Those of the earlier generation—Paul Valéry, Paul Claudel, Marcel Proust, André Gide (all born around 1870)—were either indifferent to or hostile toward his work. Valéry and Proust were indifferent. . . . Joyce had only one brief meeting with Proust, who died within months after the publication

place in the offices of *The Telegraph* [*Le télégramme*] newspaper (and not *The Tetragram*) and Bloom has just paused to watch a kind of typewriter, or rather a typesetting machine, a typographic matrix: "He stayed in his walk to watch a typesetter neatly distributing type." And as he "reads it backwards first," composing the name of Patrick Dignam, the name of the father, Patrick, from right to left, he remembers his own father reading the hagadah in the same direction. In the same paragraph, around the name of Patrick, you can follow the whole series of fathers, the twelve sons of Jacob, et cetera, and the word "practice" crops up twice to scan this patristic and *perfectly* paternal litany ("Quickly he does it. Must require some practice that." And twelve lines lower, "How quickly he does that job. Practice makes perfect.") Almost immediately after this we read, "Better phone him up first": "*plutôt un coup de téléphone pour commencer,*" the French translation says. Let's say: a phone call, rather, to begin with. In the beginning, there must indeed have been some phone call.[8]

Before the act or the word, the telephone. In the beginning was the telephone. We can hear the telephone constantly ringing, this *coup de téléphone* which plays on figures that are apparently random, but about which there is so much to say. And it sets going within itself this *yes* toward which, moving in circles around it, we are slowly returning. There are several modalities or tonalities of the telephonic *yes*, but one of them, without saying anything else, amounts to marking, simply, that we are *here*, present, listening, on the end of the line, ready to respond but not for the moment responding with anything other than the preparation to respond (hello, yes: I'm listening, I can hear that you are there, ready to speak just when I am ready to speak to you). In the beginning the telephone, yes, at the beginning of the telephone call, in the beginning, some telephone call [*au commencement du coup de téléphone*].

---

of *Ulysses*" (Fitch, *Sylvia Beach and the Lost Generation,* 95). ". . . coincidence of meeting . . . galaxy of events . . ."

8. EN One might expect the plural here—"some phone calls" (*quelque coups de téléphone*)—but the singular is in line with Derrida's use elsewhere in the essay of *de* meaning, roughly, "some" with a singular count noun (e.g., *de la marque, de l'autre;* "some mark," "some other"), indicating that we have gone beyond the literal meaning of the noun (without, however, entering the metaphorical).

A few pages after "*Shema Israel*" and the first telephone call, just after the unforgettable Ohio scene entitled "MEMORABLE BATTLES RE-CALLED" (you understand that a voice moves quickly from Ohio to the Battle of Tokyo), a certain telephonic *yes* resounds with a "Bingbang" which recalls the origin of the universe. A competent professor has just passed by "—A perfect cretic! the professor said. Long, short and long," after the cry "In Ohio!" "My Ohio!" Then, at the beginning of "O HARP EOLIAN" (*U*, 129), there is the sound of teeth trembling as dental floss is applied (and if I were to tell you that this year, before going to Tokyo, I went to Oxford, Ohio, and that I even bought some dental floss—that is to say, an eolian harp—in a drugstore in Ithaca, you would not believe me. You would be wrong; it is true and can be verified). When "the resonant unwashed teeth" vibrate to the dental floss, we hear "—Bingbang, bangbang." Bloom then asks if he may ring: "I just want to phone about an ad." Then "the telephone whirred inside." This time the eolian harp is not dental floss but the telephone, the cables of which are elsewhere "the navel cords," which connect with Eden (*U*, 43). "—Twenty eight... No, twenty... Double four... Yes." We do not know if this *Yes* is part of a monologue, approving the other within (yes, that's the right number), or if he is already in communication with the other at the end of the line. And we cannot know. The context is cut, it's the end of the section.

But at the end of the following section ("SPOT THE WINNER") the telephonic "yes" rings again in the same offices of *The Telegraph:* "Yes... *Evening Telegraph* here, Mr. Bloom phoned from the inner office. Is the boss...? Yes, *Telegraph*... To where?... Aha! Which auction rooms?... Aha! I see... Right. I'll catch him" (*U*, 130).

It is repeatedly said that the phone call is *internal.* "Mr. Bloom . . . made for the *inner* door" when he wants to ring; then "the telephone whirred *inside,*" and finally, "Mr. Bloom phoned from the *inner* office." So, a telephonic interiority: for before any appliance bearing the name "telephone" in modern times, the telephonic *technē* is at work within the voice, multiplying the writing of voices without any instruments, as Mallarmé would say, a mental telephony, which, inscribing remoteness, distance, *différance,* and spacing [*espacement*] in the *phonē, at the same time* institutes, forbids, *and* interferes with the so-called monologue. At the same time, in the same way, from the first phone call and from the simplest vocalization, from the monosyllabic quasi-interjection of the word *oui,* "yes," "ay." *A fortiori* for those *yes, yes*es which speech act theorists use as an illustration of the performative and which Molly repeats at the end of her co-called monologue, the "*Yes, Yes, I do*" that consents to marriage. When I speak of mental telephony, or even of masturbation, I am implicitly quoting "THE SINS OF THE PAST": "(*In a medley of voices*) He went through a form of clandestine marriage with at least one woman in the shadow of the Black Church. Unspeakable messages he telephoned mentally to Miss Dunne at an address in d'Olier Street while he presented himself indecently to the instrument in the callbox" (*U,* 491–92).

Telephonic spacing is particularly superimprinted in the scene entitled "A DISTANT VOICE." The scene crosses all the lines in our network, the paradoxes of competence and institution, represented here in the shape of the professor, and, in every sense of the word, the *repetition* of *yes* between eyes and ears. All these telephonic lines can be drawn from one paragraph:

A DISTANT VOICE

—I'll answer it, the professor said going.

. . .

—Hello? *Evening Telegraph* here... Hello?... Who's there?... Yes... Yes... Yes...

. . .

The professor came to the inner door. [*inner* again]

—Bloom is at the telephone, he said. (*U,* 137–38)

Bloom is-at-the-telephone. In this way, the professor defines a particular situation at a certain moment in the novel, no doubt, but as is always the case in the stereophony of a text that gives several levels to each statement and always allows metonymic extracts—and I am not the only reader of Joyce to indulge in this pursuit, at once legitimate and abusive, authorized and improper—the professor is also naming the permanent essence of Bloom. It can be read in this particular paradigm: *he is at the telephone,* he is always there, he belongs to the telephone, he is at once riveted and destined there. His being is a being-at-the-telephone. He is hooked up to a multiplicity of voices and answering machines. His being-there is a being-at-the-telephone, a being for the telephone, in the way that Heidegger speaks of the being for death of *Dasein*. And I am not playing with words when I say this: Heideggerian *Dasein* is also a being-called, it always is, as we are informed in *Sein und Zeit*, and as my friend Sam Weber has reminded me, a *Dasein* that accedes to itself only on the basis of the Call (*der Ruf*), a call which has come from afar, which does not necessarily use words, and which, in a certain way, does not say anything. To such an analysis, we could apply down to the last detail the whole of chapter 57 of *Sein und Zeit* on the subject of *der Ruf*, drawing, for example, on sentences like the following: *Der Angerufene ist eben dieses Dasein; aufgerufen zu seinem eigensten Seinkönnen (Sich-vorweg...). Und aufgerufen ist das Dasein durch den Anruf aus dem Verfallen in das Man. . .* : the called one is precisely this *Dasein*; summoned, provoked, challenged toward its ownmost possibility of being (ahead of itself). And in this way the *Dasein* is summoned by this call from or out of the fall into the "they." Unfortunately, we do not have the time to enter further into this analysis, within or beyond the jargon of authenticity (*Eigentlichkeit*), of which this university [Frankfurt] keeps some memory.

    —Bloom is at the telephone, he said.
    —Tell him to go to hell, the editor said promptly. X is Burke's public house, see? (*U*, 138)

Bloom is at the telephone, hooked up to a powerful network to which I shall return in an instant. He belongs in his essence to a polytelephonic structure. But he is at the telephone in the sense that one also *waits* at the telephone. When the professor says, "Bloom is at the telephone," and I shall shortly say, "Joyce is at the telephone," he is saying: he is waiting for someone to respond to him, waiting for an answer, which the editor—who decides the future of the text, its safekeeping or its truth—does not want to give, and who at this point sends him down to hell, into the *Verfallen*, into the hell of censured books.[9] Bloom is waiting for an answer, for someone to say, "hello, yes," that is, for someone to say, "Yes, yes," beginning with the telephonic *yes* indicating that there is indeed another voice, if not an answering machine, on the other end of the line. When, at the end of the book, Molly says, "yes, yes," she is answering a request, but a request that she requests. She is at the telephone, even when she is in bed, asking, and waiting to be asked, on the telephone (since she is alone) to say, "yes, yes." And the fact that she asks "with my eyes" does not prevent this demand being made by telephone; on the contrary: "well as well him as another and then I asked him with my eyes to ask again yes and then he asked me would I yes to say yes my mountain flower and first I put my arms around him yes and drew him down to me so he could feel my breasts all perfume yes and his heart was going like mad and yes I said yes I will Yes" (*U*, 704).

The final "Yes," the last word, the eschatology of the book, yields itself only to *reading*, since it distinguishes itself from the others by an inaudible capital letter; what also remains inaudible, although visible, is the literal incorporation of the *yes* in the eye [*oeil*] of the language, of *yes* in *eyes*. *Langue d'oeil.*

We still do not know what *yes* means and how this small word, if it is one, operates in language and in what we calmly refer to as speech acts. We do not know whether this word shares anything at all with any other word in any language, even with the word *no*, which is most certainly not symmetrical to it. We do not know if a grammatical, semantic, linguistic, rhetorical, or philosophical concept exists capable of this event marked *yes*. Let us leave that aside for the moment. Let us, and this is not merely a fiction, act *as if* this does not prevent us, on the contrary, from hearing what the word *yes* governs. We will move on to the difficult questions later, if we have time.

Yes on the telephone can be crossed, in one and the same occurrence, by a variety of intonations whose differentiating qualities are potentialized on stereophonic long waves. They may appear only to go as

9. EN "Hell," "*l'enfer,*" is the name given to the section of the Bibliothèque Nationale where questionable items are stored. For *Verfallen* see the quotation from Heidegger above.

far as interjection, the mechanical quasi-signal that indicates either the mere presence of the interlocutory *Dasein* at the other end of the line (Hello, yes?) or the passive docility of a secretary or a subordinate who, like some archiving machine, is ready to record orders (*yes sir*) or who is satisfied with purely informative answers (*yes, sir; no, sir*). Here is just one example among many. I have deliberately chosen the section where a typewriter and the trade name H. E. L. Y.'S lead us to the last piece of furniture in this vestibule or techno-telecommunicational preamble, to a certain gramophone, at the same time as they connect us to the network of the prophet Elijah. So here we are, though of course I have sectioned and selected, filtering out the noise on the line:

> Miss Dunne hid the Capel street library copy of *The Woman in White* far back in her drawer and rolled a sheet of gaudy notepaper into her typewriter.
>
> Too much mystery business in it. Is he in love with that one, Marion? Change it and get another by Mary Cecil Haye.
>
> The disk shot down the groove, wobbled a while, ceased and ogled them: six.
>
> Miss Dunne clicked at the keyboard:
>
> —16 June 1904. [almost eighty years.]
>
> Five tallwhitehhatted sandwichmen between Monypeny's corner and the slab where Wolfe Tone's statue was not, eeled themselves turning H. E. L. Y.'S and plodded back as they had come. . . .
>
> The telephone rang rudely by her ear.
>
> —Hello. Yes, sir. No, sir. Yes, sir. I'll ring them up after five. Only those two, sir, for Belfast and Liverpool. All right, sir. Then I can go after six if you're not back. A quarter after. Yes, sir. Twentyseven and six. I'll tell him. Yes: one, seven, six.
>
> She scribbled three figures on an envelope.
>
> —Mr. Boylan! Hello! That gentleman from *Sport* was in looking for you. Mr. Lenehan, yes. He said he'll be in the Ormond at four. No, sir. Yes, sir. I'll ring them up after five. (*U*, 228–29)

It is not by accident that the repetition of *yes* can be seen to assume mechanical, servile forms, often bending the woman to her master, even if any answer to the other as a singular other must, it seems, escape those forms. In order for the *yes* of affirmation, assent, consent, alliance, of engagement, signature, or gift to have the value it has, it must carry the repetition within itself. It must *a priori* and immediately confirm its promise and promise its confirmation. This essential repetition lets itself be haunted by an intrinsic threat, by an internal telephone which parasites it like its mimetic, mechanical double, like its incessant parody. We shall return to this fatality. But we can already hear a gramophony which records writing in the liveliest voice. *A priori* it reproduces it, in the absence of intentional presence on the part of the affirmer. Such gramophony responds, of course, to the dream of a reproduction which *preserves* as its truth the living *yes,* archived in the very quick of its voice. But by the same token it allows the possibility of parody, of a *yes* technique that persecutes the most spontaneous, the most giving desire of the *yes.* To meet [*répondre à*] its destination, this *yes* must reaffirm itself immediately. Such is the condition of a signed commitment. The *yes* can only state *itself* by promising itself its own memory. The affirmation of the *yes* is the affirmation of memory. *Yes* must preserve itself, and thus reiterate itself, archive its voice in order to allow it once again to be heard.

This is what I call the gramophone effect. *Yes* gramophones itself and telegramophones itself, *a priori.*

The desire for memory and the mourning of *yes* set in motion the anamnesic machine. And its hypermnesic overacceleration. The machine reproduces the living, it doubles it with its automaton. The example I have chosen offers the privilege of a double contiguity: from the word *yes* to the word *voice* and to the word *gramophone* in a sequence expressing the desire for memory, desire as memory of desire and desire for memory. It takes place in Hades, in the cemetery, at about 11 o'clock in the morning, the time reserved for the *heart* (that is, as Heidegger would put it again, the place of preserving memory and truth), here in the sense of the Sacred Heart:

> The Sacred Heart that is: showing it. Heart on his sleeve. . . .
> How many! All these here once walked round Dublin. Faithful departed. As you are now so once were we.

Besides how could you remember everybody? Eyes, walk, voice. Well, the voice, yes: gramophone. Have a gramophone in every grave or keep it in the house. After dinner on a Sunday. Put on poor old greatgrandfather Kraahraark! Hellohellohello amawfullyglad kraark awfullygladaseeragain hellohello amarawf kopthsth. Remind you of the voice like the photograph reminds you of the face. Otherwise you couldn't remember the face after fifteen years, say. For instance who? For instance some fellow that died when I was in Wisdom Hely's. (*U*, 115–16)[10]

What right do we have to select or interrupt a quotation from *Ulysses*? This is always legitimate and illegitimate, to be made legitimate like an illegitimate child. I could follow the sons of Hely (Bloom's old boss), threading them through all sorts of genealogies. Rightly or wrongly, I judge it more economical here to rely on the association with the name of the prophet Elijah, to whom a good many passages are devoted, or rather whose coming at regular intervals can be foretold. I pronounce *Elie* in the French way, but in the English name for Elijah, Molly's *Ja* can be heard echoing—if Molly gives voice to the flesh (*la chair*, hang on to this word) which always says *yes* (*stets bejaht*, Joyce reminds us, reversing Goethe's words). I shall not investigate further the part of the text where it is said, "And there came a voice out of heaven, calling: *Elijah! Elijah!* And he answered with a main cry: *Abba! Adonai!* And they beheld Him even Him, ben Bloom Elijah, amid clouds of angels" (*U*, 343).

No, without transition, I give myself up to repetition, to that which is called "the second coming of Elijah" in the brothel. The Gramophone, the character and the voice, if I can put it like this, of the gramophone has just shouted:

Jerusalem!
Open your gates and sing
Hosanna... (*U*, 472)

In the second coming of Elijah after "the end of the world," Elijah's voice acts as a kind of telephone exchange or marshalling yard. All

---

10. I am told that James Joyce's grandson is here, now, in this room. This quotation is naturally dedicated to him.

communication, transport, transfer, and translation networks go through him. Polytelephony goes through Elijah's programophony. But do not forget, whatever you do, that Molly reminds us that ben Bloom Elijah lost his job at Hely's. Bloom had thought at that time of prostituting Molly, of making her pose naked for a very rich man (*U*, 674).

Elijah is just a voice, a skein of voices. It says, "*C'est moi qui opère tous les téléphones de ce réseau-là*" in the French translation approved by Joyce for "Say, I am operating all this trunk line. Boys, do it now. God's time is 12.25. Tell mother you'll be there. Rush your order and you play a slick ace. Join on right here! Book through to eternity junction, the nonstop run" (*U*, 473). I want to insist (in French) on the fact that seats must be *booked* [*louer*], reserved with Elijah, Elijah must be *praised* [*louer*] and the *booking* [*location*] of this *praise* [*louange*] is none other than the *book* which stands in lieu of *eternity junction*, like a transferential and teleprogramophonic exchange.[11] "Just one word more," continues Elijah, who also evokes the second coming of Christ and asks us if we are ready, "Florry Christ, Stephen Christ, Zoe Christ, Bloom Christ," et cetera. "Are you all in this vibration? I say you are"—which is translated into French by "*Moi je dis que oui,*" a problematic though not illicit translation about which we must speak again. And the voice of the one who says "yes," Elijah, saying to those who are in the *vibration* (a key word in my view) that they can call him any time, straightaway, instantaneously, without using any technique or postal system, but going by the sun, by solar cables and rays, by the voice of the sun—we could say photophone or heliophone. He says "by sunphone": "Got me? That's it. You call me up by sunphone any old time. Bumboosers, save your stamps" (*U*, 473). So do not write me any letters, save your stamps, you can collect them, like Molly's father.

We have arrived at this point because I was telling you about my travel experiences, my round trip, and about a few phone calls. If I am telling stories, it is to put off speaking about serious things and because

---

11. TN The French plays upon both meanings of *louer* ("to book" or "to rent" and "to praise"), upon *location* (a "hiring" or "renting") and *louange* ("praise" or "commendation"), as well as *livre* ("book" as a noun).

I am too intimidated. Nothing intimidates me more than a community of experts in Joycean matters. Why? I wanted first of all to speak to you about this, to speak to you about authority and intimidation. The page that I am going to read was written on the plane to Oxford, Ohio, a few days before my trip to Tokyo. I had decided at that time to put before you the question of competence, of legitimacy, and of the Joycean institution. Who has a recognized right to speak of Joyce, to write on Joyce, and who does this well? What do competence and performance consist of here? When I agreed to speak before you, before the most intimidating assembly in the world, before the greatest concentration of knowledge on such a polymathic work, I was primarily aware of the honor that was being paid me. I wondered by what claim I had managed to make people think I deserved it, however minimally. I do not intend to answer this question here. But I know, as you do, that I do not belong to your large, impressive family. I prefer the word *family* to that of *foundation* or *institute*. Someone answering, yes, in Joyce's name and to Joyce's name has succeeded in linking the future of an institution to the singular adventure of a proper name and a signature, a *signed* proper name, for writing out one's name is not yet signing. In a plane, if you write out your name on the identity card which you hand in on arrival in Tokyo, you have not yet signed. You sign when the gesture with which, in a certain place, preferably at the end of the card or the book, you inscribe your name again, takes on the sense of *yes,* this is my name, I certify this, and, yes, yes, I will be able to attest to this again. I will remember later, I promise, that it is really I who signed. A signature is always a *yes, yes,* the *synthetic* performative of a promise and a memory conditioning every commitment. We shall return to this obligatory departure point of all discourse, following a circle which is also that of the *yes,* of the "so be it," of the amen and the hymen.

I did not feel worthy of the honor that had been bestowed on me, far from it, but I must have been nourishing some obscure desire to be part of this mighty family which tends to sum up all others, including their hidden narratives of bastardy, legitimation, and illegitimacy. If I have accepted, it is mainly because I suspected some perverse challenge in a legitimation so generously offered. You know better than I the disquiet regarding familial legitimation; it is this which makes *Ulysses,* as well as *Finnegans Wake,* vibrate. I was thinking, in the plane, of the challenge and the trap, because experts, I said to myself, with the lucidity and experience that a long acquaintance with Joyce confers on them, ought to know better than most to what extent, beneath the simulacrum of a few signs of complicity, of references or quotations in each of my books, Joyce remains a stranger to me, as if I did not know him. Incompetence, as they are aware, is the profound truth of my relationship to this work which I know after all only directly, through hearsay, through rumors, through what people say, second-hand exegeses, readings that are always partial. For these experts, I said to myself, the time has come for the deception to made evident, and how could it be demonstrated or denounced better than at the opening of a large symposium?

So, in order to defend myself against this hypothesis, which was almost a certainty, I asked myself: but in the end what does competence come down to in the case of Joyce? And what can a Joycean institution, a Joycean family, a Joycean international organization be? I do not know how far we can speak of the modernity of Joyce, but if this exists, beyond the apparatus for postal and programophonic technologies, it consists in the fact that the declared project of keeping generations of university scholars at work for centuries of babelian edification must itself have been drawn up using a technological model and the division of university labor that could not be that of former centuries. The scheme of bending vast communities of readers and writers to this law, of detaining them by means of an interminable transferential chain of translation and tradition, can equally well be attributed to Plato and Shakespeare, to Dante and Vico, without mentioning Hegel and other finite divinities. But none of these could calculate, as well as Joyce did, his feat, by modifying it in accordance with certain types of world research institutions prepared to use not only means of transport, of communication, of organizational programming allowing an accelerated capitalization, a crazy accumulation of interest in terms of knowledge blocked in Joyce's name, even as he lets you all sign in his name, as Molly would say ("I could often have written out a fine cheque for myself and write his name on it" [*U,* 702]), but also modes of archivization and consultation of data unheard of [*inouïes*] for all the grandfathers whom I have just named, omitting Homer.

The intimidation amounts to this: Joyce experts are the representatives as well as the effects of the most powerful project for programming over the centuries the totality of research in the onto-logico-encyclopedic field, all the while commemorating his own, proper signature. A Joyce scholar has the right to dispose of the totality of competence in the encyclopedic field of the *universitas*. He has at his command the computer of all memory, he plays with the entire archive of culture— at least of what is called Western culture, and, in it, of that which returns to itself according to the Ulyssean circle of the encyclopedia; and this is why one can always at least dream of writing *on* Joyce and not *in* Joyce from the fantasy of some Far Eastern capital, without, in my case, having too many illusions about it. The effects of this preprogramming, you know better than I, are admirable and terrifying, and sometimes of intolerable violence. One of them has the following form: nothing can be invented *on the subject* of Joyce. Everything we can say about *Ulysses,* for example, has already been anticipated, including, as we have seen, the scene about academic competence and the ingenuity of metadiscourse. We are caught in this net. All the gestures made in the attempt to take the initiative of a movement are found to be already announced in an overpotentialized text that will remind you, at a given moment, that you are captive in a network of language, writing, knowledge, and *even narration.* This is one of the things I wanted to demonstrate earlier, in recounting all these stories, true ones moreover, about the postcard in Tokyo, the trip to Ohio, or the phone call from Rabaté. We have verified that all this had its narrative paradigm and was *already* recounted in *Ulysses.* Everything that happened to me, including the narrative that I would attempt to make of it, was already pre-dicted and pre-narrated, in its dated singularity, prescribed in a sequence of knowledge and narration: within *Ulysses,* to say nothing of *Finnegans Wake,* by a hypermnesic machine capable of storing in an immense epic work Western memory and virtually all the languages in the world *including traces of the future.* Yes, everything has already happened to us with *Ulysses* and has been signed in advance by Joyce.

What remains to be seen is what happens to this signature in these conditions, and this is one of my questions.

This situation is one of reversal, stemming from the paradox of the *yes*. Moreover, the question of the *yes* is always linked to that of the *doxa,* to what is opined in opinion. So this is the paradox: just when the work of such a signature gets going—some might say submits itself, at any rate restarts *for itself,* so that it might return to itself—the most competent and reliable production and reproduction machine, it simultaneously ruins the model. Or, at least, it threatens to ruin the model. Joyce laid stakes on the modern university, but he challenges it to reconstitute itself after him. At any rate he marks the essential limits. Basically, there can be no Joycean competence, in the certain and strict sense of the concept of competence, with the criteria of evaluation and legitimation that are attached to it. There can be no Joycean foundation, no Joycean family; there can be no Joycean legitimacy. What relationship is there between this situation and the paradoxes of the *yes,* or the structure of a signature?

The classical concept of competence supposes that one can rigorously dissociate knowledge (in its act or in its positing) from the event that one is dealing with, and especially from the ambiguity of written or oral marks—let's call them gramophonies. Competence implies that a metadiscourse is possible, neutral and univocal with regard to a field of objectivity, whether or not it possesses the structure of a text. Performances ruled by this competence must in principle lend themselves to a translation with nothing left over on the subject of the corpus that is itself translatable. Above all, they should not essentially be of a narrative type. In principle, one doesn't relate stories in a university; one does history, one recounts in order to know and to explain; one speaks about narrations or epic poems, but events and stories must not be produced in the name of institutionalizable knowledge. Now with the event signed by Joyce a double bind has become at least explicit (for we have been caught in it since Babel and Homer and everything else that follows): on the one hand, we must write, we must sign, we must bring about new events with untranslatable marks—and this is the frantic call, the distress of a signature that is asking for a *yes* from the other, the pleading injunction for a counter-signature; but on the other hand, the singular novelty of any other *yes*, of any other signature, finds itself already programophoned in the Joycean corpus.

I do not notice the effects of the challenge of this double bind on myself alone, in the terrified desire I might have to belong to a family of Joycean representatives among whom I will always remain an illegitimate son; I also notice these effects on you.

On the one hand, you have the legitimate assurance of possessing, or of being in the process of constructing, a supercompetence, measuring up to a corpus that includes virtually all those bodies of knowledge treated in the university (sciences, technology, religion, philosophy, literature, and, co-extensive with all these, languages). With regard to this hyperbolic competence, nothing is transcendent. Everything is *internal*, mental telephony; everything can be integrated into the domesticity of this programotelephonic encyclopedia.

On the other hand, it must be realized at the same time, and *you realize this*, that the signature and the *yes* that occupy you, are capable—it is their destination—of destroying the very root of this competence, of this legitimacy, of its domestic interiority, capable of deconstructing the university institution, its internal or interdepartmental divisions, as well as its contract with the extra-university world.

Hence the mixture of assurance and distress that one can sense in "Joyce scholars." From one point of view, they are as crafty as Ulysses, knowing, as did Joyce, that they know more, that they always have one more trick up their sleeve. Whether it is a question of totalizing summary or subatomistic micrology (what I call the "divisibility of the letter"), no-one does it better; everything is integratable in the "this is my body" of the corpus. But from another point of view, this hypermnesic interiorization can never be closed upon itself. For reasons connected with the structure of the corpus, the project and the signature, there can be no assurance of any principle of truth or legitimacy, so you also have the feeling, given that nothing new can take you by surprise from the inside, that something might eventually happen to you from an unforeseeable outside.

And you have guests.

You are awaiting the passing through or the second coming of Elijah. And, as in all good Jewish families, you always have a place set for him. Waiting for Elijah, even if his coming is already gramophoned in *Ulysses,* you are prepared to recognize, without too many illusions, I think, the external competence of writers, philosophers, psychoanalysts, linguists. You even ask them to open your colloquia. And, for example, to ask questions like the following: what is happening today here in Frankfurt, in this city where the Joyce international, the cosmopolitan, but very American James Joyce Foundation, established Bloomsday 1967, whose president, the representative of a very large American majority, is to be found in Ohio (Ohio again!), continues its edification in a modern Babel, which is also the capital of the book fair and of a famous philosophical school of modernity? When you call on incompetents, like me, or on allegedly external competences, knowing full well that these do not exist, is it not both to humiliate them, and because you expect from these guests not only news, good news come at last to deliver you from the hypermnesic interiority in which you go round in circles like hallucinators in a nightmare, but also, paradoxically, a legitimacy? For you are at once very sure and very unsure of your rights, and even of your community, of the homogeneity of your practices, your methods, your styles. You cannot rely on the least consensus, on the least axiomatic concordat among you. As a matter of fact, you do not exist, you are not founded to exist as a foundation, which is what Joyce's signature gives you to read. And you call on strangers to come and tell you, as I am doing in replying to your invitation: you exist, you intimidate me, I recognize you, I recognize your paternal and grandpaternal authority, recognize me and give me a diploma in Joycean studies.

Of course you do not believe a word of what I am saying to you at the moment. And even if it were true, and even if, yes, it is true, you would not believe me if I told you that I too am called Elijah: this name is not inscribed, no, on my official documents, but it was given me on my seventh day. Moreover, Elijah is the name of the prophet present at *all* circumcisions. He is the patron, if we can put it like this, of circumcisions. The chair on which the new-born baby boy is held is called "Elijah's chair." This name should be given to all the "chairs" of Joycean studies, to the "panels" and "workshops" organized by your foundation. Rather than *Postcard from Tokyo*, I had thought of calling this lecture *Circumnavigation and Circumcision*. A Midrash tells how Elijah had complained about Israel's forgetting the alliance, that is, Israel's forgetting circumcision. God is then supposed to have given the order for him to be present at all circumcisions, perhaps as a punishment. This scene of signature could have been marked with blood connecting all the announced passages concerning the prophet Elijah to the event of circumcision, the moment of entry into the community, of alliance and legitimation. At least twice in *Ulysses* there are references to the "collector of prepuces" ("—The islanders, Mulligan said to Haines casually, speak frequently of the collector of prepuces" [*U*, 20]; "What's his name? Ikey Moses? Bloom./He rattled on./—Jehovah, collector of prepuces, is no more. I found him over in the museum when I went to hail the foamborn Aphrodite" [*U*, 201]). Each time, and often near the arrival of milk or foam, circumcision is associated with the name of Moses, as in this passage before "the name of Moses Herzog": "—Circumcised! says Joe./—Ay, says I. A bit off the top" (*U*, 290). "Ay, says I": yes, says I; or again I says I; or again I (says)I, yes(says)yes; I: I,yes: yes, yes, yes, I, I, etc. Tautology, monology, but surely synthetic judgment *a priori*. You might also have played on the fact that in Hebrew the word for stepfather (think back to Bloom when he declares himself in front of Stephen to be ready to go "a step farther") also refers to the circumciser. And if Bloom has a dream, it is of having Stephen as part of the family, and therefore, either by way of marriage or adoption, of circumcising the Greek.

So where are we going with the union [*alliance*] of this Joycean community? What will become of it at this pace of accumulation and commemoration in one or two centuries, taking into account new technologies for archiving and storing information? Finally, Elijah is not me, nor some stranger come to say this thing to you, the news from outside, even the apocalypse of Joycean studies, that is, the truth, the final revelation (and you know that Elijah was always associated with an apocalyptic discourse). No, Elijah is you: you are the Elijah of

Ulysses, who is presented as a large telephone exchange ("HELLO THERE, CENTRAL!" [*U*, 149]), the marshalling yard, the network through which all information must transit. We can imagine that there will soon be a giant computer of Joycean studies ("operating all this trunk line. ... Book through to eternity junction" [*U*, 473]). It would capitalize all publications, coordinate and teleprogram all communication, colloquia, theses, papers, and would draw up an index in all languages. We would be able to consult it any time by satellite or by "sunphone," day and night, taking advantage of the "reliability" of an answering machine. "Hello, yes, yes, what are you asking for? Oh, for all the occurrences of the word *yes* in *Ulysses?* Yes." It would remain to be seen if the basic language of this computer would be English and if its patent would be American, given the overwhelming and significant majority of Americans among the trustees of the Joyce Foundation. It would also remain to be seen if we could consult this computer on the word *yes* in every language, and if the *yes,* in particular the one involved in the operations of consultation, can be counted, calculated, numbered. A circle will lead me in due course back to this question.

In any case, the figure of Elijah, whether it be that of the prophet or the circumciser, of polymathic competence or of telematic control, is only a synecdoche of Ulyssean narration, at once smaller and greater than the whole.

We should, then, get rid of a double illusion and a double intimidation. (1) No truth can come from outside the Joycean community, and without the experience, the cunning, and the knowledge amassed by trained readers. But (2) inversely, or symmetrically, there is no model for "Joycean" competence, no interiority and no closure possible for the concept of such a competence. There is no absolute criterion for measuring the relevance of a discourse on the subject of a text signed by "Joyce." Even the concept of competence finds itself shaken by this event. For we must write, write in one language and respond to the *yes* and countersign in another language. The very discourse of competence (that of neutral, metalinguistic knowledge immune from all untranslatable writing, etc.) is thus incompetent, the least pertinent there is on the subject of Joyce, who, moreover, also finds himself in the same situation whenever he speaks of his "work."

Instead of pursuing these generalities, and bearing in mind time passing, I return to *yes* in *Ulysses*. For a very long time, the question of the *yes* has mobilized or traversed everything I have been trying to think, write, teach, or read. To limit myself to examples of readings, I had devoted seminars and texts to the *yes*, to the double *yes* in Nietzsche's *Zarathustra* ("Thus spake Zarathustra," Mulligan moreover says [*U*, 29]), the *yes, yes* in the marriage ceremony [*hymen*], which is still the best example, the *yes* of the great midday affirmation, and then the ambiguity of the double *yes:* one of them comes down to the Christian assumption of one's burden, the *Ja, Ja* of the donkey overloaded as Christ was with memory and responsibility, and the other light, airy, dancing, solar *yes, yes* is also a *yes* of reaffirmation, of promise, of oath, a *yes* to eternal recurrence. The difference between the two *yes*es, or rather between the two repetitions of the *yes*, remains unstable, subtle, sublime. One repetition haunts the other. For Nietzsche, *yes* always finds its chance with a certain kind of woman, and he, like Joyce, anticipated that one day professorships would be set up to study his *Zarathustra*. In the same way, in Blanchot's *La folie du jour*, the quasi-narrator attributes the power to say *yes* to women, to the beauty of women, beautiful insofar as they say *yes:* "Yet I have met people who have never said to life, "Quiet!", who have never said to death, "Go away!" Almost always women, beautiful creatures."[12]

The *yes* would then be that of woman—and not just that of the mother, the flesh, the earth, as is so often said of Molly's *yes*es in the majority of readings devoted to her: "Penelope, bed, flesh, earth, monologue," said Gilbert,[13] and many others after him and even before him, and here Joyce is no more competent than anyone else. This is not false, it is even the truth of a certain truth, but it is not all, and it is not so simple. The law of gender [*genre*] seems to me to be strongly

12. EN Maurice Blanchot, *The Madness of the Day*, trans. Lydia Davis (Barrytown, N.Y.: Station Hill Press, 1981), 7; see "The Law of Genre" above.
13. EN Stuart Gilbert, *James Joyce's "Ulysses"* (Harmondsworth: Penguin, 1963), 328. Gilbert is quoting from the schema which Joyce gave him.

overdetermined and infinitely more complicated, whether we are dealing with sexual or grammatical gender, or again with rhetorical technique. To call this a monologue is to display a somnambulistic carelessness.

So I wanted to listen again to Molly's *yes*es. But can this be done without making them resonate with all the *yes*es that prepare the way for them, correspond to them, and keep them hanging on at the other end of the line throughout the whole book? Last summer in Nice I read *Ulysses* again, first in French, then in English, pencil in hand, counting the *oui*'s and then the *yes*es and sketching out a typology. As you can imagine, I dreamt of hooking up to the Joyce Foundation computer, and the result was not the same from one language to the other.

Molly is not Elijah [*Elie*], is not *Moelie* (for you know that the Mohel is the circumciser), and she is not Joyce, but even so her *yes* circumnavigates and circumcises, encircling the last chapter of *Ulysses*, since it is at once her first and her last word, her send-off [*envoi*] and her closing fall: "Yes because he never did" and finally "and yes I said yes I will Yes" (*U*, 704). The eschatological final "Yes" occupies the place of the signature at the bottom right of the text. Even if one distinguishes, as one must, Molly's "yes" from that of *Ulysses*, of which she is but a figure and a moment, even if one distinguishes, as one must also do, these two signatures (that of Molly and that of *Ulysses*) from that of Joyce, they read each other and call out to each other. To be precise, they call to each other across a *yes*, which always inaugurates a scene of call and request: it confirms and countersigns. Affirmation demands *a priori* confirmation, repetition, safekeeping, and the memory of the *yes*. A certain narrativity is to be found at the simple core of the simplest *yes*: "I asked him with my eyes to ask again yes and then he asked me would I yes to say yes" (*U*, 704).

A *yes* never comes alone, and we never say this word alone. Nor do we laugh alone, as Freud says, and we shall come back to this. And Freud also stresses that the unconscious knows nothing of *no*. But in what way does the Joycean signature imply what we will curiously refer to here as the question of the *yes*? There is a question of the *yes*, a request of the *yes*, and perhaps, for it is never certain, an unconditional, inaugural affirmation of the *yes* that cannot necessarily be distinguished from the question or the request. Joyce's signature, or at least the one that interests me here, though I in no way claim to exhaust the phenomenon, cannot be summarized by the affixation of his seal in the form of a surname and the play of signifiers, as they say, in which to reinscribe the name "Joyce." The inferences to which these games of association and society pastimes have for a long time been giving rise are facile, tedious, and naively jubilatory. And even if they are not entirely irrelevant, they begin by confusing a signature with a simple mention, apposition, or manipulation of the officially authorized name. For neither in its juridical capacity, as I have just suggested, nor in the essential complexity of its structure, does a signature amount to the mere mention of a proper name. The proper name itself, which a signature does not merely spell or mention, cannot be reduced to a legal surname. This runs the risk of setting up a screen or mirror toward which psychoanalysts, in a hurry to conclude, would rush headlong like dazzled larks. I have tried to show this for Genet, Ponge, and Blanchot.[14] As for the scene of the surname, the opening pages of *Ulysses* should suffice to educate the reader.

Who signs? Who signs *what* in Joyce's name? The answer could not be in the form of a key or a clinical category that could be pulled out of a hat whenever a colloquium required. Nevertheless, as a modest foreword, though it might be of interest only to me, shall we say that I believed it possible to examine this question of the signature through that of the *yes* which it always implies and insofar as it here *marries* the question of knowing who is laughing and how laughter comes about *with* Joyce, *in* Joyce, in a singular way, since *Ulysses*.

Who is the man laughing? Is it a man? And that which laughs, how does it laugh? Does it laugh? For there is more than one modality, more than one tonality of laughter just as there is a whole gamut, a polygamy in the game and the gamble of the *yes*. Why gamut, game, and gamble? Because before the gramophone, just before, and before Elijah's tirade as the operator of the telephone exchange, the hobgoblin

14. EN For Ponge, see the extract from *Signsponge* below; for Blanchot see "Pas" in *Parages* (especially pp. 109–16); for Genet see *Glas*, right-hand column.

speaks the croupier's language in French: "*Il vient!* [Elijah, I suppose, or Christ] *C'est moi! L'homme qui rit! L'homme primigène! (He whirls round and round with dervish howls.) Sieurs et dames, faites vos jeux! (He crouches juggling. Tiny roulette planets fly from his hands.) Les jeux sont faits! (The planets rush together, uttering crepitant cracks.) Rien n'va plus*" (*U*, 472). "*Il vient!*", "*rien n'va plus*," in French in the original. The French translation does not include this, the French effaces the French, then, at the risk of cancelling an essential connotation or reference in this self-presentation of the man laughing.

Since we are speaking of the translation, the tradition, and the transfer of *yes*, we should remember that the same problem exists for the French version of the *yes* when this is to be found, as they say, "*en français dans le texte*," and even in italics. The effacing of these marks is even more serious in that the "*Mon père, oui*" presents the value of a quotation that shows up all the problems of the quoted *yes*. In I, 3 ("Proteus"), shortly after the evocation of the "ineluctable modality of the visible" and of the "ineluctable modality of the audible"—in other words, the ineluctable gramophony of the word *yes*—"sounds solid" enunciates the same transfer through the "navel cord" that interrogates the consubstantiality of father and son, and all of this occurs close to a scripturo-telephonic and Judaeo-Hellenic scene: "Hello. Kinch here. Put me on to Edenville. Aleph, alpha: nought, nought, one" (*U*, 43). "Yes, sir. No, sir. Jesus wept: and no wonder by Christ" (*U*, 44). On the same page (and we must for essential reasons deal here with things in accordance with contiguity) what the French translation, co-signed by Joyce, translates by "*oui*" is not *yes*, but once "I am" and once "I will." We shall return to this in a circular way. Here, then, is the passage, closely followed by the mother's postal order that Stephen cannot cash in a French post office (counter "*fermé*") and by the allusion to the "blue French telegram; curiosity to show: / —Mother dying come home father":

—*C'est tordant, vous savez. Moi je suis socialiste. Je ne crois pas à l'existence de Dieu. Faut pas le dire à mon père.*

—*Il croit?*
—*Mon père, oui.* (*U*, 47) (In French in the original.)

Since the question of the signature remains in its entirety before us, the modest but indispensable preliminary dimension of its elaboration would situate itself, I believe, at the intersection of the *yes*, of the visible *yes* and the audible *yes*, of the *oui ouï* ["heard yes"], without any etymological filiation between the two words *oui* and *ouï*, of the *yes for the eyes* and the *yes for the ears*, and of laughter, at the intersection of the *yes* and *laughter*. In sum, across the telephonic lapsus that made me say or that caused to be heard "*oui dire*" ("hearing"), it is "*oui rire*" ("yes laughter")[15] that forced its way through, the consonantal difference between *dire* and *rire*, that is, *d* and *r* (which are, moreover, the only consonants in my name).

But why laugh? Why laughter? Everything has doubtless already been said on laughter in Joyce, on parody, satire, derision, humor, irony raillery. And on his Homeric laughter and his Rabelaisian laughter. It remains perhaps to think of laughter, as, precisely, a remains. What does laughter want to say? What does laughter want? [*Qu'est-ce que ça veut dire, le rire? Qu'est-ce que ça veut rire?*] Once one recognizes that, in principle, in *Ulysses* the virtual totality of experience—of meaning, of history, of the symbolic, of languages, and of writings, the great cycle and the great encyclopedia of cultures, scenes, and affects, in short, the sum total of all sum totals—tends to unfold itself and reconstitute itself by playing out all its possible combinations, with a writing that seeks to occupy virtually all the spaces, well, the totalizing hermeneutic that makes up the task of a worldwide and eternal institution of Joyce studies will find itself confronted with what I hesitatingly call a dominant affect, a *Stimmung* or a *pathos,* a tone which retraverses all the others yet which does not participate in the series of the others since it *re-marks* all of them, adds itself to them without allowing itself to be added in or totalized, in the manner of a remainder that is both quasi-transcendental and supplementary. And it is this yes-

15. EN Derrida's coinage *oui-rire,* for which I have introduced the translation "yeslaughter," also means "to laugh yes" or "laughing yes," as *oui dire* means "saying yes."

laughter [*oui-rire*] that overmarks not only the totality of writing, but all the qualities, modalities, *genres* of laughter whose differences might be classified into some sort of typology.[16]

So why yes-laughter *before and after all,* for all that a signature is accountable for—or, rather, leaves on account? Why this remainder?

I have not the time to sketch out this work and this typology. Cutting across country, I shall say only two words on the double relationship, and therefore on the unstable relationship, which, with its double tonality, instructs my reading and my re-writing of Joyce, this time beyond even *Ulysses,* and my double relationship to this yes-laughter. My presumption is that I am not the only person to project this double relationship. It is instituted and requested, required, by the Joycean signature itself.[17]

With a certain ear, with a certain hearing [*ouïe*], I can hear a reactive, even negative, yes-laughter resonating. It takes joy in hypermnesic mastery and in spinning spiderwebs that defy all other possible mastery, as impregnable as an alpha and omegaprogramophone in which all the histories, stories, discourses, knowledges, all the signatures to come that Joycean and other institutions might address, would be prescribed, computed in advance outside the scope of any effective computer, precomprehended, captive, predicted, partialized, metonymized, exhausted, like the subjects, whether they know it or not. And science or consciousness can settle nothing—on the contrary, it merely allows its supplementary calculation to be put at the service of the master signature; it may laugh at Joyce, but it thereby indebts itself once again to him. As is said in *Ulysses,* "*Was Du verlachst wirst Du noch dienen.*[18] / Brood of mockers" (*U,* 197).

There is a James Joyce who can be heard laughing at this omnipotence, at this great *tour joué:* a trick played and a grand tour completed. I am speaking of the tricks and tours [*tours*] of Ulysses, of his ruses, his cunning [*retors*], and of the great tour he completes when on his

---

16. EN Yes-laughter, *oui-rire,* functions, that is, in a manner which is related to the operation of terms like "arche-writing," "the supplement," and *différance.* See the Introduction.

17. EN See also Derrida's "Two Words for Joyce."

18. EN "What you laugh at you will still serve"; a German aphorism.

return [*retour*], he comes back from everything. A triumphal, jubilatory laughter, certainly, but also, since jubilation always betrays some kind of mourning, the laughter of resigned lucidity. For omnipotence remains phantasmatic, it opens and defines the dimensions of phantasm. Joyce cannot *not know this*. He cannot, for example, not know that the book of all books, *Ulysses* or *Finnegans Wake,* is still a mere opuscule among the millions and millions of works in the Library of Congress, absent forever no doubt from the news agency in a Japanese hotel, and lost too in the non-book archives, the expansion of which has nothing to do with the library. Millions of tourists, American and otherwise, are less and less likely to come across this thing in some "curious meeting." And this crafty little book will be judged by some to be too ingenious, industrious, manipulatory, overloaded with knowledge impatient to reveal itself by hiding, by *adding itself on* to everything: *in sum,* poor literature, vulgar in that it never leaves its luck to the incalculable simplicity of a poem, grimacing from overcultivated and hyperscholastic technology, a doctor's literature, just a shade too subtle in other words, the literature of a Doctor Pangloss with his eyes newly opened (wasn't this Nora's opinion?), which would have had the calculated good fortune to be censored, and therefore launched, by the U.S. postal authorities.

Even in its resignation to phantasm, this yes-laughter reaffirms control of a subjectivity that draws everything together as it draws itself together, or as it delegates itself to the name, in what is merely a vast rehearsal, during the sun's movement for one day from the Orient to the Occident. It condemns and condemns itself, sometimes sadistically, sardironically, it is the cynicism of a rictus, of sarcasm, and of derision: *brood of mockers.* It overwhelms itself and loads itself down, it makes itself pregnant with the whole of memory, it takes on summary, exhaustion, the second coming. It is not contradictory to state, regarding this yes-laughter, that it is that of Nietzsche's Christian donkey, the one that cries *Ja, ja,* or even that of the Judaeo-Christian beast that wants to make the Greek laugh once he has been circumcised of his own laughter: absolute knowledge as truth of religion, shouldered memory, guilt, literature of burden [*littérature de somme*]—as we say, "beast of burden"—literature of summons [*littérature de sommation*], moment of the debt: A. E. I. O. U, *I owe you,* with the *I* constituting itself in the very debt; it only comes into its own, there where it was, on the basis of the debt.[19] This relationship between the debt and the vowels, between "I owe you" and vocalization, might have led me—but I have not got the time—to link what I have tried to say elsewhere (in *The Post Card* and "Two Words for Joyce") about "he war" and "Ha, he, hi, ho, hu" in *Finnegans Wake* with the "I, O, U" in *Ulysses,* which is a strange anagram of the French *oui,* badly and didactically translated by *"je vous dois"* in the version authorized by Joyce, the one to which he said *yes* and thus consented to.

But did he say it in French—that is, all in vowels—or in English? Laughter laughs at having got generations of heirs, readers, custodians, and Joyce scholars and writers for ever in its debt. This yes-laughter of encircling reappropriation, of omnipotent Odyssean recapitulation, accompanies the installation of a device virtually capable of impregnating in advance its patented signature, even that of Molly, with all the countersignatures to come, even after the death of the artist as an old man, who carries off only an empty shell, the accident of a substance. The machine of filiation—legitimate or illegitimate—functions well and is ready for anything, ready to domesticate, circumcise, circumvent everything; it lends itself to the encyclopedic reappropriation of absolute knowledge which gathers itself up close to itself, as Life of the Logos, that is, also in the truth of natural death. We are here, in Frankfurt, to bear witness to this in commemoration.

But the eschatological tone of this yes-laughter also seems to me to be worked or traversed—I prefer to say *haunted*—joyously ventriloquised by a completely different music, by the vowels of a completely different song. I can hear this too, very close to the other one, as the yes-laughter of a gift without debt, light affirmation, almost amnesic, of a gift or an abandoned event, which in classical language is called "the work," a lost signature without a proper name that reveals and names the cycle of reappropriation and domestication of all the paraphs only to delimit their phantasm, and does so in order to contrive the

19. EN Compare Freud's well-known slogan, "Where id was, there shall ego be."

breach necessary for the coming of the other, whom one can always call Elijah, if Elijah is the name of the unforeseeable other for whom a place must be kept, and no longer Elijah, the great operator, Elijah, the head of the megaprogramotelephonic network, but the other Elijah: Elijah, the other. But there we are, this is a homonym, Elijah can always be one and the other at the same time, we cannot invite the one, without the risk of the other turning up. But this is a risk that must always be run. In this final movement, I return then to the risk or the chance of this contamination of one yes-laughter by the other, to the parasiting of an Elijah, that is to say of a me, by the other.

Why have I linked the question of laughter, of a laughter which *remains,* as a fundamental, quasi-transcendental tonality, to that of the "yes"?

In order to ask oneself what happens with *Ulysses,* or with the arrival of whatever, whoever—of Elijah for example—it is necessary to try to think the singularity of the event, and therefore the uniqueness of a signature, or rather of an irreplaceable mark that cannot necessarily be reduced to the phenomenon of copyright, legible across a patronym, after circumcision. It is necessary to try to think circumcision, if you like, from the possibility of a mark, of a feature, preceding and providing its figure. Now if laughter is a fundamental or abyssal tonality in *Ulysses,* if the analysis of this laughter is not exhausted by any of the available forms of knowledge precisely because it laughs at knowledge and from knowledge, then laughter bursts out in the event of signature itself. And there is no signature without *yes.* If the signature cannot be reduced to the manipulation or the mention of a name, it assumes the irreversible commitment of the person confirming, who *says* or *does* yes, the token of a mark left behind.

Before asking oneself who signs, if Joyce is or is not Molly, what is the status of the difference between the author's signature and that of a figure or a fiction signed by an author; before chattering about sexual difference as duality and expressing one's conviction as to the character of Molly as "onesidedly womanly woman" (and here I am quoting Frank Budgen and others after him)—Molly, the beautiful plant, the herb or *pharmakon*[20]—or the "onesidedly masculine" character of James Joyce; before taking into consideration what Joyce says about the non-stop monologue as "the indispensable countersign to Bloom's passport to eternity" (and once again, the competence of Joyce in letters and conversations does not seem to me to enjoy any privilege); before manipulating clinical categories and a psychoanalytic knowledge that are largely derivative of the possibilities of which we are speaking here, one will ask oneself what a signature is: it requires a *yes* more "ancient" than the question "what is?" since this question presupposes it, a *yes* more ancient than knowledge. One will ask oneself for what reason the *yes* always appears as a *yes, yes*. I say the *yes* and not the word "yes," because there can be a *yes* without a word.

One ought, then, to have preceded this entire discourse with a long, learned and thoughtful meditation on the meaning, the function, above all the presupposition of the *yes:* before language, in language, but also in an experience of the plurality of languages that perhaps no longer belongs to linguistics in the strict sense. The expansion toward a pragmatics seems to me to be necessary but inadequate as long as it does not open itself up to a thinking of the trace, of writing, in a sense that I have tried to explain elsewhere and which I cannot go into here.[21]

What is it that is said, is written, occurs with *yes?*

Yes can be implied without the word being said or written. This permits, for example the multiplication of *yes*es everywhere in the French version when it is assumed that a *yes* is marked in English sentences from which the word *yes* is in fact absent. But at the limit, given that *yes* is co-extensive with every statement, there is a great temptation, in French but first of all in English, to double up everything with a kind of continuous *yes*, even to double up the *yes*es that are

20. EN Moly was the plant given by Hermes to Odysseus to protect him from Circe (see Ellmann, *James Joyce* [New York: Oxford University Press, 1982], 496–97); *pharmakon* is the drug, beneficial or harmful, that Derrida exploits in "Plato's Pharmacy."

21. EN See, especially, *Of Grammatology* and "Plato's Pharmacy"; Derrida's special use of "writing" is discussed in the Introduction, pp. 9–10 above.

articulated by the simple mark of a rhythm, intakes of breath in the form of pauses or murmured interjections, as sometimes happens in *Ulysses:* the *yes* comes from me to me, from me to the other in me, from the other to me, to confirm the primary telephonic "Hello": yes, that's right, that's what I'm saying, I am, in fact, speaking, yes, there we are, I'm speaking, yes, yes, you can hear me, I can hear you, yes, we are in the process of speaking, there is language, you are receiving me, it's like this, it takes place, it happens, it is written, it is marked, yes, yes.

But let's start out from the *yes phenomenon,* the manifest *yes* patently marked as a *word,* spoken, written or phonogramed. Such a word says but says nothing in itself, if by saying we mean designating, showing, describing some thing to be found outside language, outside marking. Its only references are other marks, which are also marks of the other. Given that *yes* does not say, show, name anything that is beyond marking, some would be tempted to conclude that *yes* says nothing: an empty word, barely an adverb, since all adverbs, in which grammatical category *yes* is situated in our languages, have a richer, more determined semantic charge than the *yes* they always presuppose. In short, *yes* would be transcendental adverbiality, the ineffaceable supplement to any verb: in the beginning was the adverb, yes, but as an interjection, still very close to the inarticulate cry, a preconceptual vocalization, the perfume of discourse.

Can one sign with a perfume? Just as we cannot replace *yes* by a thing which it would be supposed to describe (it describes nothing, states nothing, even if it is a sort of performative implied in all statements: yes, I am stating, it is stated, etc.), nor even by the thing it is supposed to approve or affirm, so it would be impossible to replace the *yes* by the names of the concepts supposedly describing this act or operation, if indeed this is an act or operation. The concept of activity or of actuality does not seem to me to be enough to account for a *yes.* And this quasi-act cannot be replaced by "approval," "affirmation," "confirmation," "acquiescence," "consent." The word *affirmative* used by the military to avoid all kinds of technical risks, does not replace the *yes;* it still assumes it: yes, I am saying "affirmative."

What does this *yes* lead us to think, this *yes* which names, describes, designates nothing, and which has no reference outside marking (which is not to say outside language, for the *yes* can do without words, or at least the word *yes*)? In its radically non-constative or non-descriptive dimension, even if it is saying "yes" to a description or a narration, *yes* is through and through and *par excellence* a performative. But this characterization seems to me inadequate. First because a performative must be a *sentence,* a sentence sufficiently endowed with meaning in itself, in a given conventional context, to bring about a determined event. Now I believe, yes, that—to put it in a classical philosophical code—*yes* is the transcendental condition of all performative dimensions. A promise, an oath, an order, a commitment always implies a *yes,* I sign. The *I* of *I sign* says *yes* and says *yes* to itself, even if it signs a simulacrum. Any event brought about by a performative mark, any writing in the widest sense of the word, involves a *yes,* whether this is phenomenalized or not, that is, verbalized or adverbalized as such. Molly says *yes,* she remembers *yes,* the *yes* that she spoke with her eyes to ask for *yes* with her eyes, et cetera.

We are in an area which is *not yet* the space where the large questions of the origin of negation, of affirmation or of denegation, can and must be unfolded. Nor are we even in the space in which Joyce was able to reverse "*Ich bin der Geist, der stets verneint*" by saying that Molly is the flesh which always says *yes.* The *yes* to which we now refer is "anterior" to all these reversible alternatives, to all these dialectics. They assume it and envelop it. Before the *Ich* in *Ich bin* affirms or negates, it poses itself or pre-poses itself: not as *ego,* as the conscious or unconscious self, as masculine or feminine subject, spirit or flesh, but as a pre-performative force which, for example, in the form of the "I" [*je*] marks that "I" as addressing itself to the other, however undetermined he or she is: "Yes-I," or "Yes-I-say-to-the-other," even if *I* says *no* and even if *I* addresses itself without speaking. The minimal, primary *yes,* the telephonic "hello" or the tap through a prison wall, marks, before meaning or signifying: "I-here," listen, answer, there is some mark, there is some other. Negatives may ensue, but even if they completely take over, this *yes* can no longer be erased.

I have had to yield to the rhetorical necessity of translating this minimal and undetermined, almost virgin, address into words, into words such as "I," "I am," "language," at a point where the position of the *I*, of being, and of language still remains derivative with regard to this *yes*. This is the whole difficulty for anyone wishing to speak on the subject of the *yes*. A metalanguage will always be impossible here insofar as it will itself assume the event of a *yes* which it will fail to comprehend. It will be the same for all accountancy or computation, for any calculation aiming to arrange a series of *yes*es according to the principle of reason and its machines. *Yes* indicates that there is address to the other. This address is not necessarily a dialogue or an interlocution, since it assumes neither voice nor symmetry, but the haste, in advance, of a response that is already asking. For if there is some other, if there is some *yes*, then the other no longer lets itself be produced by the same or by the ego. *Yes*, the condition of any signature and of any performative, addresses itself to some other which it does not constitute, and it can only begin by *asking* the other, in response to a request that has always already been made, *to ask* it to say *yes*. Time appears only as a result of this singular anachrony. These commitments may remain fictitious, fallacious, and always reversible, and the address may remain invisible or undetermined; this does not change anything about the necessity of the structure. *A priori* it breaches all possible monologue. Nothing is less a monologue than Molly's "monologue," even if, within certain conventional limits, we have the right to view it as belonging to the genre or type known as the "monologue." But a discourse embraced by two *Yes*es of different qualities, two *Yes*es with capital letters, and therefore two gramophoned *Yes*es, could not be a monologue, but at the very most a soliloquy.

But we can see why the appearance of a monologue imposes itself here, precisely because of the *yes, yes*. The *yes* says nothing and asks only for another *yes*, the *yes* of an other, which, as we will shortly see, is analytically—or by *a priori* synthesis—implied in the first *yes*. The latter only situates itself, advances itself, marks itself in the call for its confirmation, in the *yes, yes*. It begins with the *yes, yes*, with the second *yes*, with the other *yes*, but as this is still only a *yes* that *recalls* (and Molly *remembers*, *recalls* to herself from the other *yes*), we might always be tempted to call this anamnesis monologic. And tautological. The *yes* says nothing but the *yes*: another *yes* that resembles the first even if it says *yes* to the advent of a completely other *yes*. It appears monotautological or specular, or imaginary, because it opens up the position of the *I*, which is itself the condition for performativity. Austin reminds us that the performative grammar *par excellence* is that of a sentence in the first person of the present indicative: yes, I promise, I accept, I refuse, I order, I do, I will, and so on. "He promises" is not an explicit performative and cannot be so unless an *I* is understood, as, for example, in "I swear to you that he promises."

Think back to Bloom in the chemist's. Among other things, he speaks to himself about perfumes. And remember, too, that the *yes*es of Molly (moly), the herb, also belong to the element of perfume. I could (and I thought about it for a while) have turned this paper into a treatise on perfumes—that is, on the *pharmakon*—and I could have called it *On the perfumative in "Ulysses."* Remember that Molly remembers all these *yes*es, remembers herself through these *yes*es, as consenting to that which smells good, that is, to perfume: "He asked me would I yes to say yes my mountain flower [Bloom's name, Flower, in pseudonym form on the postcard in the poste restante, evaporates here] and first I put my arms around him yes and drew him down to me so he could feel my breasts all perfume yes" (*U*, 704). Right at the beginning of the book, the bed, the chair, and the *yes* are all perfume calls: "To smell the gentle smoke of tea, fume of the pan, sizzling butter. Be near her ample bedwarmed flesh. Yes, yes" (*U*, 63). The "yes I will" seems tautological, opening out the repetition called for or presupposed by the so-called primary "yes" which, in short, is only saying "I will," and "I" as "I will." I asked you to think back to Bloom in the chemist's. He is talking to himself about perfumes: ". . . had only one skin. Leopold, yes. Three we have." A line later he says, "But you want a perfume too. What perfume does your? *Peau d'Espagne*. That orangeflower" (*U*, 86). From there, he passes to the baths, then to the massage: "Hammam. Turkish. Massage. Dirt gets rolled up in your navel. Nicer if a nice girl did it. Also I think I. Yes I. Do it in the bath" (*U*, 86). If we lift out this segment (*Also I think I. Yes I*), as we are always, and never, justified in doing, we have the minimal *proposition*, which, moreover, is equivalent to the "I will," illustrating the hetero-tautology of the *yes* implied in every *cogito* as thought, self-positing, and will to self-positing. But despite the umbilical scene ("navelcord" again), despite the archi-narcissistic and auto-affective appearance of this "Yes-I" which dreams of massaging itself, of washing itself, of appropriating itself, of making itself clean, all alone even in the caress itself, the *yes* addresses itself to some other and can appeal only to the *yes* of some other; it begins by responding.

We have no more time, so I rush into an even more telegraphic style. The French translation for "I think I. Yes I" is extremely deficient, since it gives "*Je pense aussi à. Oui, je,*" instead of "*Je pense je,*" I think the *I* or the *I* thinks *I,* and so on; and the "Curious longing I" which immediately follows on becomes in French "*Drôle d'envie que j'ai là, moi.*" The response, the *yes* of the other, comes from elsewhere to bring him out of his dream, in the slightly mechanical form of a *yes* from the chemist. "Yes, sir, the chemist said," telling him twice that he must pay: "Yes, sir, the chemist said. You can pay altogether, sir, when you come back" (U, 86). The dream of a perfumed bath, a clean body, and an unguent massage continues as far as the Christly repetition of "this is my body," thanks to which he crosses himself in bliss, like the anointing of the Lord: "Enjoy a bath now: clean trough of water, cool enamel, the gentle tepid stream. This is my body" (U, 88). The following scene refers to the anointing of Christ ("oiled by scented melting soap"), the navel, the flesh ("his navel, bud of flesh": the remains of the umbilical cord as the remains of the mother), and we're at the end of the chapter with, again, the word "flower," Bloom's other signature: "a languid floating flower."

The great dream of perfumes unfolds in the Nausicaa section. Beginning with "Yes. That's her perfume" (U, 372), it illustrates a move of fidelity to Molly, and sets itself forth as a grammar of perfumes.

The self-positing of the self with regard to the *yes* crops up each time, repeatedly, differently throughout the periplus. One place, among others (I quote it because it is near to one of the A. E. I. O. U. examples), is the one which refers to the "I" as "entelechy of forms." But "I" is here at once *mentioned* and *used:*

> But I, entelechy, form of forms, am I by memory because under ever-changing forms.

I that sinned and prayed and fasted.
A child Conmee saved from pandies.
I, I and I. I.
A.E.I.O.U. (*U*, 190)

A little further: "Her ghost at least has been laid for ever. She died, for literature at least, before she was born" (*U*, 190). (This is the sequence about the ghost and the French Hamlet "*lisant au livre de lui-même,*" in which John Eglinton says about French people "Yes. . . . Excellent people, no doubt, but distressingly shortsighted in some matters" [*U*, 187]). Elsewhere, at the end of Nausicaa, Bloom writes something in the sand and then rubs it out:

Write a message for her. Might remain. What?
I. . . .
AM. A. (*U*, 379)

The self-positing in the *yes* or the *Ay* is, however, neither tautological nor narcissistic; it is not egological even if it initiates the movement of circular reappropriation, the odyssey that can give rise to all these determined modalities. It holds open the circle that it institutes. In the same way, it is not yet performative, not yet transcendental, although it remains presupposed in any performativity, *a priori* in any constative theoricity, in any knowledge, in any transcendentality. For the same reason, it is preontological, if ontology expresses what is or the being of what is. The discourse on Being presupposes the responsibility of the *yes*, yes what is said is said, I am responding to the summons of Being, the summons of Being is being responded to, and so on. Still in telegraphic style, I will situate the possibility of the *yes* and of yes-laughter in the place where transcendental egology, the ontoencyclopedia, the great speculative logic, fundamental ontology and the thought of Being open onto a thought of the gift and sending [*envoi*] which they presuppose but cannot contain. I cannot develop this argument as I would like and as I have tried to do elsewhere.[22] I shall

22. EN See, for example, "Envois" in *The Post Card,* and, on the gift, "Women in the Beehive," 198–200, and "Two Words for Joyce," 146–47.

content myself with connecting these remarks to what, at the beginning of this trip, concerned the postal networks in *Ulysses:* a postcard, letter, check, telegramophone, telegram, et cetera.

The self-affirmation of the *yes* can address itself to the other only in recalling itself to itself, in saying to itself *yes, yes.* The circle of this universal presupposition, fairly comic in itself, is like a dispatch to oneself, a sending-back [*renvoi*] of self to self, which *both never leaves itself and never arrives at itself.* Molly says to herself (apparently speaking to herself alone), she reminds herself, that she says *yes* in asking the other to ask her to say *yes,* and she starts or finishes by saying *yes* to the other in herself, but she does so in order to say to the other that she will say *yes* if the other asks her, yes, to say *yes.* These dispatches and returned dispatches [*envois et renvois*] always mime the situation of the questions/answers in scholastics. And the scene of "sending oneself to oneself, having it off with oneself,"[23] is repeated many times in *Ulysses* in its literally postal form. And it is always marked with scorn, like the phantasm and failure themselves. The circle does not close upon itself. For want of time, I shall draw on only three examples. First is the one which mentions Milly, aged four or five, sending herself love letters, and in which, moreover, she is compared to a looking glass (*"O Milly Bloom, . . . You are my looking glass"* [*U,* 65]). To this end she left "pieces of folded brown paper in the letterbox." At least that is what the French version says (*"Elle s'envoyait"*). The English text is less clear, but let us continue. As for Molly, the philatelist's daughter, she sends herself everything, like Bloom and Joyce, but this is remarked *en abyme* in the literality of the following sequence, which recounts how she dispatches herself to herself [*s'envoyer*] through the post: "like years not a letter from a living soul except the odd few I posted to myself with bits of paper in them" (*U,* 678). Four lines earlier she is sent (away) or rejected [*envoyée ou renvoyée*] by him: "but he never forgot himself when I was there sending me out of the room on some blind excuse."

It is a question, then, of self-sending [*s'envoyer*]. And in the end,

---

23. EN The French expression *s'envoyer* (literally "to send oneself" something) is used colloquially with a sexual meaning: *s'envoyer quelq'un,* to have it off with someone; *s'envoyer en l'air,* to have it off.

sending oneself someone who says *yes* without needing, in order to say it, what the French idiom or *argot* babelizes under the terms of *s'envoyer:* to "have it off" with oneself or someone else. Self-sending barely allows itself a detour via the virgin mother when the father imagines himself sending himself, getting off on, the seed of a consubstantial son: "a mystical estate, an apostolic succession, from only begetter to only begotten" (*U,* 207). It is one of the passages on *"Amor matris,* subjective and objective genitive," which "may be the only true thing in life. Paternity may be a legal fiction" (*U,* 207).

My third example precedes it slightly and comes immediately after *"Was Du verlachst wirst Du noch dienen":* "He Who Himself begot, middler the Holy Ghost, and Himself sent Himself, Agenbuyer, between Himself and others, Who . . . " (*U,* 197). Two pages later:

> —Telegram! he said. Wonderful inspiration! Telegram! A papal bull!
> He sat on a corner of the unlit desk, reading aloud joyfully:
> —*The sentimentalist is he who would enjoy without incurring the immense debtorship for a thing done.* Signed: Dedalus. (*U,* 199)

To be more and more aphoristic and telegraphic, I will say in conclusion that the Ulyssean circle of *self-sending* commands a reactive yes-laughter, the manipulatory operation of hypermnesic reappropriation, whenever the phantasm of a signature wins out, a signature gathering together the sending in order to gather itself together near itself. But when, and it is only a question of rhythm, the circle opens, reappropriation is renounced, the specular gathering together of the sending lets itself be joyfully dispersed in a multiplicity of unique yet numberless sendings, then the other *yes* laughs, the other, yes, laughs.

For here the relationship of a *yes* to the Other, of a *yes* to the other and of one *yes* to the other *yes,* must be such that the contamination of the two *yeses* remains inevitable. And not only as a threat: but also as an opportunity. With or without a word, taken as a minimal event, a *yes* demands *a priori* its own repetition, its own memorizing, demands that a *yes* to the *yes* inhabit the arrival of the "first" yes, which is never therefore simply originary. We cannot say *yes* without promising to confirm it and to remember it, to keep it safe, countersigned in another *yes,* without promise and memory, without the promise of memory. Molly remembers (and recalls herself). The memory of a promise initiates the circle of appropriation, with all the risks of technical repetition, of automatized archives, of gramophony, of simulacrum, of wandering deprived of an address and destination. A *yes* must entrust itself to memory. Having come already from the other, in the dissymmetry of the request, and from the other of whom it is requested to request a *yes,* the *yes* entrusts itself to the memory of the other, of the *yes* of the other and of the other yes. All the risks already crowd around from the first breath of *yes.* And the first breath is suspended in the breath of the other, it is already and always a second breath. It remains there out of sound and out of sight, linked up in advance to some "gramophone in the grave."

We cannot separate the twin *yeses,* and yet they remain completely other. Like Shem and Shaun, like writing and the post. Such a coupling seems to me to ensure not so much the signature of *Ulysses* but the *vibration* of an event which *succeeds only in asking.* A differential vibration of several tonalities, several qualities of yes-laughters which do not allow themselves to be stabilized in the indivisible simplicity of one sole sending, of self to self, or of one sole consigning, but which call for the counter-signature of the other, for a *yes* which would resound in a completely other writing, an other language, an other idiosyncrasy, with an other stamp.

I return to you, to the community of Joycean studies. Supposing a department of Joycean studies decides, under authority of an Elijah Professor, Chairman or Chairperson, to put my reading to the test and to institute a "program," the first phase of which would consist of putting in table form a typology of all the *yeses* in *Ulysses,* before moving on to the *yeses* in *Finnegans Wake.* The chairperson agrees (the chair, like the flesh, always says yes)[24] to buy an *n*th generation computer that would be up to the task. The operation agreed to could go very far. I could keep you for hours describing what I myself computed, a pencil in my hand: the mechanical figure of *yeses* legible

24. TN *La chair dit toujours oui:* "The flesh always says yes"; "The chair always says yes."

in the original gives more than 222 in all, of which more than a quarter, at least 79, are in Molly's so-called monologue (!), with an even greater number in French, since certain types of words or phrases or rhythmic pauses are in fact translated by *"oui"* ("ay," "well," "he nodded," for example), sometimes in the absence of the word *yes*.[25] Another count would be necessary in every language, with a special fate for those used in *Ulysses*. What would we do, for example, with *"mon père, oui,"* which is written in French in the original, or with *"O si certo"* where *yes* stands as near as possible to Satanic temptation, that of the spirit saying no ("You prayed to the devil. . . . *O si, certo!* Sell your soul for that" [*U*, 46]). Beyond this perilous counting of explicit *yeses*, the chairperson would decide on or promise two tasks which would be impossible for any computer of which we possess the concept and control today. These are two impossible tasks for all the reasons I have listed and which I reduce to two main types.

1. By hypothesis, we would have to organize the different categories of *yes* according to a large number of criteria. I found at least ten

---

25. Here are some examples; French and then English page references are given (the French edition is that published by Gallimard in 1948). 13/16 *oui* purely and simply added; 39/42 *oui* for "I am"; 39/43 *oui* for "I will"; 43/46 *oui* for "ay"; 90/93 *oui mais* for "well but"; 93/96 *Oh mais oui* for "O, he did"; 100/103 *Je crois que oui* for "I believe so"; 104/108 *Oh mais oui* for "O, to be sure"; 118/121 *fit oui de la tête* for "nodded"; 120/123 *oui* for "Ay"; 125/128 *pardi oui* for "So it was"; 164/167 *Je crois que oui* for "I believe there is"; 169/172 *oui merci* for "thank you"; *oui* for "ay"; 171/174 *oui* for "ay"; 186/189 *oui-da, il me la fallait* for "marry, I wanted it"; 191/194 *Oui. Un oui juvénile de M. Bon* for "—Yes, Mr. Best said youngly"; 195/199 *oui-da* for "Yea"; 199-203 *oh si* for "o yes"; 210/214 *Oui da* for "Ay"; 214/218 *Oh Oui* for "very well indeed"; 220/224 *Dame oui* for "Ay"; 237/242 *Elle fit oui* for "she nodded"; 238/243 *Oui, essayez voir* for "Hold him now"; 250/256 *Oui, essayez voir* for "Ay, ay"; 261/266 *oui, essayez voir* for "hold him now"; 262/268 *Mais oui, mais oui* for "Ay, ay, Mr. Dedalus nodded"; 266/271 *Oui, mais* for "But . . . "; 272/277 *Oui, certainement* for "o, certainly is"; 277/281 *Oui, chantez . . . "* for "Ay do"; 285/289 *oui, oui* for "Ay, ay"; 294/299 *oui* for "ay"; *oui* for "ay"; 305/309 *Ben oui pour sûr* for "So I would" (complicated syntax); 309/313 *Ah oui* for "Ay"; 323/328 *oui* for "ay"; *oui* for "ay"; 330/335 *oui* for "That's so"; 331/336 *oui* for "well"; 346/351 *oui* for "so I would"; 347/352 *oui* for "nay"; 363/367 *oui* for "what!"; 365/370 *Sapristi oui* for "devil you are"; *oui!* for "see!"; 374/377 *Elle regardait la mer le jour où elle m'a dit oui* for "Looking out over the sea she told me"; 394/397 *oui da* for "ay"; 429/431 *Je crois que oui* for "I suppose so"; 475/473 *je dis que oui* for "I say you are"; 522/518 *oui, je sais* for "O, I know"; 550/546 *Ben oui* for "Why"; 554/550 *Oui* for "Ay": 557/552 *si, si* for "ay, ay"; *si, si* for "ay, ay"; 669/666 *oui* for "well"; *oui bien sûr* for "but of course"; 687/684 *oui* for "ay"; 699/694 *bien oui* for "of course"; 706/701 *le disait oui* for "say they are." There are more than fifty shifts of diverse kinds. A systematic typology would be tempting.

categories or modalities.[26] This list cannot be closed, since each category can be divided into two depending on whether *yes* appears in a manifest *monologue* in response to the other *in itself* or in manifest *dialogue*.[27] We would have to take into consideration the different tonalities attributed to the alleged modalities of *yes* in English and in every language. Now supposing that we could give the computer reading-head relevant instructions to pick up subtle changes in tone, a thing which is doubtful in itself, the over-marking of every *yes* with the remains of a quasi-transcendental, *yes-laughter* can no longer give rise to a diacritical detection ruled by binary logic. The two *yes-laughters* of differing quality call one to the other, call for and imply each other irresistibly; consequently they risk, as much as they request, the signed pledge. One doubles the other, not as a countable presence, but as a

26. For example: (1) The "yes" in question form: *oui? Allo?* as in "Yes? Buck Mulligan said. What did I say?" (14); (2) the "yes" of rhythmic breathing in the form of monologic self-approbation, as in "Two in the back bench whispered. Yes. They knew . . ." (30), or "yes, I must" (44); (3) the "yes" of obedience, as in "Yes, sir" (44); (4) the "yes" marking agreement on a fact, as in "O yes, but I prefer Q. Yes, but W is wonderful" (46); (5) the "yes" of the passionate breathing of desire, as in "Be near her ample bedwarmed flesh. Yes, yes" (63); (6) the "yes" of calculatedly and precisely determined breathing, as in "yes, exactly" (81); (7) the "yes" of absentminded politeness, as in "Yes, yes" (88); (8) the "yes" of emphatic confirmation, as in "Indeed yes, Mr. Bloom agreed" (103); (9) the "yes" of open approval, as in "Yes, Red Murray agreed" (119); (10) the "yes" of insistent confidence, as in "Yes, yes. They went under" (135). This list is in its essence open, and the distinction between explicit monologue and dialogue can also lend itself to all those parasitings and grafts which are the most difficult to systematize.

27. Closure is impossible, then. It opens up new and destabilizing questions for the institution of Joyce studies. There are a number of reasons for this. First, those to which we have just referred with regard to the structure of a "yes." Then those connected with the new relationship which Joyce deliberately, maliciously instituted from a certain date between the pre-text and the so-called completed or published work. He watched over his archive. We now know that from a certain moment, conscious of the treatment to which the archive of the "work in progress" would give rise, he carried out a part of the work himself and began to save rough notes, sketches, drafts, corrections, variations and studio works (we might think here of Ponge, of *La fabrique du pré* or of the manuscripts of *La table*). In this way he deferred his signature up to the moment of readiness for the press. He has given generations of university students and professors, custodians of his "open work," a new task, a task which in principle is infinite. Rather than giving himself up by accident and posthumously to the "genetic criticism" industry, one could say that he constructed the concept and programmed the routes and the dead ends. The diachronic dimension, the incorporation or rather the addition of variants, the manuscript form of the work, the play of the proofs, even the printer's errors, point to moments which are essential in the work and not just the accident of a "This is my body."

"I am exhausted, abandoned, no more young. I stand, so to speak, with an unposted letter bearing the extra regulation fee before the too late box of the general postoffice of human life" (*U*, 486).

ghost. The *yes* of memory, with its recapitulating control and reactive repetition, immediately doubles the light, dancing *yes* of affirmation, the open affirmation of the gift. Reciprocally, two responses or two responsibilities refer to each other without having any relationship between them. The two sign yet prevent the signature from gathering itself together. They can only call up another *yes,* another signature. And, on the other hand, one cannot decide between two *yeses* that *must* gather together like twins, to the point of simulacrum, the one being the gramophony of the other.

I hear this vibration as the very music of *Ulysses.* A computer cannot today enumerate these interlacings, in spite of all the many ways it can help us out. Only an as yet unheard-of computer could, by attempting to integrate with it, and therefore by adding to it its own score, its other language and its other writing, *respond* to that in *Ulysses.* What I say or write here is merely putting forward a proposition, a small piece in regard to that other text which would be the unheard-of computer.

2.   Hence the second part of the argument. The program of the operation to be carried out on the computer or in the institute, ordered by the chairperson, in fact presupposes a *yes*—others would call it a speech act—which, responding in some way to the event of the *yeses* in *Ulysses* and to their call, to whatever in their structure is or utters a call, is *part of and not part of* the analyzed corpus. The chairperson's *yes,* like that of the program of whoever writes on *Ulysses,* responding and countersigning in some way, does not let itself be counted or discounted, no more than does the *yes* which it calls for in turn. It is not just binarity which proves to be impossible, it is, for the same reason, totalization, and the closing of the circle, and the return of Ulysses, and Ulysses himself, and the self-sending of some indivisible signature.

Yes, yes, this is what arouses laughter, and we never laugh alone, as Freud rightly said, never without sharing something of the same repression. Or, rather, this is what leads to laughter, just as it, and the id, lead to thought. And just as it, and the id, give quite simply, beyond laughter and beyond the *yes,* beyond the *yes/no/yes* of the *me/not-me, ego/not-ego* which can always turn toward the dialectic.

But can we sign with a perfume?

Only another event can sign, can countersign to bring it about that an event has already happened. This event, that we naively call the first event, can only affirm itself in the confirmation of the other: a completely other event.

The other signs. And the *yes* keeps restarting itself, an infinite number of times, even more than, and quite differently from, Mrs. Breen's week of seven *yes*es when she hears Bloom recount to her the story of Marcus Tertius Moses and Dancer Moses (*U*, 437): "MRS. BREEN (*eagerly*) Yes, yes, yes, yes, yes, yes, yes."

I decided to stop here because I almost had an accident just as I was jotting down this last sentence, when, on leaving the airport, I was driving home after the trip to Tokyo.

8

FROM

PSYCHE

INVENTION OF THE OTHER

&❧ Francis Ponge's short poem "Fable" provides an example of literary inventiveness that Derrida, in the full essay from which this is an extract, relates to the notion of "invention" in wider cultural and political senses. The text that represents to a more orthodox literary critic an instance of the "gratuitous obscurity" evident in Ponge's writing (Martin Sorrell, *Francis Ponge* [Boston: G. K. Hall, 1981], 119) is for Derrida a lucid demonstration of the enigma of invention, at once requiring and unsettling protocols and rules, at once finding something already implicit in the cultural fabric by means of which to make itself understood and bringing something wholly new into being. Like the signature, the invention is constituted by its originality (a reproduction of a signature is not a signature; a copy can never be an invention) and yet wholly dependent on recognition and legitimation (and therefore subject to codes and laws). Any invention, any poem, any reading, must be turned toward the past and the same ("invention" in its older sense of "finding" what already exists), and toward the future and the other, neither of which exists or can be known in advance. "Fable," in Derrida's reading, invents on the subject of the title, of reference, of the reflexiveness of language, of allegory, of the other, of irony—and of invention; its inventive handling of discourse enforces while it problematizes the distinction between constative and performative language.

Deconstruction—which Derrida says "is inventive or it is nothing at all"—emerges in this piece as a movement of affirmation with important political consequences, exposing the social repressiveness of the traditional concept of invention while seeking to harness the concept's problematic qualities—to "reinvent invention"—in order to make a space for an inventiveness open to the wholly other. Invention—as both discussed and exemplified in this extract—is one name for what Derrida continually aims to achieve in his responses to literary texts: an originality that respects the laws within which it finds itself, even while it probes, as anything that is new must do, those laws' differences from themselves. He finds this kind of inventiveness in the work of Paul de Man, who died shortly before "Psyche" was written. Deconstruction's work at the limits of philosophy (which is also the work of a poem like "Fable") is directed toward an undoing of closed structures in order to make possible the coming of the other; not an other which merely reinforces the same (as, notes Derrida, the other produced by racism always does), not an other which is simply outside or absolutely new, but one that displaces the very opposition of same and other, inside and outside, old and new.

&ɞ "Psyche: Invention de l'autre," originally given as two lectures at Cornell University in 1984, appears as the first text in Derrida's collection of almost the same name: *Psyché: Inventions de l'autre* ([Paris: Galilée, 1987], 11–61). The omitted section (37–58) deals with the institutional procedures of patent and copyright, with the varied meanings of the word *invention* (referring especially to the Port Royal *Logic,* to Descartes, and to Leibniz), with the attempt of modern governments to reduce invention to an exploitable program, and with the theological dimensions of the term's history (notably in Schelling). The English translation by Catherine Porter was published, as "Psyche: Inventions of the Other," in *Reading de Man Reading,* ed. Lindsay Waters and Wlad Godzich (Minneapolis: University of Minnesota Press, 1989). It has been modified slightly in the light of the published French text.

What am I going to be able to invent this time?[1]

Here perhaps we have an inventive incipit for a lecture. Imagine, if

1. EN *Que vais-je inventer encore?*: a rendering closer to the colloquial meaning would be "What am I going to be able to come up with this time?" As Derrida goes on to suggest, the implications of *encore* are multiple: "again," "once more," "still," "this time," "else" ("what else am I going to be able to invent?"). The paradoxical logic of invention—as the wholly new and the institutionally recognizable—is thus broached immediately. And this opening sentence is at once *used*—it *is* Derrida's *incipit*—and

you will, a speaker daring to address his hosts in these terms. He seems not to know what he is going to say; he declares rather insolently that he is setting out to improvise. He is going to have to invent on the spot, and he asks himself once more [*encore*] "Just what am I going to have to invent?" But simultaneously he seems to be implying, not without presumptuousness, that the improvised speech will constantly remain unpredictable, that is to say, as usual, "still" [*"encore"*] new, original, unique—in a word, inventive. And in fact, by having at least invented something with his very first sentence, such an orator would be breaking the rules, would be breaking with convention, etiquette, the rhetoric of modesty, in short, with all the conditions of social interaction. An invention always presupposes some illegality, the breaking of an implicit contract; it inserts a disorder into the peaceful ordering of things, it disregards the proprieties. Apparently without the patience of a preface—it is itself a new preface—, this is how it unsettles the givens.

The Question of the Son Cicero would certainly not have advised his son to begin this way. For, as you know, it was in responding one day to his son's request and desire that Cicero defined, on one occasion among others, oratorical invention.[2]

The reference to Cicero is indispensable here. If we are to speak of invention, we must always keep in mind the word's Latin roots, which mark the construction of the concept and the history of its problematics. Moreover, the first request of Cicero's son bears on language, and on translation from Greek to Latin ("Studeo, mi pater, Latine ex te audire ea quae mihi tu de ratione dicendi Graece tradidisti, si modo tibi est otium et si vis": "I am burning with a desire, father, to hear you say to me in Latin those things concerning the doctrine of speaking that you have given [dispensed, reported, delivered or translated, bequeathed] to me in Greek, at least if you have the time and want to do it") (*Partitiones oratoriae*, 1).

mentioned, as an example of an opening sentence; this undecidability of use and mention is another topic to be addressed later.

2. Cf. *Partitiones oratoriae*, 1–3, and *De inventione*, I, 7.

Cicero the father answers his son. He first tells him, as if to echo his request or to restate it narcissistically, that as a father his first desire is for his son to be as learned as possible, *doctissimum*. The son has then, with his burning desire, anticipated the father's wish. Since his desire is burning with that of his father, the latter takes satisfaction in it and reappropriates it for himself in satisfying it. Then the father offers the son this teaching: given that the orator's special power, his *vis,* consists in the things he deals with (ideas, objects, themes), as well as in the words he uses, *invention* has to be distinguished from *disposition*; invention finds or discovers things, while disposition places or localizes them, positions them while arranging them: "et res et verba invenienda sunt et collocanda." Yet invention is "properly" applied to ideas, to the things one is talking about, and not to elocution or verbal forms. As for disposition, which locates words as well as things, form as well as substance, it is often linked to invention, father Cicero then explains. So disposition, furnishing places with their contents, concerns both words and things. We would then have, on the one hand, the "invention-disposition" pairing for ideas or things, and on the other hand the "elocution-disposition" pairing for words or forms.

We now have in place one of the most traditional philosophical *topoi*. Paul de Man recalls that *topos* in a beautifully wrought text entitled "Pascal's Allegory of Persuasion."[3] I should like to dedicate this essay to the memory of Paul de Man. Allow me to do so in a very simple way, by trying once more to borrow from him—from among all the things we have received from him—a bit of that serene discretion by which his thought—its force and its radiance—was marked. It was in 1967, when he directed the Cornell University Program in Paris, that I first came to know him, to read him, to listen to him, and there arose between us an unfailing friendship that was to be utterly cloudless and that will remain in my life, in me, one of the rarest and most precious rays of light.

In "Pascal's Allegory of Persuasion," de Man pursues his unceasing meditation on the theme of allegory. And it is also, more or less directly,

---

3. Paul de Man, "Pascal's Allegory of Persuasion," in Stephen Greenblatt, ed., *Allegory and Representation* (Baltimore: Johns Hopkins University Press, 1981), 1–25.

invention as allegory, another name for the invention of the other, that I wish to speak of today. Is the invention of the other an allegory, a myth, a fable? After pointing out that allegory is "sequential and narrative," although "the topic of its narration" is "not necessarily temporal at all," de Man insists on the paradoxes in what we could call the task of allegory or the allegorical imperative: "Allegory is the purveyor of demanding truths, and thus its burden is to articulate an epistemological order of truth and deceit with a narrative or compositional order of persuasion" (1–2). And in the same development he encounters the classical distinction between rhetoric as invention and rhetoric as disposition: "A large number of such texts on the relationship between truth and persuasion exist in the canon of philosophy and rhetoric, often crystallized around such traditional philosophical topoi as the relationship between analytic and synthetic judgments, between propositional and modal logic, between logic and mathematics, between logic and rhetoric, between rhetoric as *inventio* and rhetoric as *dispositio,* and so forth" (2).

Had we had the time for it here, it would have been interesting to ask why and how, in the positive notion of rights that is established between the seventeenth and nineteenth centuries, the view of an author's rights, or of an inventor's proprietary rights in the realm of arts and letters, takes into account only form and composition. This law excludes all consideration of "things," content, themes, or meaning. All the legal texts, often at the price of considerable difficulty and confusion, stress this point: invention can display its originality only in the values of form and composition. As for "ideas," they belong to everyone; universal in their essence, they could not ground a property right. Is that a betrayal, a bad translation, or a displacement of the Ciceronian heritage? Let us leave this question hanging. I simply wanted to include in these opening remarks some praise for the father Cicero. Even if he never invented anything else, I find a great deal of *vis,* of inventive power, in someone who opens a discourse on discourse, a treatise on oratory art, and a text on invention, with what I shall call *the question of the son* as a question *de ratione dicendi.* This question happens to be a scene of *traditio* as tradition, transfer, and translation; we could also say it is an allegory of metaphor. The child who speaks, questions, zealously seeks knowledge—is he the fruit of an invention? Does one invent a child? This question will resurface later on. Does it first of all concern the *son* as the legitimate offspring and bearer of the name?

What am I going to be able to invent this time?

It is certainly expected of a discourse on invention that it should fulfill its own promise or honor its contract: it will deal with invention. But it is also hoped (the letter of the contract implies this) that it will put forth something brand new—in terms of words or things, in its utterance or its enunciation—on the subject of invention. To however limited an extent, in order not to disappoint its audience, it ought to invent. We expect that it state the unexpected. No preface announces it, no horizon of expectation prefaces its reception.

In spite of all the ambiguity of this word and concept, invention, you already have some sense of what I am trying to say.

This discourse must then be presented as an invention. Without claiming to be inventive through and through, and continually, it has to exploit a largely common stock of rule-governed resources and possibilities in order to sign, as it were, an inventive proposition, at least one, and that signed innovation will alone determine the extent to which it will be able to engage the listener's desire. But—and here is where the dramatization and the allegory begin—it will also need the signature or the countersignature of the other, let's say here that of the son who is not the invention of the father. A son will have to recognize the invention as such, as if the heir were the sole judge (hang on to the word *judgment*), as if the son's countersignature bore the legitimating authority.

But presenting an invention, presenting itself as an invention, the discourse I am talking about will have to have its invention evaluated, recognized, and legitimized by someone else, by an other who is not one of the family: the other as a member of a social community or of an institution. For an invention can never be *private* once its status as invention, let us say its patent or warrant, its manifest, open, public identification, has to be certified and conferred. Let us translate: as we speak of invention, that old grandfatherly subject we are seeking to reinvent here today, we ought to see this very speech acquire a sort of patent, the title of invention—and that presupposes a contract, consensus, promise, commitment, institution, law, legality, legitimation. There is no natural invention—and yet invention also presupposes originality, a relation to origins, generation, procreation, genealogy, that is to say, a set of values often associated with genius or geniality, thus with naturality. Hence the question of the son, of the signature, and of the name.

We can already see the unique structure of such an event—the occurrence of an invention—taking shape. Who sees it taking shape? The father, the son? Who finds himself or herself excluded from this scene of invention? What other of invention? Father, son, daughter, wife, brother, or sister? If invention is never private, what then is its relation with all the family dramas?

So, then, the unique structure of an event, for the speech act I am speaking of must be an event. It will be so, on the one hand, insofar as it is unique, and on the other hand, inasmuch as its very uniqueness will produce the coming or the coming about of something new. It should promote or allow the coming of what is new in a "first time ever." The full weight of the enigma condenses in every word of this cluster—"new," "event," "coming" [*venir*], "singularity," "first time" (here the English phrase "first time" marks the temporal aspect that the French *première fois* elides). Never does an invention appear, never does an invention take place, without an inaugural event. Nor is there any invention without an advent [*avènement*], if we take this latter word to mean the inauguration for the future [*avenir*] of a *possibility* or of a *power* that will remain at the disposal of everyone. *A*dvent there must be, because the *e*vent of an invention, its act of inaugural production, once recognized, legitimized, countersigned by a social consensus according to a system of conventions, must be valid *for the future*. It will only receive its status of invention, furthermore, to the extent that this socialization of the invented thing will be protected by a system of *conventions* that will ensure for it at the same time its recording in a common history, its belonging to a culture: to a heritage, a lineage, a pedagogical tradition, a discipline, a chain of generations. Invention *begins* by being susceptible to repetition, exploitation, reinscription.

We have already encountered, limiting ourselves to a network that is not solely lexical and that does not reduce to the games of a simple verbal invention, the convergence of several modes of coming [*du venir ou de la venue*], the enigmatic collusion of *invenire* and *inventio*, of *événement* ("event"), *avènement* ("advent"), *avenir* ("future"), *aventure* ("adventure"), and *convention* ("convention"). How could one translate this lexical cluster outside the Romance languages while preserving its unity, the unity linking the *first time* of invention to the *coming*, to the arrival of the future, of the event, of the advent, or the convention or of the adventure? For the most part these words of Latin origin are, for example, welcomed by English (even the term "venue," in its narrow, highly coded judicial sense, and the special sense of "advent" designating the coming of Christ); they are welcome with, however, a notable exception at the center of the grouping: the verb *venir* itself. To be sure an invention comes down [*revient*], says the *Oxford English Dictionary,* to "the action of coming upon or finding." But I can already imagine the inventiveness required of the translator of this lecture in those places where it exploits the institution of the Latin-based languages. Even if this verbal collusion appears adventurous or conventional, it makes us think. What does it make us think? What else? Whom else? What do we still have to invent in regard to the coming [*venir*]? What does it mean, *to come?* To come a first time? Every invention supposes that something or someone comes a *first time,* something or someone comes to someone, to someone else. But for an invention to be an invention, to be *unique* (even if the uniqueness has to be repeatable), it is also necessary for this first time, this unique moment of origin, to be a last time: archaeology and eschatology acknowledge each other here in the irony of the *one and only* instant.

So we are considering the singular structure of an event that seems to produce itself by speaking of itself, *by the fact of speaking of itself,* once it has begun to invent on the subject of invention, paving the way for it, inaugurating or signing its uniqueness, bringing it about, as it were, at the same moment as it also names and describes the generality of its genre and the genealogy of its *topos: de inventione,* sustaining our memory of the tradition of a genre and its practitioners. In its claim to be inventing again [*inventer encore*], such a discourse would be stating the inventive beginning by speaking of itself, in a reflexive structure that not only does not produce coincidence with or presence to itself, but which instead projects the advent of the self, of the "speaking" or "writing" of itself as other, that is to say, *in the manner of the trace*. I shall content myself with mentioning the value of "self-reflexivity" that was often at the core of Paul de Man's analyses. Doubtless more wily than it seems, it has occasioned some very interesting debates, notably in essays by Rodolphe Gasché and Suzanne Gearhart.[4] I shall try to return to these matters some other time.

But in speaking of itself, such a discourse would then be trying to gain recognition by a public community not only for the general truth value of what it is advancing on the subject of invention (the truth of invention and the invention of truth) but at the same time for the operative value of a technical apparatus henceforth available to all.

Fables: Beyond the Speech Act Without yet having cited it, I have been describing for a while now, with one finger pointed toward the margin of my discourse, a text by Francis Ponge. This text is quite short: six lines in *italics,* not even counting the title line— I shall come back in a moment to this figure 7—plus a two-line parenthesis in *roman* type. The roman and italic characters, although their positions are reversed from one edition to the next, may serve to highlight the Latin linguistic heritage that I have mentioned and that Ponge has never ceased to invoke.

To what genre does this text belong? Perhaps we are dealing with one of those pieces Bach called his *Inventions,* contrapuntal pieces in two or three voices that are developed on the basis of a brief initial cell whose rhythm and melodic contour are very clear and sometimes lend themselves to an essentially didactic writing.[5] Ponge's text *disposes* one

---

4. Rodolphe Gasché, "Deconstruction as Criticism," *Glyph* 6 (1979): 177–216, and " 'Setzung' and 'Übersetzung': Notes on Paul de Man," *Diacritics* 11.4 (Winter 1981): 36–57; Suzanne Gearhart, "Philosophy *before* Literature: Deconstruction, Historicity, and the Work of Paul de Man," *Diacritics* 13.4 (Winter 1983): 63–81.

5. We may also recall Clément Jannequin's *Inventions musicales* (circa 1545). Bach's inventions were not merely didactic, even though they were also intended to teach counterpoint technique. They may be (and often are) treated as composition exercises (exposition of the theme in its principal key, reexposition in the dominant, new developments, supplementary or final exposition in the key indicated in the signature). There

such initial cell, which is the following syntagm: *"Par le mot* par . . . ,"
i.e., *"With the word* with . . ." I shall designate this "invention" not
by its genre but by its title, that is, by its proper name: "Fable."[6]
This text is called "Fable." This proper name embraces, so to speak,
the name of a genre. A title, always unique, like a signature, is confused
here with a genre name; an apt comparison would be a novel entitled
Novel, or inventions called *Inventions.* And we can bet that this fable
entitled "Fable," and constructed like a fable right through to its
concluding "moral," will treat the subject of the fable. The fable, the
essence of the fabulous about which it will claim to be stating the truth,
will also be its general subject. *Topos:* fable.
I shall read "Fable," then, the fable "Fable."

FABLE

Par le mot par *commence donc ce texte*
Dont la première ligne dit la vérité,
Mais ce tain sous l'une et l'autre
Peut-il être toléré?
Cher lecteur déjà tu juges
Là de nos difficultés...

(APRÈS sept ans de malheurs
Elle brisa son miroir).

are inventions in A major, in F minor, in G minor, and so on. And as soon as one gives
the title *inventions* in the plural, as I am doing here, one invites thoughts of technical
virtuosity, didactic exercise, instrumental variations. But is one obliged to accept the
invitation to think what one is thus invited to think?
6. In *Proêmes,* part I, "Natare piscem doces" (Paris: Gallimard, 1948), 45. The term
proême, in the didactic sense that is emphasized by the learned *doces,* says something
about invention, about the inventive moment of a discourse: beginning, inauguration,
incipit, introduction. Cf. the second edition of "Fable," with roman and italic type
inverted, in Ponge's *Oeuvres,* vol. I (Paris: Gallimard, 1965), 114.
"Fable" finds and states the truth that it finds in finding it, that is, in stating it.
Philosopheme, theorem, poem. A very sober *Eureka,* reduced to the greatest possible
economy in its operation. In Poe's fictive preface to *Eureka* we read: "I offer this book
of Truths, not in its character of Truth-Teller, but for the Beauty that abounds in its
Truth, constituting it true. To these I present the composition as an Art-Product alone,—
let us say as a Romance; or if I be not urging too lofty a claim, as a Poem. *What I here
propound is true:*—therefore it cannot die" (*The Works of Edgar Allen Poe,* vol. 9,
Eureka and Miscellanies [Chicago: Stone and Kimball, 1895], 4). "Fable" may be called
a spongism, for here truth signs its own name (signed: Ponge), if *Eureka* is a poem.
This is perhaps the place to ask, since we are speaking of *Eureka,* what happens when
one translates *heurēma* as "inventio,"*heuretēs* as "inventor," *heurisko* as "I encounter,
I find by looking or by chance, upon reflection or by accident, I discover or obtain . . ."

FABLE

With the word with *commences then this text*[7]
Of which the first line states the truth,
But this silvering under the one and the other
Can it be tolerated?
Dear reader already you judge
There as to our difficulties...

(AFTER seven years of misfortune
She broke her mirror).

Why did I wish to dedicate the reading of this fable to the memory of Paul de Man? First of all because it deals with a text by Francis Ponge. I am thus recalling a beginning. The first seminar that I gave at Yale, at the invitation of Paul de Man who introduced me there, was on Francis Ponge. *La chose* was the title of this seminar; it continued for three years, touching upon a number of related subjects: the debt, the signature, the countersignature, the proper name, and death. To remember this starting point is, for me, to mime a starting over; I take consolation in calling that beginning back to life through the grace of a fable that is also a myth of impossible origins. In addition, I wish to dedicate this reading to Paul de Man because of the resemblance Ponge's fable, bespeaking a unique intersection of irony and allegory, bears to a poem of truth. It presents itself ironically as an allegory "of which the first line states the truth": truth of allegory and allegory of truth, truth as allegory. Both are fabulous inventions, by which we mean inventions of language (at the root of "fable"/"fabulous" is *fari* or *phanai:* to speak, to affirm) as inventions of the same and of the other, of oneself as (of) the other. This is what we are going to attempt to demonstrate.

The allegorical is marked here both in the fable's theme and in its structure. "Fable" tells of allegory, of an utterance's move to cross over to the other, to the other side of the mirror. Of the desperate effort of an unhappy utterance to move beyond the specularity that it constitutes itself. We might say in another code that "Fable" puts *into*

7. EN The translation of *par* as "with" is my own, as the usual preposition after "commence." Otherwise it follows Catherine Porter's translation.

action [*en acte*] the question of reference, of the specularity of language *or* of literature, and of the possibility of stating the other or speaking *to* the other. We shall see how it does so; but already we know the issue is unmistakably that of death, of this moment of mourning when the breaking of the mirror is the most necessary and also the most difficult. The most difficult because everything we say or do or cry, however outstretched toward the other we may be, remains *within us*. A part of us is wounded and it is with ourselves that we are conversing in the travail of mourning and of *Erinnerung*. Even if this metonymy of the other in ourselves already constituted the truth and the possibility of our relation to the living other, death brings it out into more abundant light. So we see why the breaking of the mirror is still more necessary, because at the instant of death, the limit of narcissistic reappropriation becomes terribly sharp, it increases and neutralizes suffering: let us weep no longer over ourselves, alas when we *must* no longer be concerned with the other *in ourselves,* we *can* no longer be concerned with anyone except the other *in ourselves.* The narcissistic wound enlarges infinitely for want of being able to be narcissistic any longer, for no longer even finding appeasement in that *Erinnerung* we call the work of mourning. Beyond internalizing memory, it is then necessary to *think,* which is another way of remembering. Beyond *Erinnerung,* it is then a question of *Gedächtnis,* to use a Hegelian distinction that Paul de Man was wont to recall in his recent work for the purpose of presenting Hegelian philosophy as an allegory of a certain number of dissociations, for example, between philosophy and history, between literary experience and literary theory.[8]

Allegory, before it is a theme, before it relates to us the other, the discourse of the other or toward the other, is here, in "Fable," the structure of an event. This stems first of all from its narrative form.[9] The "moral" or "lesson" of the fable, as one says, resembles the ending of a story. In the first line the *donc* appears merely as the conclusive

8. Paul de Man, "Sign and Symbol in Hegel's Aesthetics," *Critical Inquiry* 8 (1982): 761–75.
9. "Allegory is sequential and narrative" ("Pascal's Allegory of Persuasion," 1). And again: "Allegory appears as a successive mode" ("The Rhetoric of Temporality," in *Blindness and Insight,* 2d ed. [Minneapolis: University of Minnesota Press, 1983], 226).

seal of a beginning, as a logical and temporal scansion that sets up a singular consequentiality; the word *APRÈS* ("AFTER") in capital letters brings it into sequential order. The parenthesis that comes *after* marks the end of the story, but in a while we shall observe the inversion of these times.

This fable, this allegory of allegory, presents itself then as an invention. First of all because this fable is called "Fable." Before venturing any other semantic analysis, let me state a hypothesis here—leaving its justification for later. Within an area of discourse that has been fairly well stabilized since the end of the seventeenth century in Europe, there are only two major types of *authorized* examples for invention. On the one hand, people invent *stories* (fictional or fabulous), and on the other hand they invent *machines,* technical devices or mechanisms, in the broadest sense of the word. Someone may invent by fabulation, by producing narratives to which there is no corresponding reality outside the narrative (an alibi, for example), or else one may invent by producing a new operational possibility (such as printing or nuclear weaponry, and I am purposely associating these two examples, since the politics of invention—which will be my theme—is always *at one and the same time* a politics of culture and a politics of war). Invention as *production* in both cases—and for the moment I leave to the term "production" a certain indeterminacy. *Fabula* or *fictio* on the one hand, and on the other *technē, epistēmē, historia, methodos,* i.e., art or know-how, knowledge and research, information, procedure, etc. There, I would say for the moment in a somewhat elliptical and dogmatic fashion, are the only two possible, and rigorously specific, registers of all invention today. I am indeed saying "today," stressing the relative modernity of this semantic categorization. Whatever else may resemble invention will not be recognized as such. Our aim here is to grasp the unity or invisible harmony of these two registers.

"Fable," Francis Ponge's fable, invents itself as fable. It tells an apparently fictional story, which seems to last seven years, as the eighth line notes. But first "Fable" is the tale of an invention, it recites and describes itself, it presents itself from the start as a beginning, the inauguration of a discourse or of a textual mechanism. It does what it says, not being content with announcing, as did Valéry, appropriately enough *On the Subject of "Eureka,"*[10] "In the beginning was the Fable." This latter phrase, miming but also translating the first words of John's gospel ("In the beginning was the *logos*") is perhaps also a performative demonstration of the very thing it is saying. And "fable" like *logos,* does indeed say saying, speak of speech. But Ponge's "Fable," while locating itself ironically in this evangelical tradition, reveals and perverts, or rather brings to light, by means of a slight perturbation, the strange structure of the envoi or the evangelical message, in any case of its incipit which says that in the incipit there is the *logos.* "Fable," owing to a turn of syntax, is a sort of poetic performative that simultaneously describes and carries out, on the same line, its own generation.

Not all performatives are somehow reflexive, certainly; they do not all describe themselves, they do not constate themselves as performatives while they take place. This one does so, but its constative description is nothing other than the performative itself. *"With the word* with *commences then this text."* Its beginning, its invention or its first coming does not come about before the sentence that recounts precisely this event. The narrative is nothing other than the coming of what it cites, recites, constates, or describes. It is hard to distinguish the telling and the told faces of this sentence that invents itself while inventing the tale of its invention; in truth, telling and told are undecidable here. The tale is given to be read; it is itself a legend since what the tale narrates does not occur before it or outside of it, of this tale producing the event it narrates; but it is a legendary fable or a fiction in a single line of verse with two versions or two sides [*versants*] of the same. *Invention of the other in the same*—in verse the same from all sides of a mirror whose silvering could (should) not be tolerated. By its very typography, the second occurrence of the word "with" reminds us that the first "with"—the absolute incipit of the fable—is being quoted. The citation institutes a repetition or an originary reflexivity that, even as it divides the inaugural act, at once the inventive event and the relation or archive of an invention, also allows it to unfold in order to

10. EN Paul Valéry, *Oeuvres,* ed. Jean Hytier (Paris: Gallimard, 1957–60), vol. I, 867.

say nothing but the same, itself, the dehiscent and refolded invention of the same, at the very instant when it takes place. And already heralded here, expectantly, is the desire for the other—and to break a mirror. But the first "with," quoted by the second, actually belongs to the same sentence as the latter one, i.e., to the sentence that points out the operation or event, which nonetheless takes place only through the descriptive quotation and neither before it nor anywhere else. Borrowing terms employed by some proponents of speech act theory, we could say that the first "with" is used, the second quoted or mentioned. This distinction seems pertinent when it is applied to the word "with." Is it still pertinent on the scale of the sentence as a whole? The *used* "with" belongs to the mentioning sentence, but also to the mentioned sentence; it is a moment of quotation, and it is as such that it is used. What the sentence cites integrally, from "with" to "with," is nothing other than itself in the process of citing, and the use values within it are only subsets of the mentioned values. The inventive event is the quotation and the narrative. In the body of a single line, on the same divided line, the event of an utterance mixes up two absolutely heterogeneous functions, "use" and "mention," but also heteroreference and self-reference, allegory and tautegory. Is that not precisely the inventive force, the masterstroke of this fable? But this *vis inventiva,* this inventive power, is inseparable from a certain syntactic play with the places in language; it is also an art of *disposition*.

If "Fable" is both performative and constative from its very first line, this effect extends across the whole of the text. By a process of poetic generation we shall have to verify, the concept of invention distributes its two essential values between these two poles: the constative— discovering or unveiling, pointing out or saying what is—and the performative—producing, instituting, transforming. But the sticking point here has to do with the figure of co-implication, with the configuration, of these two values. In this regard *Fable* is exemplary from its very first line. That line's inventiveness results from the single act of enunciation that performs *and* describes, operates *and* states. Here the conjunction "and" does not link two different activities. The constative statement is the performative itself since it points out nothing that is prior or foreign to itself. Its performance consists in the "constatation" of the constative—and nothing else. A quite unique relation to itself, a reflection that produces the self of self-reflection by producing the event in the very act of recounting it. An infinitely rapid circulation— such are the *irony* and the temporality of this text. It is what it is, a text, this text, in as much as it *all at once* shunts the performative into the constative, and vice versa. De Man has written of undecidability as an infinite and thus intolerable acceleration. It is significant for our reading of "Fable" that he says this about the impossible distinction between fiction and autobiography:[11] the play of our fable also lies between fiction and the implicit intervention of a certain *I* that I shall bring up shortly. As for irony, de Man always describes its particular temporality as a structure of the instant, of what becomes "shorter and shorter and always climaxes in the single brief moment of a final *pointe*."[12] "Irony is a synchronic structure,"[13] but we shall soon see how it can be merely the other face of an allegory that always seems to be unfolded in the diachronic dimension of narrative. And there again "Fable" would be exemplary. Its first line speaks only of itself, it is immediately metalingual, but its metalanguage has nothing to set it off; it is an inevitable and impossible metalanguage since *there is no language before it,* since it has no prior object beneath or outside itself. So that in the first line, which states the truth of (the) "Fable," everything is put simultaneously in a first language and in a second metalanguage—and nothing is. There is no metalanguage, the first line repeats; there is only that, says the echo, or Narcissus. The property of language whereby it always can and cannot speak of itself is thus demonstrated in action and in accordance with a paradigm. Here I refer you to a passage from *Allegories of Reading* where de Man returns to the question of metaphor and the role of Narcissus in Rousseau. I shall simply extract a few propositions that will allow you to recall the thrust of his full demonstration: "To the extent that all language is conceptual, it already speaks about language and not about things. . . . All language is language about denomination, that is, a conceptual,

11. Cf. "Autobiography as De-Facement," *The Rhetoric of Romanticism* (New York: Columbia University Press, 1984), 70.
12. "The Rhetoric of Temporality," 226.
13. "The Rhetoric of Temporality," 226.

figural, metaphorical metalanguage. . . . If all language is about language, then the paradigmatic linguistic model is that of an entity that confronts itself."[14]

The infinitely rapid oscillation between the performative and the constative, between language and metalanguage, fiction and nonfiction, autoreference and heteroreference, etc., does not just produce an essential instability. This instability constitutes that very event—let us say, the work—whose invention disturbs normally, as it were, the norms, the statutes, and the rules. It calls for a new theory and for the constitution of new statutes and conventions that, capable of recording the possibility of such events, would be able to account for them. I am not sure that speech act theory, in its present state and dominant form, is capable of this, nor, for that matter, do I think the need could be met by literary theories either of a formalist variety or of a hermeneutic inspiration (i.e., semanticist, thematicist, intentionalist, etc.).

The fabulous economy of a very simple little sentence, perfectly intelligible and normal in its grammar, spontaneously *deconstructs* the oppositional logic that relies on an untouchable distinction between the performative and the constative and so many other related distinctions;[15] it deconstructs that logic without disabling it totally, to be sure, since it also needs it in order to bring about this singular event. Now in this case does the deconstructive effect depend on the force of a literary event? What is there of literature, and what of philosophy, here, in this fabulous staging of deconstruction? I shall not attack this enormous problem head on. I shall merely venture a few remarks that have some bearing upon it.

14. Paul de Man, *Allegories of Reading: Figural Language in Rousseau, Nietzsche, Rilke, and Proust* (New Haven: Yale University Press, 1979), 152–3. A note appended to this sentence begins as follows: "The implication is that the self-reflective moment of the *cogito*, the self-reflection of what Rilke calls '*le Narcisse exhaucé*,' is not an original event but itself an allegorical (or metaphorical) version of an intralinguistic structure, with all the negative epistemological consequences this entails." The equation between allegory and metaphor, in this context, poses problems to which I shall return elsewhere.

15. "The first passage (section 516) on identity showed that constative language is in fact performative, but the second passage (section 477) asserts that the possibility for language to perform is just as fictional as the possibility for language to assert. . . . The differentiation between performative and constative language (which Nietzsche anticipates) is undecidable; the deconstruction leading from the one model to the other is irreversible but it always remains suspended, regardless of how often it is repeated" ("Rhetoric of Persuasion [Nietzsche]," *Allegories of Reading*, 129–30).

1. Suppose we knew what literature is, and that in accord with prevailing conventions we classified "Fable" as literature: we still could not be sure that it is integrally literary (it is hardly certain, for example, that this poem, as soon as it speaks *of* the truth and expressly claims to state it, is nonphilosophical). Nor could we be sure that its deconstructive structure cannot be found in other texts that we would not dream of considering as literary. I am convinced that the same structure, however paradoxical it may seem, also turns up in scientific and especially juridical utterances, and indeed can be found in the most foundational or institutive of these utterances, thus in the most inventive ones.

2. On this subject I shall quote and comment briefly on another text by de Man that meets up in a very dense fashion with all the motifs that concern us at this point: performative and constative, literature and philosophy, possibility or impossibility of deconstruction. This is the conclusion of the essay "Rhetoric of Persuasion (Nietzsche)" in *Allegories of Reading:*

> If the critique of metaphysics is structured as an aporia between performative and constative language, this is the same as saying that it is structured as rhetoric. And since, if one wants to conserve the term "literature," one should not hesitate to assimilate it with rhetoric, then it would follow that the deconstruction of metaphysics, or "philosophy," is an impossibility to the precise extent that it is "literary." This by no means resolves the problem of the relationship between literature and philosophy in Nietzsche, but it at least establishes a somewhat more reliable point of "reference" from which to ask the question. (131)

This paragraph shelters too many nuances, shadings, and reserves for us to be able, in the short time we have here, to lay open all the issues it raises. I hope to deal with it more patiently some other time. For now I shall make do with a somewhat elliptical gloss. In the suggestion that a deconstruction of metaphysics is impossible "to the precise extent that it is 'literary,' " I suspect there may be more irony than first appears. At least for this reason, among others, the most rigorous deconstruction has never claimed to be foreign to literature, nor above all to be *possible*. And I would say that deconstruction loses nothing from admitting that it is impossible; also that those who would rush to delight in that admission lose nothing from having to wait. For a deconstructive operation *possibility* would rather be the danger, the danger of becoming an available set of rule-governed procedures, methods, accessible approaches. The interest of deconstruction, of such force and desire as it may have, is a certain experience of the impossible: that is, as I shall insist in my conclusion, of the other—the experience of the other as the invention of the impossible, in other words, as the only possible invention. Where, in relation to this, might we place that unplaceable we call "literature"? That, too, is a question I shall leave aside for the moment.

"Fable" gives itself then, by itself, by herself, a patent of invention. And its double strike is its invention. This singular duplication, from "with" to "*with,*" is destined for an infinite speculation, and the specularization first seems to seize or freeze the text. It paralyzes it, or makes it spin in place at an imperceptible or infinite speed. It captivates it in a mirror of misfortune. The breaking of a mirror, according to the superstitious saying, announces seven years of misfortune. Here, in typographically different letters and in parentheses, it is *after* seven years of misfortune that she broke the mirror. APRÈS—"after"—is in capital letters in the text. This strange inversion, is it also a mirror effect, a sort of reflection of time? But if the initial effect of this fall of "Fable," which in parentheses assumes the classic role of a sort of "moral," retains an element of forceful *reversal,* it is not only because of this paradox, not just because it inverts the meaning or direction of the superstitious proverb. In an *inversion* of the classical fable form, this "moral" is the only element that is explicitly narrative, and thus, let us say, allegorical. A fable of La Fontaine's usually does just the opposite: there is a narrative, *then* a moral in the form of a maxim or aphorism. But reading the narrative we get here in parentheses and in conclusion, in the place of the "moral," we do not know where to locate the inverted time to which it refers. Is it recounting what would have happened before or what happens after the "first line"? Or again, what happens throughout the whole poem, of which it would be the very temporality? The difference in the grammatical tenses (the simple past of the allegorical "moral" following a continuous present) does not allow us to answer. And there will be no way of knowing whether the "misfortune," the seven years of misfortune that we are tempted to synchronize with the seven preceding lines, is being recounted by the fable or simply gets confused with the misfortune of the narrative, this distress of a fabulous discourse able only to reflect itself without ever moving out of itself. In this case, the misfortune would be the mirror itself. Far from being expressible in the breaking of a mirror, it would consist—whence the infinity of the reflection—in the very presence and possibility of the mirror, in the specular play for which language provides. And upon playing a bit with these misfortunes of performatives or constatives that are never quite themselves because they are parasites of one another, we might be tempted to say that this misfortune is also the essential "infelicity" of these speech acts, that "infelicity" so often depicted by the authors of speech act theory as an accident.

In any case, through all these inversions and perversions, through this fabulous revolution, we have come to the crossroads of what Paul de Man calls allegory and irony. In this connection, I shall indicate three moments or motifs in "The Rhetoric of Temporality":

1. A "provisional conclusion" links allegory and irony in the discovery—we can say the invention—"of a truly temporal predicament." Here are some lines that seem to have been written for "Fable":

> The act of irony, as we now understand it, reveals the existence of a temporality that is definitely *not organic*, in that it relates to its source only in terms of distance and difference and allows for *no end, for no* totality [this is indeed the mirror, a technical and nonorganic structure]. Irony divides the flow of temporal experience into a past that is pure mystification and a future that remains harassed forever by a relapse within the inauthentic. It can know this inauthenticity but can never overcome it. It can only restate and repeat it on an increasingly conscious level, but it remains endlessly caught in the impossibility of making this knowledge applicable to the empirical world. It dissolves in the narrowing spiral of a linguistic sign that becomes more and more remote from its meaning, and it can find no escape from this spiral. The temporal void that it reveals is the same void we encountered when we found *allegory*

always implying an unreachable anteriority. Allegory and irony are linked in their common discovery of a truly temporal predicament. (222, my emphasis)

Suppose we let the word *predicament* (and the word *is* a predicament) keep all its connotations, including the most adventitious ones. Here the mirror is the *predicament:* a necessary or fateful situation, a quasi-nature; we can give a neutral formulation of its predicate or category, and we can state the menacing danger of such a situation, the technical machinery, the artifice that constitutes it. We are caught in the mirror's fatal and fascinating trap.

2. A bit later, Paul de Man presents irony as the inverted specular image of allegory: "The fundamental structure of allegory reappears here [in one of Wordsworth's Lucy Gray poems] in the tendency of the language toward narrative, the spreading out along the axis of an imaginary time in order to give duration to what is, in fact, simultaneous within the subject. *The structure of irony, however, is the reversed mirror-image of this form*" (225, my emphasis).

3. And finally, a passage bringing these two inverted mirror images together in their sameness: "Irony is a synchronic structure, while allegory appears as a successive mode capable of engendering duration as the illusion of a continuity that it knows to be illusionary. *Yet the two modes, for all their profound distinctions in mood and structure, are the two faces of the same fundamental experience of time*" (226, my emphasis).

"Fable," then: an allegory stating ironically the truth of allegory that it is in the present, and doing so while stating it through a play of persons and masks. The first four lines are in the third person of the present indicative (the evident mode of the constative, although the "I," about which Austin tells us that it has, in the present, the privilege of the performative, can be implicit there). In these four lines, the first two are indicative, the next two interrogative. Lines five and six could make the implicit intervention of an "I" explicit insofar as they address the reader; they dramatize the scene by means of a detour into apostrophe or parabasis. Paul de Man gives much attention to parabasis, notably as it is evoked by Schlegel in relation to irony. He brings it up again in "The Rhetoric of Temporality" (222) and elsewhere. Now the "you judge" [*tu juges*] is also *both* performative and constative; and "our difficulties" [*nos difficultés*] are as much the difficulties of the author as those of the implicit "I" of a signatory, those of the fable that presents itself, and those of the community of fable-author-readers. For everyone gets tangled up in the same difficulties, all reflect them, and all can judge them.

But who is the "she" of the last line? Who "broke her mirror?" Perhaps "Fable," the fable itself (feminine in French), which is here, really, the subject. Perhaps the allegory of truth, indeed Truth itself, and it is often, in the realm of allegory, a Woman. But the feminine can also countersign the author's irony. She would speak of the author, she would state or show the author himself in her mirror. One would then say of Ponge what Paul de Man says of Wordsworth. Reflecting upon the "she" of a Lucy Gray poem ("She seemed a thing that could not feel"), he writes: "Wordsworth is one of the few poets who can write proleptically about their own death and speak, as it were, from beyond their own graves. The 'she' in the poem is in fact large enough to encompass Wordsworth as well" ("The Rhetoric of Temporality," 225). Let us call the "she" in this "Fable" "Psyche," the one who appears in the *Metamorphoses* of Apuleius, the one who loses Eros, her betrothed husband, for having wished to see him in spite of the prohibition. But in French a "psyche," a homonym and common noun, is also a large double mirror installed on a rotating stand. The woman, let us say Psyche, the soul, her beauty or her truth, can be reflected there, can admire or adorn herself from head to foot. Psyche does not appear here, at least does not do so under her name, but Ponge could well have dedicated his fable to La Fontaine, who is celebrated in French literature both for his fables and his retelling of the Psyche myth. Ponge has often expressed his admiration for La Fontaine: "If I prefer La Fontaine—the slightest fable—to Schopenhauer or Hegel, I do know why." This Ponge writes in *Proêmes* (Part II, "Pages bis," V, 167).

As for Paul de Man, he does name Psyche, not the mirror, but the mythical character. And he does so in a passage that matters much to us since it also points up the distance between the two "selves," the subject's two selves, the impossibility of seeing oneself and touching oneself at the same time, the "permanent parabasis" and the "allegory of irony":

> [T]his successful combination of allegory and irony also determines the thematic substance of the novel as a whole [*La Chartreuse de Parme*], the underlying *mythos* of the allegory. The novel tells the story of two lovers who, like Eros and Psyche, are never allowed to come into full contact with each other. When they can see each other they are separated by an unbreachable distance; when they can touch, it has to be in a darkness imposed by a totally arbitrary and irrational decision, an act of the gods. The myth is that of the unovercomable distance which must always prevail between the selves, and it thematizes the ironic distance that Stendhal the writer always believed prevailed between his pseudonymous and nominal identities. As such, it reaffirms Schlegel's definition of irony as a "permanent parabasis" and singles out this novel as one of the few novels of novels, as the allegory of irony.

These are the last words of "The Rhetoric of Temporality" (228).

Thus, in the same strike, but a double strike, a fabulous invention becomes the invention of truth, of its truth as fable, of the fable of truth, the truth of truth *as fable*. And of that which in the fable depends on language (*fari*, fable). It is the impossible mourning of truth: in and through the word. For you have seen it well, if the mourning is not announced by the breaking of the mirror, but consists in the mirror, if it comes with specularization, well then, the mirror comes to be itself solely through the intercession of the word. It is an invention and an intervention of the word, and here even of the word "word." The word itself is reflected in the word *mot* as it is in the name "name." The silvering [*tain*], which excludes transparency and authorizes the invention of the mirror, is a trace of language:

> With the word *with* commences then this text
> Of which the first line states the truth,
> But this silvering under the one and the other
> Can it be tolerated?

Between the two *with*s, the silvering that is deposited under the two lines, between the one and the other, is language itself; it depends on the word, and the word "word"; it is "the word" which distributes, separates, on each side of itself, the two appearances of "with": "With the word *with* . . ." It opposes them, puts them opposite or vis-à-vis each other, links them indissociably yet also dissociates them forever. Eros and Psyche. This process does an unbearable violence that the law should prohibit (can this silvering be tolerated under the two lines or between the lines?); it should prohibit it as a perversion of usage, an overturning of linguistic convention. Yet it happens that this perversion obeys the law of language, it is a quite normal proposition, no grammar has anything to object to this rhetoric. We have to get along without that prohibition, such is both the observation and the command conveyed by the *igitur* of this fable—the simultaneously logical, narrative, and fictive *donc* of the first line: "With the word *with* commences, *then*, this text . . . "

This *igitur* speaks for a Psyche, to it/her and before it/her, about it/her as well, and *psyche* would be only the rotating *speculum* that has come to relate the same to the other: "With the word *with* . . ." Of this relation of the same to the other, we could say, playfully: it is *only* an invention, a mirage, or an admirable mirror effect, its status remains that of an invention, of a simple invention, by which is meant a technical mechanism. The question remains: is the psyche an invention?

The analysis of this fable would be endless. I abandon it here. "Fable" in speaking of the fable does not only invent insofar as it tells a story that does not take place, that has no place outside itself and is nothing other than itself in its own inaugural in(ter)vention. This invention is not only that of a poetic fiction, a work whose production becomes the occasion for a signature, for a patent, for the recognition of its status as a literary work by its author and also by its reader, the other who judges ("Dear reader already you judge . . . ")—but who judges from the point of his inscription in the text, from the place that, although first assigned to the addressee, becomes that of a counter-signing. "Fable" has this status as an invention only insofar as, from the double position of the author and the reader, of the signatory and the countersignatory, it also puts out a machine, a technical mechanism that one must be able, under certain conditions and limitations, to reproduce, repeat, reuse, transpose, set within a public tradition and heritage. It thus has the value of a procedure, model, or method, furnishing rules for exportation, for manipulation, for variations. Taking into account other linguistic variables, a syntactic invariable can, recurringly, give rise to other poems of the same type. And this *typed* construction, which presupposes a first instrumentalization of the language, is indeed a sort of *technē*. Between art and the fine arts. This hybrid of the performative and the constative that from the first line at once says *the* truth ("of which the first line states the truth," according to the description and reminder of the second line), and *a* truth that is nothing other than its own truth producing itself: this is indeed a unique event, but it is also a machine and a general truth. While appealing to a preexistent linguistic background (syntactic rules and the fabulous treasure of language), it furnishes a rule-governed mechanism or regulator capable of generating other poetic utterances of the same type, a sort of printing matrix. So we can propose the following example: "At the word *at* begins then this fable"; there would be other regulated variants, at greater or lesser distances from the model, that I do not have the time to note here. Then again, think of the problems of quotability, both inevitable and impossible, that are occasioned by a self-quoting invention. If, for example, I say, as I have done already, "With the word *with* commences then this text by Ponge entitled 'Fable,' for it commences as follows: 'With the word *with*, etc.' " This is a process without beginning or end that nonetheless does nothing but begin, but without ever being able to do so since its sentence or its initiatory phase is already secondary, already the sequel of a first one that it describes even before it has properly taken place, in a sort of exergue as impossible as it is necessary. It is always necessary to begin again in order finally to arrive at the beginning, and reinvent invention. Let us try, here in the margin of the exergue, to begin.

It was understood that we would address here the status of invention.[16] You are well aware that an element of disequilibrium is at work

---

16. EN The French *statut* covers both "status" and written "statute."

in that contract of ours, and that there is thus something provocative about it. We have to speak of the status of invention, but it is better to invent something on this subject. However, we are authorized to invent only within the statutory limits assigned by the contract and by the title (status of invention or inventions of the other). An invention refusing to be dictated, ordered, programmed by these conventions would be out of place, out of phase, out of order, impertinent, transgressive. And yet, some eagerly impatient listeners might be tempted to retort that indeed there will be no invention here today unless that break with convention, into impropriety, is made; in other words, that there will be invention only on condition that the invention transgress, in order to be inventive, the status and the programs with which it was supposed to comply.

As you have already suspected, things are not so simple. No matter how little we retain of the semantic load of the word "invention," no matter what indeterminacy we leave to it for the moment, we have at least the feeling that an invention ought not, as such and as it first emerges, have a status. At the moment when it erupts, the inaugural invention ought to overflow, overlook, transgress, negate (or, at least— this is a supplementary complication—avoid or deny) the status that people would have wanted to assign to it or grant it in advance; indeed it ought to overstep the space in which that status itself takes on its meaning and its legitimacy—in short, the whole environment of *reception* that by definition ought never be ready to welcome an authentic innovation. On this hypothesis (which is not mine, for the time being) it is here that a theory of reception should either encounter its essential limit or else complicate its claims with a theory of transgressive gaps. About the latter we can no longer tell whether it would still be theory and whether it would be a theory of something like reception. Let's stick with this commonsense hypothesis a while longer: an invention ought to produce a disordering mechanism, to open up a space of unrest or turbulence for every status assignable to it when it makes its appearance. Is it not then spontaneously destabilizing, even deconstructive? The question would then be the following: what can be the deconstructive effects of an invention? Or, conversely, in what respect can a movement of deconstruction, far from being limited to the negative or destructuring forms that are often naively attributed to it, be inventive in itself, or at least be the signal of an inventiveness at work in a sociohistorical field? And finally, how can a deconstruction of the very concept of invention, moving through all the complex and organized wealth of its semantic field, still invent? Invent over and beyond the concept and the very language of invention, beyond its rhetoric and its axiomatics?

I am not trying to conflate the problematic of invention with that of deconstruction. Moreover, for fundamental reasons, there could be no *problematic* of deconstruction. My question lies elsewhere: why is the word *invention,* that tired, worn-out classical word, today experiencing a revival, a new fashionableness, and a new way of life? A statistical analysis of the occidental *doxa* would, I am sure, bring it to light: in vocabulary, book titles,[17] the rhetoric of advertising, literary criticism, political oratory, and even in the passwords of art, morality, and religion. A strange return of a desire for invention. "One must invent": not so much create, imagine, produce, institute, but rather invent; and it is precisely in the interval between these meetings (invent/create, invent/imagine, invent/produce, invent/institute, etc.) that the uniqueness of this desire to invent dwells. To invent not this or that, some *technē* or some fable, but to invent the world—a world, not America, the New World, but a new world, another habitat, another person, another desire even. A closer analysis should show why it is then the word "invention" that imposes itself, more quickly and more often

---

17. Why have these titles proliferated in recent years? *L'invention du social* by Jacques Donzelot, *L'invention démocratique* by Claude Lefort, *L'invention d'Athènes* . . . by Nicole Loraux, *L'invention de la politique* by M. I. Finley (a title all the more significant since it was invented as the French translation of *Politics in the Ancient World*). At intervals of a few weeks there appeared Gerald Holton's *L'invention scientifique* (Paris: P.U.F., 1982; this title also having been imposed by the translation), Judith Schlanger's *L'invention intellectuelle* (Paris: Fayard, 1983), and Christian Delacampagne's *L'invention du racisme* (Paris: Fayard, 1983). Delacampagne's book reminds us that the invention of evil, like all inventions, is a matter of culture, language, institutions, history, and technology. In the case of racism in the strict sense, it is doubtless a very recent invention in spite of its ancient roots. Delacampagne connects the signifier, at least, to *reason* and *razza*. Racism is also an invention of the other, but in order to exclude it and tighten the circle of the same. A logic of the *psyche,* the topic of its identifications and projections warrants a lengthy discussion. It is the subject of all the texts in *Psyche;* for its "political" exemplification, see in particular "Racism's Last Word," "Géopsychanalyse," and "The Laws of Reflection: Nelson Mandela, In Admiration."

than other neighboring words ("discover," "create," "imagine," "produce," "institute," and so on). And why this desire for invention, which
goes so far as to dream of inventing a new desire, on the one hand
remains contemporary with a certain experience of fatigue, of weari-
ness, of exhaustion, but on the other hand accompanies a desire for
deconstruction, going so far as to lift the apparent contradiction that
might exist between deconstruction and invention.

Deconstruction is inventive or it is nothing at all; it does not settle
for methodical procedures, it opens up a passageway, it marches ahead
and marks a trail; its writing is not only performative, it produces
rules—other conventions—for new performativities and never installs
itself in the theoretical assurance of a simple opposition between performative and constative. Its *process*[18] involves an affirmation, this
latter being linked to the coming [*venir*] in event, advent, invention.
But it can only make it by deconstructing a conceptual and institutional
structure of invention that would neutralize by putting the stamp of
reason on some aspect of invention, of inventive power: as if it were
necessary, over and beyond a certain traditional status of invention, to
reinvent the future.

**Coming,
Inventing,
Finding,
Finding
Oneself**

A strange proposition. We have said that every invention tends to unsettle the status that one would like to
assign it at the moment when it takes place. We are
saying now that deconstruction must assume the task of
calling into question the traditional status of invention
itself. What does this mean?

What is an invention? What does it do? It *finds* something for the
first time. And the ambiguity lies in the word "find." To find is to
invent when the experience of finding takes place for the first time.
An event without precedent whose novelty may be either that of the
(invented) thing found (for example, a technical apparatus that did not
exist before: printing, a vaccine, nuclear weapons, a musical form, an

18. EN The French is *démarche:* gait, way of moving, step, process (as of thought).

institution—good or bad—and so on), or else the act and not the object of "finding" or "discovering" (for example, in a now dated sense, the Invention of the Cross—by Saint Helena, mother of Constantine the Great, in Jerusalem in A.D. 326—or Tintoretto's "Invention of the Body of Saint Mark"). But in both cases, from both points of view (object or act) invention does not create an existence or a world as a set of existents, it does not have the theological meaning of a veritable creation of existence *ex nihilo*. It discovers for the first time, it unveils what was already *found* there, or produces what, as *technē,* was not already found there but is still not created, in the strong sense of the word, is only put together, starting with a stock of existing and available elements, in a given configuration. This configuration, this ordered totality that makes an invention and its legitimation possible, raises all the problems you know about, whether we refer to cultural totality, *Weltanschauung,* epoch, *epistēmē,* paradigm, etc. However important and difficult these problems may be, they all call for an elucidation of what inventing means and implies. In any event, Ponge's "Fable" creates nothing, in the theological sense of the word (at least this is apparently the case); it invents only by having recourse to a lexicon and to syntactic rules, to a prevailing code, to conventions to which in a certain fashion it subjects itself. But it gives rise to an event, tells a fictional story and produces a machine by introducing a disparity or gap into the customary use of discourse, by upsetting to some extent the mind-set of expectation and reception that it nevertheless needs; it forms a beginning *and* speaks of that beginning, and in this double, indivisible movement, it inaugurates. This double movement harbors that uniqueness and novelty without which there would be no invention.

In every case and through all the semantic displacements of the word "invention," this latter remains the *coming* [*venir*], the event of a novelty that must surprise, because at the moment when it comes about, there could be no statute, no status, ready and waiting to reduce it to the same.

But this coming about [*survenue*] of the new must be due to an operation of the human subject. Invention always belongs to man as the inventing subject. This is a defining feature of very great stability, a semantic quasi-invariant that we must take rigorously into account. For whatever may be the history or the polysemy of the concept of invention as it is inscribed in the workings of Latin culture, even if not in the Latin language itself, never, it seems to me, has anyone assumed the authority to speak of invention without implying in the term the technical initiative of the being called man.[19] Man himself, and the human world, is defined by the human subject's aptitude for invention, in the double sense of narrative fiction or fable and of technical or technoepistemic innovation (just as I am linking *technē* and *fabula*, I am recalling here the link between *historia* and *epistēmē*). No one has ever *authorized* himself—it is indeed a question of status and convention—to say of God that he invents, even if, as people have thought, divine creation provides the ground and support for human invention; and no one has ever authorized himself to say of animals that they invent, even if, as it is sometimes said, their production and manipulation of instruments resemble human invention. On the other hand, men can invent gods, animals, and especially divine animals.

This techno-epistemo-anthropocentric dimension inscribes the value of invention in the set of structures that binds differently the technical order and metaphysical humanism. (By value of invention I mean its *dominant* sense, governed by conventions.) If today it is necessary to reinvent invention, it will have to be done through questions and deconstructive performances bearing upon this traditional and dominant value of invention, upon its very status, and upon the enigmatic history that links, within a system of conventions, a metaphysics to technoscience and to humanism.

. . .

Invention amounts [*revient*] to the same, and it is always possible, as soon as it can receive a status and thereby be legitimized by an institution that it then becomes in its turn. For always the objects we

19. Find *or* invent, find *and* invent. Man can invent by finding, by finding invention, or he can invent beyond what he finds and what is already to be found. Two examples: (1) Bossuet: "The deaf and the dumb find the invention of communicating with their fingers"; (2) Fénelon: "Finding the world as it is, men have had the inventiveness to adapt it to their own uses." "Human" invention often has the negative sense of the imagination, delirium, arbitrary or deceptive fiction.

invent in this way are institutions. The institutions are inventions and the inventions *on* which a status is conferred are in turn institutions. How can an invention *come back* [*revenir*] to being the same, how can the *invenire,* the advent of time-to-come, come to come back, to fold back toward the past a movement always said to be innovative? For that to happen it suffices that invention be possible and that it invent what is possible. Then, right from its origin ("With the word *with* commences then this text"), it envelops in itself a repetition, it unfolds only the dynamics of what was already *found there,* a set of comprehensible possibilities that come into view as ontological or theological truth, a program of cultural or technoscientific politics (civil or military), and so forth. By inventing the possible on the basis of the possible, we relate the new—that is, something quite other that can also be quite ancient—to a set of present possibilities, to the present time and state of the order of possibility that provides for the new the conditions of its status. This statutory economy of public invention does not break the *psyche,* does not pass beyond the mirror. And yet the logic of supplementarity introduces into the very structure of the *psyche* a fabulous complication, the complication of a fable that does more than it says and invents something other than what it offers for copyrighting. The very movement of this fabulous repetition can, through a merging of chance and necessity, produce the new of an event. Not only with the singular invention of a performative, since every performative presupposes conventions and institutional rules—but by bending these rules with respect for the rules themselves in order to allow the other to come or to announce its coming in the opening of this dehiscence. That is perhaps what we call deconstruction. The performance of the "Fable" respects the rules, but does so with a strange move—one that others would adjudge perverse, although it is thereby complying faithfully and lucidly with the very conditions of its own poetics. This move consists in defying and exhibiting the precarious structure of its rules, even while respecting them, and through the mark of respect that it invents.

A unique situation. Invention is always possible, it is the invention of the possible, the *technē* of a human subject in an ontotheological horizon, the invention in truth of the subject and of this horizon; it is the invention of the law, invention in accord with the law that confers status; invention of and in accord with the institutions that socialize, recognize, guarantee, legitimize; the programmed invention of programs; the invention of the same through which the other amounts to the same when its event is again reflected in the fable of a *psyche*. Thus it is that invention would be in conformity with its concept, with the dominant feature of the word and concept "invention," only insofar as, paradoxically, invention invents nothing, when in invention the other does not come, and when nothing comes to the other or from the other. For the other is not the possible. So it would be necessary to say that the only possible invention would be the invention of the impossible. But an invention of the impossible is impossible, the other would say. Indeed. But it is the only possible invention: an invention has to declare itself to be the invention of that which did not appear to be possible; otherwise it only makes explicit a program of possibilities within the economy of the same.[20]

It is in this paradoxical predicament that a deconstruction gets under way. Our current tiredness results from the invention of the same and from the possible, from the invention that is always possible. It is not against it but beyond it that we are trying to reinvent invention itself, another invention, or rather an invention of the other that would come, through the economy of the same, indeed while miming or repeating it ("with the word *with* . . . "), to offer a place for the other, to let the other come. I am careful to say "let it come" because if the other is precisely what is not invented, the initiative or deconstructive inventiveness can consist only in opening, uncloseting, destabilizing foreclusionary structures so as to allow for the passage toward the other. But one does not make the other come, one lets it come by preparing for

20. This economy is obviously not limited to any conscious representation and to the calculations that appear there. And if there is no invention without the stroke of what was once called genius, without, indeed, the flash of a *Witz* through which everything begins, still that generosity must no longer respond to a principle of savings and to a restricted economy of *différance*. The aleatory advent of the entirely other, beyond the incalculable as a still possible calculus, beyond the order of the calculus itself—there is "true" invention, which is no longer invention of truth and can only come about for a finite being: the very *opportunity* [*chance*] of finitude. It invents and appears to itself only on the basis of what thus *falls out* [EN *échoit;* see "Ulysses Gramophone," note 4, above on *échéance*].

its coming. The coming of the other or its coming back is the only possible arrival [*survenue*], but it is not invented, even if the inventiveness of the greatest genius is needed to prepare to welcome it: to prepare to affirm the chance of an encounter that not only is no longer calculable but is not even an incalculable factor still homogeneous with the calculable, not even an undecidable still caught up in the process of decision making. Is this possible? Of course it is not, and that is why it is the only possible invention.

A moment ago, I said we were searching to reinvent invention. No, that search cannot be an outgrowth of *research* as such, whatever Greek or Latin tradition we may find behind the politics and the modern programs of research. Nor is it any longer possible for us to say that *we* are searching: what is promised here is not, is no longer or not yet, the identifiable "we" of a community of human subjects, with all those familiar features we wrap up in the names *society, contract, institution,* and so forth. All these traits are linked to that concept of invention that remains to be deconstructed. It is another "we" that is offered to this inventiveness, after seven years of misfortune, with the mirror broken and the tain crossed, a "we" that does not find *itself* anywhere, does not invent itself: it can be invented only by the other who says "come" and to whom a response with another "come" seems to me to be the only invention that is desirable and worthy of interest. The other is indeed what is not inventable, and it is then the only invention in the world, the only invention of the world, *our* invention, the invention that invents *us*. For the other is always another origin of the world and we are (always) (still) to be invented. And the being of the *we*, and Being itself. Beyond Being.

By the other, beyond the performance and the *psyche* of "With the word *with.*" Performativity is necessary but not sufficient. In the strict sense, a performative still presupposes too much conventional institution to break the mirror. The deconstruction I am invoking only invents or affirms, lets the other come insofar as, while a performative, it is not only performative but also continues to unsettle the conditions of the performative and of whatever distinguishes it comfortably from the constative. This writing is liable to the other, opened to and by the other, to the work of the other; it is writing working at not letting itself be enclosed or dominated by that economy of the same in its totality which guarantees both the irrefutable power and the closure of the classical concept of invention, its politics, its technoscience, its institutions. These are not to be rejected, criticized, or combated, far from it—and all the less so since the economic circle of invention is only a movement for reappropriating exactly what sets it in motion, the *différance* of the other. And that movement cannot be recast as meaning, existence, or truth.

Passing beyond the possible, it is without status, without law, without a horizon of reappropriation, programmation, institutional legitimation, it passes beyond the order of demand, of the market for art or science, it asks for no patent and will never have one. In that respect it remains very gentle, foreign to threats and wars. But for that it is felt as something all the more dangerous.

Like the future. For the time to come is its only concern: allowing the adventure or the event of the entirely other to come. Of an entirely other that can no longer be confused with the God or the Man of ontotheology or with any of the figures of that configuration (the subject, consciousness, the unconscious, the self, man or woman, and so on). To say that this is the only future is not to advocate amnesia. The coming of invention cannot make itself foreign to repetition and memory. For the other is not the new. But its coming extends beyond this past present that once was able to construct—to invent, we must say—the techno-onto-anthropo-theological concept of invention, its very convention and status, the status of invention and the statue of the inventor.

What am I going to be able to invent this time, you asked yourselves, at the beginning, when it was the fable.

And to be sure, you have seen nothing come.

The other, that's no longer inventable.

"What do you mean by that? That the other will have been only an invention, the invention of the other?"

"No, that the other is what is never inventable and will never have waited for your invention. The call of the other is a call to come, and that happens only in multiple voices."

9

FROM

SIGNSPONGE

✲ Derrida's response to the writing of Francis Ponge is in part an act of recognition: recognizing the achievement of one of the most inventive and risk-taking of twentieth-century French writers, and recognizing in Ponge's texts an enactment of some of the concerns that have frequently preoccupied Derrida himself. In this extract from his book on Ponge, Derrida homes in on the closely related questions of the signature and the proper name, questions which are never far from the inescapable, if unaskable, question of the *other*—that which is absolutely heterogeneous to me, but which makes demands upon me nonetheless (all the more, in fact). In the discussion of Ponge in "Psyche: Invention of the Other" (see above) Derrida addresses the question of the other via the issue of invention; here it is implied in Ponge's concern with the *thing*, "*la chose*," and in Derrida's concern with *his* thing, Francis Ponge—author, proper name (always on the verge of dissolving into a common noun), and signed body of texts. (The original title, *Signéponge*, is untranslatable: it combines the senses of "signed, Ponge" and "sign-sponge.")

Derrida's interest is in the *structure* of the signature (the clearest exposition of which is in the closing pages of "Signature Event Context"): it is an act whereby I affirm my unique presence, here and now (often accompanied by an explicit mention of the place and date which are always, in any case, implicit), but it is an act I can perform only if I conform to a code that will allow my signature to be recognized, repeated, copied, forged, mechanically reproduced. If I merely write my name, using a graphic style that appeals to me at the moment of writing—one, perhaps, that seems to respond to my mood, the

344

surroundings, the purpose of the document, and so on—I will not have signed, and I will have failed to affirm the uniqueness and genuineness of my attestation by, paradoxically, attending too fully to the singularity of the event. But even in this case the proper name that I write in my non-signature has the same structure; it can carry out its task of uniquely specifying "me" only by participating in the linguistic code that allows it to be repeated, realized in different media, bestowed on a descendent, confused with other names, or made to serve as a quarry for common nouns. In both these cases, it will be evident that the conditions that allow for smooth functioning are exactly the same conditions that allow for breakdowns; breakdowns are therefore, Derrida argues, not accidents that befall the signature and the proper name, but a necessary precondition of their very existence, both making them possible and preventing them from achieving the pure authenticity they claim to possess.

The structure traced here is not limited to these cases, however; Derrida refers to the "general signature" (much as he refers to "general writing" or the "general text"), the signature-like property (and propriety) of all writing, which affirms its here-and-now as writing, as a writing, unique, localized, dated. (The datedness of writing is a topic in the extract from *Shibboleth* included in this volume.) In so doing it also asserts itself as other, other than the total embodiment of an intention, other than a code simply to be read off by any reader. And this marking of itself—which is related to the generic marking discussed in "The Law of Genre"—involves a placing *en abyme*: any reference (explicit or implicit) by the writing to itself as writing is an inclusion of the whole within a part of the whole, upsetting the logic of identity upon which its unique status seemed to rest. (Of course, a particular kind of reading is implied here; a response, or recognition, which countersigns the work—see "Ulysses Gramophone"—affirming and endorsing its signature, though only by means of a gesture that itself partakes of the same self-divided structure.)

The fascination of Ponge's procedures, for Derrida, is that they do not merely play out these structural paradoxes; they play with them, or perhaps play them, offering a series of unique, signed, dated, placed texts that, as they affirm the uniqueness and otherness of the things to which they respond, exhibit for our pleasure and fascination the curious logic of their responding. A series of texts very like Derrida's, that is.

&⚬ *Signéponge* was first delivered as a lecture at a colloquium on Ponge held at Cerisy-la-Salle in 1975; and first published in its full form in a bilingual edition, *Signéponge/Signsponge* (1984), translated by Richard Rand. The French text was subsequently published in France in 1988 (Paris: Seuil), incorporating slight changes. The extract that follows—pp. 24–64 of the bilingual edition—has been revised by Richard Rand in the light of these changes. Quotations from Ponge have been translated by Rand; sources of the original French texts cited are listed at the end of the extract.

My object, my thing, that which is going to prescribe a rhetoric proper to this event, if it takes place, would be Francis Ponge. If I had asked, as at the outset of a conference or a course, what are we going to talk about? what is the subject today? the answer would have come very quickly: about Francis Ponge, or about the texts of Francis Ponge. But will the question have been about whom or about what?

We always pretend to know what a corpus is all about. When we put the texts of Francis Ponge on our program, we are assured, even if we dismiss the author's biography, of knowing at least what the link is, be it natural or contractual, between a given text, a given so-called author, and his name designated as proper. The academic conventions of literary biography presuppose at least one certainty—the one concerning the signature, the link between the text and the proper name of the person who retains the copyright. Literary biography begins after the contract, if one may put it like this, after the event of signature. All the philological fuss about apocryphal works is never bothered by the slightest doubt, on the contrary, it is set in movement by an absence of doubt as to the status (further on we shall have to say the statue) of a paraph.[1] They certainly ask whether or not it has taken place, this paraph, but as to the very strange structure of this place and this taking-place, the critic and the philologist (and various others), do not as such

---

1. EN The French *parafe* means, most commonly, the initials one puts on a legal document; it can also mean—as it does in English—a flourish added to a signature to guard against forgery.

ask themselves a single question. They may wonder whether a certain piece of writing is indeed assignable to a certain author, but as regards the event of the signature, the abyssal machinery of this operation, the commerce between the said author and his proper name, in other words, whether he signs when he signs, whether his proper name is truly his name and truly proper, before or after the signature, and how all this is affected by the logic of the unconscious, the structure of the language, the paradoxes of name and reference, of nomination and description, the links between common and proper names, names of things and personal names, the proper and the nonproper, no question is ever posed by any of the regional disciplines which are, as such, concerned with texts known as literary.[2]

The Francis-Ponge-text (at the moment I can only designate it by means of a double hyphen) not only furnishes an example, but also *opens up* a science of these questions. Which it puts into practice and into the abyss. For me, Francis Ponge is someone first of all who has known that, in order to know what goes on in the name and the thing, one has to get busy with one's own, let oneself be occupied by it (he has said elsewhere, I no longer know exactly where, and the connection is not an accident, that he was never occupied with anything except death). Occupied with his name, he has taken account of his engagement as subject-writer-in-a-language, *at work.*

He is always at work. With the supplementary trap or abyss effect that I spoke of, he has unceasingly explained, exhibited, turned what he did inside out. And without effacing his name, he has nonetheless effaced it by showing that the stony monumentalization of the name was a way of losing the name; I shall say, by way of anticipating a bit, a way of sponging his signature. And, of course, and this is the twist of the signature, *vice versa.* Thanks to the idiom, "the complete work of an author," he says, still in *Reasons for Living Happily,* "can in its turn be considered as a thing."

Is the signature gained or lost by becoming a thing?

He, to begin with (and what I assume, as I open it up at this point,

---

2. EN For a discussion of some of the issues pertaining to the event of the signature, see Derrida's "Signature Event Context."

by saying *he* from now on about my thing, is praise for the renown that he has made for himself, and I designate him, just as he does the thing in *The Third Person Singular,* which was the first title for *Oral Essay:* "There," he says, "you have to take the thing in the singular; it is amusing because third person . . . singular at the same time . . .")— he, to begin with, engaged himself (I insist on the gage that marks here the immemorial contract, the debt, the duty, the law, the trial aiming for acquittal, I do not speak of nonsuit); he has resolutely engaged himself (resolution is his obstinate watchword, we shall have to ask ourselves why); with resolution, then, with this unceasingly reaffirmed taste for the *frank* act, he is *himself* engaged, has engaged *himself*— and in the face of what and of whom if not of an instance represented by his proper name—*engaged in his name,* not to write anything, not to produce anything that he could not sign, he himself and no one else, anything that, from that point on, could not be absolutely proper to himself, reserved for himself alone, even if, by chance, and this was not in play at the outset, this should remain not much. Slightly before "you have been remarked by F. Ponge" [in *The Notebook of the Pine Forest*]: "Bring out only that which I am the only one to say." And after having recited a whole poetical anthology on the Seine: "But certainly, also, songs of this sort are not, properly speaking, for us. We are not particularly marked out to recite them. And so it does not interest us very much to recite them. Nor you to hear them from us."

It is therefore in the abyss of the proper that we are going to try to recognize the impossible idiom of a signature.[3]

He will have speculated as no one else on the proper, the proper way to write and the proper way to sign. No longer separating, within the proper, the two stems of *propriety* and *property.*[4]

---

3. TN Derrida uses two spellings of the French word for "abyss," *abyme* and *abîme.* The former is the specifically heraldic term for the device whereby the image of a shield is represented on the surface of that shield. *Mise en abyme,* or "placement in abyss," designates the way in which the operations of reading and writing are represented in the text, and *in advance,* as it were, of any other possible reading.

4. EN The adjective *propre* can mean both "clean" and "own," giving rise to two different nouns, *propreté,* "cleanliness, propriety" and *propriété,* "ownership, property." The English word "proper" includes both of these among its older senses, and will be used in this translation.

The only difference, after all, between the one and the other, is an I out of which we can always make some dead wood. He has treated the I in every way, in every language, in *upper case* ("I (i), J (*je*), I (one): one, simple, single, singularity. . . . Chaos of the matter of the I (one). . . . This I is my likeness . . ." [*Joca Seria*]); in *lower case*, taking it off in order to write, in the *Pre*, "a verdant verity";[5] playing with its frail or fresh erection in *the Making of the Pre*: "Difference between the liquid drop or accent (acute here) dot on the i and the virgule of the grass. Virgule, verge.[6]

"On the wet grass there is a dot of dew on the i," this grass, this herb, rising up here with this "something male" that he will have discerned in the opening of his *Malherbe*. If we had time to describe all the "woods" and "trees" in Ponge, we would see all the implications of dead wood (take it also as an order)[7] where he, the I, is erected again; but we shall see, from among these trees, only the family tree, to which it is not a matter of reducing everything else. Here is just one, because it bears, like the proprietary aspect of the proper, an I *in its center*: "Pine (I would not be far from saying) is the elementary idea of tree. It is an I, a stem, and the rest is of little importance. This is why it supplies—among its obligatory developments along the horizontal—so much dead wood."

And so he loves *the proper:* what is proper to himself, proper to the other, proper, that is, to the always singular thing, which is proper in that it is not dirty, soiled, sickening, or disgusting. And he demands the proper in all these states, but with an obstinacy so obsessive that one has to suspect, in this agonistic insistence, some hand-to-hand conflict with the impossible, with something which, within the proper, within the very structure of the proper, is produced only by shifting into its opposite, by being set in abyss, by being inverted, contaminated,

5. TN In French, *pré* means "prairie" or "meadow," but also the prefix "pre-." In the phrase *une vérité qui soit verte,* translated here as "a verdant verity," the word *verte* ("green") is the word *vérité* ("truth") minus the letter *i*.
6. EN *Virgule, vergette:* literally, "comma, small cane (or penis)."
7. TN The French phrase *bois mort* means "dead wood" but also "drink, dead man!" (It links up, thematically, with the homophone *pain/pin,* "bread"/"pine.")

and divided. And one has to suspect that the grand affair of the signature is to be found there.

I am proceeding slowly. I do not want it to seem as if I were explaining him, still less as if I were explaining *to* him what it is, with him or of him, that is taking place here, as one of those professors or metaphysicolicians that he particularly denounces—complaining also (but the case is too complicated for today) that too much has been said about him—would be tempted to do.

He is right not to tolerate explication, and in effect he does not tolerate it ("There are moments when I feel altogether pricklish [defensively] at the idea of being *explained;* and other moments when this subsides, when I feel discouraged and inclined to let it happen..."). I do not dare to imagine the condition in which this colloquium will have taken or left him, but I believe that in fact he cannot be explained, having readied everything for this in various texts which explain themselves very well, and in such a way that everything can be found there, in addition to that remainder which prevents an explanatory discourse from ever attaining saturation. What I am doing here, in the matters of explanation, professors, academic discourse, the academic figure *par excellence* who is the philosopher, and the philosopher *par excellence* known as Hegel, is to ask why, among all the reproaches addressed to them, we meet up with the following: Hegel (the philosopher) is not very proper, and after reading him you have to wash up, to wash your hands of him, you might even say. *Repeated Pages* from *Proems:* "If I prefer La Fontaine—the slightest fable—to Schopenhauer or Hegel, I certainly know why.

"It seems to me: 1. less tiring, more fun; 2. more proper, less disgusting. . . . The trick, then, would be to make only 'small writings' or '*Sapates,*'[8] but ones that would *hold*, satisfy, and at the same time relax, cleanse after reading the grrand metaphysicolicians."

Why, along with all their other shortcomings, would philosophers be unclean?

In explaining this, I must also refuse to be the philosopher that, in

---

8. TN "*Sapates*"— a kind of Christmas stocking found in southern France, and also, according to Littré, a big gift disguised as a small one, as when a diamond is concealed within a lemon. The reference is to Ponge's poem "Preface to the Sapates."

the light of some appearances, I am thought to be, and above all I must make a scene in which I oblige him not to wash his hands any more of the things I say here, be they proper or improper. And to do this, I have to have it out with the signature, with his, with mine, perhaps, and with the other's, since one of the reasons (perhaps) that philosophers as such are a little disgusting is that none of them, as philosophers (this being a part of philosophy), will have known how to cut short, to stop (whence the "volumeinseveraltominous" character of their work, there is only one *Volume One* by Ponge), or to cut, and thereby to shorten and to sign. In order to sign, one has to stop one's text, and no philosopher will have signed his text, resolutely and singularly, will have spoken in his own name, accepting all the risks involved in doing so. Every philosopher denies the idiom of his name, of his language, of his circumstance, speaking in concepts and generalities that are necessarily improper.

Francis Ponge, for his part, would wish to sing the praises and fame only of those who sign. And twice even more so than once, causing us to suspect that you never get there on the first try, supposing that you ever get there at all.

From the outset, however, *For a Malherbe* is caught in an indecision—something that resoluteness will always want to resolve—between a certain *effacing* of the signature that will transform the text into a thing, as ought to be—or into a legendary, proverbial, oracular inscription—and a stubborn *redoubling* of the signature, it being my hypothesis here that these end up as somewhat the same, or do not, in any case, lend themselves to a simple distinction. "The silent world is our only homeland [hence a silent homeland, without language, without discourse, without family name, without a father, but then we were warned beforehand: "We who only get the word from the silent world, our only homeland, are not so stupid, and you can count on it, Gentlemen Critics, as not to observe that we use it according to a particular idiom, and that our books end up being put on the French shelf of the universal library."] The only homeland, moreover, never to proscribe anyone, except perhaps the poet who leaves it in search of other honors. But does one not, perhaps, proscribe oneself from it by signing only with one's name? This is an idea held by certain absolutist thinkers, who tend to proverbs, that is to say, to formulas so striking (so authoritarian) and so evident, that they can do without the signature. But a poet of this sort no sooner calls upon something in the silent world (no, not no sooner! with great difficulty, in fact, and forcibly!) than he produces an object-work that re-enters it, the silent world, that is; a work which, objectively, reinserts itself into that world. This is what justifies the indifference of ambiguity and self-evidence in poetic texts, their oracular character, shall we say."

And so you must certainly sign, but it is as well also not to sign, to write things that, finally, are things, worthy of going without your signature. There is thus a good way of signing, a bad way of signing. The bar does not pass between the signature and the absence of signature, but *through the signature*. Which is therefore always overflowing. Before asking how this can be, I note that it may in part account for the ambiguity of his link with philosophers who do not sign, who have a way of signing without signing: ". . . it seems to me that philosophy belongs to literature as one of its genres... And . . . there are others that I prefer. . . . It remains the case that I have to remain a philosopher *in petto*, worthy, that is—convinced though I am of philosophy's and the world's absurdity—of pleasing my philosophy professors, so as to remain a good man of letters, and so give pleasure to you..." (*Repeated Pages* from *Proems*).

And after naming the *chaos* which Malherbe, like the rest of us, had to pull himself out of, "let us add that he signed his name, and twice rather than once."

The process of transforming a work into a thing—mute, therefore, and silent when speaking, because dispensing with the signature—can only be brought about by inscribing the signature *in the text*, which amounts to signing twice in the process of not signing any more. We shall have to pass through this point once again.

To be more demonstrative, in the effusiveness of my praise, I shall now bring out the resoluteness with which he will have taken sides with the proper against the dirty, or rather against the soiled, the sullied, a distinction which reveals a whole story, one that takes time and decomposes itself: there is no dirty thing, only a soiled thing, a proper thing which is made dirty. Which is moiled,[9] since impurity, as we shall show, often comes about through liquid means, and so should be absorbed by a cloth which is appropriate. Appropriating. The proper is moiled. That which is soiled is moiled.

This is the first meaning of proper, which then goes on to thicken with the other meaning (the proper of property), but thickens in a strange way, one which, to my way of thinking (an objection which I lack the time to develop), produces something entirely different from semantic density, let alone this semantic materialism whose simplification he has endorsed too quickly.

He has everywhere sung the praises of that which would be proper. I will let you multiply the examples. Consider *The Washing Machine*,[10] which, like all his objects, is, in addition or beforehand, a writing as well, one that is standing, stable, stabile, a stance on the page. The washing machine is "very impatiently written": "Should we not beforehand, however—as well as we could as on its tripod—have set up, in this way, trunconically, our washing machine in the middle of the page?"

The operation or scene of writing that the washing machine turns into (though never reducing itself to this, and we shall see why) is a *reappropriation*.

And the fact that it renders linen, tissue, or cloth clean and proper is something that matters to us a great deal, not only in light of the affinity which we have so overused of late between text and tissue, to say nothing as yet of the sponge-towel,[11] but also because the appropriation of linen draws us toward the underclothes of this kind of writing. "The washing machine is so conceived that, having been filled with a heap of *ignoble* tissue [I underline *ignoble*—J. D.], the inner emotion, the boiling indignation that it feels from this, when channelled to the

9. EN The French *se mouille* means "gets wet"; Derrida exploits the rhyme of *mouiller*, "to wet," and *souiller*, "to dirty." The English transitive verb "to moil" means to wet or to dirty.

10. TN *La lessiveuse*—not only a washing machine, but also a washerwoman, whence the erotic scene that follows.

11. TN *Serviette-éponge* is translated as "sponge-towel" instead of the more correct "Turkish towel," for the obvious reasons. [EN In a later part of this text, not reprinted here, Derrida makes much of the texture of the sponge-towel.]

upper part of its being, falls back as rain on the heap of *ignoble* tissue turning its stomach—more or less perpetually—it being a process that should end up with a purification.

"So here we are at the very heart of the mystery. The sun is setting on this Monday evening. Oh housewives! And you, near the end of your study, how tired your backs are! But after grinding away all day long like this (what is the demon that makes me talk this way?) look at what clean and proper arms you have, and pure hands, worn by the most moving toil!"

And to telescope the erotic scene that brings the signer into the text every time, and *on the side* of the washing machine, placing his hands "on your dear hips" (the housewife is a washer "releasing the spigot" before untying the apron "of a blue just like the noble utensil's"), but figuring also the signer hard at the work of reappropriation, and always from both sides (he, facing the washing machine, is the washing machine that describes the washing machine, which, however, can do very nicely without him)—here, to telescope this erotic scene, is the rinsing process: ". . . yes, we have to come back again to our object; once again we have to rinse our idea in clear water:

"Certainly the linen, once it went into the washing machine, had already been cleaned, roughly. The machine did not come into contact with filthiness as such, with snot, for example, dried out, filthy, and clinging to the handkerchiefs.

"It is still a fact, however, that the machine experiences an idea or a diffuse feeling of filthiness about the things inside of itself, which, through emotions, boilings, and efforts, it manages to overcome—in separating the tissue: so much so that, when rinsed in a catastrophe of *fresh* water, these will come to seem extremely white...

"And here, in effect, is the miracle:

"A thousand white flags are suddenly unfurled—attesting not to defeat, but to victory—and are not just, perhaps, the sign of bodily propriety among the inhabitants of the neighborhood."

The moment of rinsing, always in *fresh* water (I have underlined it), is decisive, by which I mean that it carries with it a decision, placed at the end of the text. As in *Soap,* at the end of the "intellectual toilet," after the "exhaustion of the subject." The *Rinse* fits into one page, the last: "... *We have to finish up. Toiled skin, though very proper. We have obtained what we wanted from the soap. And even a little more, maybe.*" [This is the little more *that (than) the signature requires*—a scoured paraph, such is the formula. And the word *paraph* is the same, in its origin, as *paragraph*.] "A paragraph of fresh water. A rising *a)* of the body—*b)* of the soap..."

Soap, that *sort-of-stone-but* that figures the subject, washing and washed, has to be rinsed as well: "Would it not be his entry into society, then, his being put into company with some other (being or thing), with some object, finally, that might enable a person to conceive of his own personal identity, to disengage it from what it is not, to scour and to decarbonize it? To signify himself?"

To signify oneself in the insignificant (outside meaning or concept), isn't this the same thing as signing? Somewhere he says that the insignificant is "hygienic." We will find this word useful later on.

The desire for the proper that necessarily fastens on to linen and freshness (but also, as always, onto the words *linen* and *fresh*) is always at work here (among its other under-determinations, I pass over, for the time being, the hidden, phonic, semantic and graphic thread in the word *linen* that joins the linen-pin (the clothespin) to the sponge-towel: it can wait[12])—at work here, in other words threatened, extended, and trembling in front of *The Carnation:* "At the end of the stem, out of an olive, of a supple nut of leaves, the marvelous luxury of linen comes unbuttoned.

"Carnations, these marvelous rags.

"How proper they are.

. . .

"Inhaling them, you feel a pleasure whose opposite would be a sneeze.

"Seeing them, the pleasure you feel when you see the panties, torn into lovely shreds,[13] of a young girl taking care of her linen."

Let us wait, patiently, between the legs of this "young girl" [*fille*

12. EN Derrida picks up this thread in the later part of the text, not reprinted here.
13. EN The phrase *déchirée à belles dents,* here translated literally, is usually employed figuratively to mean "slandered."

jeune] (he does not tell us whether she is a virgin [*jeune fille*]), and try, in the meantime, to find some sponge-cloth there. Meanwhile, on the facing page (where there are some notes on the carnation that begin by defining the engagement to write as "an affair of self-esteem, nothing more"), from among some words classed and grouped in the dictionary (his most beautiful objest,[14] made for sinking all illiterate scientisms into the greatest confusion), I notice that all the words beginning in *fr*, like freshness [*fraîcheur*], describe a certain way of handling linen:

"*Frounce* [*Froisser*]: to rumple, to cause to assume irregular folds. (The origin is a noise.)

"*Frizz* [*Friser*] (a towel): to fold it in such a way as to form small curls.

"*Frip* [*Friper*], in the sense of rumple, is confused with *fespe*, from *fespa*, which means rags and also fringe, a kind of plush.

"*Fringes* [*Franges*]: etymology unknown..."

This last word, with a so-called unknown genealogy, bears the closest resemblance to the given name of the signer, and the fringes signal, in their margins, as much on the side of fracture, fraction, or the fragment that you know to be cut, as on the side of frankness or franchise, which is just as good for cutting as for freeing and affranchising (liberating, emancipating, stamping, paying off a debt).

If he writes, as he says, "against the spoken word, the eloquent spoken word," he also writes, in the same gesture, against dirt. Dirt takes place, its place, first of all, closest to the body, as in dirty linen. Whence *The Practice of Literature*: "And often after a conversation, after talking, I have the feeling of dirt, of insufficiency, of muddled things; even a conversation that has moved forward a bit, that has gone just a bit toward the bottom of things, and with intelligent people. We say so many stupid things. . . . This is not proper. And often my taste for writing comes when I return to my house after a conversation in which I had the impression of taking old clothes, old shirts from one trunk and putting them into another, all this in the attic, you know, with lots of dust, lots of dirt, sweating a little and dirty, feeling uncom-

---

14. EN Derrida has earlier coined the term *objeu* from the words *objet* ("object") and *enjeu* ("stake, in a bet").

fortable. I see a piece of white paper and I say: 'Maybe, with a little attention, I can write something proper, something neat and clean.' This, is it not, is often the reason, maybe one of the principal reasons, for writing.'"

The fragment from *Proems* with the very title *Reasons for Writing* says almost the same thing, but I want to take some tweezers from it which, like clothespins, describe very well the instruments with which he treats the French language when it is too dirty, so as to reappropriate it, or in other words refrancify it: "In all deference to the *words* themselves, *given the habits they have contracted in so many foul mouths,* it takes a certain courage to decide not only to write but even to speak. *A pile of dirty rags, not to be picked up with tweezers; this is what they offer us for stirring, shaking, and moving from place to place.* In the secret hope that we will fall silent. Well, let us take up the challenge, then!"

To take up the challenge, resolutely, will consist in grabbing the tweezers and treating words between quotation marks, in the first place as a generalized citation of the French language. Even his signature, included within the text, will be held in quotation marks.

How can the signature be caught, by the signer, between quotation marks?

I am not pushing things too far when I compare quotation marks to tweezers. He has done it himself, and precisely around the word "proper" in the expression "proper name"—"this is done in quotation marks, in other words with tweezers."

And so he does not run away from dirt, he writes with dirt, against dirt, on dirt, about dirt. It is his matter.

This is set down in *The Augean Stables:* "Alas, as a crowning horror, the same sordid order speaks *within our very selves.* . . . It all happens to us as if we were painters who had only one single immense pot at their disposal for soaking their brushes, in which, from the night of ages, everyone would have had to thin out their colors. . . . It is not a matter of cleansing the Augean stables, but of painting them in fresco with the medium of the manure proper to them."

To paint in fresco—in other words, with fresh charges yet again. The fresco directly kneads (he loves this word for all that it kneads) the *fresh,* as its name indicates; it mixes color with the humid freshness of moiled paste, in the crases of earth and water. In this sense *The Pre* will also give rise, among other things, to fresco.

"It is not a matter of cleansing the Augean stables, but of painting them in fresco with the medium of the manure proper to them."

Their proper manure. The word *proper* plays, expropriating itself and reappropriating itself to itself, right in the manure.

It works right into the matter.

In the linen (of the body), its tissue, its text, *proper* envelops both propriety and property. Property: the *idion* of the thing which dictates, according to its muteness, in other words singularly, a description of itself or rather a writing of itself that would be idiomatic, appropriate to the thing and appropriated by the thing, to the signer and by the signer. This double appropriation of the *idion* is prescribed right here in the overture to *The Carnation,* a little before the ecstacy induced by the "propriety" of "linen": "to take up the *challenge* of things to language. . . . Is *that* poetry? . . . For me it is a need, an *engagement,* a rage, an affair of self-esteem, nothing more. . . . Once a thing has been given—no matter how ordinary it may be—I find that it always presents some truly particular qualities . . . those are the ones that I try to draw out and disengage.

"What *interest* is there in *disengaging* them? To cause the human mind to gain those qualities of which it is *capable* and which its routine alone prevents from appropriating to itself." I underline *challenge, engagement, interest,* and *disengaging.*

(That this process promises to engage in the production of events, and even revolutions, along with the placement in abyss that will necessarily ensue, is something that we would have to put into colloquy—elsewhere, and in another tone—with the *Aneignung* of Marx or the *Ereignis* [*Ring,* annular object, and *Reigen des Ereignens,* propriation as well as event] of the Heideggerian thing.[15])

Why is this wager impossible, and why does this impossibility make possible, cause to rise, to become erect and then extended, the signature

15. TN Marx refers to *Aneignung* ("appropriation") throughout *Capital,* and Heidegger to *Ereignis* ("event") throughout his later writings.

of a Ponge, granting it a stature both monumental and mortuary? What is the interest in this gage? What is the risk in this wager?

I hasten the answer a bit even at the cost of some disorder.

He has to acquit himself of an infinite debt. And we are, anyway, always fascinated, under the law of someone who will have known how to incur a debt.

He is undebted.[16]

The twist here lies in the fact that an infinite debt is canceled by itself and is never effaced, which oddly amounts to the same thing. He, therefore, is undebted. With respect to what he calls the thing. The thing dictates its conditions, silent though it is, and being silent, does not enter into the contract. It is irresponsible, he alone being responsible from the outset toward the thing, which remains entirely other, indifferent, never engaging itself. "To acknowledge the greatest right of the object, its imprescribable right, opposable to any poem... ... The object is always more important, more interesting, more capable (full of rights): it has no duty toward me, it is I who am entirely duty-bound in its regard." (*Banks of the Loire,* or how to be beaten by the thing, regularly, without ever "sacrificing" it to "the putting in value of some verbal find," returning always to "the object itself, to whatever it has that is raw, *different:* different in particular from what I have already [up to this moment] written about it.")

The law is all the more imperious, unlimited, insatiably hungry for sacrifice, in that it proceeds from something entirely other (the thing) which demands nothing, which does not even have a relationship to itself, which does not exchange anything either with itself or with any person, and which—death, in short—is not a subject (anthropomorphic or theomorphic, conscious or unconscious, neither a discourse nor even a form of writing in the current sense of the word). Demanding everything and *nothing,* the thing puts the debtor (the one who would wish to say properly *my thing*) in a situation of absolute heteronomy and of infinitely unequal alliance. So that, to be acquitted, for him, or

16. TN The phrase *lui s'endette* ("he is indebted") can also be heard as *lui sans dette* ("he without debt").

at least "to pick up the challenge," would not be to obey a verbal contract which has never been signed, but rather to do, he himself, in signing, what is *necessary* so that, in the end, in the orgastic jubilation of what he calls the truth, he could not only sign his text, imposing or apposing his signature, but also, by transforming his text into a signature, he could *oblige* the thing, oblige-it-to, yes, to do nothing less than sign itself, to signify itself (see the extraordinary *Appendix V to Soap*), to become a writing-signature, and so to contract with Francis Ponge the absolute idiom of a contract: one single countersigned signature, one single thing signing double. But this contract, of course, is really nothing of the sort: in a certain manner, nothing is exchanged in exchange for the signatures; and, on the other hand, since the event is idiomatic every single time, neither thing nor person is engaged beyond the momentary singularity of a certain coitus of signatures. And since the confusion of signatures only gains its value by causing the entirely-other to come into the event, this entirely-other remains, on both sides, outside the contract, indifferent, unconcerned. The countersignature lets it be (lets it live, as is said of the object of love in *Proems*). This is just as true for Ponge's side as it is for the side of the thing, whence this feeling, when we read him, of vital engagement *and* flippancy, as of someone who knows at once how to be here and how to be disengaged, who knows that he is disengaged. Whence this inimitable intonation, serious and light at the same time, of a "take it or leave it," all and nothing, all or nothing, everything said and done.

The structure of the placement in abyss, such as he practices it, seems to me to repeat this scene every time: every time, but every time in a necessarily idiomatic fashion, the "differential quality" affecting the very form of the signature, this latter remaining *the other's*. From this comes the infinite monumentalization of the signature, and also its dissipation without return, the signature no longer being tied to a single proper name, but to the atheological multiplicity of a new *signatura rerum*.

What is singular about this tyrannical *thou must* of the thing is exactly its singularity. The singularity of a command which is irreplaceable each time—its rarity—prevents it from becoming law. Or rather, if you prefer, it is a law that is immediately transgressed (let us say, more precisely, *freed up* [*franchie*]), the one who responds being placed, immediately, in a singular link with it, whereby he frees himself from the tyranny even as he experiences and approves it. And then the law will be freed up a second time when—we will get to this later on—the signer will make the thing sign, will make it enter into a singular contract and transform the singular demand into law by means of the placement in abyss. The transgression that enfranchises and frees up will be the law of repetition in abyss.

And, properly, the step, the stop, of Ponge.[17]

This reading hypothesis has two preliminary consequences. In the very first place, it is on the basis of his debt, and of the fact that he puts himself into debt without debt, that, at the very point where he seems to flare up against prescription (didactic, ethical, political, philosophical, etc.), his texts also engage, prescribe, oblige, and teach in the form of a lesson and a morality. See what he says about *duty* and *difference* in the *Preface* to the *Making of the Pre*. He assumes the duty and the need, therefore, to dictate a duty of some kind, according to "what it would, no doubt, be pretentious to call my ethic" (*For a Malherbe*). We must accept the fact, as he does, that he gives a lesson (ethical, political, rhetorical, poetical, etc.): not in order to receive it, but in order to understand the basis on which—the formula, the ring (the debt undebts itself)—one can give and receive a lesson. Imperious, gentle, intractable. His lesson (his ethic, his politics, in other words his philosophy) is less interesting to me (I do not, in fact, always listen to it without murmuring) than the basis on which it is constituted, and which he expounds better than anyone, thereby showing—and we are too readily dubious about this—that the ethical instance is at work in the body of literature. Which is why, rather than *listen* to the lesson he gives, I prefer to *read* it, as a lesson, in other words, *on* morals, and no longer *of* morals, *on* the genealogy of morals that he has drawn, as we shall see, from a morals of genealogy.

Second consequence: since the two (engaged-disengaged) entirely others are outside of the contract process, are inaccessible, and since we can never do anything other than let them be (he and the thing),

17. EN *Le pas de Ponge:* both the step and the negative, the "no," of Ponge.

that which interests, or interests us, and engages us in reading, is inevitably what happens in the middle, *between them:* the intermediaries (names and things), the witnesses, the intercessors, the events that go on *between them,* the interested parties.

I return to this point by taking a step, a stop, backwards.

How is the proper double or double proper (propriety and idiomatic property, but also the double *of* the proper *that is placed in abyss*) produced in signature?

We can, as a first and insufficient approach, distinguish three modalities of signature. The one that we call the signature in the proper sense represents the proper name, articulated in a language and readable as such: the act of someone not content to write his proper name (as if he were filling out an identity card), but engaged in authenticating (if possible) the fact that it is indeed he who writes: here is my name, I refer to myself, named as I am, and I do so, therefore, in my name. I, the undersigned, I affirm (yes, on my honor). The line between the autography of one's proper name and a signature poses (*de facto* and *de jure*, therefore) redoubtable problems, which I do not wish to evade, as is always being done (on the contrary, it is *my* question here), but which, for the moment, I pass over.

The second modality, a banal and confused metaphor for the first, is the set of idiomatic marks that a signer might leave by accident or intention in his product. These marks would have no essential link with the form of the proper name as articulated or read "in" a language. But then the inclusion of the proper name "in" a language never happens as a matter of course. We sometimes call this the style, the inimitable idiom of a writer, sculptor, painter, or orator. Or of a musician, the only one who is incapable, as such, of inscribing his signature in the first sense, his nominal signature, that is, upon the work itself: the musician cannot sign within the text. He lacks the space to do so, and the spacing of a language (unless he overcodes his work on the basis of another semiotic system, one of musical notation, for example). This is also his opportunity.

In keeping with this second sense, let us say that the work is signed Ponge or X without having to read the proper name.

Thirdly, and it is more complicated here, we may designate as general signature, or signature of the signature, the fold of the placement in abyss where, after the manner of the signature in the current sense, the work of writing designates, describes, and inscribes itself as *act* (action and archive), signs itself before the end by affording us the opportunity to read: I refer to myself, this is writing, *I* am a writing, this is *writing*—which excludes *nothing* since, when the placement in abyss succeeds, and is thereby decomposed and produces an event, it is the other, the thing as other, that signs. This does not just happen in books, not only, but also in revolutions, or between the *Sapates* of Francis Ponge.

These three modalities are, in principle, structurally distinct. But I want to show how Francis-Ponge (I put a hyphen between his first name and his last name)—and this is what constitutes his style, his paraph, or, if such a thing exists, his own particular operation—is able to fold all three into a single one, or in any case combine them in the same scene for the same drama and the same orgasm.

The law producing *and* prohibiting the signature (in the first modality) of the proper name, is that, by not letting the signature fall outside the text any more, as an undersigned subscription, and by inserting it into the body of the text, you monumentalize, institute, and erect it into a thing or a stony object. But in doing so, you also lose the identity, the title of ownership over the text: you let it become a moment or a part of the text, as a thing or a common noun. The erection-tomb falls.[18] Step, and stop, of man [*pas d'homme*].

Hence the signature has to remain and disappear at the same time, remain in order to disappear, or disappear in order to remain. *It has to do so, it is lacking,*[19] this is what matters. It has to, it fails to, *remain by disappearing, it has to have to disappear, it has to have yet to disappear,* a simultaneous and double demand, a double and contradictory postulation, a double obligation, a *double bind* which I translated in *Glas* as the *double band* of the signature, the double band, the double band(s), hence the double(s) band. There has to be a signature

18. EN *L'érection-tombe:* both "the erection-tomb" and "the erection falls."
19. TN *Il faut* means both "it is lacking" and "it has to, one must"; it is also a homophone of *il faux* "it (is) faulty." (EN See Derrida's note on the earlier form of this phrase, *Ci falt;* "Before the Law," note 19, above.)

so that it can remain-to-disappear. It is lacking, which is why there has to be one, but it is necessary that it be lacking, which is why there does not have to be one.

It has to   write that as you wish,   such is the countersigned signature, useless and indispensable, supplementary.

Let us begin with a point of departure that is somewhat aleatory, though not any more so, perhaps, than a proper name; and which is, moreover, sufficiently motivated by the figure of the "geneanalogical" tree (*Interviews of Francis Ponge with Philippe Sollers*); let us begin with one of the oldest archives, with the tree from *Reasons for Living Happily* (1928–29).

After appealing to the *idion,* and to the "unique circumstances" which, "at the same moment," create "the motive for making me seize my pencil"—along with a "new tool on our bench" (wood on wood) for describing things "from their own point of view," so as to give "the impression of a new idiom"—he explains the conditions under which, "later on, the complete work of an author" may "be considered a thing in its turn": "not only a rhetoric per poem" or "a manner per year or per work."

The figure of the tree then imposes itself, as if by chance: ". . . like the successive rinds of a tree, detaching themselves at each period through the natural effort of the tree." Now the tree, whose elementary idea, as we recall, is one of pine wood, from which we make dead wood (coffins and tables also), turns up again in 1941, in a letter announcing the rule of the counter-rule: ". . . every writer 'worthy of the name' must write *against* all writing that precedes him (*must* in the sense of *is forced to, is obliged to*)—notably against all existing rules." (What we have to remember here is Ponge against the rules, right up against the origin of rules). The letter continues: "But I favor one technique per poet, and even, at the limit, one technique per poem— which its object would determine.

"Thus, for *The Pine Forest,* if I may be permitted to put it so—is it not the pine tree that furnishes (during its lifetime) *the most dead wood?* . . .

"The ultimate preciosity?—No doubt. But what can I do? Having

once imagined this kind of difficulty, honor requires us to confront it
... (and then again, it's fun)."

Fun is not an accessory value here. And once again, as if by chance
and for the sake of amusement, the *Oral Essay,* when speaking of the
"duty of trees" (to make branches and leaves), and of "this tree which
is my friend," inscribes on a leaf (of a tree, of course), the common
noun that is closest, nearest to the proper given name of the author,
except for a gender and an aitch.[20] It is presented as a "small apologue,"
but we read an apologia as well: "Let us suppose that I had a friend
(I have friends: I have them in literature, philosophy, politics, journalism). But let us suppose that this friend of mine is a tree. What is the
duty of trees, the point about trees? It is to make branches, then leaves;
this, of course, is their duty. Now then, this tree, who is my friend,
thought that he had written on his leaves, on each of his leaves (in the
language of trees, everyone knows what I mean), that he had written
franchise on a leaf ... "[21]

This is the first example, the last one being "neither executioner nor
victim."

Now the sequel to the apologue tells how, in brief, the tree becomes
an executioner and a victim at one and the same time, signing itself
and bleeding to death from the very moment that the woodcutter, after
making off with one of its branches, turns it into a hatchet [*hache*]
with which he then tries to cut down the tree. The eyes of the tree
"fasten on to the axe held by the woodsman—something the tree
almost failed to remark the first time—and it recognizes, in the brand-
new handle of this axe the wood of the branch that was removed in
the first place." "Almost failed to *remark...*"

The end of the apologue suggests that we should not "push metaphors too far. It is one of their hazards that we can take them in all
senses."

---

20. TN The French word for the letter *h* is *hache,* and the same word means "hatchet";
this pun becomes crucial later on.

21. TN In translating *franchise* I have retained the *faux ami* "franchise" in preference
to its proper meaning of "frankness." "Francis" plus an "h" plus the final "e" signaling
the feminine gender in French produces *franchise.*

But we can stay here right next to what is nearest. For "it becomes tragic at the moment when our tree, not content with complaining, with saying: *Tu quoque, fili mi,* reaches the point where it thinks: *Am I the wood, then, that hatchets [haches] are made of?* That, that's terrible." What comes back to cut the tree, and then to put it to death, is thus a part of the tree, a branch, a son, a handle, a piece detached from the tree which writes, which writes itself on itself, on its leaf, its first leaf, *franchise.* The tree itself, the signer, cuts itself, and the torn-off piece with which it cuts itself to death is also a hatchet, an aitch, a letter subtracted from the *franchise* written on the tree, what has to be cut away from this common noun so that the noun can become, or very nearly so, a proper given name. But the supplementary hatchet, the aitch, by making dead wood, confers a monumental stature on the apologetic tree.

The phallic character of the I, of pine wood, the incisor of the cutting and resolute franchise, the sharpened decision of the hatchet or aitch that the tree allows to be turned against itself—all this is understood according to the male value, the cutting virility recognized in frankness and francity. If all this were not regularly put, so as to invert itself, in abyss, according to a necessary law which has indeed to be explained, we would see once again affirmed, with the greatest force, the desire for the proper joined with the most fully assumed phallocentrism.

After having, for example, as he often does, decomposed and analyzed the proper name of Malherbe into an adjective and a common noun (male/herb)—the splitting up, or the process of naturalization, transforming the name at once into a blazon or legendary *rebus,* as happens elsewhere with the names of Spada (this time, once again, the phallic sword)[22]; of Picasso ("This is also the reason why, at the outset of this text, I had to plant this name, and *first of all its initial capital* [also his own, as if by chance] like, on the tip of a pike [*pique*] [this time, a piece picked out from the pronounceable name is also the graphic and visible form of the initial], an oriflamme: that of the intellectual offensive" [here the whole word—not pronounced, and, as

---

22. I thought I read this in "For Marcel Spada" (preface to "At the Carrot Festival"). I do not find it there. I must have heard Ponge talking about it.

always, under-written, discreetly left to be guessed at, without insistence or bad taste—this whole word, *assault*, is a piece of Picasso,[23] and he recalls further on that this is the representation of a "pennant"]); of Braque, always on the frank attack for renown ("Bracket [*Braquet*] the range, to disengage yourself")—very well, he associates, on the page of male/herb, the frank, the male, the resolute: "Pride. Resolution. Its way of menacing, teasing, when women resist." And toward the end of the book: "The hard kernel of Francity. Enlightened patriotism.

"Poetry of the certainty. Articulation of the *Yes*. . . . Something magisterial. An unmistakable tone of superiority. Something male as well." The *yes* (affirmed, approved, signed), is associated with the inscription of his proper name, with the autographic signature, as at the end, for example, of the *Braque*. Let us not hasten to link this francity to its poorly enlightened national referent, since we ought at least to guide it through this detour of the proper forename which, for Malherbe and for Ponge, was also almost shared in common. An almost common given name if we compare François to Francis, "Eldest son of the great Logos . . . François, in whom your presence bathes me on this beautiful day. . ." But an altogether common proper given name, since it is twice relatinized on the pedestal, or the epitaph: "*Primus Franciscus Malherba*" and "*Franciscus Pontius/Nemausensis Poeta*," according to the first publication of *The Fig* (*Dried*).

To be frank, French, free, and disengaged is also to know how to cut, to transgress, to infringe the law or to cross [*franchir*] the line: he plays with this at the end of the *Prose on the Name of Vulliamy* ("If at last the step from voyance to your vuillance is one that only a poet could freely take [*faire franchir*], and since Francis at least makes you dare at last to take it, vuillingly take it in your turn, my friend").

Over the single instance of the given name, we have already seen, on the one hand, the double band of the signature stretched between the need to become a thing, the common name of a thing, or the name of a generality losing the *idion* in order to inscribe the colossal, and, on the other hand, the contrary demand for a pure idiomaticity, a capital

23. EN The French word *assaut* ("assault") is pronounced in the same way as the ending of "Picasso."

letter unsoiled by the common, the condition of the signature in the proper sense. The *rebus* signature, the metonymic or anagrammatic signature, these are the condition of possibility and impossibility. The *double bind* of a signature event. As if the thing (or the common name of the thing), ought to absorb the proper, to drink it and to retain it in order to keep it. But, in the same stroke, by keeping, drinking, and absorbing it, it is as if the thing (or its name) lost or soiled the proper name.

French Sources

Ac   *L'atelier contemporain*. Paris: Gallimard, 1977

E   *Entretiens de Francis Ponge avec Philippe Sollers*. Paris: Gallimard/Seuil, 1970. (*Interviews of Francis Ponge with Philippe Sollers*)

Fp   *La fabrique du pré*. Geneva: Skira, 1971. (*The Making of the Pre*)

M   *Méthodes*. Paris: Gallimard (Collection Idées), 1971.

NR   *Nouveau recueil*. Paris: Gallimard, 1967.

P   *Pièces*. Paris: Gallimard (Collection Poésie), 1962.

PM   *Pour un Malherbe*. Paris: Gallimard, 1965. (*For a Malherbe*)

S   *Le savon*. Paris: Gallimard, 1976. (*Soap*)

Tp   *Tome premier*. Paris: Gallimard, 1965. (*Volume One*) This volume includes *Proêmes* (117–252).

"Berges de la Loire." *Tp*, 255–58. (*Banks of the Loire*)

"Braque ou la méditation-à-l'oeuvre." *Ac*, 283–317. (*Braque*)

"Le carnet du bois de pins." *Tp*, 325–82. (*The Notebook of the Pine Forest*)

"Les écuries d'Augias." *Tp*, 175–76. (*The Augean Stables*)

"La figue (sèche)." *P*, 179–82. (*The Fig [Dried]*)

"Joca Seria." *Ac*, 153–90. (*Joca Seria*)

"La lessiveuse." *P*, 72–76. (*The Washing Machine*)

"L'œillet." *Tp*, 289–304. (*The Carnation*)

"La pratique de la littérature." *M*, 269–93. (*The Practice of Literature*)

"Le pré." *NR*, 201–09; *Fp*, 201–02. (*The Pre*)

"Préfaces aux sapates." *Tp*, 126–27. (*Prefaces to the Sapates*)

"Prose sur le nom de Vulliamy." *Ac*, 78–79. (*Prose on the Name of Vulliamy*)

"Raisons de vivre heureux." *Tp*, 188–90. (*Reasons for Living Happily*)

"Tentative orale." *M*, 223–68. (*Oral Essay*)

IO

FROM

Shibboleth

FOR PAUL CELAN

 ❧ Paul Celan's poems enact with peculiar intensity the paradox which lies at the heart of Derrida's sense of literature: each one is imbued with a quality of uniqueness, of here-and-nowness, while at the same time owing that quality to the cultural and linguistic crossroads that constitute it, and from which it speaks to us, in our equally singular and situated place and time. In this lecture Derrida focuses this dual quality by means of a number of motifs drawn from the poems, including the password *shibboleth,* circumcision, ash ("that remainder without remainder"), and the date. It is what Derrida calls "the enigma of the date" which figures most extensively in the portion of the text—approximately its first half—reprinted here.

Paul Celan, who grew up in an orthodox Jewish family in Romania and survived the German occupation and the murder of his parents by the S.S., shows in his poetry and his comments on art a concern not only with the dates of European history but with the date as a phenomenon not reducible to the systems of history (or philosophy). Derrida discusses *The Meridian,* Celan's 1960 address on the occasion of the award of the Georg Büchner Prize (an address which, for Derrida, is as much a poem as a treatise), and some poems which name particular dates. But the significance of the date extends well beyond specific mentions and uses of it; it is a term—like "the signature" and "the proper name"—which Derrida employs, in a complex strategy of reapplication, for that characteristic of literature which renders it ungraspable by philosophy, making philosophy both possible and, in terms of its own goals, impossible. For what philosophy attempts, in its most fundamental mission, is a writing without a date, a writing that transcends the here-and-now of its coming-into-existence, and the heres-and-nows of the acts which confirm, extend, and renew that existence. ("Date" can be used, in English as in French, to refer to place as well as time.) But all writing is a dating (as it is a signing), every text has a provenance, and the date, like the signature, exhibits the counter-logic of iterability: serving to fix for the future a specific and unique time and place, it can do so only on the basis of its readability, which is to say that it has to remain open to repetition and reinscription; its repeatability is a condition of its singularity, its effacement a condition of its legibility. Like literature in the question "What is literature?" the date pre-dates the "what is?" of philosophy. Later in the lecture, Derrida points out that "a formal poetics" is in the same situation as philosophy: in spite of their project of transcendence, "both presuppose the date, the mark incised in language, of a proper name or an idiomatic event" (*Schibboleth*, 89).

It is in poetry such as Celan's that the functioning of the date is especially evident. In a passage not reprinted here Derrida writes:

> Radicalizing and generalizing, we may say, without artifice, that poetic writing offers itself up, in its entirety, to dating. The Bremen address recalls this: a poem is en route from a place toward "something open" ("an approachable you"), and it makes its way "across" time, it is never "timeless." It is all cipher of singularity, offering its place and recalling it, offering and recalling its time at the risk of losing them in the holocaustic generality of recurrence and the readability of the concept, in the anniversary repetition of the unrepeatable. (*Schibboleth*, 87)

The date implies, for Celan and for Derrida, the possibility of encounter (including the encounter with the absolutely other), and of the anniversary, the gathering together of events across historical boundaries; it is figured in circumcision, an act of incision in the body that happens only once, yet a "once" that is never pure; it is a kind of *shibboleth*, a border-crossing test at which it is not enough to *know* (as philosophy does) since one has to succeed in *doing* (and a doing that is bodily, not simply mental). Derrida generalizes the *shibboleth* to include "every insignificant, arbitrary mark" as it "becomes discriminative, decisive, and divisive." It thus signifies the condition of language, the divisions between and within languages (translation is another topic raised here); it also signifies an always possible abuse of language in a discriminatory politics. The poem as date, as *shibboleth*, both secret and open, commemorates that which is destined to be forgotten; and the remainder of this lecture, violently excised here due to the exigencies of space, commemorates as it explores Celan's Jewishness, his rings, hours, words, circumcisions, ashes.

ᴥ *Shibboleth* was first given as a lecture at an international conference on the work of Celan at the University of Washington, Seattle, on October 14, 1984. (Derrida dates the text carefully.) An English translation by Joshua Wilner of the text as given at the Seattle conference was published in *Midrash and Literature,* ed. Geoffrey H. Hartman and Sanford Budick (New Haven: Yale University Press, 1986). Derrida subsequently published a revised and expanded version of the text as *Schibboleth: Pour Paul Celan* (Paris: Galilée, 1986), stating in a prefatory note: "Despite certain revisions and some new developments, the plan of exposition, the rhythm, and the tone of the lecture have been preserved as far as possible." The extract that follows (comprising pp. 11–62 of the French volume) is taken from Wilner's hitherto unpublished translation of the revised text. (The full translation will be published in *Word Traces,* ed. Aris Fioretis [Baltimore: Johns Hopkins University Press].) A long footnote on the work of Jean Greisch, Martin Heidegger, and Paul Ricoeur has been omitted. Quotations from Celan are taken from *Gesammelte Werke in fünf Bänden,* ed. Beda Allemann and Stefan Reichert with the assistance of Rudolf Bücher (Frankfurt am Main: Suhrkamp, 1983) (*GW*); and translations from *Poems of Paul Celan,* trans. Michael Hamburger (New York: Persea, 1988) (*P*); *Paul Celan: Collected Prose,* trans. Rosmarie Waldrop (Manchester: Carcanet, 1986) (*CP*); *65 Poems: Paul Celan,* trans. Brian Lynch and Peter Jankowsky (Dublin: Raven Arts, 1985) (*65*); and *Speech-Grille, and Selected Poems,* trans. Joachim Neugroschel (New York: Dutton, 1971) (*SG*). Translations have occasionally been modified in the interest of a more exact articulation between Derrida's text and the passage he cites. Otherwise unidentified translations are by Joshua Wilner.

I

One time alone: circumcision takes place but once.

Such, at least, is the appearance we receive, and the tradition of the appearance, we do not say of the semblance.

We will have to circle around this appearance. Not so much in order to circumscribe or circumvent some *truth* of circumcision—that must be given up for essential reasons. But rather to let ourselves be approached by the resistance which "once" may offer thought. And it is a question of offering, and of that which such resistance *gives* one to think. As for resistance, this will be our theme as well, calling up the last war, all wars, clandestine activity, demarcation lines, discrimination, passports and passwords.

Before we ask ourselves what, if anything, is meant by "once," and the word *time* in "one time alone"; before interpreting, as philosophers or philosophers of language, as hermeneuts or poeticians, the meaning or truth of what one speaks of in English as "once," we should keep, no doubt, a long and thoughtful while to those linguistic borders where, as you know, only those who know how to pronounce *shibboleth* are granted passage and, indeed, life. "Once," "one time"—nothing, one would think, could be easier to translate: *une fois, einmal, una volta.* We will find ourselves returning more than once to the vicissitudes of latinity, to the Spanish *vez,* to the whole syntax of *vicem, vice, vices, vicibus, vicissim, in vicem, vice versa,* and even *vicarius,* to its turns, returns, replacements and supplantings, voltes and revolutions. For the moment, a single remark: the semantic registers of all these idioms do not *immediately* translate each other; they appear heterogeneous. One speaks of "time" in the English "one time," but not in "once," or *einmal,* or any of the French, Italian, or Spanish locutions. The Latin idioms resort rather to the figure of the turn or the volte, the turnabout. And yet, despite this border, the crossing of ordinary translation takes place every day without the least uncertainty, each time that the semantics of the everyday imposes its conventions. Each time that it effaces the idiom.

If a circumcision takes place one time only, this time is thus, *at once, at the same time,* the first and last time. This is the appearance—

archaeology and eschatology—that we will have to circle around, as around the ring which it traces, carves out, or sets off. This ring or annulation is at once the seal of an alliance,[1] or wedding band, the circling back on itself of an anniversary date, and the year's recurrence.

I am going to speak then about circumcision and the one-and-only time, in other words, of what *comes* to mark itself as the one-and-only time: what one sometimes calls a *date*.

My main concern will not be to speak about the date so much as to listen to Celan speak about it. Better still, to watch as he gives himself over to the inscription of invisible, perhaps unreadable, dates: anniversaries, rings, constellations, and repetitions of singular, unique, *unrepeatable* events: *unwiederholbar,* this is his word.

How can one date what does not repeat if dating also calls for some form of recurrence, if it recalls in the readability of a repetition? But how date anything else than that which does not repeat?

Having just named the unrepeatable (*unwiederholbar*) and marked the borders of translation, I am led to cite here the poem which Celan entitled, in French, "A la pointe acérée,"[2] not because it has any direct connection with the surgery of circumcision, but because it seeks its way in the night along paths of questions "*Nach / dem Unwiederholbar,*" after the unrepeatable. I will limit myself at first to these small pebbles of white chalk on a board, a sort of non-writing in which the concretion of language hardens:

> Ungeschriebenes, zu
> Sprache verhärtet . . . (GW, I, 251)
>
> (Unwritten things, hardened
> into language . . .) (P, 195)

---

1. TN *Alliance* denotes a broader range of meanings in French than in English, including marriage, wedding ring, and the Biblical covenant.
2. The title of the poem alludes to Baudelaire's "*Confiteor* de l'artiste": "*et il n'est pas de pointe plus acérée que celle de l'Infini*" ("and there is no point more piercing than that of the Infinite") (*Oeuvres complètes,* ed. Claude Pichois [Paris: Gallimard, 1975], I, 278), as confirmed by Werner Hamacher's very beautiful text, "The Second of Inversion: Movements of a Figure through Celan's Poetry" (*Yale French Studies* 69 [1985]): "Celan reported in conversation that he borrowed this text's title from a note by Baudelaire, cited in Hofmannsthal's journal under the date June 29, 1917" (308).

Without writing, un-writing, the unwritten switches over to a question of reading on a board or tablet which you perhaps are. You are a board or a door: we will see much later how a word can address itself, indeed confide itself to a door, count on a door open to the other.

> Tür du davor einst, Tafel
>
> (Door you in front of it once, tablet)

(And with this *einst* it is again a question of one time, one time alone)

> mit dem getöteten
> Kreidestern drauf:
> ihn
> hat nun ein—lesendes?—Aug. (*GW*, I, 251)
>
> (with the killed
> chalk star on it:
> that
> a—reading?—eye has now.) (*P*, 195 [translation
>   modified])

We could have followed in this poem the ever discrete, discontinuous, *cesuraed*, elliptical circuitry of the hour (*Waldstunde*), or of the trace, and of the track of a wheel that turns on itself (*Radspur*). But here what I am *after* is the question which seeks its way *after* (*nach*) the unrepeatable, through beechmast (*Buchecker*). Which may also be read as book corners or the sharp, gaping edges of a text:

> Wege dorthin
> Waldstunde an
> der blubbernde Radspur entlang.
> Auf-
> gelesene
> kleine, klaffende
> Buchecker: schwärzliches
> Offen, von
> Fingergedanken befragt
> nach—

wonach?

Nach
dem Unwiederholbaren, nach
ihm, nach
allem.

Blubbernde Wege dorthin.

Etwas, das gehn kann, grusslos
wie Herzgewordenes,
kommt. (*GW*, I, 251–52)

(Ways to that place.
Forest hour alongside
the spluttering wheeltrack.
Col-
lected
small, gaping
beechnuts: blackish
openness, asked of
by fingerthoughts
after—
after what?

After
the unrepeatable, after
it, after
everything.

Spluttering tracks to that place.

Something that can go, ungreeting
as all that's become heart,
is coming.) (*P*, 195 [translation modified])

Ways (*Wege*): something comes, which can go (*Etwas, das gehn kann, . . . kommt*). What is going, coming, going to come, going and coming? and becoming heart? What coming, what singular event is in question? What impossible repetition (*Nach / dem Unwiederholbaren, nach / ihm*)?

How to "become heart"? Let us not, for the moment, invoke Pascal or Heidegger—who in any case suspects the former of having yielded too much to science and forgotten the original thinking of the heart. Hearing me speak of the date and of circumcision, some might rush on to the "circumcised heart" of the Scriptures. That would be moving too fast and along a path of too little resistance. Celan's trenchant ellipsis requires more patience, it demands more discretion. Cesura is the law. It gathers, however, in the discretion of the discontinuous, in the cutting in of the relation to the other or in the interruption of address, as address itself.

It makes no sense, as you may well suppose, to dissociate in Celan's writings those *on the subject* of the date, which name the theme of the date, from the poetic traces of dating. To rely on the division between a theoretical, philosophical, hermeneutic, or even technopoetic discourse concerning the phenomenon of the date, on the one hand, and its poetic implementation,[3] on the other, is to no longer read him.

The example of *The Meridian* warns us against such a misconstruction. It is, as they say, a "discourse": one pronounced on a given occasion and at a given date—that is, an address. Its date is that of the conferral of a prize (*Rede anlässlich der Verleihung des Georg-Büchner-Preises, am 22. Oktober 1960* [GW, III, 187]). On October 22, 1960, this address deals, in its way, with art or more precisely with the memory of art, perhaps with art as a thing of the past, Hegel would have said, "art as we already know it," but as "also a problem, and, as we can see, one that is variable, tough, longlived, let us say, eternal" (*GW, III, 188 / CP, 38*). The thing of the past: "*Meine Damen und Herren! Die Kunst, das ist, Sie erinnern sich . . .,*" "Art, you will remember . . . " (*GW, III, 187/CP, 37*). The ironic attack of this first sentence seems to speak of a history gone by, but it does so in order to call on the memory of those who have read Büchner. Celan announces that he is going to evoke several appearances of art, in particular in *Woyzeck* and *Leonce und Lena:* you remember. A thing from our past that comes back in memory, but also a problem for the future, an eternal problem, and above all a way toward poetry. Not poetry, but a way in view of poetry, one way only, one among others and not

3. TN *Mise en oeuvre:* that is, "setting-to-work," but also, in the idiom of this text, "setting-(in)to-(the)-work." In subsequent occurrences, I have simply retained the French phrase.

the shortest. "This would mean art is the distance poetry must cover, no less and no more. / I know that there are other, shorter, routes. But poetry, too, can be ahead. *La poésie, elle aussi, brûle nos étapes*" (*GW*, III, 194 / *CP*, 44–45).

At this crossing of ways between art and poetry, in this place to which poetry makes its way at times without even the patience of a path, lies the enigma of the date.

It seems to resist every philosophical question and mode of questioning, every objectification, every theoretico-hermeneutic thematization.

Celan shows this poetically: by a *mise-en-oeuvre* of the date. In this address itself. He begins by citing several dates: 1909, the date of a work devoted to Jakob Michael Lenz by a university lecturer in Moscow, M. N. Rosanov; then the night of May 23–24, 1792, a date itself cited, already mentioned in this work, the date of Lenz's death in Moscow. Then Celan *mentions* the date which appears this time on the first page of Büchner's *Lenz*, "the Lenz who 'on the 20th of January was walking through the mountains' " (*GW*, III, 194 / *CP*, 46).

Who was walking through the mountains, *on this date?*

He, Lenz, Celan insists, he and not the artist preoccupied by questions of art. He, as an "I," "*er als ein Ich.*" This "I" who is not the artist obsessed by questions of art, those posed him by art—Celan does not rule out that it may be the poet; but in any case it is not the artist.

The singular turn of this syntagm, "he as an I," will support the whole logic of individuation, of that "sign of individuation" which each poem constitutes. The poem is "one person's language become shape" (*gestaltgewordene Sprache eines Einzelnen*) (*GW*, III, 198 / *CP*, 49). Singularity but also solitude: the only one, the poem is alone ("*einsam*"). And from within the most intimate essence of its solitude, it is en route ("*unterwegs*"), "aspiring to a presence," following the French translation of André du Bouchet[4] (*und seinem innersten Wesen nach Gegenwart und Präsenz*) (*GW*, III, 194 / *CP*, 46). Insofar as alone, the only one, the poem would keep itself then, perhaps, within the "secrecy of encounter."

4. *Le méridien* in *Strette* (Paris: Mercure de France, 1971), 191.

The only one: singularity, solitude, secrecy of encounter. What assigns the only one to its date? For example: there was a 20th of January. A date of this kind will have allowed of being written, alone, unique, exempt from repetition. Yet this absolute property can be transcribed, exported, deported, expropriated, reappropriated, repeated in its utter singularity. Indeed, this has to be if the date is to expose itself, to risk losing itself in readability. This absolute property can enunciate, as its sign of individuation, something like the essence of the poem, the only one. Celan prefers to say, of "every poem," better still, of "each poem." *"Vielleicht darf man sagen, dass jedem Gedicht sein '20. Jänner' eingeschrieben bleibt?"*: "Perhaps we can say that each poem remains marked by its own '20th of January?' " (*GW*, III, 194 / *CP*, 47 [translation modified]). Here is a generality: to the keeping of each poem, thus of every poem, the inscription of a date, of this date, for example a "20th of January," is entrusted. But despite the generality of this law, the example remains irreplaceable. And what must remain, committed to the keeping, in other words to the truth of each poem, is the irreplaceable itself: the example offers its example only on condition that it holds for no other. But it offers its example in that very fact, and the only example possible, the one that it alone offers: the only one.

Today, on this day, at this date. And this marking of today tells us perhaps something of the essence of the poem today, for us now. Not the essence of poetic modernity or postmodernity, not the essence of an epoch or a period in some history of poetry, but what happens "today" "anew" to poetry, to poems, what happens to them at this date.

What happens to them at this date, is precisely the date, a certain experience of the date. One no doubt very ancient, dateless, but absolutely new at this date. And new because, for the first time, it here shows itself or is sought after "most plainly" (*"am deutlichsten"*). Clarity, distinction, sharpness, readability, this is what today would be *new*. What thus becomes readable is not, it must be understood, the date *itself*, but only the poetic experience of the date, that which a date, *this one*, ordains in our relation to it, a certain poetic seeking. "Perhaps the newness of poems written today is that they try most plainly to be mindful of this kind of date?" (*Vielleicht is das Neue an den Gedichten, die heute geschrieben werden, gerade dies: dass hier am deutlichsten versucht wird, solcher Daten eingedenk zu bleiben?*) (*GW*, III, 196 / *CP*, 47).

This question concerning the date, this hypothesis ("Perhaps . . . ") is dated by Celan; it relates *today* to every poem *today*, to what is new in each poetic work of our time, each of which, at this date, would share the singularity of dating (transitively), of remaining mindful of dates (*Daten eingedenk zu bleiben*). The poetic today would perhaps be dated by an inscription of the date or at least a certain coming to light, newly, of a poetic necessity which, for its part, does not date from today. Granted.

But—the sentences which we have just heard are followed by three "Buts": three times "But."

The first, the least energetic and the least oppositional, raises again the same questions concerning the traces of the other *as I:* how can some *other* irreplaceable and singular date, the date of the other, the date for the other, be deciphered, transcribed, or appropriated? How can I appropriate it for myself? Or rather, how can I transcribe myself into it? And how can the memory of such a date still dispose of a future? What dates to come do we prepare in such a transcription? Here, then, is the first "But." The ellipsis of the sentence is more economical than I can convey and its gripping sobriety can only register, which is to say date itself, from within its idiom, a certain way of inhabiting and dealing with its idiom (signed: Celan from a certain place in the German language, which was his property alone). "But do we not all transcribe ourselves out of such dates? And to what dates to come do we ascribe ourselves?" (*Aber schreiben wir uns nicht alle von solchen Daten her? Und welchen Daten schreiben wir uns zu?*) (*GW*, III, 196 / *CP*, 47 [variant translation])

Here the second "But" is sounded, but only after a blank space, the mark of a very long silence, the time of a meditation through which the preceding question makes its way. It leaves the trace of an affirmation, over against which arises, at least to complicate it, a second affirmation. And its force of opposition reaches the point of exclamation: "*Aber das Gedicht spricht ja! Es bleibt seiner Daten eingedenk, aber—es spricht. Gewiss, es spricht immer nur in seiner eigenen, aller-eigensten Sache.*" ("But the poem speaks! It is mindful of its dates, but it speaks. True, it speaks only on its own, its very own behalf") (*GW,* III, 196/*CP,* 48 [translation modified]).

What does this "but" mean? No doubt that *despite* the date, in spite of its memory rooted in the singularity of an event, the poem speaks; to all and in general, to the other first of all. The "but" seems to carry the poem's utterance beyond its date: if the poem recalls a date, calls itself back to its date, to the date *when* it writes or *of which* it writes, as of [*depuis*] which it is written, nevertheless it speaks! to all, to the other, to whoever does not share the experience or the knowledge of the singularity thus dated: *as of* [*depuis*] or *from* a given place, a given day, a given month, a given year. In the preceding phrase, the ambiguous force of *von* collects in itself in advance all of our paradoxes (*Aber schreiben wir uns nicht alle von solchen Daten her?*): we write *of* the date, *about* certain dates, but also *as of* [*depuis*] certain dates, *at* [*à*] certain dates. But the English "at," like the French *à,* may be turned by the ambiguous force of its own idiom, toward a future of unknown destination, something which was not literally said by any given sentence of Celan's, but which doubtless corresponds to the general logic of this discourse, as made explicit in the sentence which follows, "*Und welchen Daten schreiben wir uns zu?*" To what dates do we ascribe ourselves, what dates do we appropriate, now, but also, in more ambiguous fashion, turned toward what dates to come do we write ourselves, do we transcribe ourselves? As if writing *at* a certain date meant not only writing on a given day, at a given hour, but also writing *to* [*à*] the date, addressing oneself to it, committing oneself to the date as to the other, the date past as well as the promised date.

What is this "to" of "to come"[5]—as date?

Yet the poem speaks. Despite the date, even if it also speaks thanks to it, of it, as of it, to it, and speaks always of itself, "on its own, its very own behalf" (*CP,* 48), "*in seiner eigenen, allereigensten Sache,*" in its own name, without ever compromising with the absolute singularity, the inalienable property of that which convokes its. And yet, the

5. TN *L'à venir* ("the 'to come' "); cf. *l'avenir* ("the future").

inalienable must speak of the other, and to the other, it must speak. The date provokes the poem, but the latter speaks! And it speaks of what provokes it, *to* the date which provokes it, thus convoked from the future of the *same* date, in other words from its recurrence at *another* date.

How are we to understand the exclamation? Why this exclamation point after the "but" of what in no way would seem to be a rhetorical objection? One might find it surprising. I think that it confers the accent, it accentuates and marks the tone, of admiration, of astonishment in the face of poetic exclamation itself. The poet exclaims—faced with the miracle which makes clamor, poetic acclamation, possible: the poem speaks! and it speaks to the date of which it speaks! Instead of walling it up and reducing it to the silence of singularity, a date gives it its chance, its chance to speak to the other!

If the poem is *due* its date, *due to* its date, owes itself to its date as its own inmost concern (*Sache*) or signature, if it owes itself to its secret, it speaks of this date only insofar as it acquits itself, so to speak, of a given date—of that date which was also a gift—releasing itself from the date without denying it, and above all without disavowing it. It absolves itself of it so that its utterance may resonate and proclaim beyond a singularity which might otherwise remain undecipherable, mute, and immured in its date—in the unrepeatable. One must, while preserving its memory, speak of the date which already speaks of itself: the date, by its mere occurrence, by the inscription of a sign as memorandum, will have broken the silence of pure singularity. But to speak of it, one must also efface it, make it readable, audible, intelligible *beyond the pure singularity* of which it speaks. Now the beyond of absolute singularity, the chance of the poem's exclamation, is not the simple effacement of the date in a generality, but its *effacement faced with* another date, the one *to which* it speaks, the date of an other strangely wed or joined in the secrecy of an encounter, a chance secret, with the same date. I will offer—by way of clarification—some examples in a moment.

What takes place in this experience of the date, experience itself? and of a date which must be effaced in order to be preserved, in order to preserve the commemoration of the event, that advent of the unique in thrall to the poem which must exceed it and which alone, by itself, may transport it, offer it up to understanding beyond the unreadability of its cipher? What takes place is perhaps what Celan calls a little further on "*Geheimnis der Begegnung*," "the secrecy of encounter" (*GW*, III, 194 / *CP*, 49 [translation modified]).

Encounter—in the word *encounter* two values meet without which there would be no date:[6] "encounter" as it suggests the random occurrence, the chance meeting, the coincidence or conjuncture which comes to seal one or more than one event *once*, at a given hour, on a given day, in a given month, in a given region; and "encounter" as it suggests an encounter with the other, the ineluctable singularity out of which and destined for which the poem speaks. In its otherness and its solitude (which is also that of the poem, "alone," "solitary"), it may inhabit the conjunction of one and the same date. This is what happens.

What happens, if something happens, is this; and this encounter, in an idiom, of all the meanings of encounter.

But—a third time, a third "but" opens a new paragraph. It begins with a "But I think," it closes with a "today and here," and it is the signature of an "*Aber ich denke*" . . . "*heute und hier*":

> But I think—and this will hardly surprise you—that the poem has always hoped, for this very reason, to speak also on behalf of the *strange*—no, I can no longer use this word here—*on behalf of the other*—who knows, perhaps of an *altogether other*.
> This "who knows" which I have reached is all I can add here, today, to the old hopes. (*GW*, III, 196 / *CP*, 48)

The "altogether other" thus opens the thought of the poem to some thing or some concern (*Sache*: "*in eines Anderen Sache* . . . *in eines ganz Anderen Sache*") the otherness of which must not contradict but rather enter into alliance with, in expropriating, the "inmost concern" just in question, that due to which the poem speaks at its date, as of

---

6. TN The distinction which Derrida develops in the following paragraph is clearer in French, since the French word for "encounter," *rencontre*, is also employed in the phrase *de rencontre*, meaning "chance," "passing," "casual," etc. Thus, for example, "*le secret d'une* rencontre" is "the secrecy of an *encounter*"; "*un secret* de rencontre" is "a chance secret" (see the two previous paragraphs).

its date, and always *in seiner eigenen, allereigensten Sache*. Several singular events may conjoin, enter into alliance, *concentrate* in the same date, which thus becomes both the same and other, altogether other as the same, capable of speaking to the other of the other, to the one who cannot decipher one or another absolutely closed date, a tomb closed over the event which it marks. This gathered multiplicity Celan calls by a strong and charged name: *concentration*. A little further on he speaks of the poem's "attentiveness" (*Aufmerksamkeit*) to all that it encounters. This attentiveness would be rather a kind of concentration which remains mindful of "all our dates" (*eine aller unserer Daten eingedenk bleibende Konzentration*) (*GW*, III, 198 / *CP*, 50). The word can become a terrible word for memory. But one can understand it *at once* in that register in which one speaks of the gathering of the soul, or of the heart, and of "spiritual concentration," as, for example, in the experience of prayer (and Celan cites Benjamin citing Malebranche in his essay on Kafka: "Attention is the natural prayer of the soul" [*GW*, III, 198 / *CP*, 50]), and in that other sense in which concentration gathers around the same anamnesic center a multiplicity of dates, "all our dates" coming to conjoin or constellate in a single occurrence or a single place: in truth in a single poem, in *the only one,* in that poem which is each time, we have seen, alone, the only one, solitary and singular.

This perhaps is what goes on in the exemplary act of *The Meridian*. This discourse, this address, this speech act (*Rede*) is not—not only— a treatise or a metadiscourse *on the subject of* the date, but rather the habitation, by a poem, of its own date, its poetic *mise-en-oeuvre* as well, making of a date which is the poet's own a date for the other, the date of the other, or, inversely, for the gift comes around like an anniversary, a step by which the poet ascribes or commits himself to the date of the other. In the unique ring of its constellation, one and the "same" date commemorates heterogeneous events, each suddenly neighboring the other, even as one knows that they remain, and must continue to remain, infinitely foreign. It is just this which is called the encounter, the encounter of the other, "the secrecy of encounter"— and precisely here the Meridian is discovered. There was a 20th of January, that of Lenz who "on the 20th of January was walking through the mountains." And then at the *same* date, on *another* 20th of January, Celan encounters, he encounters the other and he encounters himself at the intersection of this date with itself, with itself as other, as the date of the other. And yet this takes place but once, and always anew, each time once alone, the *each-time-once-alone* constituting a generic law. One would have to resituate here the question of the transcendental schematism, of the imagination and of time, as a question of the date—*of the once*. And one would have to reread what Celan had said earlier about images:

> Then what are images?
> What has been, what can be perceived, again and again, and only here, only now. Hence the poem is the place where all tropes and metaphors want to be led *ad absurdum*. (GW, III, 199 / CP, 51)

This radical *ad absurdum*, the impossibility of that which, each time once alone, has meaning only on condition of having no meaning, no ideal or general meaning, or which has meaning only so it can invoke, in order to betray it, the concept, law, or genre, is the pure poem. Now the pure poem does not exist, or rather, it is "what there isn't!" (*das es nicht gibt!*). To the question: of what do I speak when I speak not of poems but of the poem, Celan answers: "I speak of the poem which does not exist! / The absolute poem—no, it certainly does not, cannot exist!" (GW, III, 199 / CP, 51 [translation modified]).

But if the absolute poem does not take place, if there is none (*es gibt nicht*), there is the image, the each time once alone, the poetic of the date and the secrecy of encounter: the other-I, a 20th of January which was also mine after having been that of Lenz. Here:

> Several years ago, I wrote a little quatrain:
>
> > "Voices from the path through nettles:
> > *Come to us on your hands.*
> > Alone with your lamp
> > Only your hand to read."

> And a year ago, I commemorated a missed encounter in the Engadine valley by putting a little story on paper where I had a man "like Lenz" walk through the mountains.

Both the one time and the other, I had transcribed myself from a "20th of January," from my "20th of January."
I... encountered myself. (*GW*, III, 201 / *CP*, 52–53 [translation modified])

I encountered myself—myself *like* the other, one 20th of January *like* the other, and *like* Lenz, like Lenz *himself*, "*wie Lenz*": the quotation marks around the expression set off, in the text, what is strange in the figure.

This "like" is also the signal of another appearance summoned within the same comparison. This man whom I described, wrote, signed, was *just like* Lenz, almost like Lenz himself, *as* Lenz. The *wie* almost has the force of an *als*. But *at the same time,* it is myself since in this figure of the other, as the other, it is myself whom I encountered at this date. The "like" is the co-signature of the date, the very figure or image, each time, of the other, "the one time and the other," one time *like* the other time (*das eine wie das andere Mal*). Such would be the anniversary turn of the date. In *The Meridian,* it is also the find, the encountering of the place of encounter, the discovery of the meridian itself:

I am also, since I am again at my point of departure, searching for my own place of origin.
I am looking for all of this with my imprecise, because nervous, finger on a map—a child's map, I must admit.
None of these places can be found. They do not exist. But I know where they ought to exist, especially now and... I find something else!
. . . I find something which consoles me a bit for having walked this impossible road in your presence, this road of the impossible.
I find the connective which, like the poem, leads to encounters.
I find something—like language—immaterial, yet earthly, terrestrial, in the shape of a circle which, via both poles, rejoins itself and on the way serenely crosses even the tropics: I find... a *meridian.* (*GW*, III, 202 / *CP*, 54–55 [translation modified])

Almost the last word of the text, near the signature. What Celan finds or discovers *all at once,* invents if one may say so, more and less than a fiction, is not only a meridian, the Meridian, but the word and the image, the trope "meridian" which offers the example of the law, in its inexhaustible polytropy, and which *binds* (*das Verbindende*, both that which binds and that which connects or acts as intermediary), which provokes in broad daylight, *at noon,* at midday, the encounter of the other in a single place, at a single point, that of the poem, of this poem: ". . . in the here and now of the poem—and the poem has only this one, unique, momentary present—even in this immediacy and nearness, that which is addressed gives voice to what is most its own: its time, the time of the other," (*GW*, III, 198–99 / *CP*, 50 [translation modified]).

II

A date would be the gnomon of these meridians.

Does one ever speak of a date? But does one ever speak without speaking of a date? Of it and as of it?

Whether one will or no, whether one knows it, acknowledges it or dissembles it, an utterance is always dated. What I am going to hazard concerning the date in general, concerning that which a generality may say or gainsay where the date is concerned, concerning the gnomon of Paul Celan,[7] will all be dated in its turn.

Under certain conditions at least, what dating comes to is signing. To inscribe a date, to enter it, is not simply to sign as of a given year, month, day, or hour (all words which haunt the whole of Celan's text), but also to sign from a given place. Certain poems are "dated" Zürich, Tübingen, Todtnauberg, Paris, Jerusalem, Lyon, Tel Aviv, Vienna, Assisi, Cologne, Geneva, Brest, etc. At the beginning or at the end of a letter, the date consigns a "now" of the calendar or of the clock (" *'alle Uhren und Kalender'* ": second page of *The Meridian* [*GW*, III, 1884 / *CP*, 38]), as well as the here, in their proper names, of the country, region, or house. It marks in this way, at the point of the gnomon, the provenance of what is *given,* or, in any case, sent; of what is, whether or not it arrives, destined. *Addressing its date,* what an address or discourse declares about the concept or meaning of the

---

7. TN The phrase *au gnomon de Paul Celan* resonates with *au nom de Paul Celan*— "in the name of Paul Celan."

date is not, by this fact, dated, in the sense in which one says of something that it dates in order to imply that it has aged or aged badly; in speaking of a discourse as dated, our intention is not to disqualify or invalidate it, but rather to signify that it is, at the least, marked by its date, signed by it or re-marked in a singular manner. What is thus remarked is its point of *departure*, that to which it no doubt belongs but from which it departs in order to address itself to the other: a certain imparting.[8]

It is concerning this singular remarking that I am going to hazard in my turn some remarks—in memory of some missives dated from Paul Celan.

What is a date? Do we have the right to pose such a question, and in this form? The form of the question "what is" has a provenance. It has its place of origin and its language. It dates. That it is dated does not discredit it, but if we had the time, we could draw certain philosophical inferences from this fact, inferences indeed *about* the philosophical regime which this question governs.

Has anyone ever been concerned with the question "what is a date?" The "you" who is told "*Nirgends / fragt es nach dir—,*" nowhere is there any asking about you, nowhere any concern with you, is a date, of that we may be certain *a priori*. This you, which must be an I, like the *er als ein Ich* of a moment ago, always figures an irreplaceable singularity. Only another singularity, just as irreplaceable, can take its place without substituting for it. One addresses this you as one addresses a date, the here and now of a commemorable provenance.

As it reaches me, at least, the question "What is a date?" presupposes two things.

First of all, the question "What is . . . ?" has a history or provenance; it is signed, engaged, or commanded by a place, a time, a language or a network of languages, in other words by a date in relation to whose essence this question's power is hence limited, its claim finite, and its very pertinence contestable. This fact is not unrelated to what our symposium calls "the philosophical implications" of Celan's work.

8. TN *Partage* in French signifies at once division, participation through sharing in what is divided, and the share apportioned. It will be translated in most cases by either "imparting" or "partaking."

Perhaps philosophy, as such, and insofar as it makes use of the question "What is . . . ?," has nothing essential to say about what bears Celan's date or about what Celan says or makes of the date—and which might in its turn say something to us, perhaps, about philosophy.

On the other hand, and this is a second presupposition, in the inscription of a date, in the explicit and coded phenomenon of dating, *what is dated must not be dated.* The date: yes and no, Celan would say, as he does more than once.

> Sprich—
> Doch scheide das Nein nicht vom Ja.
> Gib deinem Spruch auch den Sinn:
> gib ihm den Schatten.
>
> Gib ihm Schatten genug,
> gib ihm so viel,
> als du um dich verteilt weisst zwischen
> Mittnacht und Mittag und Mittnacht. (*GW*, I, 135)
>
> (Speak—
> But keep yes and no unsplit.
> And give your say this meaning:
> give it the shade.
>
> Give it shade enough,
> give it as much
> as you know has been dealt out between
> midnight and midday and midnight.) (*P*, 99)

Again the meridian. It is necessary that the mark which one calls a date be *marked off*, in a singular manner, detached from the very thing which it dates; and that in this de-marcation, this deportation, it become readable, that it become readable, precisely, as a date in wresting or exempting itself from itself, from its immediate adherence, from the here and now; in freeing itself from what it nonetheless remains, a date. It is necessary that the unrepeatable (*das Unwieder-holbare*) be repeated in it, effacing in itself the irreducible singularity which it denotes. It is necessary that in a certain manner it divide itself in repeating, and by the same stroke encipher or encrypt itself. Like *phusis,* a date likes to encrypt itself. It must efface itself in order to become readable, to render itself unreadable in its very readability. For if it does not annul in itself the unique marking which connects it to an event without witness, without other witness, it remains intact but absolutely indecipherable. It is no longer even what it has to be, what it will have had to be, its essence and its destination, it no longer keeps its promise, that of a date.

How, then, can that which is dated, while at the same time marking a date, not date? The question, whether one finds this hopeful or troubling, cannot be formulated in this way in all languages. It remains scarcely translatable. I insist on this because what a date, always bound up with some proper name, gives us to think, commemorate, or bless, as well as to cross in a possible-impossible translation, is, each time, an idiom. And if the idiomatic form of my question may appear un-translatable, this is because it plays on the double functioning of the verb "to date." In French or in English. Transitively: I date a poem. Intransitively: a poem dates if it ages, if it has a history, and is of a certain age.

To ask "What is a date?" is not to wonder about the meaning of the word "date." Nor is it to inquire into an established or putative etymology, though this may not be without interest for us. It might, in fact, lead us to think about gifts and literality, and, in particular, the giving of the letter: *data littera,* the first words of a formula for indicat-ing the date. This would set us on the trace of the first word, of the initial or the opening of a letter, of the first letter of a letter—but also of something given[9] or sent. The sense of the date as something given or sent will carry us beyond the question given in the form "what is?" A date is not something which is there, since it withdraws in order to appear, but if *there is no* absolute poem (*Das absolute Gedicht—nein, das gibt es gewiss nicht, das kann es nicht geben!*), says Celan, perhaps there are (*es gibt*) dates—even if they do not exist.

I will associate for the moment, in a preliminary and disorderly way,

---

9. EN "Date" derives from the Latin *data,* "given," used in the formula indicating the time and place of a letter.

the values of the given and the proper name (for a date functions like a proper name) with three other essential values.

1. That of the missive within the strict limits of the epistolary code.

2. The re-marking of place and time, at the point of the here and now.

3. The signature: if the date is an initial, it may come at the letter's end and in all cases, whether at the beginning or the end, have the force of a signed commitment, of an obligation, a promise or an oath (*sacramentum*). In its essence, a signature is always dated and has value only by virtue of this. It dates and it has a date. And prior to being mentioned, the inscription of a date (here, now, this day, etc.) always entails a kind of signature: whoever inscribes the year, the day, the place, in short the present of a "here and now," attests thereby to his or her own presence at the act of inscription.

Celan dated all his poems. I am not thinking here, in the first place, of a kind of dating which one might—mistakenly, but conveniently— call "external," that is, the mention of the date on which a poem was written. In its conventional form this mention lies in some ways outside the poem. One is certainly not entitled to push to its limit the distinction between this external notation of the date and a more essential incorpo- ration of the date within a poem wherein it forms a part, a poem itself. In a certain way, as we will see, Celan's poetry tends to displace, indeed to efface, such a limit. But supposing we maintain for clarity of exposition the provisional hypothesis, we will concern ourselves first of all with a dating which is registered *in* the body of the poem, *in* one of its parts and under a form which accords with the traditional code (for example, "the 13th of February"), and then with a nonconven- tional, noncalendrical form of dating, one which would merge entirely, without residue, with the general organization of the poetic text.[10]

In "Eden," that memorable reading of the poem from *Schneepart*, "Du liegst im grossen Gelausche" (*GW*, II, 334), Szondi recalls that an indication of date accompanied its first publication: "*Berlin 22./23.*

---

10. EN The second, "noncalendrical," form of dating is discussed in the section of the text not reprinted here.

12. 1967."[11] We know how Szondi turned to account these dates and his chance to have been the intimate witness of, and at times actor in, or party to, the experiences commemorated, displaced, and ciphered by the poem. We also know with what rigor and modesty he posed the problems of this *situation,* both with regard to the poem's genesis and with regard to the competence of its decipherers. Like him, we must take into account the following fact: as the intimate and lucid witness of all the chance happenings and all the necessities which intersected Celan's passing through Berlin *at this date,* Szondi was the only one able to bequeath us the irreplaceable passwords of access to the poem, a priceless *shibboleth,* a luminous, clamorous, swarm of notes, so many signs of gratitude for a deciphering and translation of the enigma. And yet, left to itself without witness, without the alerted complicity of a decipherer, without even the "external" knowledge of its date, a certain internal necessity of the poem would nonetheless *speak* to us, in the sense in which Celan says of the poem, "But it speaks!" beyond what appears to confine it within the dated singularity of an individual experience.

Szondi was the first to acknowledge this. He set this enigma before him with an admirable lucidity and prudence. How is one to give an account of this: concerning the circumstances in which the poem was written, or better, concerning those which it names, codes, disguises or dates in its own body, concerning the secrets of which it partakes, witnessing is *at once* indispensable, *essential* to the reading of the poem, to the partaking which it becomes in its turn, and finally *supplementary, nonessential,* merely the guaranty of an excess of intelligibility which the poem can also forego. *At once* essential and inessential. This *at once* derives, this is my hypothesis, from the structure of the date.

(I will not here give myself over to my own commemorations, I will not give over my dates. Permit me nevertheless to recall here that in my encounter with Paul Celan and in the friendship which subsequently bound us, such a short time before his death, Peter Szondi was always the mediator and witness, the common friend who presented us to one

11. TN Peter Szondi, *Schriften*, ed. Wolfgang Fietkau (Frankfurt am Main: Suhrkamp, 1978), II, 390.

another in Paris, though we were already working there at the same institution. And this took place a few months after a visit which I made to the University of Berlin, at Szondi's invitation, in July 1968, just a short time after the month of December 1967 of which I spoke a moment ago.)

What does Szondi recall for us, from the outset of his reading? That Celan suppressed the poem's date for the first collection. It does not figure in the *Ausgewählte Gedichte* edited by Reichert in 1970.[12] This conforms, according to Szondi, with Celan's customary practice: "The poems are dated in the manuscript, but not in the published versions" ("Eden," 391).

But the retraction of what we are calling the "external" date does not do away with the internal dating. And while the latter harbors in its turn, as I will try to show, a force of self-effacement, what is involved in that case is another structure, that of the inscription of the date itself.

We are going to be concerned then with the date as a cut or incision which the poem bears in its body like a memory, like, at times, several memories in one, the mark of a provenance, of a place and of a time. To speak of an incision or cut is to say that the poem is entered into, that it begins in the wounding of its date.

If we had the time, we should patiently analyze the modalities of dating. There are many. In this typology, the most conventional form of dating, dating in the so-called literal or strict sense, involves marking a missive with coded signs. It entails reference to charts, and the utilization of systems of notation and spatio-temporal plottings said to be "objective": the calendar (year, month, day), the clock (the hours, whether or not they are named—and how often will Celan have named them, here or there, but only to restore them to the night of their ciphered silence: "*sie werden die Stunde nicht nennen*," "They will not name the hour" [*GW*, I, 125 / *P*, 91]), toponomy, and first of all the names of cities. These coded marks all share a common resource, but also a dramatic and fatally equivocal power. Assigning or consigning

12. TN *Ausgewählte Gedichte*, ed. Klaus Reichert (Frankfurt am Main: Suhrkamp, 1970).

absolute singularity, they must mark themselves off simultaneously, *at one and the same time,* and from themselves, by the possibility of commemoration. In effect, they mark only insofar as their readability enunciates the possibility of a recurrence. Not the absolute recurrence of that which precisely cannot return: a birth or circumcision takes place but once, nothing could be more self-evident. But rather the spectral return of that which, unique in its occurrence, will never return. A date is a specter. But the spectral return of this impossible recurrence is marked *in* the date, it seals or specifies itself in the sort of anniversary ring secured by the code. For example by the calendar. The anniversary ring inscribes the possibility of repetition, but also the circuit of return to the city whose name a date bears. The first inscription of a date signifies this possibility: that which cannot come back will come back as such, not only in memory, like all remembrance, but also at the same date, at an in any case analogous date, for example each February 13... And each time, at the same date, what one commemorates will be the date *of* that which could never come back. This latter will have signed and sealed the unique, the unrepeatable; but to do so, it will have had to offer itself for reading in a form sufficiently coded, readable, and decipherable for the indecipherable to *appear* in the analogy of the anniversary ring (February 13, 1962, is *analogous* to February 13, 1936), even if it appears *as* indecipherable.

One is tempted to associate here all of Celan's rings with this alliance between the date and itself *as* other. There are ever so many and they are all unique. I will cite only one; it imposes itself here, since it seals in the same beeswax—and the fingers themselves are of wax—the alliance, the letter, the ciphered name, the hive of the hours, and the writing of what is not written:

MIT BRIEF UND UHR

Wachs,
Ungeschriebnes zu siegeln,
das deinen Namen
erriet,
das deinen Namen
verschlüsselt.

Kommst du nun, schwimmendes Licht?
Finger, wächsern auch sie
durch fremde,
schmerzende Ringe gezogen.
Fortgeschmolzen die Kuppen.

Kommst du, schwimmendes Licht?

Zeitleer die Waben der Uhr,
bräutlich das Immentausend,
reisebereit.

Komm, schwimmendes Licht. (*GW*, I, 154)

(WITH LETTER AND CLOCK

Wax
To seal the unwritten
that guessed
your name,
that enciphers
your name.

Swimming light, will you come now?

Fingers, waxen too,
drawn
through strange, painful rings.
The tips melted away.

Swimming light, will you come?

Empty of time the honeycomb cells of the clock,
bridal the thousand of bees,
ready to leave.

Swimming light, come.) (*P*, 107)

Clock and ring are quite close again in "Chymisch" (*GW*, I, 227–28 / *P*, 178–81). A ring awakens on our finger, and the fingers are the ring itself, in "Es war Erde in ihnen" (*GW*, I, 211 / *P*, 153). But above all, since a date is never without a letter to be deciphered, I think of the ring of the carrier-pigeon at the end of "La Contrescarpe." The carrier-pigeon transports, transfers, or translates a coded message, but this is not a metaphor. It departs at its date, that of its sending, and it must return from the other place to the same one, that from which it came, completing a round trip. Now the question of the cipher is posed by Celan not only with regard to the message but also with regard to the ring itself, sign of belonging and alliance, and condition of return. The cipher of the seal, the imprint of the ring, *counts,* perhaps more than the content of the message. As with *shibboleth,* the meaning of the word matters less than, let us say, its signifying form once it becomes a password, a mark of belonging, a manifestation of an alliance:

> Scherte die Brieftaube aus, war ihr Ring
> zu entziffern? (All das
> Gewölk um sie her—es war lesbar.) Litt es
> der Schwarm? Und verstand,
> und flog wie sie fortlieb? (*GW,* I, 282)

> (Did the carrier pigeon sheer off, was its ring
> decipherable? (All that cloud around it—it was
>   readable.) Did the
> flock endure it? And understand,
> and fly as the other went on?)

A date gets carried away, transported; it takes off, takes itself off— and thus effaces itself in its very readability. Effacement is not something that befalls it like an accident; it affects neither its meaning nor its readability; it merges, on the contrary, with reading's very access to that which a date may still signify. But if readability effaces the date, the very thing which it offers for reading, this strange process will have begun with the very inscription of the date. The date must conceal within itself some stigma of singularity if it is to last longer—and this lasting is the poem—than that which it commemorates. This is its only chance of assuring its spectral return. Effacement or concealment, this annulment in this annulation of return belongs to the movement of dating. And so what must be commemorated, *at once* gathered together and repeated, is, *at the same time,* the date's annihilation, a kind of nothing, or ash.

Ash awaits us.

III

Let us keep for the moment to those dates which we recognize through the language-grid of the calendar: the day, the month, and sometimes the year.

First case: a date relates to an event which, at least *in appearance and outwardly,* is distinct from the actual writing of the poem and the moment of its signing. The metonymy of the date (a date is always also a metonymy) designates part of an event or a sequence of events by way of recalling the whole. The mention "13th of February" forms a part of what happened on that day, only a part, but it stands for the whole in a given context. What happened on that day, in the first case which we are going to consider, is not, in appearance and outwardly, the advent of the poem.

The example then is that of the first line of "In eins" ("In One"). It begins with "*Dreizehnter Feber,*" "Thirteenth of February."

What is gathered and commemorated in the single time of this "In eins," at one poetic stroke? And is it a matter, moreover, of one commemoration? The "in one," "all at once," several times at once, seems to constellate in the uniqueness of a date. But this date, in being unique and *the only one,* all alone, the lone of its kind—is it one?

And what if there were more than one February 13?

Not only because February 13 recurs, becoming each year its own revenant, but first of all because a multiplicity of events, dispersed (for example, on a political map of Europe) among diverse places, at different periods, in foreign idioms, may have conjoined at the heart of the same anniversary.

> IN EINS
>
> Dreizehnter Feber. Im Herzmund
> erwachtes Schibboleth. Mit dir,
> Peuple
> de Paris. *No pasarán.* (GW, I, 270)
>
> (IN ONE
>
> Thirteenth of February. In the heart's mouth

an awakened shibboleth. With you,
Peuple
de Paris. *No pasarán*.) (*P*, 206)

Like the rest of the poem, and well in excess of what I could say concerning them, these first lines are *evidently* ciphered.

Ciphered, in full evidence: in several senses and in several languages.

Ciphered, first of all, in that they include a cipher, the cipher of the number thirteen. This is one of those numbers where chance and necessity cross and in crossing are both at once consigned. Within its strictures a ligament binds together, in a manner at once significant and insignificant, fatality and its opposite: chance and coming-due, coincidence in the event, what *falls*—well or ill—together.

> DIE ZAHLEN, im Bund
> mit der Bilder Verhängnis
> und Gegen-
> verhängnis. (*GW*, II, 17)

> (THE NUMBERS, bonded
> with the images' doom
> and their counter-
> doom.) (65, 49)

> Und Zahlen waren
> mitverwoben in das
> Unzählbare. Eins und Tausend... (*GW*, I, 280)

> (And numbers were
> interwoven into the
> numberless. One and a thousand...)

Even before the number thirteen, the "one" of the title, "IN EINS," announces the con-signing and co-signing of a multiple singularity. From the title and the opening on, cipher, and then date, are incorporated in the poem. They give access to the poem which they are, but a ciphered access.

These first lines are ciphered in another sense: more than others, they are untranslatable. I am not thinking here of all the poetic challenges with which this great poet-translator confronts poet-translators. No, I will limit myself to the aporia (to the barred passage, *no pasarán:* this is what "aporia" means). What seems to bar the passage of translation is the multiplicity of languages in a single poem, all at once. Four languages, like a series of proper names or signatures, like the face of a seal.

Like the title and the date, the first line is in German. But with the second line, a second language, an apparently Hebrew word, arises in the "heart's mouth": *shibboleth.*

> Dreizehnter Feber. Im Herzmund
> erwachtes Schibboleth. Mit dir, . . .
>
> (Thirteenth of February. In the heart's mouth
> an awakened shibboleth. With you, . . .)

This second language could well be a first language, the language of the morning, the language of origin speaking of the heart, out of the heart and out of the East. "Language" in Hebrew is "lip," and does not Celan elsewhere (we will come to it) call words circumcised, as one speaks of the "circumcised heart"? Let this be for the moment. *Shibboleth,* this word I have called Hebrew, is found, as you know, in a whole family of languages: Phoenician, Judaeo-Aramaic, Syriac. It is traversed by a multiplicity of meanings: river, stream, ear of grain, olive-twig. But beyond these meanings, it acquired the value of a password. It was used during or after war, at the crossing of a border under watch. The word mattered less for its meaning than for the way in which it was pronounced. The relation to the meaning or to the thing was suspended, neutralized, bracketed: the opposite, one could say, of a phenomenological *epochē* which preserves, first of all, the meaning. The Ephraimites had been defeated by the army of Jephthah; in order to keep the soldiers from escaping across the river (*shibboleth* also means river, of course, but that is not necessarily the reason it was chosen), each person was required to say *shibboleth.* Now the Ephraimites were known for their inability to pronounce correctly the *shi* of *shibboleth,* which became for them, in consequence, an "unpronounceable name"; they said *sibboleth,* and, at that invisible border between *shi* and *si,* betrayed themselves to the sentinel at the risk of death. They betrayed their difference in rendering themselves indifferent to the diacritical difference between *shi* and *si;* they marked themselves as unable to re-mark a mark thus coded.

This happened at the border of the Jordan. We are at another border, another barred passage in the fourth language of the strophe: *no pasarán.* February 1936: the electoral victory of the *Frente Popular,* the eve of civil war. *No pasarán:* la Pasionaria, the no to Franco, to the Phalange supported by Mussolini's troops and Hitler's Condor legion. Rallying cry and sign, clamor and banderoles during the siege of Madrid, three years later, *no pasarán* was a *shibboleth* for the Republican people, for their allies, for the International Brigades. What passed this cry, what passed despite it, was the Second World War, the war of extermination. A repetition of the first, certainly, but also of that dress rehearsal [*répétition générale*], its own future anterior, which was the Spanish Civil War. This is the dated structure of the dress rehearsal: everything happens as if the Second World War had already begun in February of 1936, in a slaughter at once civil and international, violating or reclosing the borders, leaving ever so many wounds in the body of a single country—grievous figure of a metonymy. Spanish is allotted to the central strophe, which transcribes, in short, a kind of Spanish *shibboleth,* a password, and not a word in passing, but a silent word transmitted like a symbolon or handclasp, a rallying sign, a sign of membership and political watchword.

> . . . er sprach
> uns das Wort in die Hand, das wir brauchten, es war
> Hirten-Spanisch, darin,
>
> im Eislicht des Kreuzers "Aurora" . . .
>
> (. . . into our hands
> he spoke the word that we needed, it was

shepherd-Spanish, and in it

in icelight of the cruiser "Aurora" . . .)[13]

Amidst the German, the Hebrew, and the Spanish, in French, the People of Paris:

> . . . Mit dir,
> Peuple
> de Paris. *No pasarán.*
>
> (. . . With you,
> Peuple
> de Paris. *No pasarán.*)

It is not written in italics, no more than is *shibboleth*. The italics are reserved for "*No pasarán*" and the last line, "*Friede den Hütten!*," "*Peace to the cottages!*," the terrible irony of which must surely aim at someone.

The multiplicity of languages may concelebrate, *all at once,* at the same date, the poetic and political anniversary of singular events, spread like stars over the map of Europe, and henceforth conjoined by a secret affinity: the fall of Vienna and the fall of Madrid, for as we will see, Vienna and Madrid are associated in the same line by another poem, entitled "Schibboleth"; and still other memories of February, the beginnings of the October Revolution with the incidents tied not only to the cruiser Aurora and to Petrograd, both of which are named in the poem, but in fact to the Peter and Paul Fortress. It is the last stanza of "In eins" which recalls other "unforgettable" singularities, the Tuscan for example, which I will not here undertake to decipher.

> . . .
>
> "Aurora":
> die Bruderhand, winkend mit der
> von den wortgrossen Augen
> genommenen Binde—Petropolis, der

13. Martine Broda devotes "a long parenthesis" to this "shepherd-Spanish" in "Bouteilles, caillous, schibboleths: un nom dans la main," in *Dans la main de personne* (Paris: Cerf, 1986), 95–105.

Unvergessenen Wanderstadt lag
auch dir toskanisch zu Herzen

Friede den Hütten!

(. . .
                    "Aurora":
the brotherly hand, waving with
the blindfold removed from
his word-wide eyes—Petropolis, the
roving city of those unforgotten,
was Tuscanly close to your heart also.

Peace to the cottages!)

But already within the habitation of a single language, for example French, a discontinuous swarm of events may be commemorated all at once, *at the same date,* which consequently takes on the strange, coincident, *unheimlich* dimensions of a cryptic predestination.

The date itself resembles a *shibboleth.* It gives ciphered access to this collocation, to this secret configuration of places for memory.

The series thus constellated becomes all the more ample and numerous as the date remains relatively indeterminate. If Celan does not specify the day (13), and says only "February," (*Februar,* this time and not *Feber*), as in the poem entitled "Schibboleth," the memory swells even further of demonstrations of the same kind, with the same political significance, which were able to bring the People of Paris, that is, the people of the left, together in the surge of a single impulse to proclaim, like the Republicans of Madrid, *No pasarán.* One sole example: it is on the twelfth of February, 1934, after the failure of the attempt to form a Common Front of the Right, with Doriot, after the riot of February 6, that a huge march takes place which spontaneously regroups the masses and the leadership of the parties of the left. This was the origin of the Popular Front.

But if, in "In eins," Celan specifies the thirteenth of February (*Dreizehnter Feber*), one may think of February 13, 1962. I consign this hypothesis to those who may know something about or can testify to the so-called "external" date of the poem; I am unaware of it, but even should my hypothesis be factually false, it would still designate the power of those dates to come to which, Celan says, we write and ascribe ourselves. A date always remains a kind of *hypothesis,* the support for a, by definition, unlimited number of projections of memory. The slightest indetermination (the day and the month without the year, for example) increases the chances, and the chances of a future anterior. The date is a future anterior, it gives the time one assigns to anniversaries to come. Thus, on February 13, 1962, Celan was in Paris. *Die Niemandsrose,* the collection in which "In eins" appears, is not published until 1963. On the other hand, in moving from one poem to the other, from "Schibboleth," published eight years before, to "In eins," Celan specifies "Thirteenth of February" where the earlier poem said only "February." Thus something must have happened. February 13, 1962 is the day of the funeral for the Métro Charonne massacre victims, an anti-OAS demonstration at the end of the Algerian war. Several hundred thousand Parisians, the People of Paris, are marching. Two days after, the meetings begin which lead to the Evian accords. These People of Paris are still the People of the Commune, the People with whom one must band together: *with you, Peuple de Paris.* In the same event, at the same date, national war and civil war, the end of one and the beginning—*as* the beginning of the other.

Like the date, *shibboleth* is marked several times, several times in one, "in eins," *at once.* A marked multiplicity but also a marking one.

On the one hand, within the poem, it names, as is evident, the password or rallying cry, a right of access or sign of membership in all the political situations along the historical borders which are brought together in the poem's *configuration.* This *visa,* it will be said, is the *shibboleth,* it determines a theme, a meaning or a content.

But on the other hand, as cryptic or numerical cipher, *shibboleth* also spells the anniversary date's singular power of gathering together. The anniversary grants access to the date's memory, its future, but also to the poem—itself. *Shibboleth* is the *shibboleth* for the right to the poem which calls itself a *shibboleth,* its own *shibboleth* at the very moment that it commemorates others. *Shibboleth* is its title, whether or not it appears in that place, as in one of the two poems.

This does not mean—two things.

On the one hand, this does not mean that the events commemorated in this fantastic constellation are nonpoetic events, suddenly transfigured by an incantation. No, I believe that for Celan the signifying conjunction of all these dramas and historical actors will have *constituted* the dated signature, the dating of the poem.

Nor does this mean, on the other hand, that possession of the *shibboleth* effaces the cipher, holds the key to the crypt, and guarantees transparency of meaning. The crypt remains, the *shibboleth* remains secret, the passage uncertain, and the poem only unveils this secret to confirm that there is something secret there, withdrawn, forever beyond the reach of any hermeneutic exhaustion. A non-hermetic secret, it remains, and the date with it, heterogeneous to all interpretative totalization, eradicating the hermeneutic principle. There is no one meaning, from the moment that there is date and *shibboleth*, no longer a sole originary meaning.

A *shibboleth*, the word *shibboleth*, if it is one, names, in the broadest extension of its generality or its usage, every insignificant arbitrary mark, for example the phonemic difference between *shi* and *si*, as that difference becomes discriminative, decisive and divisive. The difference has no meaning in and of itself, but it becomes what one must know how to recognize and above all to mark if one is to get on, to get over the border of a place or the threshold of a poem, to see oneself granted asylum or the legitimate habitation of a language. So as no longer to be an outlaw there. And to inhabit a language, one must already have a *shibboleth* at one's disposal: not simply understand the meaning of the word, not simply *know* this meaning or know how a word *should* be pronounced (the difference of *h* between *shi* and *si:* this the Ephraimites knew), but *be able* to say it as one ought, as one ought to be able to say it. It does not suffice to know the difference, one must be capable of it, one must be able to do it, or know how to do it—and doing here means *marking*. It is this differential mark which it is not enough to know like a theorem which is the secret. A secret without secrecy. The right of alliance involves no hidden secret, no meaning concealed in a crypt.

In the word, the difference between *shi* and *si* has no meaning. But it is the ciphered mark which one must *be able to partake of* with the other, and this differential power must be inscribed in oneself, that is to say in one's body itself, just as much as in the body of one's own language, and the one to the same extent as the other. This inscription of difference in the body (for example by the phonatory ability to pronounce this or that) is nonetheless not natural, is in no way an innate organic faculty. Its very origin presupposes participation in a cultural and linguistic community, in a milieu of apprenticeship, in short, an alliance.

Shibboleth does not cipher something, it is not only a cipher, and the cipher of the poem; it is now, emerging from non-meaning where it keeps itself in reserve, the cipher *of* the cipher, the ciphered manifestation of the cipher as such. And when a cipher manifests itself as what it is, that is to say, in encrypting itself, this is not in order to say to us: I am a cipher. It may still conceal from us, without the slightest hidden intention, the secret which it shelters in its readability. It moves, touches, fascinates, or seduces us all the more. The ellipsis and cesura of discretion inhabit it, there is nothing it can do about it. This pass is a passion before becoming a calculated risk, prior to any strategy, any poetics of ciphering intended, as with Joyce, to keep the professors busy for generations. Even supposing that this exhausts Joyce's first and true desire, something I do not believe, nothing seems to me more foreign to Celan.

Multiplicity and migration of languages, certainly, and within language itself. Babel: named in "Hinausgekrönt," after the "*Ghetto-Rose*" and that phallic figure knotted in the heart of the poem ("*phallisch gebündelt*"), this is also its last word, both its address and its envoy.

> Und es steigt eine Erde herauf, die unsre,
> diese.
> Und wir schicken
> keinen der Unsern hinunter
> zu dir,
> Babel. (GW, I, 272)

> (And an earth rises up, ours,
> this one.
> And we'll send

none of our people down
to you,
Babel.) (*P*, 211)

Address and envoi of the poem, yes, but what seems to be said to
Babel, addressed to it, is that nothing will be addressed to it. One will
send it nothing, nothing from us, none of ours.

Multiplicity and migration of languages, certainly, and within language. Your country, it says, migrates all over, like language. The
country itself migrates and transports its borders. It displaces itself like
those names and stones which one gives as a pledge, from hand to
hand, and the hand is given too, and what gets detached, sundered,
torn away, can gather itself together anew in the symbol, the pledge,
the promise, the alliance, the imparted word, the migration of the
imparted word.

> —was abriss, wächst wieder zusammen—
> da hast du sie, da nimm sie dir, da hast du alle beide,
> den Namen, den Namen, die Hand, die Hand
> da nimm sie dir zum Unterpfand,
> er nimmt auch das, und du hast
> wieder, was dein ist, was sein war,
>
> Windmühlen
>
> stossen dir Luft in die Lunge . . . (*GW*, I, 284)
>
> (—what was severed joins up again—
> there you have it, so take it, there you have them
>   both,
> the name, the name, the hand, the hand,
> so take them, keep them as a pledge,
> he takes it too, and you have
> again what is yours, what was his,
>
> windmills
>
> push air into your lungs . . .) (*P*, 217)

Chance and risk of the windmill—language which holds as much of
wind and of illusion as it draws from breath and spirit, from the

breathing bestowed. We will not recall all the coded trails of this immense poem ("Es ist alles anders..."), from Russia—"the name of Osip"—to Moravia, to the Prague cemetery ("the pebble from / the Moravian hollow / which your thought carried to Prague, / on to the grave, to the graves, into life") and "near Normandy-Niemen," the French squadron in war exile in Moscow, etc. Only this, which speaks of the emigration of the country itself, and of its name. Like language:

> wie heisst es, dein Land
> hinterm Berg, hinterm Jahr?
> Ich weiss, wie es heisst.
> . . .
> es wandert überallhin, wie die Sprache,
> wirf sie weg, wirf sie weg,
> dann hast du sie wieder, wie ihn,
> den Kieselstein aus
> der Mährischen Senke,
> den dein Gedanke nach Prag trug . . . (*GW*, I, 285)

> (What is it called, your country
> behind the mountain, behind the year?
> I know what it's called.
> . . .
> It wanders off everywhere, like language,
> throw it away, throw it away,
> then you'll have it again, like that other thing,
> the pebble from
> the Moravian hollow
> which your thought carried to Prague . . .) (*P*, 219)

Multiplicity and migration of languages, certainly, and within language itself, Babel within *a single* language. *Shibboleth* marks the multiplicity within language, insignificant difference as the condition of meaning. But by the same token, the insignificance of language, of the properly linguistic body: it can only take on meaning in relation to a *place*. By place, I mean just as much the relation to a border, country, house, or threshold, as any site, any *situation* in general from within which, practically, pragmatically, alliances are formed, contracts, codes and conventions established which give meaning to the insignificant, institute passwords, bend language to what exceeds it, make of it a moment of gesture and of step, secondarize or "reject" it in order to find it again.

Multiplicity within language, or rather heterogeneity. One should specify that untranslatability is connected not only with the difficult passage (*no pasarán*), the aporia or impasse which would isolate one poetic language from another. Babel is also this *possible impossible step*,[14] beyond hope of transaction, tied to the multiplicity of languages within the uniqueness of the poetic inscription: several times in one, several languages in a single poetic act. The uniqueness of the poem, itself yet another date and *shibboleth*, forges and seals, in a single idiom, *in eins,* the poetic event, a multiplicity of languages and of equally singular dates. "In eins": within the unity and within the uniqueness of this poem, the four languages are certainly not untranslatable, neither among themselves nor into other languages. But what will always remain untranslatable into any *other* language whatsoever, is the marked difference of languages in the poem. We spoke of the *doing* which does not reduce to *knowing,* and of that *being able to do the difference* which is what *marking* comes to. This is what goes on and what comes about here. Everything seems, in principle, by right, translatable, except for the mark of the difference among the languages within the same poetic event. Let us consider for example the excellent French translation of "In eins." The German is translated into French, as is normal. *Schibboleth* and *no pasarán* are left untranslated, which respects the foreignness of these words in the principal medium, the German idiom of what one calls the original version. But in preserving, and how could one not, the French of this version in the translation, "*Avec toi, / Peuple / de Paris,*" the translation must efface the very thing which it preserves, the foreign effect of the French (unitalicized) in the poem, and that which places it in configuration with all those ciphers, passwords, and *shibboleths* which date and sign the poem, "In eins," in the at once dissociated, rent, and adjoined, rejoined, regathered unity of its singularities. There is no remedy to which translation

14. TN In French, "*ce pas impossible*": i.e., both "this impossible step" and "this not impossible."

could have recourse here, none at least in the body of the poem. No one is to blame, moreover there is nothing to bring before the bar of translation. The *shibboleth,* here again, does not resist translation by reason of some inaccessibility of its meaning to transference, by reason of some semantic secret, but by virtue of that in it which forms the cut of a nonsignifying difference in the body of the written or oral mark, written in speech as a mark within a mark, an incision marking the very mark itself. On both sides of the historical, political, and linguistic border (a border is never natural), the meaning, the different meanings of the word *shibboleth* are known: river, ear of grain, olive twig. One even knows how it should be pronounced. But a single trial determines that some cannot while others can pronounce it with the heart's mouth. The first will not pass, the others will pass the line—of the place, of the country, of the community, of what takes place in a language, in languages as poems. Every poem has its own language, it is one time alone its own language, even and especially if several languages *are able* to cross there. From this *point of view,* which may become a watch tower, the vigilance of a sentinel, one sees well: the value of the *shibboleth* may always, and tragically, be inverted. Tragically because the inversion sometimes overtakes the initiative of subjects, the good will of men, their mastery of language and of politics. Watchword or password in the struggle against oppression, exclusion, fascism, and racism, it may also corrupt its differential value, which is the condition of alliance and of the poem, making of it a discriminatory limit, the grillwork of policing, of normalization and of methodical subjugation.

IV

Inserted in the second line of "In eins," the word *schibboleth* forms the title of a longer and earlier poem, published in 1955 in the collection *Von Schwelle zu Schwelle. Shibboleth* could also serve, by metonymy, as the title of the collection. It speaks in effect of the threshold, of the crossing of the threshold (*Schwelle*), of that which permits one to pass or to cross, to transfer from one threshold to another: to translate. One meets here in the earlier poem with more or less the same configuration of events, sealed by the same February anniversary, the linking of the capitals of Vienna and Madrid substituted perhaps for the linking, in "In eins," of Paris, Madrid and Petropolis. *No pasarán* already figures in close conjunction with *shibboleth*. Again we are dealing, no doubt, with the memory of February 1936–39, though this time neither the day (13), nor the year appear. Which leads one to think, given the seeming absence of references to France and the French language, that, in fact, another date is in question, this time, in the otherness of which other Februaries, and then a certain thirteenth of February, come together, overdetermining the *Sprachgitter* of the signature. The play of resemblances and differences, the *shibboleth between* the two poems, could occasion an interminable analysis.

Apart from its presence as title, the word *shibboleth* almost directly precedes "February" and *no pasarán*, in a strophe which one might call open-hearted, opened here again through the heart, through the single word "heart" (in "In eins," it will also be "Im Herzmund," in the heart's mouth, in the first line):

> Herz:
> gib dich auch hier zu erkennen,
> hier, in der Mitte des Marktes.
> Ruf's, das Schibboleth, hinaus
> in die Fremde der Heimat:
> Februar. No pasarán. (*GW*, I, 131)

> (Heart:
> make yourself known even here,
> here, in the midst of the market.
> Call it out, the shibboleth,
> into the alien homeland strangeness:
> February. No pasarán.) (*SG*, 73)

Strangeness, estrangement in one's own home, not being at home, being called away from one's homeland or away from home in one's homeland, the "shall not" pass [*ce pas du "ne pas"*] which secures and threatens every border crossing in and out of oneself, this moment of the *shibboleth* is re-marked in the date in the month of and in the word February. The difference is hardly translatable: *Februar* in "Schibboleth," *Feber* ("*Dreizehnter Feber*") in "In eins," a *shibboleth in Febru-ary* perhaps leading back, through a play of archaism and Austrian, to some no doubt falsely attributed etymology of *februarius* as the mo-ment of fever, access, crisis, inflammation.[15]

The two poems beckon to one another, kindred, complicitous, allies, but as different as is possible. They bear and do not bear the same date. A *shibboleth* secures the passage from one to the other in the difference, within sameness, of the same date, between *Februar* and *Feber*. They speak, in the same language, two different languages. They partake of it.

We make use here of "partaking," as elsewhere "imparting," to render the ambiguities of the French *partage*,[16] a word which names difference, the line of demarcation, the parting of the waters, scission, cesura as well as participation, that which is divided because it is shared or held in common, imparted and partaken of.

Fascinated by a resemblance at once semantic and formal and which nonetheless has no linguistico-historical explanation, I will hazard a comparison between the imparted or partaken as *shibboleth* and as *symbolon*. In both cases of S-B-L, a pledge is transmitted to another, "*er sprach / uns das Wort in die Hand*" ("he spoke / the word in our hand"), a word or piece of a word, the complementary part of an object divided in two to seal an alliance, a tessera. This is the moment of engagement, of signing, of the pact or contract, of the promise, of the ring.[17]

15. *Feber:* Austrian dialect for *Februar. Jänner,* occurring in other poems, goes back (like *Jenner*) to the beginnings of Middle High German and remains in use up through the nineteenth century, and even today in Austria, and here and there in Switzerland and Alsace.

16. TN In the French, Derrida refers here to Jean-Luc Nancy's use of "partage" in *Le partage des voix* (Paris: Galilée, 1982). Among its other meanings, "partage des voix" is the French idiom for a split, that is to say tied, vote.

17. It would have been appropriate to do it everywhere, but I choose to recall Freud's *shibboleths* here, at the moment of this allusion to the ring, for example the one symbolizing the alliance of the founders of psychoanalysis. Freud often used this word, *shibboleth*, to designate that which "distinguishes the followers of psychoanalysis from those who are opposed to it" (*Three Essays on the Theory of Sexuality,* in *The Standard Edition of the Complete Psychological Works of Sigmund Freud,* ed. and trans. James Strachey [London: The Hogarth Press, 1953–66], VII, 226n2; *Gesammelte Werke* [London: Imago, 1940–68], V, 128n2) or "dreams, the shibboleth of psychoanalysis" (*On the History of the Psycho-Analytic Movement, Standard Edition,* XIV, 57; *Gesammelte Werke,* X, 102). Cf. also *The Ego and the Id (Standard Edition,* XIX, 13; *Gesammelte*

The signature of the date plays a role here. Beyond the singular event which it marks and of which it would be the detachable proper name, capable of outliving and thus of calling, of recalling, the vanished as vanished, its very ash, it gathers together, like a title (*titulus* includes a sense of gathering), a more or less apparent and secret conjunction of singularities which partake of, and in the future will continue to partake of, the *same date*.

There is no limit assignable to such a conjunction. It is determined by the future to which a fracture promises it. No testimony, no knowledge, not even Celan's, could by definition exhaust its deciphering. First of all because there is no absolute witness for an external decoding. Celan may always have imparted one more *shibboleth:* under cover of a word, a cipher, or a letter. Second, he would not have claimed himself to have totalized the possible and compossible meanings of a constellation. Finally and above all, the poem is destined to remain *alone,* it is destined for this from its first breath, alone with the vanishing of the witnesses and the witnesses of witnesses. And of the poet.

The date is a witness, but one may very well bless it without knowing all of that for which and of those for whom it bears witness. It is always possible that there may no longer be any witness for this witness. We are going to slowly approach this affinity between a date, a name— and ash. The last words of "Aschenglorie":

> Niemand
> zeugt für den
> Zeugen. (*GW*, II, 72)
>
> (No one
> bears witness for
> the witness.) (*SG*, 241)

Folded or refolded in the simplicity of the singular, a certain repetition thus assures the minimal and "internal" readability of the poem,

Werke, XIII, 239) and *New Introductory Lectures on Psychoanalysis* (*Standard Edition*, XXII, 7; *Gesammelte Werke*, XV, 6). The motif of the *shibboleth* was discussed during a seminar arranged around Wladimir Granoff, Marie Moscovici, Robert Pujol and Jean-Michel Rey in conjunction with a symposium at Cerisy-la-Salle. Cf. *Les fins de l'homme* (Paris: Galilée, 1981), 185–89.

even in the absence of a witness, of a signatory or of anyone who might have some knowledge concerning the historical reference of the poetic legacy. This in any case, is what is *signified,* if one can still speak in this way, by the word or title *shibboleth.* Not this or that meaning derived from its language of origin: river, ear of grain, olive-twig, or indeed the other meanings which it takes on in the poem. It signifies: there is *shibboleth,* there is something of a crypt, it remains incalculable, it does not conceal a single determinate secret, a semantic content waiting for the one who holds a key behind the door. If there is indeed a door, it does not present itself in this way. If this crypt is symbolic, this does not in the last analysis derive from some tropic or rhetoric. To be sure, the symbolic dimension never disappears, and at times it takes on thematic values. But what the poem marks, what enters and incises languages in the form of a date, is that there is partaking of the *shibboleth,* a partaking at once open and closed. The date (signature, moment, place, gathering of singular marks) always functions as a *shibboleth.* It shows that there is something not shown, that there is ciphered singularity: irreducible to any concept, to any knowledge, even to a history or tradition, be it of a religious kind. A ciphered singularity which gathers a multiplicity *in eins,* and through whose grid a poem remains readable: *"Aber das Gedicht spricht ja!"* The poem speaks, even should none of its references be intelligible, no other than the Other, the one to whom it addresses itself and to whom it speaks in saying that it speaks to him. Even if it does not reach and leave its mark on, at least it calls to, the Other. Address takes place.

In a language, in the poetic writing of a language, there is nothing but *shibboleth.* Like the date, like a name, it permits anniversaries, alliances, returns, commemorations—even if there should be no trace, what one commonly calls a trace, the subsistent presence of a remainder, even if there should be scarcely an ash of what we thus still date, celebrate, commemorate, or bless.

Seattle, October 14, 1984

Aphorism Countertime

⬥ "L'aphorisme à contretemps" came into being in 1986 when Derrida was invited to write a piece on *Romeo and Juliet* for a production of the play in Paris by Daniel Mesguich, and its specificity is signaled by the irreducibly personal note with which it ends. Derrida has remarked that although he probably would not have written about *Romeo and Juliet* had he not been asked to do so, he had been aware for a long time that Shakespeare's play represented something he wanted to discuss (see the Interview above). It is both a text which articulates certain problems that run through the entire history of Western culture, and one of that culture's most familiar and endlessly recirculated icons. Derrida responds to, and connects, these twin features of the play by means of a focus on *contretemps,* a word which in French can mean both "mishap" and "syncopation," while the phrase *à contretemps* suggests both "inopportunely" and, in a musical sense, "out of time" or "in counter-time." For many more than have seen or read the play, the story of *Romeo and Juliet* has become a byword for love blighted by mischance and destroyed by unfortunate timing; and it is notable that Derrida focuses his attention on the scene that, more than any other, has become a cultural commonplace. Close attention to the verbal interchange in the balcony scene, and to the question of the *name* in particular, leads to an understanding of the force of *contretemps* both in the play and in the institutional and intellectual context within which, and by means of which, we experience it. Derrida examines the contradictory force of naming (in both literal and more general senses) as a cultural practice: in instituting and enforcing temporal and spatial homogeneity, it brings into being the possibility of the very accidents—including death as we understand it—which it is designed to prevent. The names of Romeo and Juliet, Montague and Capulet, produce both the desire that drives the events of the play and the tragic mischances that thwart it. In their confounding of homogeneous time and place, therefore, countertime and mishap echo an absolute heterogeneity which is "anterior" to times and happenings, and the various labels by which we try to order them. Love and hate are to be understood neither as arbitrary individual emotions nor as determined cultural products, but as powerful effects of chance built into the network of names and dates that make relations both possible and impossible. (For a further discussion of the date which is closely related to this discussion of the name, see the extract from *Shibboleth* above; "Ulysses Gramophone" is also concerned with networks and accidents.)

The traditional critical essay, too, is an attempt to produce a homogeneous spatiotemporal continuum, and Derrida chooses in its stead an aphoristic form characterized by disjunction and heterogeneity. (The question of the aphorism—which for Derrida is the question of the mark in general—is also raised aphoristically in "Fifty-Two Aphorisms.") The aphoristic voice is one which asserts and delimits, functioning like the name; and like the name, it is never far from *contretemps* and death. Aphorisms and proper names are characterized by their capacity for surviving the deaths of those who employ them or are designated by them, and are therefore structured by the possibility of death; they thus exhibit in a particularly striking way the working of iterability that makes possible any utterance or recognizable act. So do plays, for they live on in the repetition of dramatic productions, each one affirming in a different way the uniqueness of the text they repeat, and each one repeating differently the play's staging of theatricality itself. Derrida's "Aphorism Countertime" is another such singular staging of Shakespeare's play.

"L'aphorisme à contretemps" was first published in *Roméo et Juliette* (Paris: Papiers) in 1986, and collected in *Psyché: Inventions de l'autre* (519–33). This is its first appearance in English translation. The translator, Nicholas Royle, would like to thank Geoffrey Bennington and James Raeside for all their invaluable criticisms and suggestions made in the course of his work on this translation.

1. Aphorism is the name.

2. As its name indicates, aphorism separates, it marks dissociation (*apo*), it terminates, delimits, arrests (*horizō*). It brings to an end by separating, it separates in order to end—and to define [*finir—et définir*].

3. An aphorism is a name but every name can take on the figure of aphorism.

4. An aphorism is exposure to contretemps.[1] It exposes discourse— hands it over to contretemps. Literally—because it is abandoning a word [*une parole*] to its letter.

(Already this could be read as a series of aphorisms, the alea of an initial anachrony. In the beginning there was contretemps. In the beginning there is speed. Word and deed are *overtaken*. Aphorism outstrips.)

5. To abandon speech [*la parole*], to entrust the secret to letters— this is the stratagem of the third party, the mediator, the Friar, the matchmaker who, without any other desire but the desire of others, organizes the contretemps. He counts on the letters without taking account of them:

> In the meantime, against thou shalt awake,
> Shall Romeo by my letters know our drift,
> And hither shall he come. (IV, i, 113–15)[2]

6. Despite appearances, an aphorism never arrives by itself, it doesn't come all alone. It is part of a serial logic. As in Shakespeare's play, in the *trompe-l'oeil* depth of its paradigms, all the *Romeo*

---

1. TN The word *contretemps* signifies, in English as well as French, "an inopportune occurrence; an untoward accident; an unexpected mishap or hitch" (*OED*), but in French it also refers to being "out of time" or "off-beat" in the musical sense, to a sense of "bad or wrong time," "counter-time."

2. TN References to Shakespeare's *Romeo and Juliet* are to the Arden text, ed. Brian Gibbons (New York: Methuen, 1980).

*and Juliet*s that came before it, there will be several series of aphorisms here.

7. Romeo and Juliet, the heroes of contretemps in our mythology, the positive heroes. They missed each other, how they missed each other! Did they miss each other? But they also survived, *both of them,* survived *one another,* in their name, through a studied effect of contretemps: an unfortunate crossing, by chance, of temporal and aphoristic series.[3]

8. Aphoristically, one must say that Romeo and Juliet will have lived, and lived on, through aphorism. *Romeo and Juliet* owes everything to aphorism. Aphorism can, of course, turn out to be a device of rhetoric, a sly calculation aiming at the greatest authority, an economy or strategy of mastery which knows very well how to potentialize meaning ("See how I formalize, in so few words I always say more than would appear"). But before letting itself be manipulated in this way, aphorism hands us over, defenseless, to the very experience of contretemps. Before every calculation but also across it, beyond the calculable itself.

9. The aphorism or discourse of dissociation: each sentence, each paragraph dedicates itself to separation, it shuts itself up, whether one likes it or not, in the solitude of its proper duration. Its encounter and its contact with the other are always given over to chance, to whatever may befall, good or ill. Nothing is absolutely assured, neither the linking nor the order. One aphorism in the series can come before or after the other, before *and* after the other, each can survive the other—and in the other series. Romeo and Juliet *are* aphorisms, in the first place in their name, which they are not (Juliet: " 'Tis but thy name that is my enemy" . . . Romeo: "My name, dear saint, is hateful to myself, / Because it is an enemy to thee. / Had I it

3. TN Derrida's text works with several senses of the verb *survivre:* "to survive," "to survive beyond" or "survive through," "to live on," and so forth. For a fuller account of "living on" and the related double-notion of "death sentence" and "arrest of death" [*l'arrêt de mort*], see Derrida's "Living On/Borderlines."

written, I would tear the word" [II, ii, 38, 55–57]), for there is no aphorism without language, without nomination, without appellation, without a letter, even to be torn up.

10. Each aphorism, like Romeo and Juliet, each aphoristic series has its particular duration. Its temporal logic prevents it from sharing all its time with another place of discourse, with another discourse, with the discourse of the other. Impossible synchronization. I am speaking here of the discourse of time, of its marks, of its dates, of the course of time and of the essential digression which dislocates the time of desires and carries the step of those who love one another off course. But that is not sufficient to characterize our aphorism, it is not sufficient that there be language or mark, nor that there be dissociation, dislocation, anachrony, in order for aphorism to take place. It still must have a determined form, a certain mode. Which? The bad aphorism, the *bad* of aphorism is sententious, but every apho-rism cuts and delimits by virtue of its sententious character:[4] it says the truth in the form of the last judgment, and this truth carries [*porte*] death.[5] The death sentence [*l'arrêt de mort*], for Romeo and Juliet, is a contretemps which condemns them to death, both of them, but also a contretemps which arrests death, suspends its coming, secures for both of them the delay necessary in order to witness and survive the other's death.

11. Aphorism: that which hands over every rendezvous to chance. But desire does not lay itself open to aphorism by chance. There is no time for desire without aphorism. Desire has no place without aphorism. What Romeo and Juliet experience is the exemplary anach-rony, the essential impossibility of any absolute synchronization. But

4. TN The French phrase here is *caractère de sentence*, which can also mean "quality of judgment"; "*sentence*" carries the sense of "moral saying" as well as "judgment."

5. TN "Aphorism Countertime" contains—or carries—a certain play on the verb *porter*, corresponding in some ways to the English verb "to bear" ("to carry" as well as "to wear [clothes]"). *Porter* is the verb used to designate, for example, being called by, having, or bearing a name [*porter le nom*], as well as being in mourning [*porter le deuil*]. Derrida treats the idea of the name as bearing death within it—and as being structurally conditioned to survive its bearer—in several of his works: among others, *Signéponge/Signsponge*, "Otobiographies," and *Mémoires*.

at the same time they live—as we do—this disorder of the series. Disjunction, dislocation, separation of places, deployment or spacing of a story because of aphorism—would there be any theater without that? The survival of a theatrical work implies that, theatrically, it is saying something about theater itself, about its essential possibility. And that it does so, theatrically, then, through the play of uniqueness and repetition, by giving rise every time to the chance of an absolutely singular event as it does to the untranslatable idiom of a proper name, to its fatality (the "enemy" that "I hate"), to the fatality of a date and of a rendezvous. Dates, timetables, property registers, place-names, all the codes that we cast like nets over time and space—in order to reduce or master differences, to arrest them, determine them—these are also contretemps-traps. Intended to avoid contretemps, to be in harmony with our rhythms by bending them to objective measurement, they produce misunderstanding, they accumulate the opportunities for false steps or wrong moves, revealing and simultaneously increasing this anachrony of desires: *in the same time.* What is this time? There is no place for a question in aphorism.

12.   Romeo *and* Juliet, the conjunction of two desires which are aphoristic but held together, maintained in the dislocated now of a love or a promise. A promise in their name, but across and beyond their given name, the promise of *another name,* its request rather: "O be some other name . . . " (II, ii, 42). The *and* of this conjunction, the theater of this "and," has often been presented, represented as the scene of fortuitous contretemps, of aleatory anachrony: the failed rendezvous, the unfortunate accident, the letter which does not arrive at its destination, the time of the detour prolonged for a *purloined letter,*[6] the remedy which transforms itself into poison when the stratagem of a third party, a brother, Friar Laurence, proposes simultaneously the remedy and the letter ("And if thou dar'st, I'll give thee remedy. . . . In

6. TN English in original. This is an allusion to Derrida's "Le facteur de la verité," a text concerned with Edgar Allan Poe's short story "The Purloined Letter," and Jacques Lacan's "Seminar on 'The Purloined Letter' " (the latter partly translated in *Yale French Studies* 48 [1973]: 38–72). "Aphorism Countertime" follows Shakespeare's text in focusing on the (tragic, comic, ironic, and above all *necessary*) possibility that a letter can always *not* reach its destination.

the meantime, against thou shalt awake, / Shall Romeo by my letters know our drift, / And hither shall he come . . ." [IV, i, 76, 113–15]). This representation is not false. But if this drama has thus been imprinted, superimprinted on the memory of Europe, text upon text, this is because the anachronous accident comes to illustrate an essential possibility. It confounds a philosophical logic which would like accidents to remain what they are, accidental. This logic, at the same time, throws out into the unthinkable an anachrony of structure, the absolute interruption of history as deployment of *a* temporality, of a single and organized temporality. What happens to Romeo and Juliet, and which remains in effect an accident whose aleatory and unforeseeable appearance cannot be effaced, at the crossing of several series and beyond common sense, can only be what it is, accidental, insofar as it has *already* happened, in essence, before it happens. The desire of Romeo and Juliet did not encounter the poison, the contretemps or the detour of the letter by chance. In order for this encounter to take place, there must *already* have been instituted a system of marks (names, hours, maps of places, dates and supposedly "objective" place-names) to thwart, as it were, the dispersion of interior and heterogeneous durations, to frame, organize, put in order, render possible a rendezvous: in other words to deny, while taking note of it, non-coincidence, the separation of monads, infinite distance, the disconnection of experiences, the multiplicity of worlds, everything that renders possible a contretemps or the irremediable detour of a letter. But the desire of Romeo and Juliet is born in the heart of this possibility. There would have been no love, the pledge would not have taken place, nor time, nor its theater, without discordance. The accidental contretemps comes to *remark* the essential contretemps. Which is as much as to say it is not accidental. It does not, for all that, have the signification of an essence or of a formal structure. This is not the abstract condition of possibility, a universal form of the relation to the other in general, a dialectic of desire or consciousnesses. Rather the singularity of an imminence whose "cutting point" spurs desire at its birth—the very birth of desire. I love because the other is the other, because its time will never be mine. The living duration, the very presence of its love remains infinitely distant from mine, distant from itself in that which stretches it toward mine and even in what one might want to describe as amorous euphoria, ecstatic communion, mystical intuition. I can love the other only in the passion of this aphorism. Which does not happen, does not come about like misfortune, bad luck, or negativity. It has the form of the most loving affirmation—it is the chance of desire. And it not only cuts into the fabric of durations, it spaces. Contretemps says something about topology or the visible; it opens theater.

13. Conversely, no contretemps, no aphorism without the promise of a now in common, without the pledge, the vow of synchrony, the desired sharing of a living present. In order that the sharing may be desired, must it not first be given, glimpsed, apprehended? But this sharing is just another name for aphorism.[7]

14. This aphoristic series crosses over another one. Because it traces, aphorism *lives on,* it lives much longer than its present and it lives longer than life. Death sentence [*arrêt de mort*]. It gives and carries death, but in order to make a decision thus on a sentence [*arrêt*] of death, it suspends death, it stops it once more [*il l'arrête encore*].

15. There would not be any contretemps, nor any anachrony, if the separation between monads only disjoined interiorities. Contretemps is produced at the intersection between interior experience (the "phenomenology of internal time-consciousness"[8] or space-consciousness) and its chronological or topographical marks, those which are said to be "objective," "in the world." There would not be any series otherwise, without the possibility of this marked spacing, with its social conventions and the history of its codes, with its fictions and its simulacra, with its dates. With so-called proper names.

---

7. EN *Partage,* the usual word for "sharing," also signifies "division"; see the extract from *Shibboleth* above, note 8.
8. TN The reference is to Husserl. See, for example, *The Phenomenology of Internal Time-Consciousness,* trans. James S. Churchill (Bloomington: Indiana University Press, 1964). See also Derrida's *Edmund Husserl's "Origin of Geometry": An Introduction,* 57, and chapter 5 ("Signs and the Blink of an Eye") of his *Speech and Phenomena.*

16. The simulacrum raises the curtain, it reveals, thanks to the dissociation of series, the theater of the impossible: two people each outlive the other. The absolute certainty which rules over the *duel* (*Romeo and Juliet* is the *mise-en-scène* of all duels) is that one must die before the other. One of them must see the other die. To no matter whom, I must be able to say: since we are two, we know in an absolutely ineluctable way that one of us will die before the other. One of us will see the other die, one of us will live on, even if only for an instant. One of us, only one of us, will carry the death of the other—and the mourning. It is impossible that we should each survive the other. That's the duel, the axiomatic of every duel, the scene which is the most common and the least spoken of—or the most prohibited—concerning our relation to the other. Yet *the impossible happens*—not in "objective reality," which has no say here, but in the experience of Romeo and Juliet. And under the law of the pledge, which commands every given word. They live *in turn* the death of the other, for a time, the contre-temps of their death. Both are in mourning—and both watch over the death of the other, attend to the death of the other. Double death sentence. Romeo dies before Juliet, whom he has seen dead. They both live, outlive the death of the other.

17. The impossible—this theater of double survival—also tells, like every aphorism, the truth. Right from the pledge which binds together two desires, each is already in mourning for the other, entrusts death to the other as well: if you die before me, I will keep you, if I die before you, you will carry me in yourself, one will keep the other, will already have kept the other from the first declaration. This double interiorization would be possible neither in monadic interiority nor in the logic of "objective" time and space. It takes places nevertheless every time I love. Everything then begins with this survival. Each time that I love or each time that I hate, each time that a law *engages* me to the death of the other. And it is the same law, the same double law. A pledge which keeps (off) death can always invert itself.[9]

9. TN The French text reads: *Un gage peut toujours s'inverser qui garde de la mort.* This double bind of what keeps off death and at the same time keeps it might be further elucidated by way of Derrida's *Mémoires,* where for example he explores the notion that

18. A given series of aphorisms crosses over into another one, the same under different names, under the name of the name. Romeo and Juliet love each other across their name, despite their name, they die on account of their name, they live on in their name. Since there is neither desire nor pledge nor sacred bond (*sacramentum*) without aphoristic separation, the greatest love springs from the greatest force of dissociation, here what opposes and divides the two families in their name. Romeo and Juliet bear these names. They bear them, support them even if they do not wish to assume them. From this name which separates them but which will at the same time have tightened their desire with all its aphoristic force, they would like to separate themselves. But the most vibrant declaration of their love still calls for the name that it denounces. One might be tempted to distinguish here, another aphorism, between the proper forename and the family name which would only be a proper name in a general way or according to genealogical classification. One might be tempted to distinguish Romeo from Montague and Juliet from Capulet. Perhaps they are, both of them, tempted to do it. But they don't do it, and one should notice that in the denunciation of the name (Act II, scene ii), they also attack their forenames, or at least that of Romeo, which seems to form part of the family name. The forename still bears the name of the father, it recalls the law of genealogy. Romeo *himself,* the bearer of the name is not the name, it is *Romeo,* the name which he bears. And is it necessary to call the bearer by the name which he bears? She calls him by it in order to tell him: I love you, free us from your name, Romeo, don't bear it any longer, Romeo, the name of Romeo:

> JULIET.
> O Romeo, Romeo, wherefore art thou Romeo?
> Deny thy father and refuse thy name.
> Or if thou wilt not, be but sworn my love
> And I'll no longer be a Capulet. (II, ii, 33–36)

She is speaking, here, in the night, and there is nothing to assure her that she is addressing Romeo himself, present in person. In order to

"*already* you are *in memory of* your own death; and your friends as well, and all the others, both of your own death and already of their own through yours" (87*n*2).

ask Romeo to refuse his name, she can only, in his absence, address his name or his shadow. Romeo—himself—is in the shadow and he wonders if it is time to take her at her word or if he should wait a little. Taking her at her word will mean committing himself to disowning his name, a little later on. For the moment, he decides to wait and to carry on listening:

> ROMEO [*aside*].
> Shall I hear more, or shall I speak at this?

> JULIET.
> 'Tis but thy name that is my enemy:
> Thou art thyself, though not a Montague.
> What's Montague? It is nor hand nor foot
> Nor arm nor face nor any other part
> Belonging to a man. O be some other name.
> What's in a name? That which we call a rose
> By any other word would smell as sweet;
> So Romeo would, were he not Romeo call'd,
> Retain that dear perfection which he owes
> Without that title. Romeo, doff thy name,
> And for thy name, which is no part of thee,
> Take all myself.

> ROMEO.
>   I take thee at thy word.
> Call me but love, and I'll be new baptis'd:
> Henceforth I never will be Romeo.

> JULIET.
> What man art thou that thus bescreen'd in night
> So stumblest on my counsel?

> ROMEO.
>   By a name
> I know not how to tell thee who I am:
> My name, dear saint, is hateful to myself
> Because it is an enemy to thee.
> Had I it written, I would tear the word.

JULIET.
My ears have yet not drunk a hundred words
Of thy tongue's uttering, yet I know the sound,
Art thou not Romeo, and a Montague?

ROMEO.
Neither, fair maid, if either thee dislike.
(II, ii, 37–61)

19. When she addresses Romeo in the night, when she asks him "O Romeo, Romeo, wherefore art thou Romeo? / Deny thy father and refuse thy name," she seems to be addressing *him, himself,* Romeo bearer of the name Romeo, the one who is not Romeo since he has been asked to disown his father and his name. She seems, then, to call him beyond his name. He is not present, she is not certain that he is there, *himself,* beyond his name, it is night and this night screens the lack of distinction between the name and the bearer of the name. It is in his name that she continues to call him, and that she calls on him not to call himself Romeo any longer, and that she asks him, Romeo, to renounce his name. But it is, whatever she may say or deny, he whom she loves. Who, him? Romeo. The one who calls himself Romeo, the bearer of the name, who calls himself Romeo although he is not only the one who bears this name and although he exists, without being visible or present in the night, outside his name.

20. Night. Everything that happens at night, for Romeo and Juliet, is decided rather in the penumbra, between night and day. The indecision between Romeo and the bearer of this name, between "Romeo," the name of Romeo and Romeo himself. Theater, we say, is visibility, the stage [*la scène*]. This drama belongs to the night because it stages what is not seen, the name; it stages what one calls because one cannot see or because one is not certain of seeing what one calls. Theater of the name, theater of night. The name calls beyond presence, phenomenon, light, beyond the day, beyond the theater. It keeps—whence the mourning and survival—what is no longer present, the invisible: what from now on will no longer see the light of day.

21. She wants the death of Romeo. She will have it. The death of his name ("'Tis but thy name that is my enemy"), certainly, the death of "Romeo," but they will not be able to get free from their name, they know this without knowing it [*sans le savoir*]. She declares war on "Romeo," on his name, in his name, she will win this war only on the death of Romeo himself. Himself? Who? Romeo. But "Romeo" is not Romeo. Precisely. She wants the death of "Romeo." Romeo dies, "Romeo" lives on. She keeps him dead in his name. Who? Juliet, Romeo.

22. Aphorism: separation in language and, in it, through the name which closes the horizon. Aphorism is at once necessary and impossible. Romeo is radically separated from his name. He, his living self, living and singular desire, he is not "Romeo," but the separation, the aphorism of the name remains impossible. He dies without his name but he dies also because he has not been able to set himself free from his name, or from his father, even less to renounce him, to respond to Juliet's request ("Deny thy father and refuse thy name").

23. When she says to him: my enemy is only your name, she does not think "my" enemy. Juliet, herself, has nothing against the name of Romeo. It is the name which she bears (Juliet and Capulet) that finds itself at war with the name of Romeo. The war takes place between the names. And when she says it, she is not sure, in the night, that she is making contact with Romeo himself. She speaks to him, she supposes him to be distinct from his name since she addresses him in order to say to him: "You are yourself, not a Montague." But he is not there. At least she cannot be sure of his presence. It is within herself, deep down inside, that she is addressing him in the night, but still him in his name, and in the most exclamatory form of apostrophe: "O Romeo, Romeo, wherefore art thou Romeo?" She does not say to him: why are you called Romeo, why do you bear this name (like an article of clothing, an ornament, a detachable sign)? She says to him: why *are you* Romeo? She knows it: detachable and dissociable, aphoristic though it be, his name is his essence. Inseparable from his being. And in asking him to abandon his name, she is no doubt asking him to live at last, and to live his love (for in order to live oneself truly, it is necessary to elude the law of the name, the familial law made for survival and constantly recalling me to death), but she is *just as much* asking him to die, since his life *is* his name. He exists in his name: "wherefore art thou Romeo?" "O Romeo, Romeo." Romeo is Romeo, and Romeo is not Romeo. He is himself only in abandoning his name, he is himself only in his name. Romeo can (be) call(ed) himself only if he abandons his name, he calls himself only *from* his name. Sentence of death and of survival: twice rather than once.

24. Speaking to the one she loves within herself and outside herself, in the half-light, Juliet murmurs the most implacable analysis of the name. Of the name and the proper name. Implacable: she expresses the judgment, the death sentence [*l'arrêt de mort*], the fatal truth of the name. Pitilessly she analyzes, element by element. What's Montague? Nothing of yourself, you are yourself and not Montague, she tells him. Not only does this name say nothing about you as a totality but it doesn't say anything, it doesn't even name a part of you, neither your hand, nor your foot, neither your arm, nor your face, nothing that is human! This analysis is implacable for it announces or denounces the inhumanity or the ahumanity of the name. A proper name does not name anything which is human, which belongs to a human body, a human spirit, an essence of man. And yet this relation to the inhuman only befalls man, for him, to him, in the name of man. He alone gives himself this inhuman name. And Romeo would not be what he is, a stranger to his name, without this name. Juliet, then, pursues her analysis: the names of things do not belong to the things any more than the names of men belong to men, and yet they are quite differently separable. The example of the rose, once more. A rose remains what it is without its name, Romeo is no longer what he is without his name. But, for a while, Juliet makes out as if Romeo would lose nothing in losing his name: like the rose. But like a rose, she says to him in short, and without genealogy, "without why." (Supposing that the rose, all the roses of thought, of literature, of mysticism, this "formidable anthology," absent from every bouquet...)

25. She does not tell him to lose all names, rather just to change names: "O be some other name." But that can mean two things: take another proper name (a human name, this inhuman thing which belongs only to man); *or*: take another kind of name, a name which is not that of a man, take the name of a thing then, a common name which, like the name of the rose, does not have that inhumanity which consists in affecting the very being of the one who bears it even though it names nothing of himself. And, after the colon, there is the question:

> O be some other name:
> What's in a name? That which we call a rose
> By any other word would smell as sweet;
> So Romeo would, were he not Romeo call'd,
> Retain that dear perfection which he owes
> Without that title.[10]

26. The name would only be a "title," and the title is not the thing which it names, any more than a title of nobility participates in the very thing, the family, the work, to which it is said to belong. *Romeo and Juliet* also remains the—surviving—title of an entire family of plays. We must apply what goes on in these plays also to the plays themselves, to their genealogy, their idiom, their singularity, their survival.

27. Juliet offers Romeo an infinite deal, what is apparently the most dissymmetrical of contracts: you can gain all without losing anything, it is just a matter of a name. In renouncing your name, you renounce nothing, nothing of you, of yourself, nor anything human. In exchange, and without losing anything, you gain me, and not just a part of me, but the whole of myself: "Romeo, doff thy name, / And for thy name, which is no part of thee, / Take all myself." He will have

---

10. TN I have followed the text of Derrida's quotation here, thus preserving the colon at the end of the first line. The Arden version, already cited, gives a full stop. As Brian Gibbons points out (Arden, 129), there have been several variants and varying hypotheses regarding these lines of the play. Confusingly perhaps, Q2–4 and F in fact give: "ô be some other name / Belonging to a man."

gained everything, he will have lost everything: name and life, and Juliet.

28. The circle of all these names in *o: words, Romeo, rose, love*. He has accepted the deal, he *takes her at her word* ("I take thee at thy word") at the moment where she proposes that he *take* her in her entirety ("Take all myself"). Play of idiom: in taking you at your word, in taking up the challenge, in agreeing to this incredible, priceless exchange, I take the whole of you. And in exchange for nothing, for a word, my name, which is nothing, nothing human, nothing of myself, or else nothing for myself. I give nothing in taking you at your word, I abandon nothing and take absolutely all of you. In truth, and they both know the truth of aphorism, he will lose everything. They will lose everything in this aporia, this double aporia of the proper name. And for having agreed to exchange the proper name of Romeo for a common name: not that of *rose*, but of *love*. For Romeo does not renounce all of his name, only the name of his father, that is to say his proper name, if one can still say that: "I take thee at thy word. / Call me but love, and I'll be new baptis'd: / Henceforth I never will be Romeo." He simultaneously gains himself and loses himself not only in the common name, but also in the common law of love: *Call me love.* Call me your love.

29. The dissymmetry remains infinite. It also hangs on this: Romeo does not make the same demand of her. He does not request that this woman who is secretly to be his wife renounce her name or disown her father. As if that were obvious and there was no call for any such rift [*déchirement*] (he will speak in a moment of tearing [*déchirer*] his name, the writing or the letter of his name, that is if he had written it himself, which is just what is in principle and originarily excluded). Paradox, irony, reversal of the common law? Or a repetition which on the contrary confirms the truth of this law? Usually, in our cultures, the husband keeps his name, that of his father, and the wife renounces hers. When the husband gives his name to his wife, it is not, as here, in order to lose it, or to change it, but to impose it by keeping it. Here it is she who asks him to renounce his father and to change his name. But this inversion confirms the law: the name of the father should be kept by the son, it is from him that there is some sense in tearing it away, and not at all from the daughter who has never been put in charge of it. The terrible lucidity of Juliet. She knows the two bonds of the law, the *double bind,* which ties a son to the name of his father. He can only live if he asserts himself in a singular fashion, without his inherited name. But the writing of this name, which he has not written himself ("Had I it written, I would tear the word"), constitutes him in his very being, without naming anything of him, and by denying it he can only wipe himself out. In sum, at the very most he can deny it, renounce it, he can neither efface it nor tear it up. He is therefore lost in any case and she knows it. And she knows it because she loves him and she loves him because she knows it. And she demands his death from him by demanding that he hold onto his life because she loves him, because she knows, and because she knows that death will not come to him by accident. He is doomed [*voué*] to death, and she with him, by the double law of the name.

30. There would be no contretemps without the double law of the name. The contretemps presupposes this inhuman, too human, inadequation which always dislocates a proper name. The secret marriage, the pledge (*sacramentum*), the double survival which it involves, its constitutive anachrony, all of this obeys the same law. This law, the law of contretemps, is double since it is divided; it carries aphorism within itself, as its truth. Aphorism is the law.

31. Even if he wanted to, Romeo could not renounce his name and his father *of his own accord.* He cannot want to do so of his own accord, even though this emancipation is nevertheless being presented to him as the chance of at last being himself, beyond the name—the chance of at last living, for he carries the name as his death. He could not want it himself, in himself, because *he is not without* his name. He can only desire it from the call of the other, in the name of the other. Moreover he only hates his name starting from the moment Juliet, as it were, demands it from him:

My name, dear saint, is hateful to myself
Because it is an enemy to thee.
Had I it written, I would tear the word.

32. When she thinks she recognizes him in the shadow, by moon-light, the drama of the name is consummated (Juliet: "My ears have yet not drunk a hundred words / Of thy tongue's uttering, yet I know the sound. / Art thou not Romeo, and a Montague?" Romeo: "Neither, fair maid, if either thee dislike"). She recognizes him and calls him by his name (Are you not Romeo and a Montague?), she *identifies* him on the one hand by the timbre of his voice, that is to say by the words she hears without being able to see, and on the other hand at the moment when he has, obeying the injunction, renounced his name and his father. Survival and death are at work, in other words the moon. But this power of death which appears by moonlight is called Juliet, and the sun which she comes to figure all of a sudden carries life *and* death *in the name of the father*. She kills the moon. What does Romeo say at the opening of the scene (which is not a scene since the name destines it to invisibility, but which is a theater since its light is artificial and figurative)? "But soft, what light through yonder window breaks? / It is the east, and Juliet is the sun! / Arise fair sun and kill the envious moon, / Who is already sick and pale with grief . . . " (II, ii, 2–5).

33. The lunar face of this shadow play, a certain coldness of *Romeo and Juliet*. Not all is of ice or glass, but the ice on it does not come only from death, from the marble to which everything seems doomed (*the tomb, the monument, the grave, the flowers on the lady's grave*), in this sepulchrally statuesque fate which entwines and sepa-rates these two lovers, starting from the fact of their names. No, the coldness which little by little takes over the body of the play and, as if in advance, cadaverizes it, is perhaps irony, the figure or rhetoric of irony, the contretemps of ironic consciousness. It always places itself disproportionately between finitude and infinitude, it makes use of inadequation, of aphorism, it analyzes and analyzes, it analyzes the law of misidentification, the implacable necessity, the machine of the proper name that obliges me to live through precisely that, in other words my name, of which I am dying.

34. Irony of the proper name, as analyzed by Juliet. Sentence of truth which carries death, aphorism separates, and in the first place separates me from my name. I am not my name. One might as well say that I should be able to survive it. But firstly it is destined to survive me. In this way it announces my death. Non-coincidence and contretemps between my name and me, between the experience according to which I am named or hear myself named and my "living present." Rendezvous with my name. *Untimely*, bad timing, at the wrong moment.

35. Changing names: the dance, the substitution, the masks, the simulacrum, the rendezvous with death. *Untimely. Never on time.*

36. Speaking ironically, that is to say in the rhetorical sense of the figure of irony: conveying the opposite of what one says. Here, the *impossible* then: 1) two lovers both outlive each other, each seeing the other die; 2) the name constitutes them but without being anything of themselves, condemning them to be what, beneath the mask, they are not, to being merged with the mask; 3) the two are united by that which separates them, etc. And they state this clearly, they formalize it as even a philosopher would not have dared to do. A vein, through the sharp tip of this analysis, receives the distilled potion. It does not wait, it does not allow any time, not even that of the drama, it comes at once to turn to ice the heart of their pledges. This potion would be the true poison, the poisoned truth of this drama.

37. Irony of the aphorism. In the *Aesthetics,* Hegel pokes fun at those who, quick to heap praises on ironists, show themselves not even capable of analyzing the analytical irony of *Romeo and Juliet.* He has a go at Tieck: "But when one thinks one has found the perfect opportunity to show what irony is, for example in *Romeo and Juliet,* one is disappointed, for it is no longer a question of irony."[11]

38. Another series, which cuts across all the others: the name, the law, the genealogy, the double survival, the contretemps, in short the aphorism of *Romeo and Juliet.* Not of Romeo and of Juliet but of *Romeo and Juliet,* Shakespeare's play of that title. It belongs to a series, to the still-living palimpsest, to the open theater of narratives which bear this name. It survives them, but they also survive thanks to it. Would such a double survival have been possible "without that title," as Juliet put it? And would the names of Matteo Bandello or Luigi da Porto survive without that of Shakespeare, who survived them?[12] And without the innumerable repetitions, each staked in its particular way, under the same name? Without the grafting of names? And of other plays? "O be some other name . . ."

39. The absolute aphorism: a proper name. Without genealogy, without the least copula. End of drama. Curtain. Tableau (*The Two Lovers United in Death* by Angelo dall'Oca Bianca). Tourism, December sun in Verona ("Verona by that name is known" [V, iii, 299]). A true sun, the other ("The sun for sorrow will not show his head" [V, iii, 305]).

---

11. TN See G. W. F. Hegel, *Aesthetics: Lectures on Fine Art,* trans. T. M. Knox, vol. I (Oxford: Clarendon Press, 1975), 69.
12. EN Bandello and da Porto were the authors of two of the many earlier versions of the Romeo and Juliet story.

A Selected Bibliography of Derrida's Writing

(with particular reference to the question of literature)

The following is a telegraphically annotated list of texts by Derrida that engage with literary works and with the question of literature, augmented by other texts by Derrida referred to in the course of this book; it will thus serve as both a guide for further reading and a list of works cited. (It should be added that none of Derrida's writings can be said to be *wholly* irrelevant to the question of literature.) Wherever there is an English translation in existence, this is the text that is cited. In the case of books first published in French, the date of the original publication is given after the title. Although the texts included in this volume are mentioned here, the bibliographical information provided in the headnotes is not duplicated. (A bibliography of Derrida's publications from 1962 to 1990, compiled by Albert Leventure, appears in *Textual Practice* 5.1 [Spring 1991].)

"Afterword: Toward an Ethic of Discussion." In *Limited Inc,* 111–60.

Altérités. With Pierre-Jean Labarrière, Francis Guibal, and Stanislas Breton. Paris: Editions Osiris, 1986. Includes transcripts of discussions on such topics as the other, undecidability, ethics, responsibility, Necessity.

"Aphorism Countertime." Included in this volume.

"Before the Law." Included in this volume.

"Che cos'è la poesia?" In *A Derrida Reader*, 223–37. Derrida's response to the question "What is poetry?": the poem, the "poematic," learning by heart.

"*Chôra.*" *Poikilia: Etudes offertes à Jean-Pierre Vernant.* Paris: EHESS, 1987. 265–96.

"Circonfession." *Jacques Derrida.* Geoffrey Bennington and Jacques Derrida. Paris: Seuil, 1991. An exploration/explosion of the autobiographical mode. English translation in preparation.

"The Deaths of Roland Barthes." *Philosophy and Non-Philosophy Since Merleau-Ponty.* Ed. Hugh J. Silverman. New York: Routledge, 1988. 259–96. This tribute to Barthes includes some speculations on the question of reference which are highly relevant to Derrida's readings of literary texts.

"Declarations of Independence." *New Political Science* 15 (Summer 1986): 7–15. On the act of founding an institution.

"Deconstruction and the Other." *Dialogues with Contemporary Continental Thinkers.* Ed. Richard Kearney. Manchester: Manchester University Press, 1984. 105–26. Touches at several points on the importance of literature in Derrida's work.

"Deconstruction in America: An Interview." *Critical Exchange* 17 (Winter 1985): 1–33. Among other issues Derrida discusses the significance of literature for deconstruction.

A Derrida Reader: Between the Blinds. Ed. Peggy Kamuf. New York: Columbia University Press, 1991. An invaluable anthology, covering a wide range of work, mostly in the form of excerpts. Includes "Che cos'è la poesia?" and "Letter to a Japanese Friend."

"Différance." In *Margins*, 1–27, and *Speech and Phenomena*, 129–60. An essay of major significance in Derrida's oeuvre; relevant to his work on literature and everything else.

Dissemination (1972). Trans. Barbara Johnson. Chicago: University of Chicago Press; London: Athlone, 1981. Comprises "Outwork," "Plato's Pharmacy," "The Double Session," and "Dissemination."

"Dissemination." In *Dissemination*, 287–366. A highly citational engagement with *Nombres*, an unorthodox "literary" text by Philippe Sollers.

"The Double Session." In *Dissemination*, 173–285. Mallarmé and the question of literature; extract included in this volume ("The First Session").

Du droit à la philosophie. Paris: Galilée, 1990. A substantial collection of pieces on the institutions of philosophy and the university. Translation in progress, together with additional material, for *Institutions of Philosophy.*

The Ear of the Other: Otobiography, Transference, Translation (1982). Ed. Christie V. McDonald. Trans. Avital Ronell and Peggy Kamuf. New York: Schocken Books, 1985. Derrida's lecture on Nietzsche, "Otobiographies," is followed by two roundtable discussions—on autobiography and translation—to which he makes extended contributions.

"Economimesis." *Diacritics* 11.2 (Summer 1981): 3–25. A discussion of Kant's aesthetic theory, and its imbrication with economics.

"Edmond Jabès and the Question of the Book." In *Writing and Difference,* 64–78. On the writing of Jabés, especially the first volume of *Le livre des questions.*

Edmund Husserl's "Origin of Geometry": An Introduction (1962). Trans. John P. Leavey, Jr. Stony Brook: Nicolas Hays, 1978.

"Ellipsis." In *Writing and Difference,* 294–300. Short piece on Jabès's *Le retour au livre* (the third volume of *Le livre des questions*).

"Envois." In *The Post Card,* 1–256. An epistolary work ranging across, and exemplifying, a number of concerns with implications for literature; Joyce, in particular, features occasionally by name and throughout by implication.

"Le facteur de la vérité." In *The Post Card,* 411–96. A lengthy engagement with Lacan's discussion of a Poe story, "The Purloined Letter." (An earlier translation was entitled "The Purveyor of Truth.")

Feu la cendre. Paris: Des Femmes, 1987. A "conversation" around the term *cendre* ("ash"), with several literary references (including Virginia Woolf). English translation in preparation.

"Fifty-Two Aphorisms for a Foreword." *Deconstruction: Omnibus Volume.* Ed. Andreas Papadakis, Catherine Cooke, and Andrew Benjamin. New York: Rizzolli; London: Academy Editions, 1989. 67–69. Aphorisms on architecture, prefaces, the work of the International College of Philosophy—and on the aphorism.

"Forcener le subjectile." *Antonin Artaud: Dessins et portraits.* Paule Thévenin and Jacques Derrida. Paris: Gallimard, 1986. 55–108. On the drawings, and associated texts, of Artaud. English translation in preparation.

"Force of Law: The 'Mystical Foundation of Authority,' " *Cardozo Law Review* 11 (1990): 919–1045. On Benjamin's "Critique of

Violence"; includes an analysis of *judgment* that is highly relevant to literary criticism.

"Géopsychanalyse 'and the rest of the world,' " In *Psyché*, 327–52. English translation to appear in *Negotiations*.

Glas (1974). Trans. John P. Leavey, Jr., and Richard Rand. Lincoln: University of Nebraska Press, 1986. The right-hand column constitutes one of Derrida's most extended engagements with a literary *oeuvre*, that of Jean Genet (particularly *Funeral Rights, Miracle of the Rose, Our Lady of the Flowers,* and *The Thief's Journal*).

Of Grammatology (1967). Trans. Gayatri Chakravorty Spivak. Baltimore: Johns Hopkins University Press, 1976. Writing and the sign, especially in texts by Saussure, Lévi-Strauss, and—predominantly—Rousseau. A chapter—". . . That Dangerous Supplement . . ."—included in this volume.

"An Idea of Flaubert: 'Plato's Letter.' " *MLN* 99 (1984): 748–68. Flaubert's interest in, and relation to, philosophy.

Institutions of Philosophy. Ed. Deborah Esch and Thomas Keenan. Cambridge, Mass.: Harvard University Press, forthcoming. An expanded English version of *Du droit à la philosophie.*

"An Interview with Derrida." *Derrida and "Différance."* Ed. David Wood and Robert Bernasconi. Evanston: Northwestern University Press, 1988. 71–82. Some comments on the importance of literature for Derrida, in an interview with *Le nouvel observateur.*

"Interview with Jean-Luc Nancy." *Topoi* 7 (1988): 113–21. On the question of the "subject." Reprinted in *Who Comes After the Subject?,* ed. Eduardo Cadava, Peter Connor, and Jean-Luc Nancy (New York: Routledge, 1991).

"Languages and Institutions of Philosophy." *Recherches sémiotiques/ Semiotic Inquiry* 4 (1984): 91–154.

"The Laws of Reflection: Nelson Mandela, in Admiration." *For Nelson Mandela.* Ed. Jacques Derrida and Mustapha Tlili. New York: Seaver Books/Henry Holt, 1987. 11–42.

"Letter to a Japanese Friend." *Derrida and "Différance."* Ed. David Wood and Robert Bernasconi. Evanston: Northwestern University Press, 1988. 1–5. Reprinted in *A Derrida Reader,* 270–76. A useful clarification of the term *deconstruction.*

Limited Inc. Ed. Gerald Graff. Evanston: Northwestern University Press, 1988. Includes "Signature Event Context," "Limited Inc a b c . . . ," and "Afterword: Toward an Ethic of Discussion."

"Limited Inc a b c ... " In *Limited Inc,* 29–110. A response to John Searle's attack on "Signature Event Context."

"Living On/Borderlines." *Deconstruction and Criticism.* Harold Bloom et al. New York: Continuum, 1979. 75–176. Concerning Shelley's "The Triumph of Life" and Blanchot's *The Madness of the Day* and *Death Sentence;* and in a continuous footnote, the question of translation.

"Mallarmé." Included in this volume.

Margins—of Philosophy (1972). Trans. Alan Bass. New York: University of Chicago Press; Brighton: Harvester, 1982. Includes "Tympan," "Différance," "White Mythology," "Qual Quelle," and "Signature Event Context."

Mémoires d'aveugle: L'autoportrait et autres ruines. Paris: Réunion des musées nationaux, 1990. The catalogue of an exhibition of drawings at the Louvre, chosen and discussed by Derrida; the organizing topic of blindness embraces a number of literary artists as well, including Milton, Marvell, Joyce, and Borges. English translation in preparation.

Mémoires: For Paul de Man. Trans. Cecile Lindsay, Jonathan Culler, and Eduardo Cadava. New York: Columbia University Press, 1986. A range of topics of relevance to literature, including de Man's work in relation to Derrida's, the poetry of Hölderlin, and deconstruction in America.

"*Mochlos*—or The Conflict of the Faculties." *Our Academic Contract.* Ed. Richard Rand. Lincoln: University of Nebraska Press, forthcoming. On the question of academic responsibility and the place of philosophy in the university.

Negotiations: Writings. Ed. Thomas Keenan and Deborah Esch. Minneapolis: Minnesota University Press, forthcoming. A collection of texts by Derrida on political questions.

"No Apocalypse, Not Now (Full Speed Ahead, Seven Missiles, Seven Missives)." *Diacritics* 14.2 (Summer 1984): 2–31. Includes a remarkable discussion of the nuclear age as the "age of literature."

"Ocelle comme pas un." Published as a preface to a fictional work by Jos Joliet, *L'enfant au chien-assis.* Paris: Galilée, 1980. 9–43. No English translation.

"Otobiographies: The Teaching of Nietzsche and the Politics of the Proper Name." In *The Ear of the Other,* 1–38. The unfixable boundary of "life" and "works"; the role of the other in the meaning of a text.

"Outwork, prefacing." In *Dissemination,* 1–59. The question of the "book" and its limits; includes discussions of Lautréamont, Novalis, and Mallarmé.

Parages. Paris: Galilée, 1986. Four texts on Blanchot's fictions, three of which have been translated separately ("Living On/Borderlines," "The Law of Genre," and "Title [to be specified]"). As yet untranslated is "Pas," which elaborates upon the *viens* (come) and the *pas* (step/no) in/of Blanchot. A translation of the volume is in preparation.

"La parole soufflée." In *Writing and Difference,* 169–95. Artaud's theater as both a fulfillment and a disruption of metaphysics.

"Plato's Pharmacy." In *Dissemination,* 61–171. Plato's attempt to discredit writing; constantly relevant to the question of literature, if not directly addressed to it.

"The Politics of Friendship," *The Journal of Philosophy* 85 (1988): 632–44. A discussion of some texts on friendship which has a bearing on the ethics of literary criticism.

Positions (1972). Trans. Alan Bass. Chicago: University of Chicago Press; London: Athlone, 1981. Three interviews with Derrida, in which the question of literature is frequently broached.

The Post Card: From Socrates to Freud and Beyond (1980). Trans. Alan Bass. Chicago: University of Chicago Press, 1987. Includes "Envois" and "Le facteur de la vérité."

"The Principle of Reason: The University in the Eyes of Its Pupils." *Diacritics* 13.3 (Fall 1983): 3–20. The role of reason in the functioning of the university.

"Psyche: Invention of the Other." Extract included in this volume.

Psyché: Inventions de l'autre. Paris: Galilée, 1987. A large collection of pieces published over ten years, including "Psyche," "Aphorism Countertime," "Fifty-Two Aphorisms for a Foreword," and several others that are relevant to the question of literature.

"Qual Quelle: Valéry's Sources." In *Margins,* 273–306. The question of the "I" as source or origin, with special reference to Valéry's *Notebooks.*

"Racism's Last Word." *Critical Inquiry* 12 (1985): 290–99.

"The *Retrait* of Metaphor." *Enclitic* 2.2 (1978): 4–33. A postscript to

"White Mythology" and further discussion of metaphor, especially in Heidegger.

Shibboleth: For Paul Celan. Extract included in this volume.

"Signature Event Context." In *Margins,* 307–30, and *Limited Inc,* 1–23 (different translations). Also reprinted in *A Derrida Reader,* 82–111. Though not specifically concerned with literature, this essay is one of the best introductions to deconstruction's relation to philosophy, and in particular to the operations of iterability and the signature.

Signéponge/Signsponge. Trans. Richard Rand. New York: Columbia University Press, 1984. The writing of Francis Ponge; extract included in this volume.

"Some Questions and Responses." *The Linguistics of Writing: Arguments between Language and Literature.* Ed. Nigel Fabb, Derek Attridge, Alan Durant, and Colin MacCabe. Manchester: Manchester University Press, 1987; New York: Routledge, 1988. 252–64. An interview on aspects of deconstruction and linguistics.

"Some Statements and Truisms about Neologisms, Newisms, Postisms, Parasitisms, and Other Small Seismisms." *The States of "Theory."* Ed. David Carroll. New York: Columbia University Press, 1990. 63–94. Theory—or rather "theory"—in America.

Speech and Phenomena, and Other Essays on Husserl's Theory of Signs (1967). Trans. David B. Allison. Evanston: Northwestern University Press, 1973.

Spurs: Nietzsche's Styles (1978). Trans. Barbara Harlow. Chicago: University of Chicago Press, 1979. The question of style, the question of woman, in Nietzsche.

"Telepathy." *Oxford Literary Review* 10 (1988): 3–41. Presented as an "accidentally" omitted portion of "Envois," this epistolary essay is concerned with the question of touching at a distance.

"The Theater of Cruelty and the Closure of Representation." In *Writing and Difference,* 232–50. Artaud's theory of a "theater of cruelty" as marking the limits of mimesis and representation.

"The Time of a Thesis: Punctuations." *Philosophy in France Today.* Ed. Alan Montefiore. Cambridge: Cambridge University Press, 1982. 34–50. Derrida's thesis defense; includes comments on the place of literature in his work.

"Title (to be specified)." *Sub-stance* 31 (1981): 5–22. On titles: Blanchot's *The Madness of the Day* via Baudelaire and Ponge.

"Des Tours de Babel." *Difference in Translation.* Ed. Joseph F. Graham. Ithaca: Cornell University Press, 1985. 165–207. The question of translation, particularly with reference to Benjamin.

The Truth in Painting (1978). Trans. Geoff Bennington and Ian McLeod. Chicago: University of Chicago Press, 1987. Writings on painting (and on writings on painting). The discussion of framing in Kant's aesthetic theory—"Parergon" (15–147)—is particularly pertinent to considerations of literature.

"Two Words for Joyce." *Post-structuralist Joyce: Essays from the French.* Ed. Derek Attridge and Daniel Ferrer. Cambridge: Cambridge University Press, 1984. 145–59. Both a general response to Joyce and a focused account of two "words" in *Finnegans Wake.*

"Tympan." In *Margins,* ix–xxix; reprinted in *A Derrida Reader,* 148–68. The question of the limit; discussed in counterpoint with a passage from Michel Leiris's *Biffures.*

"Ulysses Gramophone: Hear Say Yes in Joyce." Included in this volume.

"White Mythology: Metaphor in the Text of Philosophy." In *Margins,* 207–71. Metaphor as philosophical, philosophy as metaphorical; the question of metaphor and mimesis. Not, however, a "literary" reading of philosophy, as the subtitle might suggest.

"Women in the Beehive: A Seminar." *Men in Feminism.* Ed. Alice Jardine and Paul Smith. New York: Methuen, 1987. 189–203. An interview which raises questions of feminism, the law, and the gift.

Writing and Difference (1967). Trans. Alan Bass. Chicago: University of Chicago Press; London: Routledge & Kegan Paul, 1978. Includes "Edmond Jabès and the Question of the Book," "La parole soufflée," "The Theater of Cruelty and the Closure of Representation," and "Ellipsis."

INDEX OF NAMES

  Texts included in this collection are indicated by bold type; references to the introduction and headnotes are in italics.

INDEX OF TOPICS

psychoanalysis 56, 93n, 99, 103–05,
194, 289, 296, 411n
psychobiography 103
psychology 2, 90, 103, 105, 153

quasi-transcendental 71, 239, 291, 295,
307

racism 39, *311*, 336n, 409
readability *15*, 68, 197, 379, 389–90,
405
reader *17*, 74–75
reading 3–4, *14–17*, 51, 69, 104, 115,
176–80, 216, 274
as production 101–2, 108
transcendent 43–47, 104
real, the *16n*, 35, 77, 102, 140, 157
reason 3, 88–92, 96, 191, 299
récit 186, 226, 227, 228, 231–42, 247–
49, 251–52; *see also* relation; story
reference (referentiality) *110*, 113, 152–
53, 213, 241–42, 298, 321
without referent 157, 163, 172
suspension of 41, 44–48
referent *16n*, *24n*, 44–45, 102, 121,
148–49, 152, 156; *see also* the real;
reference without referent
relation 186, 191; *see also récit;* story
remaining (remainder, remains) 37, 61,
291, 295, 370, 413
re-mark (double mark, remark) 9, *15*–
16, 48, 115, 121–22, 142–43, 291,
365, 400, 420
and date 388, 391
and genre 229–30
and translation 257
repetition (recurrence) *16*, 69, 226, 316,
340, 394, 419
and date 374, 389
of the dramatic work 69, *415*, 433
of "yes" 272, 275–76, 287, 299–
300, 304
see also iterability
representation (representative) 82–83,
89, 91, 96, 162; *see also* law,
representatives of
repression 56, 193–94, 308
respect 190, 196, 200, 203, 211, 340
response 5, *17–20*, 66, 70, 254, 299,
301, 308; *see also* countersignature

responsibility 5, 20, 27, 38, 51, 55, 70,
90, 206, 359
rhetoric *7n*, *13*, 50, *111*, 113–14, 121,
125–26, 314, 333, 417
rhyme 116
Romance languages 317
ruin 42, 53, 282

sacrifice 80, 359
same *see* other vs. same
"say everything" (*tout dire*) 36–39, 40
seal 35, 289, 394–96, 399, 411
secrecy (secret) 205, 372, 378–79, 382–
85, 392, 404–05, 412–13
self 95, 99, *255*, 298; *see also* the
subject
self-affirmation 303
self-presence *2n*, 76
self-referentiality *15–16*, 47, 152–53,
211–12, 324, 326
sending (dispatch, *envoi*, missive) 302,
303–04, 391
sensible *see* intelligible vs. sensible
sexual identity 59
sexual difference 295; *see also* gender
share *see* division
shibboleth 370–72, 373, 392, 396, 399–
413
sign *16*, 78–9, 83, 86, 92, 96–97, 99,
113, 116, 121, 159
signature (paraph) *18–20*, 35, 113, *255*,
260, 281–84, 344–45, 360–64
and act *2n*, 363
and date *370–71*, 387, 391, 404,
412–13
and invention *310*, 315–16, 333
and the literary text 43, 58, 66–67,
69–70, 288, 304, 352, 357
and philosophy 352
and the proper 348–51, 362
and proper name 279, 289, *345*,
346–47, 360, 362, 367–78
and "yes" *255*, 257, 279, 282–83,
288–89, 291, 295, 298–99, 308
see also counter-signature; the other
and signature; proper name and
signature
signified 90, 102, 103–04, 159
signifier *4n*, *16n*, 103–04, 114, 121–23,
145, 149, 159